Second-Rate Nation

By the Same Author

Organizing Educational Research
(with Paul F. Lazarsfeld)

Reforming the University: The Role of the Research Center

The School in Society: Studies in the Sociology of Education
(with David E. Wilder)

Bureaucracy and the Dispersed Organization
(with Karen Seashore Louis)

Fatal Remedies: The Ironies of Social Intervention

*A Gathering of Giants: The Intercultural Invention of Western Civilization
in the Middle East and Europe* (forthcoming)

SECOND-RATE NATION

FROM THE AMERICAN DREAM TO THE AMERICAN MYTH

SAM D. SIEBER

Paradigm Publishers

BOULDER • LONDON

Copyright © 2005 Paradigm Publishers

Published in the United States by Paradigm Publishers, 3360 Mitchell Lane, Suite C, Boulder, CO 80301 USA.

Paradigm Publishers is the trade name of Birkenkamp & Company, LLC, Dean Birkenkamp, President and Publisher.

ISBN 1-59451-090-3 (hardback)
ISBN 1-59451-091-1 (paperback)

Library of Congress Cataloging-in-Publication Data has been applied for.

Printed and bound in the United States of America on acid-free paper that meets the standards of the American National Standard for Permanence of Paper for Printed Library Materials.

Designed and typeset by Jack Sieber.

To

my family and friends whose encouragement and
assistance have made it possible for me to
prepare this book

and

the loving memories of
David Caplovitz and Robert Alford

The United States is the single surviving model of human progress.

George W. Bush, President

We are loathed, and I think the world has every right to loathe us, because they see us as greedy, self-interested and almost totally unconcerned about poverty and suffering.

Frank Griswold, Presiding Bishop
of the Episcopal Church

American power and influence are actually very fragile, because they rest upon an idea, a unique and irreplaceable myth: that the United States really does stand for a better world and is still the best hope of all who seek it.

Tony Judt, *The New York Review of Books*

Contents

Acknowledgments   xi

About the Author   xii

Introduction   xiii

1 **Overview of an Inferior Nation**   1

   Conflicting Images and Misplaced Priorities   1
   Comparative and Absolute Standards   4
   Past Trends   9
   Sources of the Myth's Robustness   11
   The Informational Defaults of the Media and Government   14
   An Integrated Power Structure   17
   The Facts   19

2 **The Economy, Work, Recent Federal Budgets, and Business and**
  Government   23

   The Paradox of Poverty in the Midst of Wealth   23
     Wealth   23
     Poverty   24
   Income Inequality and Social Mobility   29
   The Rollover from Record Budget Surplus to Record Budget Deficit
     in Two Years   33
   The National Debt   35
   The Trade Deficit   37
   State Deficits   38
   Bankruptcies   38
   Productivity, Job Stress, and Child Care for Working Parents   39
   Unemployment   42
   Other Comparisons with Europe   44
     Inflation and Deflation   44
     Contribution of Employers to Social Security   46
     Gross Domestic Product (GDP)   46
   Consumer Confidence and Spending   49
   Recent Federal Budgets   50
   Consumption and Happiness   56

Enron and Beyond: Corporate Fraud, Regulatory Laxity, and Tax
    Evasion   57
Corporations as Persons and Their Political Ascendancy   64

3   Health, Health Care, and Costs   75

Leading Causes of Death, Major Illnesses, and Disabilities   76
Mental Illness   81
Domestic Violence   82
Child Abuse   83
Alcohol and the Use of Illicit Substances   83
Prevention of Illness, Deferment of Death   84
The Cost of Health Care   86
    Overall Costs   87
    Distribution of Health Costs   87
The Quality of Health Care   98
The Health of Americans Compared with That of Citizens of Other
    Advanced Nations   100
An Afterword on the Medicare Prescription Drug and Modernization
    Act of 2003   104

4   Education   107

Educational Achievement Compared with Other Nations   107
Spending on Education as a Measure of National Commitment   110
Factors Related to School Achievement   112
Innovation and the Organization of Education   115
Dropping Out of Secondary Education and the Negative Role of the
    Federal Government   117
Access to Higher Education   121

5   Crime and Punishment   125

Crime, Its Fluctuation, and Its Costs   125
Imprisonment, Rehabilitation, and Parole   127
Privatization of Prisons   132
Drug Control: Enforcement or Prevention, Crime or Disease?   135
Capital Punishment   137

6   The Environment, Energy, and Natural Resources   143

Energy Consumption, Pollution, and Global Warming   143
Actions of the Current Administration That Endanger the Nation's
    Environment   155
Other Crises of the Global Environment and America's Response   157

7 **Foreign Affairs—Selected Issues** **163**

Foreign Assistance to Poor and Developing Countries 163
Economic, Social, and Environmental Deprivation in the World 163
The U.S. Response to the Need for Assistance 167
Public Attitudes toward Foreign Assistance 175
The Afghanistan War: A Case Study of Military Mismanagement
with Tragic Consequences 178
An Afterword on Civilian Casualties 196
The Iraq War of 2003 and More Military Mismanagement 197
Corporate Influence on Military Preparedness 211
The Sanctions Alternative 214
Unilateralism 215

8 **Racial, Ethnic, and Gender Inequality** **223**

Black Inequality 223
Other Victims of Ethnic or Racial Prejudice and Discrimination 232
Gender Inequality 234

9 **Civil Liberties** **241**

The Bill of Rights vs. the Patriot Act and Other Government Policies
and Regulations 241
Anecdotal Evidence of Abuse 247
Public Reaction to Curtailment of Civil Liberties 251

10 **The Media and Their Relationships with Corporations, the
Government, and the Public** **255**

Media Mediocrity and Concentration 255
The Media and Corporate Enterprise 261
A Brief History of Corporate Control of the Media 269
The Media and Government 274

11 **Democracy** **283**

The American Model 283
To Vote or Not to Vote 289
Filling the Electoral Power Vacuum with Special-Interest Wealth and
Influence 293
What Difference Does It Make If Democracy Is Weak? 298
Where the Rubber Hits the Road: The Elusive Realm of Bureaucratic
Performance 304

12 **Conclusions and a New Beginning**   **311**

    Notes   **321**

       Introduction   321
       1. Overview of an Inferior Nation   321
       2. The Economy, Work, Recent Federal Budgets, and Business and
          Government   323
       3. Health, Health Care, and Costs   334
       4. Education   343
       5. Crime and Punishment   346
       6. The Environment, Energy, and Natural Resources   350
       7. Foreign Affairs—Selected Issues   355
       8. Racial, Ethnic, and Gender Inequality   365
       9. Civil Liberties   369
       10. The Media and Their Relationships with Corporations, the
          Government, and the Public   371
       11. Democracy   376
       12. Conclusions and a New Beginning   380

    Index   **381**

Acknowledgments

I am indebted above all to several members of my family who not only believed in the value of the book in progress but participated in bringing it to fruition. Mary Sieber was an ardent editor who drew upon her many years of book editing, particularly of technical and scholarly works, to make my book as literate, accurate, and up to date as possible given my rather haphazard writing and clerical styles. My brother, John, also played an editorial role, but more as an intellectual gadfly, scrutinizer of ideas and arguments, and watchdog of tone and equanimity. My nephew Jack volunteered to perform the wizardry of converting a misshapen work into an attractive, electronic, camera-ready format in collaboration with the publisher and also provided unflagging assistance in overcoming many computer-related problems in preparation of the manuscript. Another nephew, Todd Fredricks, facilitated my perilous transition from printed matter and 3x5 cards to the computer through donation of his replaced equipment, basic instructions in its use, and constant readiness to give advice. My niece Ann's assistance with the lengthy index was indispensable at a critical time, and her efforts to publicize the book through her friends and professional contacts are also greatly appreciated. Caroline Persell and Lynette Stone offered valuable information and advice pertaining to certain parts of the book; and Judy Campbell and Ron Nyburg kept me supplied with numerous articles from the media bearing on a range of topics. Without the help of all those named above, the final product would have suffered greatly. Finally, several former colleagues, including Frances Fox Piven, Herbert Gans, Catherine Bodard Silver, and Seymour Spilerman, were helpful in my search for a publisher or agent, for which efforts I am very grateful.

The selection, treatment, and interpretation of the data, as well as all conclusions and opinions, are, unfortunately, entirely my own responsibility.

About the Author

Sam Sieber is a retired Senior Research Associate and Lecturer on the Graduate Faculty of Columbia University (with stints at New York University and other institutions of higher education) where he was a Program Director at the Bureau of Applied Social Research. He was also a frequent adviser to the National Institute of Education and numerous other educational agencies across the country, federal evaluator of university and regional R&D centers, published author of five books and numerous professional articles and research reports on social theory, research methods, the organization of R&D centers, policy research, labor economics, and school systems, and a forthcoming book on ancient history. In addition, he founded and served for several years as Executive Director of a community action agency that dealt with crime, drug abuse, and mental illness.

For thirty years he homesteaded on a Caribbean island while studying and writing history and sociological works. *Second-Rate Nation* is his first major work to be published after returning from the island in 1999 and discovering the research and publication potential of the Web.

He is presently residing in Texas where he was born and raised, and his free time is spent composing and playing the piano. His doctoral degree was received from Columbia University in the discipline of sociology.

Introduction

In 1999 I moved back to the States after living and studying elsewhere for nearly 30 years. During those years, my knowledge of current affairs in America was drawn from only a few mainstream media sources. Moreover, my short, occasional visits to my family in Texas, where I was born and raised, and to Washington, D.C., where I periodically consulted for the National Institute of Education, afforded only limited opportunity to bring myself up to date. Consequently, I was unprepared for what I discovered when I resumed residence after a lapse of many years. As I read, watched, and listened to media reports, I detected signs of multiple fractures in the body politic. And when my curiosity prompted me to delve beneath the superficial news of the mainstream media by recourse to the Internet, these signs grew to alarming proportions.

The numbers of Americans whom I now discovered to be suffering from homelessness, hunger, imprisonment, unaffordable illnesses, growing income inequality, job stress, mental disorders, poor education, lack of representation, and so on, struck me as oddly incompatible with the economic prosperity that I had heard about only a few years earlier as ushering in a new era of growth and utopia. In fact, the data seemed to inhabit a realm of reality remote from the preoccupations of the mass media, especially on television, where most Americans now gathered their news. And the deeper I delved, the more it emerged that, in spite of its posture of greatness, America was in fact *lagging behind* most other democratic, industrial nations on numerous indicators of national performance, a backward member of the advanced international community in all but gross wealth, military firepower, and an embarrassingly outdated reputation for justice, civil liberties, equality, democracy, and compassion for the downtrodden— a state of affairs that I painstakingly document in this book. Especially curious was the smug self-assurance with which the media, the nation's leaders, and the great majority of the public ignored or dismissed the unequivocal evidence of the country's slide into mediocrity and either ignored or cast aspersions on anyone who tried to open their eyes to it.

How could this have happened in such a short span of time? I asked myself. What were the causes of the nation's extensive impairment that made it fall significantly behind other nations? What was the meaning of an unabashed self-esteem and a habit of self-advertisement that did not mirror reality, especially in recent years when the discrepancy had grown larger than ever before? And, finally, why were the great majority of the people and their leaders intent upon ignoring or denying the country's predicament? Like other Americans, I had once believed that America was Number One. So I felt alarmed and even faintly betrayed by what seemed to be unacknowledged deterioration. Having left my research and teaching position at Columbia during the final, turbulent years of the Vietnam War, and having been somewhat apolitical, I had welcomed the opportunity to retreat to a place where I could devote my time to scholarship without distraction. But the country that I returned to seemed to be suffering from an even greater crisis than the Vietnam War. Of the two types of national crises, those that are acknowledged and those that are not, the latter are by far the more threatening and puzzling, and this seemed to me to be the case with America at the turn of the millennium. The challenge presented to me as a sociologist and cultural historian, together with my desire to be of some service to my country, made the subject irresistible. Hence the present book.

Was America's exaggerated self-image the effect only of a prolonged celebration of its victory in the Cold War and its subsequent triumph over the geopolitical world? I asked myself. Perhaps this simple explanation was the answer to the puzzle, or at least part of it. But upon further examination of events as they had unfolded in the past several decades, and particularly in the early period of the George W. Bush presidency, and upon further pondering of the clash between self-celebration and reality, together with the emphatic, glib denial of that reality, it occurred to me that the problem might be just the opposite, namely, that America was simply whistling on a high wire, trying to buck up its courage in a period of global ascendancy that was at bottom stressful, unfulfilling, and potentially disastrous.

My research had unquestionably turned up long-term trends indicative of underlying insecurity and distress at home in spite of the end of the Cold War. (A summary of these trends is given in chapter 1 and documented in the chapters that follow.) And it will be recalled that during the prolonged standoff with the Soviet Union, America had been obsessed with preserving its "credibility" in Korea, the Congo, Nicaragua, Laos, Vietnam, and other places.[1] All of this suggested to me that our recurrent crises in foreign affairs, which have increasingly occupied the attention of the American public and the world, might be part of a syndrome of deeply felt peril and limited potency that has infected the people and their leaders since the Vietnam War—a mood of unjust vulnerability in need of a compensatory sense of inherent superiority so robust that it could overwhelm a battalion of facts. As a historian of the Cold War has observed, "The deeper reasons for America's fixation with its presumed vulnerability, at a time when its power was actually at its peak, probably lie more within the realm of social psychology than within the realms of geopolitics or political economy."[2]

Indicative of America's incertitude in the early '90s was the fact that the demise of Soviet Communism was not greeted by the U.S. Defense Department with unalloyed joy, but rather in a mood of wary dread. In particular, among defense planners under *père* Bush, the waning of the Soviet menace aroused fear that some new foe would fill the vacuum, a prospect that evoked a firm resolve of "never again"—testimony to the trauma of the preceding 45 years under the Communist threat combined with uncertainty about the "new world order" proclaimed by the president. This trepidation even revived the old, pre-UN idea in the minds of certain members of the first Bush administration of taking preemptive action whenever it was deemed necessary, a rather clear sign of deep perturbation. As for the public, the ferocious spectacles of ethnic cleansing and genocide on TV, and the increasing concern about nuclear proliferation and anti-Western protest among a rising medley of nations and peoples in the midst of domestic economic insecurity, dampened jubilation after the fall of the Soviet Union.[3] A prominent question became: Where and when will the new enemy appear? In other words, the nation's attention had shifted from a known enemy to an unknown one, from focused fear to free-floating anxiety.

Apparently, the Cold War's culture of antagonism between the two major powers had ironically become a source of meaningful order that had been undermined by the disappearance of one of the antagonists. As a Soviet official quipped in 1987, "We are going to do the worst thing we possibly can to America—we are going to take away their enemy." Indeed, America had benefited from the Soviet threat by playing the role of "the leader of the free world," which allowed it to enforce acquiescence of non-Soviet bloc nations to its own geopolitical and economic interests. When the Cold War ended, America lost this fulcrum of power and prestige, thereby allowing other nations to assert their independence and undermine our de facto hegemony. (For a more thorough discussion of this point, see Wallerstein.[4])

In the final analysis, instead of giving Americans a feeling that they had at last gained control over their destiny, the end of the Cold War evoked a sense of impotence in the employment of the nation's superior strength, especially in the minds of government leaders, and a new form of global apprehension on the part of everyone. This sense of lost direction was aggravated by domestic economic troubles induced by excessive defense spending during the final years of the Cold War and foreign competition. Not even the victory in the first Gulf War prevented Americans from having a feeling of drift and dread. In March 1995, a *Business Week*/Harris Poll found that more than 70 percent of the public felt gloomy about the future.[5] And another pollster in the same year concluded that "anxiety may replace anger as the dominant voter emotion in 1995."[6]

European nations also suffered from various forms of the "post–Cold War jitters," as Kevin Phillips[7] has called it. But they did not have the vaunted status of a superpower at stake. Indeed, Americans were ready to fight a war to guarantee their nation's safety and to preserve the global supremacy that they felt they had earned by right—possibly even if they had to blind-side the enemy by initiating aggression themselves. For notably lacking in the nation's adjustment to the loss of its familiar enemy was any notion of fitting into the global community on an equal footing. Its privileged status as a triumphant "superpower" (although all it had really done was outspend the Soviet Union) was not to be abdicated. The current administration's unilateralism is simply the logical unfolding of that presumption.

As a matter of fact, America's fighting spirit following the demise of the Soviet Union was almost unique among advanced nations. When asked in 1991 if they were willing to go to war for their country, 77 percent of Americans said yes, the highest percentage by far of 17 advanced countries with the exception of Israel (89%), a country perennially besieged.[8] And from 1990 to 1994 alone, America engaged in six military interventions. One suspects that only a people who felt profoundly insecure and zealously protective of their global standing would be so strongly disposed toward militarism.

The area of the world that was most threatening to the security and status of the nation was the Middle East, owing to America's dependency on the region's oil and its commitment to Israel. A bellicose Iraq thus unwisely placed itself in the crosshairs of the American defense establishment when it invaded Kuwait, and especially in the minds of certain defense planners when Hussein was allowed to remain in power. These same planners eventually became President George W. Bush's top advisers. In short, the long-term goal of these planners became "regime change" in Iraq as early as *1991*, ostensibly as a means of bringing democracy to the region and reducing the threat to America. More fundamentally, a policy of ensuring that America would never again be confronted with a military rival for global supremacy, especially when basic resources and an ally were at stake, became the driving force of American foreign policy following the Cold War. Some form of control over the Middle East seemed vital, therefore, and it appears that Iraq obligingly played the quarry in the early '90s. Subsequently, the nation's pride over the high-tech prosecution of the first Gulf War and the later business boom reinforced the delusion of inherent superiority.

That this Middle Eastern policy was uppermost in the second Bush administration's stance toward Iraq *prior* to 9/11, regardless of any later reasons given for its 2003 invasion, is shown by a policy statement of Bush's security advisers (the same who had worked for the first Bush administration) that was written two months *before* the son's election: "While the unresolved conflict with Iraq provides the immediate justification, the need for a substantial American force presence in the Gulf transcends the issue of the regime of Saddam Hussein."[9] Quite obviously, the later 9/11 attacks conveniently advanced the administration's goal from "force presence" to outright military occupation of a Middle Eastern country, with the ultimate payoff of a military base in Iraq. (As it turned out, plans for six bases were later announced by the military in late 2003, and in early 2004 it was alleged that a total of 14 bases were under construction. Conceivably, these bases were a basic, if not the sole, reason for the invasion of Iraq.)

Our military success in the first Gulf War was followed by the humiliating losses in Somalia and the terrorist attacks on New York and Washington. The latter attacks raised the anxiety of Americans to a level comparable to that after Pearl Harbor and galvanized the defense planners who had served in the first Bush administration into finalizing plans for an attack on Iraq as well as Afghanistan. By confirming the nation's sense of vulnerability, especially to shadowy assailants whose ingenuity of planning, low-tech weapons (box cutters!), and scale of impact were clearly a blow to America's superpower stature, 9/11 sharply boosted the tendency of Americans to indulge in defensive fantasies of superiority and self-righteousness, two of the most telling symptoms of national humiliation, pain, and dread. As if to protest stridently, "You can't do this to me! I'm the boss and benefactor of this town!" America seemed determined to assert in no uncertain terms its ascendancy over the planet. And so, with the wholehearted support of the public's renewed sense of wounded greatness, the nation's leaders now seized the opportunity to leap boldly into the international arena in a spirit of naked unilateralism, exceptionalism, preemptive prerogative, and crusading jingoism. In short, almost all trappings of modern statesmanship were discarded. Even the United Nations was ultimately ignored in the nation's lust for vengeance, restored credibility, and a piece of the Middle East. In effect, the Cold War model of hair-trigger readiness to unleash overwhelming military power held sway. America's confrontation with demonic forces abroad was resurrected literally with a vengeance as the public's need to preserve its self-anointed greatness swelled. The nation hungered for a triumph that would eradicate all the pain and humiliation of the past 30 years.

Then matters went from bad to worse. America's new preemptive, go-it-alone approach to international problem-solving under George W. Bush seemed to reveal a basic immaturity that crippled its ability to assume the role of world leadership. (This point will be elaborated in chapter 7.) Meanwhile, at home, conditions for millions of Americans continued to deteriorate in almost every facet of the nation's life, as documented in this book. And yet, money was not only withheld from longstanding domestic needs that had become increasingly urgent over the past few decades, but was also subtracted from the levels of past, inadequate expenditures and turned over to the military. It is as if the nation's voracious fear of the Middle East as a successor to the old Communist foe had finally been able to gorge on Osama bin Laden, Saddam Hussein, and terrorism regardless of the cost to the treasury or domestic exigencies. War had been given full vent, and anyone who doubted America's absolute innocence, surpassing feats, or the wisdom of its leaders was accused of negativism at best and disloyalty at worst. These, too, were signs of an aberrant national mood that resembled a combination of paranoia and delusions of grandeur in individual psychology.

At some point in this unwinding skein I recalled a recurrent pattern in history. When an exceptional society is no longer able to sustain its customary level of aspiration, accomplishment, or international respect, because of internal weakness, a threat from without, or overextension of its hegemony (a fate that has befallen superpowers since the dawn of civilization), it resorts to *myth* to reassure itself and others in the world of its undiminished potency. When it loses the ability to realize its goals, it preserves its sense of exceptional worth by celebrating the past and scorning current realities. This is consistent with America's blind self-celebration and its negative impact on foreign relations. Thus, in some ways America's mood is reminiscent of the nostalgic (literally "home-grief") movements of national reassertion, including antiquarianism and the purging of foreign elements, that swept the ancient Near East in the seventh and eighth centuries BCE when the entire region fell under the shadow of Assyrian domination (and even earlier in Assyria itself). While the threat to those ancient kingdoms was usually from without, in America it has been both from without (foreign military misadventures, failures of engagement in the global economy, and terrorism) and from within (social deterioration and political polarization). The sustained outburst of patriotic nostalgia in response to the sixtieth anniversary of D-Day and the death of former President Reagan, at a time when affairs in Iraq had turned especially ugly, attests vividly to America's desperate need for the Myth's reassurance. In addition to the usual patriotic evocations of past triumphs, evidence of nostalgia in America soon after the loss of the Vietnam War comes from an unusual source: the Broadway musical. Musical theater, always a popular barometer of America's mood, went into a tailspin of highly successful "revivals" of musical shows reaching back many years that continued for about a decade.[10]

America's condition also brought to mind the spectacular rise in Greece of burlesque comedy, with ridicule and lampooning of former leaders and policies following Sparta's conquest of Athens after years of horrific war (similar to the shock of our losing the Vietnam War). I was also reminded of Gilbert Murray's "failure of nerve" that gripped the West after the breakdown of the classical Greek consensus during the wars of the Diadochi and the spread of Roman brutality, a period marked by mysticism, astrology, superstition, belief in Fortune, and salvationism. (Judging from the unique role of religion in the lives of Americans, as measured by international surveys and the increasing strength of fundamentalism, belief in supernatural intercession as a means of salvation is far more widespread in America than in any other advanced Western nation.) Finally, a modern parallel that one tries in vain to resist is Nazism's convulsion of nostalgic posturing (i.e., Aryan supremacy) in response to the humiliating loss of World War I and the Versailles Treaty, and also to the Soviet threat, including the latter's control of major oil reserves in the Crimea.

Although certain aspects of these periods were germane to America's new mood, each period as a whole was far from being a perfect match for it. Perhaps developments in America were a peculiar combination of *elements* from each of these troubled historical periods—periods that had in common an imperiled sense of lost potency.

It then dawned on me that what might have happened in our own period of ineffectual disorientation was a gradual shift from the traditional American Dream to a full-blown American Myth. This shift might have been initiated by America's social turmoil of the '60s and its defeat in Vietnam; then augmented by political and economic crises and by the specter of a new enemy who might fill the vacuum left by a familiar, longtime foe; the waning of an indispensable international role of anticommunist leadership; military blunders and increasing terrorism abroad; the growing hostility of rapidly advancing nations; and, finally, the 9/11 attacks in spite of an enormous intelligence bureaucracy and military establishment. Accompanying this tectonic shift in the nation's foreign affairs has been an increase in domestic disarray that has sapped both its moral and its pragmatic confidence. All these circumstances seemed to have undermined America's sense of control over its destiny, in spite of its wealth and military firepower, and to have given rise to anxieties that required the consolation of a compelling bogus reality. The recent burdens and setbacks of two military interventions in the Middle East have only added fuel to this long-developing, deep-seated vein of dismay and reaching for solace.

The spectacular rise of conservatism in the past three decades was in large part an outcome of this sense of having lost control amidst eroding pieties, welfare statism, aggressive egalitarianism, foreign blunders, and economic troubles (both at home and abroad), including the stagflation and OPEC oil embargo of the '70s. It was this latter period of economic anxiety that more than any other induced big business to mount a long and arduous climb toward deunionization, political dominance, and increasing privatization, which it achieved remarkably well with Reagan and the Bushes, and to supplement its political power by enrolling the nativistic retreatism of a large segment of the public. Thus, it is not surprising that the greatest outpouring of blood-and-soil patriotism has emanated from conservatives rather than liberals, pushing the American Myth into high gear.

While the American Dream was itself never an accurate reflection of one's chances for success and happiness in America, the American Myth that largely succeeded it is a caricature of the Dream inasmuch as it is farther removed from reality, expresses a wholly different mood, and serves quite different needs. A dream is a confident vision of a better world or way of life that is available to all who persevere. A myth is a denial of the dream's betrayal and the realities of age or circumstance that have undermined it. A dream is nurtured by hope. A myth is prompted by anxiety. A dream is a heartfelt commitment. A myth is a heartfelt lie. A dream embraces risk. A myth aspires to retrenchment. The chief function of a dream is to inspire the greatest number to fulfill their potential in a just and orderly world. The chief function of a myth in a country whose glory seems to have passed is to comfort its people with reiterated assurances that nothing has changed, all is well, and the best is yet to come. A dream is a voluntary commitment. A myth is a civic obligation. Both dream and myth can be exploited by leaders to serve their political ends, but a dream is exploited by igniting hope, while a myth is exploited by stoking the coals of insecurity. A dream is a fond vision of the future. A myth is a theatrical celebration of past and present with little substance, and in fact conceals the emptiness of the present under false colors of greatness as a means of assuaging anxiety.

On a more personal level, the waning of a solid sense of civic engagement seemed to have fostered myths of happiness that offered sanctuary in manic distractions, timeworn pieties, religious salvation, competitive consumption, high-stakes scheming, or the most harmful escape route of all: legal and moral deviance, including the concealment of motives and the manipulation of others for one's selfish benefit. This impression of a high rate of legal and moral deviance is confirmed to some degree by a review of research by Bok[11] in 1996: "Whether one looks at stealing, cheating on exams, paying taxes . . . by almost any measure . . . Americans appear to be less responsible than citizens of other advanced nations . . ."

In addition, during my years of long absence Americans seemed to have lost much of their youthful vitality, creativity, and idealism, and lost also the sheer spunk to engage in vigorous protest and organization in making a stand against economic and civil oppression or official incompetence and political self-interest. (This might have been associated with increased centrism on the part of the Democrats as well as the economic boom in the '90s.) At best, they had occasionally mocked the power elite, but at the same time, by not voting, had refused to play the game of politics and had rallied round the nation's leaders only when the country was attacked by outsiders. In fact, later on, they seemed almost to have despaired of both the ability and the obligation of government to do anything substantial about the country's domestic tribulations. In short, Americans had apparently subsided into a mood of personal, isolated self-interest and gratification, with one exception: preoccupation with the nation's efforts to provide *security.* For the only institution that has tended to retain America's trust in spite of its ups and downs, according to polls, is the military, a symptom, in all probability, of the ascendancy of a sustained, widespread spirit of apprehension.

All these domestic retreats occurred while the nation was falling demonstrably behind the rest of the advanced world in social achievement and the decent opinion of mankind. Yet, none of its domestic or foreign troubles caused it to revoke or even moderate its self-image as the bearer of the torch of greatness, a reputation earned a half century earlier—before the shocks of Vietnam, Watergate, stagflation, OPEC's oil price increase, the Teheran hostages, Somalia, Lebanon, Enron, the flagrant 2000 presidential election, and, as I write, perhaps

Iraq. On the contrary, a *magnification* of this self-image had become the nation's defense against the gnawing disappointments and anxieties aroused by an accumulation of debacles, abasements, and threats. Self-delusion has evidently bestowed an imaginary salvation from the evils of downtrends, corrosive current events, a reduction in international clout, and a growing sense of having lost direction. Consequently, the compensatory American Myth grew in strength even as America's true character declined.

The American Myth is the American Dream running on empty, so to speak. Like the three monkeys of folk wisdom, America's leaders do not want to see it, the media do not want to say it, and the people do not want to hear it. Which leaves us in a state of existential gridlock, because the Myth is a basic obstacle to the healing of our country. An illness denied is an illness untreated. Only by facing the reality of our inferiority as a national enterprise and then rejuvenating hope, strengthening civil liberties and democracy, cooperating with international partners, and insisting that our government do its part on behalf of all its people and the suffering masses of the world (and do so without seeking more riches or power or causing the massacre of more innocents in war) will America be able to reclaim a mood of genuine and merited pride and restore its credibility in the eyes of the world. At this historical moment, however, the country that I returned to in 1999 seems to be basking in ignorance or denial of its deterioration, trembling behind its ramparts, and indulging in the saddest, most undeserved fantasy of all: that it is the greatest nation that has ever graced the planet.

1

Overview of an Inferior Nation

Conflicting Images and Misplaced Priorities

Beyond the ordinary assets of ample physical and human resources, productive labor, basic infrastructure and technology, and at least formal democracy, the greatness of a modern nation is measured by its willingness constantly to monitor itself and to take bold and imaginative action to readjust its course, not only for the well-being of all its citizens, but for the poor and oppressed outside its borders who are deeply afflicted for reasons beyond their control. Most people would agree, I think, that greatness is not measured by displays of collective self-love, self-righteousness, or self-pity; or by exhibitions of disdain for, or violence against, global neighbors; or by ingenuity in the means of self-enrichment. Above all, sheer force on the international stage is often worthless. Unless power has authority, which is bestowed only by those subject to its influence, it will succumb to evasion, subversion, or open attack. In the final reckoning, a nation that wages peace and hope will become great, but one that wages war and fear will become only notorious. If the American nation heeds these simple precepts, it will not only survive but triumph, because it will truly overawe the world and gain the applause of history.

Many Americans, and very likely the great majority, believe that our country has already achieved this pinnacle of reputability, that America is a benign, circumspect, good-natured, and generous giant; a beacon of liberty and justice; a land of widespread prosperity and equal opportunity; a nation whose values, institutions, and way of life are worthy of universal emulation. This proud presumption and its uniquely strong showing in America can be detected in the responses to an international poll conducted in 1995. As the pollsters discovered: "90% of Americans would rather be citizens of the United States than of any other country. That rating is the highest of the 23 nations studied . . . "[1] The belief in America's exalted status is held so strongly by a significant number of citizens that criticism from abroad tends to be received with amazement, hurt, or outrage. In particular, an assertion that our policies have contributed to the belligerence that we sometimes encounter in the world is dismissed as either sour grapes or virulent conspiracy. At the very least, severe criticism is simply in-

1

comprehensible. As President George W. Bush said in October 2001, "I'm amazed that people would hate us. Like most Americans I just can't believe it. Because I know how good we are."[2] And on another occasion the president stated, as quoted in one of my opening epigraphs, "The United States is the single surviving model of human progress."

The extraordinarily high regard in which the president holds the United States was shared by a comfortable majority (62%) of college students in a 2002 poll, who agreed that "in spite of its flaws, the United States is the best country in the world." Here we find the American Myth in full bloom. However, there were also signs of the Myth's ultimate fragility when confronted with higher education—as indicated by the fact that the frequency of the students' positive response to this question was by no means overwhelming. Further, a sizable proportion of the students had reservations about the notion of America's moral superiority and innocence of wrongdoing. Seventy-one percent disagreed that "the values of the U.S. are superior to the values of other nations," and 79 percent did not believe that American culture was superior to Islamic culture. In addition, a majority (57%) felt that the policies of the United States were "at least somewhat responsible" for the September 11 attacks; and fully 60 percent agreed that, according to a summary of responses, "developing a better understanding of the values and history of other cultures and nations that dislike us is a better approach to preventing terrorism than investing in strong military and defense capabilities." Finally, more than a third (37%) of the students said that they would try to avoid the draft if called up.[3]

In spite of the mixed results of this survey, the students' responses ignited a storm of condemnation from conservatives that included epithets like "stupid," "crazy," and "cowardly college pukes."[4] The conservative head of the organization commissioning the study concluded that "college students need to know many things better."[5] Clearly, the American Myth of supremacy and virtue sprang to its own defense with gusto. Interestingly enough, the finding that most of the students still tended to regard America as "the best in the world" was ignored by the critics. Evidently, the Myth requires total endorsement, a lockstep commitment, whereas the students taken as a whole seemed to have gotten their right and left feet mixed up, so to speak.

Conservative commentators in the mainstream media are, of course, outspoken publicists for the idea that America excels in the cardinal virtues when compared with other countries. As an op-ed columnist of the *New York Times* put it in late 2003: "American life has improved in almost every measurable way, and far from regressing toward the mean, the U.S. has become an exceptional nation."[6] As we shall see, there is abundant reason to believe that this sentiment falls mortifyingly short of reality. Clearly, thanks to the Myth, the inclination of many conservatives is to be fashionably aloof from the problems that assail us.

Not surprisingly, the Myth has little resonance outside America. According to a poll in late 2002, a majority of the public in each of six European countries believed that American foreign policy contributed to the 9/11 attacks.[7] The approximate percentage of Europeans who felt this way was 55%, virtually the same level as among the college students in America who were polled in the same period. More tellingly, a 2002 survey in 44 countries found that the spread of U.S. influence was viewed unfavorably by a majority almost everywhere in the world.[8] These high levels of blame signify that America's iconic stature has become vulnerable, even in the eyes of a moderate majority of its most promising youth, although the latter still tend to cling to the core belief of the Myth that America is the "best country in the world."

It seems safe to say that the 9/11 attacks unleashed a frenzy of patriotism among the great majority of Americans that invigorated the American Myth. This is hardly surprising. Every kind of human community—from street corner gangs and families to nations and ethnic regions of the world—closes ranks and celebrates itself when attacked. As a consequence, however, Americans might now be even less inclined to countenance criticism of their way of life. Owing to an entrenchment of predisposition made all the more impassioned by anxiety and defensiveness toward the persistent rumblings on the horizon of disdain or hatred of the United States punctuated with random acts of mass violence, Americans might be especially unwilling to engage in objective study of their tenuous situation. A similar entrenchment of predisposition occurred in the Arab world as a consequence of the West's cultural and political triumph and the end of Ottoman rule in the early 20th century. *These two culturally defensive reactions are now confronting one another across half the globe.* Unfortunately, this crucial, historical point is rarely expressed or understood in America. If the causes of war can be reduced to honor, interest, and fear, as claimed by Thucydides, then we would do well to pay more attention to the role of wounded honor—ours and theirs—in our conflict with the Middle East.

It is therefore urgent that we reexamine our behavior, priorities, and allocation of resources in an objective search for solid evidence of an exemplary society, one that we can honorably display to the world. And if we have difficulty adducing such evidence in certain quarters, what better time to redouble our efforts of reform so that America may deserve the laurels that it earned in the distant past?

In the wake of 9/11, international affairs stole the limelight from domestic issues, although the balance seems to have been somewhat restored more recently. If people begin to believe that the economy is gaining strength and that their economic future can be faced with confidence, then attention could be mainly focused again on the international scene where matters seem to be steadily worsening. In any case, the idea that foreign and domestic policies are separate and distinct domains with little interplay is a dangerous notion. Unless we can develop and mobilize the resources and commitment of the great majority of our people, how can we meet the growing cost of defense, man (and woman) the military if a substantial number of young people try to avoid the draft, raise the level and quality of exports, supply scientists, technicians, and other professionals needed by our global businesses, avoid widespread unemployment if jobs are exported overseas to low-wage markets, reduce our trade deficit and federal debt, and offer a model that will inspire other nations and elicit their support and cooperation when needed in foreign affairs? Our foreign relations are tied closely to our domestic affairs, and vice versa. In terms of government policy, this means that an excessive attention to one sector while scanting the other could have disastrous consequences. And yet, that seems to have been our inclination, an inclination that has been dictated to a large degree by our leaders when they wished to divert our attention from shortcomings in one sector by highlighting the other, one of the oldest tricks of demagogy in the history of the world.

And yet, today, our resources cannot be fully tapped for either domestic or foreign purposes because a significant number of the population are physically or mentally ill or disabled, poorly educated, malnourished, afflicted with obesity, poisoned by pollution, inclined to violence and criminality, imprisoned and subsequently stripped of civil rights, beset with racial and ethnic prejudice and discrimination, stressed out by the job or marital difficulties, unsheltered and unemployed, alienated by the failure of our democratic system to reflect needs and desires, discouraged by lack of economic betterment (and often even losing ground) in spite of hard work, or fearful of investing because of the crookedness of corporate multimillionaires and their colluding accountants. A country that aspires to greatness cannot afford such symptoms of rot. Instead of an icon, it could well become a monstrous pariah enraged by self-inflicted blindness.

This work marshals a large number of social indicators that illuminate both the state of American society and its relations with the world at the turn of the millennium. Its purposes are to evaluate the nation's performance and to see how well the idealistic picture of America matches reality, to try to understand why there are discrepancies between ideal and reality, and to inspire reform.

Comparative and Absolute Standards

Evaluation implies the existence of acceptable standards or yardsticks. Three types of yardstick are employed here, which may be called comparative, pragmatic, and moral. The use of a comparative standard involves examining a nation's standing vis-à-vis other industrial societies, especially those that share its cultural background. It answers such questions as how the infant mortality rate compares with that of other countries. Pragmatic standards imply levels of functioning that are widely regarded as necessary for achievement in the modern world in such areas as research and development, educational achievement in basic subjects, and economic vitality. And moral standards refer to basic values held by a society, such as democracy, nonviolence, respect for law, compassion for the weak or poor, honesty and integrity on the part of private and public elites, human and civil rights, and norms of justice and fairness.

Performance according to pragmatic and moral standards can be assessed comparatively if the data exist, but even in the absence of such data it is possible to reach a judgment about moral or pragmatic performance in terms of a society's own standards. For example, the level of child abuse, homicide, or homelessness relative to general moral expectations can serve alone as a basis for evaluation, as can the level of manufacturing output or balance of trade relative to pragmatic standards. Moreover, even though pragmatic and moral standards sometimes overlap (ideas like "free enterprise," for example, have both moral and pragmatic elements, and these may even conflict), for the most part the two standards are separable. Math proficiency, for example, is evaluated solely according to a pragmatic standard.

In sum, a conclusion that America is a great nation or only a second-rate one can be studied, not only comparatively, but in terms of certain standards that are held by Americans themselves. My own conclusion that America is second-rate at best will, of course, generate disagreement; but disagreement carries with it the obligation to present alternative facts or analyses according to the standards set forth above; and the factual record shows that a great deal is awry in America. Indeed, the magnitude of our domestic and foreign disarray is matched only by the magnitude of our wealth and military might, which may or may not be a coincidence.

At this point the reader might begin to wonder whether the author is simply another perverse alarmist, or "declinist," who is chronically ill-disposed toward his native land, or one of that tribe of "nattering nabobs of negativism" (scorned by a former vice president) who has embraced the glib anti-Americanism of Europeans and, therefore, might be labeled an avatar of ethnodistalism.

To any such charge I would answer as follows: Americans who share the widespread assumption that their country is the best in the world are headed for the same jolt that I received when I began routing out the facts. Although this work was not undertaken to shock, debunk, or demolish, but only to illuminate the state of a nation that seemed to be in trouble, it is bound to be discomforting in view of the central message conveyed by the facts when laid out in serried ranks and carefully examined: America is seriously defective when compared on a host of measures with other economically advanced countries (and occasionally even mediocre when compared with many other countries in the world), or also when it is held up to its own standards of either pragmatic or moral achievement.

In comparative terms, here are some 50 dimensions on which America is found to lag behind *most* other advanced nations reporting and frequently even to fall close to the rear (if not at the rear). In this list, America ranks low on dimensions that are positively expressed (e.g., democratic representation) and high on ones that are negatively expressed (e.g., homicide rate) after taking into account population size. (The order in the list follows the order of discussion in the text as indicated by page numbers.)

social expenditures by government, 7, 11, 53
social reports of national performance, 14, 15
child poverty, 25
hunger, 26
income inequality, 29
progressive taxation, 30
national debt, 35
trade deficit, 37
savings rate, 38
working time, 39–41
worker morale/job stress, 41
subsidized child care for working parents, 41
unemployment insurance, 44
inflation (2002), 44
contribution of employers to Social Security, 46
obesity, 79
teenage suicide, 81
teenage drug use, 83, 84
premature mortality due to inadequate preventive care, 84, 85
cost of health care and prescription drugs, 86, 92
hospital beds per capita, 89
physicians per capita, 89
cost of health insurance, 95
life expectancy, 100
infant mortality, 100
AIDS, 100
accidental child deaths, 101
deaths caused by motor vehicles, 101
teenage depression, 101–102
supportive teenage companionship, 102
fatherless families, 102
getting care when needed, 103
attitudes toward health care, 104
teenage exercise (lowest) and TV watching (second highest), 102, 114

educational achievement scores, 107–109
reading apart from classroom requirements, 108
gap between educational achievement and expenditure level, 110
influence of background on children's literacy scores, 112
high-school-dropout rate, 117
enjoyment of school, 118
incidence of crime, 125
homicide rate, 125
imprisonment rate, 127
capital punishment, 137
pollution (and global effects), 143
use of public transportation, 146
percentage of gross national product (GNP) devoted to foreign aid, 167
women's parliamentary representation, 235
preservation of civil liberties, 241
freedom of the press, 280
voter turnout, 291
democratic representation, 283–310 (chapter 11)

This distressingly poor showing for America is by no means the product of current affairs only. Research findings from the '80s and mid-'90s reveal a very similar pattern. In those periods, the United States was in the *bottom third* among industrialized democratic countries with regard to the rich-poor ratio, energy efficiency, voter turnout, incarceration, foreign aid as a percentage of GNP, women's parliamentary representation, divorce rate, spending on education or health as a percentage of GNP, number of scientists and technicians per capita, book publications per capita, growth rate of exports, social expenditures by government, income growth in the lower half of the scale, government support of the arts, waste recycling, and success in solving crime.[9] Including an earlier period (1960–1990), Bok reported in 1996 (in *The State of the Nation*) that the United States was not just below average, but "at or near the bottom" in more than half of roughly 60 comparisons with other leading industrial nations.

Since America has been lauded for its commitment to R&D, this indicator deserves special attention. America's spending for nondefense R&D as a percentage of GDP has been less than Japan's and about the same as that of Germany and France for two decades (1981–2001).[10] And it has been markedly skewed toward health, as distinct from the physical sciences and engineering, over the same period.[11] In China and India, about 35 percent of college graduates are in engineering or technology fields, compared with only 5 percent in the United States.[12] In America in the past six years alone, there has been a 16 percent drop in the number of citizens or permanent residents acquiring a doctorate in science and engineering, with a "25% decline in math and computer science

PhDs." And over the past 10 years, "federal spending [in R&D] on civilian non-health areas such as energy has risen much less slowly than GDP . . . "[13] Moreover, if the current administration's use of science for policymaking is an indication of its support of R&D, then the nation is in considerable trouble on this score. A 2004 report by the Union of Concerned Scientists, which includes 20 Nobel laureates, has excoriated the administration for manipulating the application of science to policy by placing unqualified or interest-conflicted people on boards, disbanding advisory groups, censoring and suppressing reports and scientists, and not seeking independent advice.[14]

On a related subject, America's physical infrastructure has been in crisis for years, with almost a third of our bridges being "structurally deficient," three-quarters of our school buildings needing extensive repairs or replacement, only about a quarter of Superfund sites having been cleaned up in 1980–98 (and still less than half cleaned up by 2002), with potable drinking water facing an $11 billion annual shortfall (as of 2001), a fifth of buses and almost a quarter of rail vehicles in deficient condition, our electrical transmission capacity having an annual shortfall of 30 percent, and an overall grade of "D+" for America's infrastructure from the American Society of Civil Engineers.[15]

In view of our sorry showing on all these measures, it is not surprising that an index of City Quality of Life found our cities far down the list of the world's 51 major metropolises in 2002. The index was developed and applied by a human resource consulting agency that advises international businesses on such matters as the compensation required for employees who live in various cities of the world.[16] Its 39 criteria include political, social, economic, and environmental factors, personal safety and health, education, transportation, and other public services. Owing to the many ties among cities in their scores, only 17 ranks, or levels, occurred among the top 51 cities in 2002. Although the differences in scores between these ranks were almost negligible, it is still noteworthy that only two American cities, Honolulu and San Francisco, ranked as high as 9th out of 17 ranks, while New York, Boston, and Chicago ranked next to the bottom. (A recent updating of these findings shows essentially the same pattern.)

In other words, we have "scored" poorly on all the aforementioned measures when compared with other advanced countries, in spite of our being the richest country in the world. And what does our enviable wealth really amount to? The economic growth of the '90s, the one major socioeconomic dimension on which America greatly excelled in the past 30 years, was due to the investments of foreigners who now own perhaps a third of the nation's assets, exposing us to considerable risk. (See, for example, the case of Argentina.) The United States cannot even meet the limit on foreign debt for membership in the European Union. Simply put, we are a debtor nation. As for personal assets, just 1 percent of the population has 40 percent of the wealth, the greatest inequality of income distribution among the advanced industrial nations. (See chapter 2.)

Past Trends

The poor showing of America on so many critical dimensions is not just a contemporary anomaly but the culmination of a number of socioeconomic and social psychological trends. These trends have marked the unraveling of an ideal, or fading of a dream, that motivated generations of Americans, and that gave special meaning to and evoked confident pride in being a member of American society. As argued in the Introduction, however, the dream has not been totally abandoned, but has been transformed into a myth that covers up harsh realities, such as those cited above—a shift from confident hope to wishful defiance of the truth that sometimes rises to a level of stridency in its defensive reaffirmation of patriotism. What are some of these long-term trends (over the past 10, 20, or 30 years) that might have contributed to or reflect a fading of the traditionally optimistic American Dream? To anticipate later chapters where the data are presented, some of the key developments are the following.

There have been clear-cut *increases* in income inequality, the cost of higher education, and other impediments to upward mobility; in deep poverty and child poverty, consumer debt, the cost of medical insurance and drugs, working hours, cuts in government benefits, and tax relief to big business; in nonunionized workers, the unaffordability of rental housing for lower-income families (particularly for those dropped from the welfare rolls in the '90s), violent crime in major cities, imprisonment and lack of rehabilitation programs, and the influence of wealth and interest groups on elections and legislation (judging from the enormous increase in campaign and lobbying outlays and the actions of individual officeholders); in the loss of jobs through the hiring of cheap foreign labor by American companies, the deterioration of infrastructure, the concentration of media ownership, segregation in public education, AIDS, and long-term unemployment in manufacturing and, more recently, throughout the economy. An index of Social Health, developed at Fordham University, which included such measures as homicide, child poverty, job satisfaction, drug use, etc., showed a decline of *45 percent from 1979 to 1999.*[17]

At the same time, and possibly owing to these trends as well as other, more recently emergent conditions, Americans have apparently become more alienated or, put somewhat differently, more likely to sense "disempowerment." Thus, according to surveys, we have become increasingly distrustful of each other, more likely to perceive income inequality, more likely to feel powerless, more fearful of foreign attack, more likely to believe that government tends to represent big-business interests, less likely to trust most major institutions, including religion and civic institutions (but, significantly, excepting the military), and less likely to vote. In addition, there has been more drug use among younger teenagers, more suicide (especially among the young), and more child abuse. And most of these trends have been quite marked.

To be sure, some indicators have shown improvement over a number of years, such as infant mortality, poverty among the elderly, teenage pregnancy, drug use among college students, and air quality. Indeed, one recent book[18] by a journalist and fellow at the Brookings Institute argues that "practically every-thing [is] getting better" (the title of his chapter 2). But a close reading of this work reveals a pattern of flaws. Since the book demonstrates how staunch dedi-cation to the American Myth can blur one's vision of reality, it is worth devoting some attention to it here.

In the first place, the author has a tendency to mitigate certain downtrends and signs of stagnation—for example, by noting that mental stress is not neces-sarily bad, that the unaffordability of prescription drugs (many of which are life-saving) has "countervailing benefits," or that educational test scores show "guarded" improvement when, in fact, it would take 222 years for eighth graders to achieve a perfect score at the recently reported rate of negligible progress. (See my chapter 3 on education.)

Moreover, a large number of worsening conditions, such as growing barri-ers to upward mobility, seem to be omitted altogether from the book, and some are even flatly denied. An example of the latter is the author's handling of inter-national relations. The reader is assured that "in the last decade, almost every-thing in international affairs has gone spectacularly well" (p. 68). This judgment is rendered in spite of America's failure to stem terrorism (culminating in 9/11 and two Middle Eastern wars), to resolve or even ease the Israeli-Palestinian conflict, to reduce negative public opinion toward America in almost every na-tion in the world, to pacify Somalia, to lower our spectacular trade deficit, to stem the decline of our global economic strength, to prevent the emergence of hard-line policies toward America in Indonesia, Russia, Brazil, Korea, and Ar-gentina, and so on. And the fact that widespread unemployment is scarcely men-tioned in a volume published in 2003 requires no comment. As for the larger issue of an *occupational* crisis because of job stress, excessive hours of work, and the need to hold two jobs, among other problems (as discussed in my chap-ter 2), this issue apparently was not even detected by the author.

Finally, by often lumping together American and European trends under "Western society," the author obscures the fact that Europe has *drawn ahead* of America in a variety of significant ways, as documented by Derek Bok.[19] From his extensive examination of numerous international comparisons, Bok con-cluded in 1996 that "our society could not manage during the past several dec-ades to make important advances that other nations made toward basic goals that Americans share with people throughout the industrialized world."[20] This sig-nificant conclusion from research is not mentioned in the book under discussion. As a general rule, caution is advised in accepting references to long-term im-provement in certain conditions as showing a nation's special vitality, for the same condition could have improved at a considerably *greater* rate in other advanced nations; and, indeed, this has been the case with respect to a number of dimensions on which America is still behind *in spite of* improvements.

My earlier summary of downtrends in America suggests a growing gap between our idealization of the nation and the realities of American life; and additional data on strictly current conditions (that is, without reference to past trends) throughout the chapters of this book will supplement these long-term trend data. The gap has grown so large that only mythology can preserve any vestige of the older American Dream.

If the current U.S. government were mobilizing society to handle these mounting problems, as the New Deal attacked social breakdown in the '30s, one might feel confident that any decline would be halted or reversed. But under the present administration, social and environmental expenditure by government is stagnant or negative; and in 1992 the United States was *already next to last* in its social expenditures among 19 advanced nations. The faltering economy at the turn of the century, of course, has aggravated the situation as states' services have succumbed to growing deficits and the federal government has turned its attention to a war on terrorism and defense spending. Is it too extreme to characterize this situation as a recipe for social implosion? One of the chief means by which implosion has been postponed is entrenchment under the banner of the American Myth—which brings us to the question of why the Myth, which presents a picture of America so at odds with reality, is so enduring. The answer lies in the benefits that it bestows.

Sources of the Myth's Robustness

The strength of the American Myth resides in its serving a multiplicity of interests and needs—personal, societal, political, and economic—and its *politicization* and *sacralization* have gone far beyond the conventional American Dream. It provides security, pride, and a sense of belonging to a national community that can allegedly solve any problem, assuage any suffering, or throw back any foe. On the societal level, it integrates the diverse elements of the nation (which is especially useful in a pluralistic society with many immigrant groups and opposing interests) and thereby discourages overt discord, contributing to quiescence and conformism. (Philadelphia proclaimed itself the "City of Brotherly Love" precisely because of the potential for conflict among its many different national groups, sects, classes, and so forth.) Occasionally, a movement has emerged that espoused particularistic values, such as the multicultural movement of the '90s, the feminist movement of the '60s and '70s, and the Black Power and hippy movements of the '60s. But all such movements are eventually swamped by the strong undercurrent of identity with a triumphant destiny shared by all Americans. In effect, we regard ourselves as the secular version of the

Chosen People of ancient Israel, a great privilege not to be spurned lightly, even by dissenters. Indeed, both the left and the right are united in their devotion to the idea of America's supremacy as a national enterprise—which explains why the thesis of the present book has never, to the best of my knowledge, been debated nor even alluded to in public political discourse.

Another societal benefit of the Myth is a dampening of widespread resentment of, and protest against, income inequality, inasmuch as it promises untrammeled opportunity to get ahead. Indeed, it motivates economic and other efforts in spite of insurmountable hurdles, spawning frustrations that are transformed into *fantasies of overcoming* (including the vicarious enjoyment of violence against fictionalized oppressors or enemies, as in the endless stream of movies where the hero portrays a consummate overcomer). When one fails to achieve the American Dream, the Myth deflects blame from society to oneself. At the same time, it reassures the more privileged members of society that opportunity is available to those at the bottom of the ladder, thereby relieving any pangs of conscience. Thus, the Myth is a defender of the status quo in spite of the level of suffering or disaffection.

The Myth also fuels patriotism, of course, which lends itself to strong, uncompromising commitment to the nation in a confrontation with outsiders, regardless of the latter's cause or justification for complaint. In fact, because we can do no wrong (by virtue of our virtue, so to speak), our leaders feel that they can lecture, bully, snub, or exploit other nations with confidence that most of the public will stand behind them; and even launch a war that resembles an Islamic Holy War in its righteousness. Indeed, the Myth can maintain support for an enormous military machine, provided the people can be kept in a mood of insecurity by their leaders, with the indispensable help of the mass media.

Since America lacks a single, overarching religious identity (as is provided by Islam in Middle Eastern countries), the Myth serves as a substitute for shared devotion to a set of beliefs, practices, and symbols that confers an aura of divine sanction on the nation. It becomes the rock of a civil religion. Thus, the Constitution, a major piece of holy writ in the scripture of the American Myth, is referred to as "sacred," as are our flag and national monuments, and especially our military graveyards and battlefields, which are widely referred to as "hallowed" ground. In short, the Myth provides the basis for an integrative civil religion.

This overheated reverence affords numerous opportunities for opportunists, as alluded to above, to invoke the sanctity of social institutions as a means of self-enrichment or empowerment, and above all as a reason for either preserving things as they are or entrusting their protection to an even more devout believer of their choosing. Accordingly, a recurrent stimulus of the Myth is the reiteration of the "greatness of America" by politicians who seek support by flattering the public for creating such an exceptional society. In fact, the aura of sanctity can be extended even to our economic system. "I believe in God and I believe in free markets," intoned Ken Lay, the super-exploitative CEO of Enron, with reference to one of the shibboleths of the Myth. Placing the wonders of free enterprise on a par with God's benefactions is one of the greatest achievements of the American Myth.

Indeed, faith in the American Myth is fused with the state in much the same way as faith in Islam is fused with the state in Middle Eastern countries. That their faith is formally religious while ours is secular makes little difference. Both faiths are devoid of empirical foundation, which is precisely why both provide a virtually endless array of psychological, social, economic, military, political, cultural, and aesthetic benefits. For both partake of the realm of "the Other," that marvelous alternative world where anything goes and everything is possible.

In spite of all these benefits of the American Myth, it is the most destructive element in our culture today because it blinds us to the perils of domestic and international backwardness and lends support to leaders who contribute to our inferiority by commission or omission. In fact, one of the most detrimental impacts of the Myth on our public life is the compulsion felt by our leaders to conceal, defend, mitigate, and distort the nation's most lackluster or reprehensible actions. If one is at the helm of a country that purports to be infallible by dint of historical singularity, then the only recourse in response to criticism or failure is *denial* with every ounce of Machiavellian cunning that a consummate politician can muster. (The persistent refusal of President Bush to apologize for, or even acknowledge, the administration's failures that permitted the 9/11 attacks to occur is a case in point.) Yet, without bold recognition of our failures and second-rate standing among advanced nations, including our lack of maturity in foreign relations, measures necessary to remedy our current impairments will never be undertaken.

Fortunately, unlike religion, the American Myth is not only a faith, but also a secular ideology inasmuch as it *purports* to be an accurate description of the real world. Consequently, it has a fatal vulnerability. Even though it has survived unscathed for years and provides an array of benefits, it is still susceptible to being hauled into the court of social science and impartially judged for its truth-value. And that is the central purpose of this book.

There is a problem, however, with any effort to examine the Myth critically, no matter how factual the basis or judicious the argument. It imposes a duty on the believer to demonize anyone who speaks out against it. Consequently, the mildest expression of skepticism *reinforces* the Myth's strength by confirming the existence of enemies who must be rebuffed. Thus, its contempt for verity and for those who would try to express it is automatically refreshed. This is a built-in feature of all doctrinaire ideologies and reflects their felt indispensability for preserving social and psychological stability: there shalt be no naysayers. This spirited defense is totally understandable, since nobody wants to have their

Weltanschauung shaken. In this respect, the American Myth is not only a strongly held belief system but a self-enhancing lie.

As we shall see, the data for testing the Myth are easily accessible, if one but has the time and inclination. Although the basic reason for a lack of inclination to debunk the Myth is its multifunctional nature, giving it an aura of indispensability, the failure of Americans even to *receive information* that might challenge it is an important supplement to the Myth's potency. And why should that be? For example, why is it that so many of us are sublimely ignorant of more than a fraction of the startling facts in the lengthy list presented earlier? And I have little doubt that other surprising discoveries await the average reader in the following chapters.

The Informational Defaults of the Media and Government

Two reasons that so many unwelcome and even shocking facts have failed to cross the threshold of the public's attention are: (a) the extremely limited acquaintance of the public with data from the social sciences and government publications, mainly because of the government's failure to summarize data in annual "social reports," as is done in most European countries; and (b) the reluctance of the news media, especially television (where most Americans now obtain their news), to report the great majority of social trends and current conditions in the country, particularly negative ones, that are not embraced by their beloved "leading economic indicators." These two reasons for the public's limited knowledge of social conditions in America are intertwined, of course. (Since it would be utterly futile to expect our locally controlled, public educational system to dispense unsavory facts about contemporary society—racism, poverty, corporate control of government, etc.—I do not even bother to charge it with failing to do so. It is, and probably always will be, irrelevant to many of the realities of contemporary life in America.)

The media are mesmerized by economics as if it were the only realm of significance to the well-being of the nation. Yet history has repeatedly shown that even a flourishing economy can harbor widespread social injustice, poverty, and disaffection. But this fact is generally overlooked by economists, the media, and most policymakers. In fact, periods of economic upturn, because they afford a false sense of security concerning the welfare of large population groups, can allow matters to worsen for these groups more so than in times of poor economic conditions, when compunction dictates that they be given some attention.

Indeed, technology-driven booms have often *increased* inequality and its consequences, a situation neglected by the media. During the recent economic boom, for example, there were approximately two million homeless people in a year, and 25 percent of the requests for emergency shelter went unmet in 30 cities. (See chapter 2.) In 1996–98, the poverty rate for families with children in New York City was 32 percent.[20] And a more recent study reported that "despite the strong economy [in the '90s], the number of people classified as poor in the 2000 census was slightly higher than the number counted a decade earlier."[21] Even in that period of exceptionally high demand for workers in America, we ranked 11th among 30 industrial nations in the wages paid to manufacturing workers.[22] Finally, over a 30-year period (ca. 1966–96), an index of the nation's "social health," designed by Miringoff and Miringoff,[23] showed that the index *fell* for a number of years while the GDP *rose,* and then at least leveled off while the GDP continued to rise.

As a social philosopher has reminded us (as cited by Miringoff and Miringoff), "life is more than a set of commercial relations."[25] However, commercial relations can be joyful for some people while being distressful for others. Thus, mergers, downsizing, exploitation of low-wage workers, cuts in nonwage (e.g., health care) benefits, longer working hours, multiple job holding, and so forth, can fuel a booming economy while causing great social harm. The fact that social harm has risen while commercial relations were thriving, according to Miringoff and Miringoff's research, would seem to bear this out; and if one needed further proof, one need only recall that the great, booming Industrial Revolution of England was not exactly a godsend for the factory workers, including the child laborers. In short, an emphasis on economic indicators along with a neglect of social indicators is completely unwarranted on any rational grounds whatsoever. (Some reasons for the mainstream media's reluctance to allot serious coverage to social suffering and protest are discussed in chapter 10.)

It would be possible, of course, for the media themselves to combine certain indicators into an index of social well-being, and to report the results regularly. Any number of social scientists could show them how to do it or provide the index themselves. Imagine this report on the evening news: "The index of social well-being dropped 30 points last month, mainly due to an increase in child abuse and hate crimes, although there was a slight decrease in job stress, which might be related to increased productivity." Alternatively, the media could use the Miringoff index mentioned above, the Index of Sustainable Economic Welfare (which has been provisionally applied in several countries, including the United States[26]), or the Genuine Progress Indicator (see my discussion of this last-named index in chapter 2).

These considerations raise a point that is pertinent to my argument that America is a second-rate nation. In the first paragraph of this chapter, I mentioned a "nation's willingness to monitor itself" as a paramount feature of a great society. And no doubt the reader assented mechanically to this principle on the assumption that this was already the case in America. I also mentioned earlier that it is true that our government collects a wide range of both economic and social data about our country through a number of agencies. But does it select and summarize these data in a meaningful way under such basic goal-oriented categories as "social equality" that can be used by the public, policy-makers, journalists, and so on, to keep up-to-date with current social conditions and make comparisons with the past or with other nations? The answer is that it does not. But that is not all: America is one of the very few advanced countries that does *not* produce an annual "social report" of this kind. Although proposed here in 1968, the idea fell on deaf ears. In the very next year, however, the Netherlands took up the idea, and since then almost every European nation has followed suit.[27] In the past decade, a number of American communities have begun to produce such reports about *local* conditions.[28] But the federal government has not done so with regard to *nationwide* conditions. It is as though the nation was trying to retreat from the facts of life, an ostrich-like posture that the American Myth would like to preserve as long as possible.

Even if an annual report by the government is not available to the media, there is nothing to prevent them from reporting rates of homelessness, poverty, job stress, suicide, infant mortality, mental illness, arrests and recidivism, pollution levels, dropout rates, separation and divorces, child abuse, motor vehicle injuries, class mobility, and other indicators of the social health of our allegedly superior society, and to do so on a *regular* basis. And where are the comparisons with other advanced countries? Information on these matters is as near as one's computer or as distant as the breadth of one's complacency. Indeed, how many media people are aware that for decades regular soundings of the happiness of the population have been taken by one of our leading university survey research agencies? And yet everyone is attentive to the merest quaver in the Dow Jones Average or the index of Consumer Confidence—a fixation, I hardly need add, that is not prompted by solicitude for others. Perhaps the same deficit of solicitude is responsible for America's indifference to a "social report." We are in the habit of decrying the censorship of authoritarian regimes. But is de facto censorship any different from de jure censorship *in its consequences*? (For more on the media's omissions and distortions, see chapter 10.)

It is possible that America's geographical isolation from Europe has deprived it of the moderating effects of information sharing and peer comparison and pressure that would have prevented some of the unique excesses and deficiencies I have mentioned and will discuss fully in the following chapters. In short, our isolation might help explain why America has fallen behind modern Europe in so many ways and remained ignorant of this developmental fact. But the American mainstream media have played a role here as well, for clearly they have failed remarkably to keep Americans informed about events in Europe—apart, that is, from strikes, bad weather, street demonstrations (which are explained only superficially), the British monarchy, and the anti-American comments of political leaders. Our educational system has done little better with regard to contemporary affairs and quality of life in Europe. By and large,

Americans of all classes have been obliged to view contemporary Europe through the eyes of soldiers, tourist guidebook writers, novelists, and movie-makers. In this age of instantaneous, global electronic communication, our ignorance is due more to the failure of our educational system and our mainstream media than to sheer distance. In any case, the effects of geography are quite difficult to measure and will have to await more focused investigation than I can give here.

An Integrated Power Structure

I have devoted special attention to the media because they form one of the four pillars of the American structure of power that are jointly responsible for the nation's failure to live up to its ideals and self-advertisements. The other three pillars, or major power sectors, are: large corporations, government (including the military) acting under the authority of an outmoded constitution, and a poorly informed and usually acquiescent public (including its many intermediate, nongovernmental organizations). Each sector views the others as exploitable assets, which locks them together in a system of reciprocities or codependencies that defies readjustment. This formulation, although highly simplified, might help to explain America's astounding resistance to social or political reform—that is, the reason it continues to proceed on its present course in spite of demonstrable failure in almost every institutional realm, rapidly changing circumstances, popular dissent at home and abroad, and the distress of our disadvantaged subcultures.

That the public exercises power in a democratic polity, and should therefore be counted as one of the four power sectors, might seem to be obvious. But a significant part of that role is overlooked. For it is not true that the American people exercise power only through such activities as voting, writing to officials and representatives, organizing pressure groups, lobbying, contributing to campaigns, and so on. In fact, these actions constitute a limited part of the true power wielded by the public. The larger part inheres in its *acquiescence* to the performance and policies of the three other power sectors (including government), amounting to de facto approval of these sectors and delegation of responsibilities to them for "governing" the nation.

Apathy and acquiescence are evidence not of a *lack* of power, but of *passive power* or power by default—the power of implicit endorsement of the status quo by allowing, tolerating, and even suffering it to prevail. In fact, voter apathy probably has been more responsible for the outcomes of elections in America than all the informed voting of the active electorate put together. Thus, in a nation where fewer than half the electorate votes in presidential elections (see chapter 11), the overt expression of desires may be secondary to the power of silent assent or submission. This is no doubt an unorthodox way of measuring power or, if one prefers, influence; but it is nevertheless essential to an understanding of the American power structure. For the strength of the other, more active power sectors depends on public acquiescence to their performance and policies, regardless of how well the public understands what these sectors are up to or why.

The reason that passive power has remained unspoken in conventional political discourse (except for Nixon's claim of support for his Vietnam policy by the "silent majority") is because it refutes the Myth's assurance of *democratic vitality,* which vitality is supposed to be represented by vigorous and widespread participation. And if federal officeholders ever complained or even mentioned that less than half of the electorate votes in federal elections, they would be exposing themselves as not really representing the electorate and therefore imposters. Which, of course, is the case. Further, it should be reiterated that the effects of public acquiescence reach far beyond formal politics and government to the implicit endorsement, and thus emboldening, of the other dominant sources of power in our nation. In other words, the people are deeply implicated in their own fate whether they like it or not and whether they consciously foster it or not. That is the unavoidable burden of membership in a democratic society.

The ethical implication of this conception of the public's power needs to be candidly confronted: *All* the people of a democracy who are legally qualified to participate should be held accountable for the state of the nation's affairs even if they do not play an *active* part in shaping those affairs. In both ethical philosophy and law, acts of omission with dire consequences are as incriminating as acts of commission with equally dire consequences. The people should not be treated with contempt, but they should not be romanticized either, although one of the major effects of the American Myth is to do precisely that.

Codependencies among the power sectors will be referred to throughout the text. Moreover, owing to the transformative effects of this symbiotic system, it will be argued that it no longer makes sense to analyze each sector apart from the others. By "transformative" I mean the gradual absorption of the values and styles of one sector by another with which it is symbiotically related, or what might be called a cultural convergence. Thus, the values of business and the style of the media are assimilated by government, while big business and the media share political functions with government. Even the public adopts the jargon, outlooks, and modes of thought that originate in the media and government. As with any tightly integrated system, the parts are far from being autonomous, for they gather strength and direction from their relations with other parts while the boundaries between them become increasingly blurred.

If the American Myth provides the ideological barrier to reform, then the interlocking of power sectors provides the structural barrier. In fact, the two barriers reinforce one another, as culture and social structure invariably do in a reasonably stable society. In other words, beliefs, values, and norms (culture) are expressed in the way that society is organized (social structure), and the latter sustains and protects the former from attack and in turn is itself protected by the beliefs, values, and norms. In the final analysis, stability tends to triumph at the expense of needed change until dysfunctions reach a head that can no longer be ignored. Rather than presenting the facts of America's condition in terms of this theoretical system, however, I have chosen to present them with reference to each of several major domains like health care, education, the media, and the economy that are readily comprehensible to the reader. References to the Myth and to the power structure, therefore, are editorially subordinated to discussion of particular problems in each of these familiar areas that demonstrate the failure of America to live up to its self-image.

The Facts

Since the statistical data presented in the following chapters are not complex, but simple distributions of percentages, rankings, ratios, averages, and the like, I do not expect the educated reader to have the least trouble understanding them. My hope is that by bringing them together in one place, and by focusing on many measurements that have been ignored by the mainstream media or deflected by the government, the book will contribute to a more accurate and coherent picture of America at the turn of the millennium than can be achieved by random bits of information found in scattered and often unreliable sources. I especially hope that, by presenting an abundance of empirical evidence, the American Myth will begin to be exorcised from the mental world of Americans so that urgently needed reforms can proceed, and, additionally, so that the present interlocking structure of power, which sits like an incubus on American progress, will be exposed and lifted.

In accordance with these goals, it should be borne in mind that the facts I have gathered are not intended to cover every institutional domain in the depth or breadth that would be required for a full-dress, analytical portrait of the nation. Instead, the intention has been to provide *sufficient, representative* documentation to support the central thesis, namely, that we are failing to meet standards shared with most other advanced industrial countries in almost every important area of our national existence. This focus means that certain problems and issues are not explicated in depth, and that others, regrettably, are only alluded to or omitted altogether. Thus, the work is not a textbook on American institutions, although it provides a broad sweep of the American panorama. My long-range goal has been to overcome the nation's resistance to the idea that it suffers from afflictions that need urgent attention lest it become an eccentric relic of the past century.

The standard of representativeness, however, means that problem areas that are more *familiar* to readers often receive a degree of attention similar to those that are less so. While this has been done mainly to provide a fuller picture of current conditions, it also affords a factual *resource* for readers engaged in policymaking, teaching, report writing, journalism, public speaking, and so on. If the reader feels well informed on a particular topic, therefore, he or she might wish to skip over it and move on to less familiar territory. However, caution should be exercised in this regard inasmuch as I have included certain facts in familiar areas that extend, underscore, or elaborate what is already widely known or, alternatively, challenge the conventional wisdom—in other words, facts that are *not* familiar. Thus, the reader might shun familiar problem areas at the risk of failing to be exposed to a more complete record or even to a new slant on the subject.

A few words should also be said about the up-to-dateness of the data. Since the book draws on social and economic statistics pertaining to contemporary affairs, the reader might feel that the data should be as up-to-date as the morning paper or the nightly news show. This is impossible, of course, because of delays in publication due to, first, researching, summarizing, and interpreting a range of information over a period of many months and, second, producing a book and arranging for its distribution. This delay is not necessarily a drawback in the present case, however, because my thesis does not depend upon up-to-the-minute documentation as much as it does on the detection of persistent patterns. Thus, the period from roughly 1996 to 2004 sets our main boundaries, a time that encompasses the turn of the millennium. Earlier years are by no means ignored but are treated as either the womb of the present or as conduits for trends that are still discernible today. The events of this focal period, I believe, are sufficient to support my argument that America has fallen significantly behind other advanced nations and is failing to meet its proclaimed goals. Even if the George W. Bush administration vanished into oblivion at the end of its first term, the widespread support of its atavistic policies would be indicative of the troubled state of America in the early first decade of the millennium. Moreover, whether certain conditions in the nation have worsened or improved over the past decade or so, admittedly an important issue, is secondary to proving my thesis of persistent inferiority in comparison with other advanced nations and persistent failure to realize national goals. In short, I have been concerned with identifying an underlying pattern of mediocrity, if not outright inferiority, in spite of our national self-image as the world's most outstanding country and in spite of scattered improvements that we might have enjoyed over the past several years. It is the fundamental character of our national life that concerns me.

On the issue of objectivity, undoubtedly some degree of bias has been introduced by the manner in which I have selected and arranged the data. I can only plead that I have been alert to this danger and sought to limit it by not wrenching statements of fact out of context to promote a particular viewpoint, and by not omitting facts that challenge what appears to be the consensus, the general tendency of the data, or the most respectable source of documentation as well as my own predilections. At several points I have corrected what might be called "politically correct" and "fashionably aloof" viewpoints (depending on one's political position) by injecting common sense or more complete information into the discussion. Moreover, I have been prolific with references to sources, and even with the exact words of the sources, and have resorted to paraphrase or synopsis only when the data were complex or their full presentation would be unnecessarily lengthy. In short, I have tried to abide by the usual canons of representativeness, reliability, and validity while also practicing literate concision and cogency.

This does not mean, however, that I have shirked responsibility for drawing the *ethical* implications of certain findings of fact and sharing them with the reader. For we are dealing here with the manner in which humans are affected by forces larger than themselves, including personal agents, and clinical detachment in the face of needless suffering or official lies is not necessarily a virtue. Comments that reflect my own judgments should be clearly recognizable, however. Thus, the reader is free either to dismiss or refute them, and I have little doubt that many will endeavor to do one or the other.

Finally, it would be foolish to claim categorically that the text is devoid of all statistical, clerical, and interpretative errors. A book that bristles with numbers and details of complex situations, legal matters, and controversial events and policies, and which leans heavily on documentation by others, is bound occasionally to err, in spite of the fact that I and others have devoted many hours to checking and rechecking our sources.

Any outstanding errors that the reader can bring to my attention, therefore, are welcome and will benefit the preparation of any possible future editions. Please send e-mail to: feedback@SecondRateNation.com.

In sum, in my effort to inform the public, I have tried to take seriously that wise maxim of Americans when confronted with painful allegations: "Show me the facts"; and I have done so in the hope that, if America really has the moral and pragmatic fortitude that it boasts, it will endeavor to do something about them.

2

The Economy, Work, Recent Federal Budgets, and Business and Government

The American economy has long been regarded as the greatest engine of prosperity in the history of the world, and not just for the few but for the many. It was the primary, structural basis of the American Dream of upwards and onwards for all, the golden spur of an exceptionally achievement-oriented society. In the past several decades, however, this picture of the economy has become cracked and frayed, and the Dream has been preserved only by robust myth. The inequitable distribution of wealth and the declining vitality of economic processes have been accompanied by widespread social afflictions that distinguish America from other advanced nations.

The Paradox of Poverty in the Midst of Wealth

Wealth

America bestrides the world like a Croesus, the renowned king of the ancient land of Lydia that was credited by Xenophanes with the invention of standardized lucre. Since it has the largest treasury in the world, it might seem as if America itself invented money. The following facts attest to America's preeminent wealth at the dawn of a new century of fractious globalization.

The total wealth of the United States far surpasses that of other nations. In spite of having only 5 percent of the world's population, it generates 30 percent of the world's Gross Product and consumes nearly 30 percent of the world's oil production.[1] In terms of gross domestic product, America's $35,831 per person in 2001 was exceeded only by tiny Luxembourg's $35,894 per person.[2] (The United States is the third largest country in the world in terms of both its population of 285 million and its size.) In comparison with the mean GDP per capita of

18 European countries, the United States is almost twice as rich, namely, 1.9 times richer than its European motherland.[3]

If we compare the United States with the world's lowest-income countries, each person in the United States has 75 times the average annual income of an inhabitant of those countries.[4] As a reference point, it should be noted that "of the 6.2 billion people in today's world, 1.2 billion [19.4 %] live on less than $1 per day."[5] Moreover, "the richest 10 percent of Americans . . . have an income greater than the poorest 43 percent of the world's people. . . ."[6]

These figures on wealth suggest a land of riches and luxury where an ancient king would feel like a humble pensioner. But the truth of the matter is that America also presents a picture of widespread poverty, one that is unique among the advanced industrial nations of the world.

Poverty

Poverty in America is a difficult concept for Americans to grasp and even more difficult to absorb, and the fact that our teachers, mass media, and leaders would prefer not to discuss it (except for brief references during political campaigns) is no help. Among many who are better off and have never experienced its grip, it is dismissed as a sign of indolence and over-procreation, posing the threat of welfare cheating. From this viewpoint, the worst thing one can do is pamper the poor with assistance. A somewhat more sympathetic diagnosis is that poverty is a temporary condition of immigrants or persons who have fallen willy-nilly on evil days, but who will eventually become beneficiaries of the American Dream if only they have the will. In contrast to both of these explanations is the notion of structural conditions in American society that produce, preserve, and even deepen poverty in many cases. This view is not very attractive to many Americans, and indeed is simply indigestible to a staunch minority. One reason for its lack of popularity is that it is less satisfying than blame-oriented explanations that implicitly self-congratulate the accuser for having avoided the poor house. In short, the structural viewpoint undermines the complacent idea that poverty is a matter only of bad habits instead of bad luck, which idea is one of the axioms of the American Myth. Finally, the notion that class privilege and power, and the barriers to upward mobility that these impose on others, could be even remotely operative is repudiated as an outmoded bit of European ideology inspired by radical angst.

Whatever the view from the veranda, however, it is a common habit of Americans to avert their eyes from the facts about poverty "on the ground." So let us begin by looking squarely, first, at the prevalence of poverty; second, at its impact on those who suffer it; and finally, at some of its structural sources in recent American history. While blame may be appropriate in some cases, this is not the business that we are in. The clearly patterned distribution of life chances among certain social categories—ethnic or racial groups, educational levels, neighborhoods, etc.—signifies that social factors are far more powerful predictors of life chances than personal traits.

It has been said that America "discovered poverty" when Michael Harrington's book *The Other America* appeared in 1962 and helped launch the War on Poverty of the Johnson administration. It can be said with equal cogency today that America has lost sight of poverty once again. So here are some figures that might remind us of the conditions we have turned our backs on in our wholehearted devotion to the American Myth.

In 2000, the poverty rate was 11.3 percent and in 2001 it rose to 11.7 percent; in 2002, it rose another 0.4 percent to 12.1 percent. The number of persons below the poverty threshold in 2002 was 34.6 million.[7] The poverty rate for children, namely, 16.3 percent, was higher than for any other age group in 2001,[8] and from 1979 to 1998 it had increased by 15 percent nationally and by over 40 percent in at least a dozen states.[9] A *third* of Americans have fallen below the poverty line at least once.[10] Moreover, 10 percent of American children live in extreme poverty, that is, in families with incomes below 50 percent of the poverty level.[11] In 2004, the poverty level in America was the highest of 17 OECD countries with available data.[12] The percentage of the poor in "deep poverty" in this country has increased in the past 15 years from less than 33 percent of all poor people to about 40 percent.[13] So much for the wonderful '90s. The undeniable picture, then, is of numerous poor in America and many more *becoming* poor every year. These statistics may be shocking, but at least they are not deceptive.

But, then, isn't the notion of "poverty" just an invention of statisticians? It is certainly true that definitions vary, and the one I am using here—income below the official poverty line for different sizes of household—is a conservative one. One often-cited study defines poverty as living in a household whose income is less than half the median income of a nation. If we were to use this definition, child poverty in America would be hovering around 20 percent, while that of other nations would be a good deal lower. In fact, the current measure of the poverty threshold is 40 years old, and the National Academy of Sciences has estimated that it would be *45 percent higher* if it were updated.[14] But regardless of exact numbers, we can rest assured that being poor is a special state of existence that many millions of Americans share.

Then again, one might ask, what difference does it really make in the richest nation on earth? After all, one never sees a poor person on television, and the mainstream media and our leaders almost never refer to poverty. This, too, is true, but it does not alter the fact that poor people exist even if they are not covered by the media or invited to TV studios, or because our leaders tend to shun the whole issue. Our masses of the poor suffer from distinctive conditions that set them apart from other members of society; and many of these conditions entail severe psychological distress, physical suffering, and even premature death. Let us look at some of these conditions in wealthy America.

First, there is the simple problem of being unable to afford shelter. One and a third million children are homeless in a given year,[15] and in 1999 it was estimated that there were "700,000 people homeless on any given night and up to 2 million people who experience homelessness during one year,"[16] figures that are no doubt much higher today. In 27 cities in 2001, emergency shelter was unavailable for 52 percent of all family requests.[17] Especially shocking is the fact that 33 percent of the homeless in New York are veterans of the military,[18] and Congresswoman Cynthia McKinney of Georgia asserted in a public address in 2002 that nationwide the percentage of the homeless who are veterans was 25 percent. Moreover, more than a quarter of the persons who were homeless in 2002, according to a survey in 27 cities, were employed, which was probably because people forced to leave welfare for low wages could not afford housing costs.[19] Indeed, "14 million households spend more than half of their income on housing or live in severely substandard conditions . . . [a total of] one in every seven renters in America."[20] The rental cost of housing in 39 states, it should be borne in mind, is twice the minimum wage, and in 9 states it is three times the minimum wage.[21] Consequently, evictions climbed precipitously in the late '90s owing to President Clinton's elimination of Aid for Families with Dependent Children. In Milwaukee, for example, with an allegedly model program, evictions increased 200 percent from 1997 to 2000.[22]

What about hunger? "About 12 million families worried [in 2002] that they did not have enough money for food," according to a recent report by the Department of Agriculture.[23] And the percentage of Americans who reported being unable to afford food at some time in the past year, namely, 15 percent, was higher than for citizens of any other advanced nation.[24] Further, while the largest federal food program is the food stamp program, the average benefit each month is only $180. For elderly persons living alone, it is $50; and slightly more than a third of these persons receive an average benefit of just $10.[25]

In case you think you've wandered into the wrong classroom, let me assure you that we are talking about America here, the land of riches and opportunity. But there is more. How about one's health and chances of sheer physical survival?

According to a government research report, the likelihood of being in good health increases with each increment of income or education.[26] Not surprisingly, then, children at or above the poverty line are about 20 percentage points more likely to be in very good or excellent health than those below the poverty line.[27] A study in 1994 by the Children's Defense Fund found that poor children were 8 times more likely than children in families of average income to be victims of homicides, 4.5 times more likely to be abused, and 3 times more likely to die in childhood or to have only fair or poor health.[28] Moreover, poor Americans are much more vulnerable than similar citizens in other advanced nations because of their inability to afford private health insurance and the limited availability of government-subsidized insurance. More than 43 million Americans, including 8 million children, have no health insurance[29] because, as one congressman succinctly put it, "The United States is the only major nation on earth that does not have a national health care program that guarantees health care to all."[30] This deficit in health care assistance goes a long way toward explaining why the poorest men (bottom 10%) with serious health problems are *three times* more likely to die from their condition than the richest (top 10%).[31]

The elderly in particular suffer from the lack of affordable prescription drug coverage. According to a study reported by the American Association of Retired Persons,[32] among older Americans with diabetes, 31 percent without coverage do not fill all their prescriptions "because of cost," compared with 14 percent of those with coverage. Comparable rates for high blood pressure are 28 percent vs. 12 percent; and for congestive heart failure, 25 percent vs. 14 percent. (For much more on drug costs, health insurance, and the new Medicare and drug insurance law of 2003, see chapter 3.)

One consequence of being unable to afford regular care by a physician for standard ailments is that the emergency rooms of America have been overwhelmed by the poor for every kind of health problem. Thus, emergency room visits increased by 5 million in 2001, according to the American College of Emergency Physicians.[33] (The problem of dwindling emergency room capacity is also discussed in chapter 3.) And no doubt partly as a result of the lack of accessible care, we are confronted with the shocking fact that the infant mortality rate is higher in America than in 19 other countries, including the UK, Germany, France, Italy, Belgium, Denmark, and Japan. In fact, our infant mortality rate is the same as that in Martinique, Malta, New Caledonia, Cuba, and the Republic of Korea.[34]

Then there are large categories of Americans who tend to be disadvantaged in addition to their poverty, such as single mothers, the mentally ill, and many blacks and Hispanics. With regard to the mentally ill, poverty may not only deprive them of basic services but subject them to inhumane and even illegal treatment. It was found in New York State, for example, that

> Hundreds of patients released from state psychiatric hospitals in New York in recent years are being locked away on isolated floors of nursing homes, where they are barred from going outside on their own, have almost no contact with others and have little ability to contest their confinement . . .[35]

As for disadvantaged minorities, one of the common attributes of their poverty is the mortal danger of violence. In fact, the leading cause of death among young black men, and the second leading cause among young Hispanic men, is murder.[36] And the fate of many black, single mothers dropped from welfare by the Clinton administration has been homelessness, hunger, and unaffordable illness.

But the ramifications of poverty go far beyond personal handicaps to affect the welfare of the entire nation. Apart from the erosion of able manpower, the toll in crime, and the drag on the economy and on resources for public assistance, there is the problem of an uninformed and uninvolved citizenry in a presumably democratic country. And this can affect even those who are struggling to hold on to a tenuous position in society by extraordinary effort. This problem has been stated cogently by Barbara Ehrenreich, who conducted research on the working poor by immersing herself in their world and sharing their travails. One lesson she learned is the following:

> You can't have a democracy unless you have an engaged and informed citizenry. And you can't be an engaged and informed citizen if you are working two jobs, or you get home from work and immediately have to do all the household chores. To be a participant in the real sense, you have to have some leisure time to read, to think, to talk with your neighbors.[37]

The problem of poverty is by no means new. Meditating on the history of poverty and labor in America in the past century, a historian has made a depressing observation: "A hundred years after the United States became the world's greatest industrial power, the American economy still does not provide many of its people with the security they seek for themselves and their families. That scar remains as raw as it was when the century began."[38]

Which raises an interesting question. How did this predicament of widespread poverty arise in America, particularly in the recent past, which included a period of economic flourishing? Here is a synopsis by one historian of poverty:

> Among the most significant factors affecting poverty rates over the last twenty years or so are the shift to a more vulnerable (i.e., female-headed) family structure, decreasing government benefits and transfer payments for the poor, and decreasing wages for the working poor (especially men). The decline in the percentage of workers who belong to labor unions—from an all-time high in the early 1950s of about one-third the work force, to about 10 percent today—has played a role in this overall wage decline.[39]

As discussed later, this decline in union membership also helped foster the rise of corporations to their current pinnacle of political power.

If America's great wealth does not reach every American, one might ask, where does it go? Which brings us to another of the outstanding features of American society, that referred to as "income inequality."

Income Inequality and Social Mobility

Here again we encounter a dimension on which America stands out strikingly from other advanced industrial societies. Concisely put by an historian in 2002, "The disparity between rich and poor is vastly greater in the U.S. than anywhere in continental Europe (or than it was in the U.S. twenty years ago)."[40] And as the economist Lester Thurow has noted, "Probably no country has ever had as large a shift in the distribution of wealth without having gone through a revolution or losing a major war."[41]

Here are some stark statistics on the situation in 2002. The top fifth in income earned 11 times more than the bottom fifth. Just 1 percent of the top had 40 percent of the wealth.[42] From only 66 billionaires and 31.5 million people living in poverty in 1989, we progressed ten years later to 268 billionaires and 34.5 million living in poverty.[43] In the years 1997–2000 the average daily increase of wealth of the Forbes' 400 richest Americans was reported to be $1,920,000 per person.[44] As for the notion that the American stock market has democratized capitalistic ownership, the harsh truth is that in 1999 "nearly 90 percent of all shares were held by the wealthiest 10 percent of all households."[45] Being the richest nation in the world, in other words, really means that we have the highest concentration of the super rich.

But isn't this happening everywhere in the economically advanced countries? The answer is yes, but not nearly to the extent as in America, where the top CEOs live like monarchs compared to the lordlings of Europe. The CEOs of seven large foreign firms were earning between 4 percent and 27 percent of the earnings of the average American CEO in 1998. And according to the same source, the ratio of CEO earnings to blue-collar workers' earnings in Japan was about 20 to 1 and in Great Britain 35 to 1, while in America it was 419 to 1.[46]

The trend toward greater income inequality between American CEOs and their workers had taken off like a rocket over the previous two decades. In 1980 the average chief executive made 42 times what the average hourly worker made, but in 2000, according to *Business Week*, he or she made 1,531 times what the hourly worker made.[47] Inasmuch as CEOs select the members of their boards of directors (who set salaries), and also serve on the members' own boards, it is hardly surprising that they should cordially boost one another's salary, stock options, etc., over the years. A vote for higher compensation for a chairman of the board is tantamount to a vote for one's own higher compensation as a reward. To make these statistics a little more lifelike, let's look at some particular cases of individual wealth and broaden our scope from CEOs to baseball players, congressmen, and members of the current administration in Washington (my own words are in brackets).

[In 2001] the chairman of Citigroup collected 18 million dollars in salary and bonuses . . .[48]

[The CEO of Disney] received 723 million dollars in salary, bonuses, and stock options from 1996 to 2001, a yearly average of roughly 145 million. That could pay the yearly wages of more than three thousand coal miners . . .[49]

[The average annual income for major league baseball players is $2.5 million. The minimum wage allowed is $350,000.][50]

[Forty percent of U.S. senators are millionaires (23 Republicans and 17 Democrats). Twenty-five percent are multimillionaires, and 10 percent have $10 million or more.][51]

[Vice President Cheney's income from the Halliburton Oil Company in 2000 was $36,086,635.][52]

[The personal wealth of one-third of President Bush's cabinet is more than $10 million and that of another third is $1–5 million.][53]

Now, for an overall picture of what has happened to all of us:

The average after-tax, annual income [adjusted for inflation] of the richest 1 percent of Americans grew by $414,000 from 1979 to 1997. [During the same period,] the poorest 20 percent saw their after-tax income shrink by $100 a year, while those in the middle saw a gain of $3,400. In percentage terms, the rich saw a 157% boost in their annual, after-tax income, the middle saw only a 10% gain, and the poor stayed just as poor . . . During the same period . . . the richest 1% saw the biggest drop in tax obligation.[54]

The boom of the '80s and '90s was supposed to have benefited everyone, or at least that has been the assumption. Not so, according to another researcher, who paints an even more dismal picture than the preceding one: "While those in the fast lane enjoyed large increases in wealth over the two decades, the wealth of much of the rest of the population did not simply grow more slowly; it actually fell . . ."[55] From 1992 to 2000 alone the average income of the 400 richest Americans increased almost fourfold.[56]

A significant part of this boost to income inequality is caused by the tax structure of America, which departs from that of many other nations. To wit: "America has one of the world's least progressive tax structures . . . the payroll tax wreaks havoc with marginal tax rates."[57] It has even been estimated that when one includes payroll taxes, the bottom fifth in income pay virtually the same percentage of their income as the top fifth. And as we shall see later, the corporate world is extraordinarily adept at avoiding the payment of taxes. Furthermore, the tax cuts that began under the Bush administration did nothing whatsoever to reduce income inequality. On the contrary, as a result of the Bush tax cuts and rebates of 2001 (Bush's first round of tax cutting), no rebates were received by almost half of the bottom 60 percent of earners, which comprised more than 32 million individuals and families. The final distribution of benefits was as follows:[58]

Income group	% of benefits
Top 1%	37.6
Top 10%	56.5
Bottom 60%	14.7

Out of the $1.3 billion tax cut by President Bush in 2001, 35 million Americans did not receive any rebates at all.[59] In 2003, taxpayers with incomes over $100,000 received 60 percent of the tax cut.[60]

Cuts in top tax rates have been justified by some as providing a "trickle-down" effect that will eventually benefit the average worker and reinvigorate the economy. Unfortunately, statistical evidence for this effect on the economy does not exist. Steadily declining taxes for the well-to-do over the past 50 years are not correlated with GDP growth rate, income growth rate, hourly wage growth, or change in unemployment.[61] And yet, the current administration's economic growth package over the rest of the decade calls for a 17 percent cut in taxes for the richest 1 percent and a 5 percent cut for everyone else.[62]

At the same time as the wealthy have been favored with tax reductions, the likelihood of their being audited has also diminished and is now lower than that of the working poor. In 2001, more than half of all IRS audits were of the working poor. One in 174 returns of persons in this category was selected for audit, compared with one in 208 among those with incomes over $100,000.[63]

Although America has the greatest disparity of income in the industrialized world, this disparity also increased in several European countries in recent decades, as alluded to earlier. This increase has had profound implications for "upward class mobility," which is the primary measure of equal opportunity in a society. With regard to America, in the '90s a senior economist of the U.S. Labor Department reported that in the '80s as compared with the '70s "your chances of success became much better the higher up you started off." He also noted that the bottom quintile was especially likely to suffer a decrease in income over the '80s as compared with the '70s. Thus, the percentage of the poor with lower incomes at the end of the '80s was 53 percent, compared with 33 percent at the end of the '70s. Even for society as a whole, however, 36 percent of prime-age males experienced a decline in income in the '80s, as compared with 33 percent at the end of the '70s. The inescapable conclusion to be drawn from these data is that "income inequality did indeed go up and it became harder for people to succeed."[64]

This pattern continued in the '90s, and more recent data are even more disturbing. A survey in 2003 found that only 10 percent of adult men whose father had been in the bottom quartile of income had risen to the top quartile. In 1978 this figure was 23 percent, or more than *twice* the rate in 2003.[65] As for our famously praised entrepreneurial model of economic advancement, two-thirds of small businesses fail within six years after start-up. In the year 2003, 10 percent were predicted to fail by the Small Business Administration. "In fact," reported an Internet business news source in November 2003, "businesses are failing faster than they are being created."[66]

Concerning Europe, large increases in income inequality have occurred since the '70s in the UK, Denmark, Netherlands, and Sweden, and smaller increases in other OECD countries.[67] But Americans have not only sustained a much greater increase, but are less likely than Europeans to think that anything should be done about it, according to international polls: "Whereas fewer than one American in three supports significant redistribution of wealth, 63 percent of Britons favor it and the figures are higher still on the European continent."[68]

Nor is this due to simple ignorance about the state of affairs. When asked, "Are we a 'Have/Have-Not' society?" 44 percent of Americans replied yes in 2001, compared with 39 percent in 1999, 26 percent in 1988, and 31 percent in 1984.[69] Thus the perception of inequality has tended to spread. And in 2003 as many as 69 percent agreed that "the rich get richer and the poor get poorer."[70] But inasmuch as Americans have not shown an inclination to agitate for redistribution of wealth, this growing perception of inequality is apparently mitigated by the siren song of the American Myth of upward mobility for everyone, including the illusion that one has *already* achieved the upper reaches of income in America. In other words, why worry if we ourselves are among the very well off or will join them soon enough? This conclusion is supported by the following astounding results of another survey: "Fully 19 percent of the adult population claim to be in the richest 1 percent of the nation—and a further 20 percent believe they will enter that 1 percent in their lifetime!"[71] Here we see the work of the American Dream, but in such an absurdly exaggerated form (especially in light of the growing gap between rich and poor, the downward wage trend over the past several decades, and the high failure rate of small businesses) that it must be labeled a "myth."

One of the more cunning tricks of the American Myth is to ban the use of the term "class" to refer to any segment of American society except the "middle class." Reference to a "lower class" is a violation of gentility, and reference to an "upper class" smacks of either snobbism or radicalism, depending on whether one is rich or poor, respectively. Thus, in everyday usage there is only a single class in America—the middle one. This act of semantic purgation makes it possible to avoid the indecent topics of class conflict, class consciousness, class barriers, and other troubling Marxist notions that arise from the simple recognition of an unjust distribution of opportunities owing to sheer wealth and its rewards of power. (The *ideology* of Marxism is something entirely different from its strictly sociological observations and nomenclature, although to many the former taints the latter.) For the Myth is emphatic on one point: that we are a nation of amicable bourgeoisie with equal life chances. Yet the fact remains that social classes, in the sense of distinctive combinations of wealth, lifestyles, life chances, and common interests, do exist. And it is also true that they do not get along very well with one another and, as a matter of fact, segregate themselves from one another in all kinds of ways. Semantic prohibitions can make us feel better, but they cannot alter the reality of a social system.

Is it possible that income inequality, reduced upward mobility, and business failures have been allowed to gain the upper hand in America because the people are so well indoctrinated with the American Myth that they cannot imagine that *class barriers* might deny them the winnings of the great sweepstakes of life in America and that these barriers have *increased* over the past 30 years? And could this faith also be responsible for the scant concern for our roughly 33 million poor, inasmuch as they too might be presumed by most people to have a very good chance of rising to the top *if only they tried.* Structural barriers, in other words, are simply denied.

Much of our unrealistic estimate of the chances of becoming rich is founded on our extraordinary overall wealth as a nation, no doubt. So let us now turn to the true character of our wealth, and ask where it is coming from and how much longer we will be able to enjoy it. Indeed, let us look at the possibility that the American Dream has evolved into a nightmare for many as their economic security and personal assets have dwindled. We start by considering the question of domestic and foreign deficits and the cumulative national debt.

The Rollover from Record Budget Surplus to Record Budget Deficit in Two Years

As is generally known, our national debt has mushroomed in the past three years after the spending of a very healthy surplus that had only recently been realized. Here is a chronology of how it happened.[72]

Background note: Under the presidencies of Reagan and the first Bush, the national debt had quadrupled in 12 years.

May 2000   President Clinton announces that the government will pay off $216 billion of debt this year, bringing to $355 billion the out-of-debt payoff since the government balanced its budget and began having surpluses. This amounts to the largest debt reduction in history, yielding the largest surplus as a percentage of GDP since 1948. The debt is now $2.4 trillion lower than projected when Clinton first took office.

Jan. 2001   *George W. Bush takes office as president.* The Congressional
                 Budget Office projects a surplus for 2001–2011 of $5.6 tril-
                 lion.

June 2001   President Bush cuts taxes (with a retroactive date for rate
                 cuts) at a cost of $1.3 trillion over the next 10 years. Tax
                 rebates are planned to follow from July 20 to September 21,
                 2001.

July 2001   The budget surplus is projected to be $200 billion in fiscal
                 2001 instead of the $275 billion projected in September
                 2000, a shortfall of 27 percent.

Aug. 2001   The surplus is announced as $153 billion, or 24 percent
                 lower than the amount projected in the previous month for
                 fiscal 2001 as a whole. The Congressional Budget Office
                 says the government will have to dip into the Social Security
                 trust fund (with IOUs, which increase the debt).

Sept. 2001   *Terrorists attack* New York City and Washington, D.C.

Oct. 2001   America attacks the Taliban in Afghanistan in a war that will
                 cost about $1 billion a month.

Oct. 2001   A budget surplus of $127 billion is announced for fiscal 2001
                 instead of the $200 billion projected in July, a shortfall of 36
                 percent.

Mar. 2002   A budget *deficit* is projected for 2002 through 2012 of $1.3
                 trillion.

May 2002   A deficit of $100 billion is estimated for fiscal 2002, once
                 again far in excess of what had been projected.

June 2002   It is reported that the first eight months of the fiscal year in-
                 creased the deficit to $149 billion.

July 2002   A deficit of $165 billion is announced, an 11 percent increase
                 over the previous month. Since January 1 there has been a 60
                 percent increase in the deficit. The administration asserts that
                 the Bush tax cut will account for only 15 percent of the pro-
                 jected deficit in 10 years; but this figure is revised upward to

40 percent when challenged by the *New York Times*'s columnist Paul Krugman on the basis of the White House Budget Office's own figures.

Aug. 2002   The deficit is projected to be $450 billion over the next four years, which represents the largest drop in a budget surplus since 1946. The single largest source of the shortfall, according to the Congressional Budget Office, was the tax cut, which represented 56 percent of the deterioration that was attributable to legislation.

Jan. 2003   "The White House projects a federal deficit of more than $200 billion," which will probably exceed $300 billion next year, "the single largest budget shortfall in dollar terms in history," according to the *New York Times*. And this projection does not include the cost of a war with Iraq.

What does all this mean in terms of the national debt, which represents the accumulated deficits over the years?

The National Debt

One way to grasp the debt's magnitude and import is to compare it with our national budget. The total federal budget in 2002 was about $1.9 trillion. In that year the national debt was $6.2 trillion. Thus, the debt was roughly more than three times the budget. In early 2004, the debt was $7 trillion, an increase of 13 percent in two years.[73] If one believes that it is perilous to live so far beyond one's budget, then one would conclude that, according to this pragmatic standard at least, America is walking on the edge of a precipice. But distress will come only *if* we lose our ability to attract capital from abroad, *if* the deficit continues to grow (which the long-term tax cuts seem to guarantee), and *when* we must start repaying the trust fund, from which we have been borrowing. Meanwhile, it is clear that we are a *debtor nation*.

Another way of looking at the debt is in terms of each citizen's share. In 2002, the national debt came to $21,440 per citizen's share, and had increased an average of $1,111 million per day since September 29, 2001.[74] (By 2004, the debt came to $24,301 per American.)

It is noteworthy that in January 2001, the debt was projected to be eliminated in 10 years. But in September of the same year, the Congressional Budget Office projected a debt of $3.2 trillion over the same period, due in large part, as mentioned above, to the tax cuts of the Bush administration.[75] In July 2003, the debt was projected to be $9.8 trillion by 2008.[76] In fiscal 2002, the Treasury Department had already spent $299 billion on interest payments.[77]

Yet, even the 2003 figures greatly *understated* the national debt, which is probably why they were figures released to the public instead of the real figures. For what these published figures omitted were the long-term obligations to Medicare and Social Security due to borrowing. Information about the obligations to these two programs, which were arrived at after months of calculations by economic consultants for the White House, was deleted from the 2003 budget a few weeks before the budget was announced. This information showed that including these obligations would have increased the deficit figure by a factor of 10.[78] In short, it would appear that the government concealed from the public the true magnitude of the national debt by defining Medicare and Social Security out of the picture. Inasmuch as the current administration is borrowing from the Social Security surplus to pay for its other expenses, and the program is so popular, it is understandable that it would wish to obscure the added burden to the deficit incurred by this practice of robbing Peter.

As a consequence of the deficit crunch, in 2002 the Republicans in Congress expressed a desire to *increase* the debt limit by $750 billion, and in January 2003, the national debt reached its legal limit of $6.4 trillion. So on May 27 the president signed into law a bill to increase the debt limit.

Forty-three percent of the national debt in 2002 was owed to foreign parties.[79] This meant that in 2003 "foreigners now own . . . about $800 trillion of U.S. financial assets, including 13 percent of all stocks and 24 percent of corporate bonds . . . they also own 43 percent of Treasury Bonds. Additionally, they own real estate and factories."[80]

The main worry of Alan Greenspan, the Federal Reserve chairman, concerning the deficit has been its impact on interest rates in the event that the deficit continues to grow. (This assumes that the economy will regain its strength in the not-too-distant future and that deflation will not occur. On this latter point, see later.) His chief recommendation, therefore, has been that the government curb its spending. But this advice is no doubt interpreted by the conservative Republican party, which controls both houses, to mean resistance to spending on social programs, not on defense or tax cuts. Thus, while Greenspan has endeavored to restrict his vision to traditional economic matters (or at least to give the impression of doing so), these matters automatically have profound implications for the social pain to society of spending restrictions. This happens because economic data and recommendations are received within a political context, and are therefore inevitably interpreted in terms of partisan political interests. It is naïve to think otherwise. Consequently, when conservatives are in control, an increasing deficit can have a huge depressing impact on social expenditures, even though it has been persuasively argued that our recent deficits have stemmed to a significant degree from tax cuts by the current administration.

The exact relationship between the national debt and the trade deficit is a matter of dispute among economists. It is clear, however, that the trade deficit has its own foreboding features.

The Trade Deficit

In 2003, the U.S. trade deficit climbed to $489.4 billion, with China alone accounting for $100 billion.[81] This imbalance between the value of what we sell and what we buy abroad is unique among advanced industrial countries. United States' exports in 2000 were only 11.2 percent of its GDP, compared with 36.6 percent for the European Union.[82] In fact, the so-called economic miracle of the '90s was made possible by the nation's receiving $1.2 billion per day that was necessary to cover the trade deficit. Moreover, "it is these huge inward investment flows that have kept share prices up, inflation and interest rates down, and domestic consumption booming. . . . If a European, Asian or Latin American country ran comparable trade deficits, it would long since be in the hands of the International Monetary Fund."[83]

About a year after the above assessment, we were borrowing an additional $1 billion a year from abroad, which meant selling off more American assets. As a co-director of the Center for Economic and Policy Research has written: "If the trade deficit remains at its current level, within a decade forcigners will own the entire stock market, much of the government debt and many of our homes."[84]

How did we get into this situation? Basically, by our consumption binge of the past decade, abetted by "over-valuation of the dollar [which makes imports cheap and exports expensive], a low U.S. saving rate [which reduces capital for domestic investment], and the slow growth of Europe and Japan [which attracts investors to America]."[85] The eroding manufacturing base because of our diminished exports makes balancing trade especially difficult, since manufactured goods account for about 60 percent of our exports.[86] According to two Nobel Prize–winning economists, the large and growing trade deficit is "the greatest potential danger facing the economy in the years to come."[87] Should foreigners begin reducing their investments in America's assets, economic trouble could rise to a level of considerable distress.

Currently, the states also suffer from deficits, and reductions in federal expenditures for vital public services, as well as unfunded federal mandates, have driven the states to cut many services and raise taxes.

State Deficits

Forty-five of the states were reported in deficit in mid-2002,[88] and the total deficit for all state budgets was calculated at about $45 billion.[89] In the 2002 budget year, most states had already spent what they had laid aside as a hedge against recession, and 11 states planned "to eliminate health coverage for 1 million people living near the poverty level."[90] Cuts in vital services escalated in 2003, including reductions of health benefits for the poor and the closing of emergency rooms and hospitals. A 2003 study of all 50 states by the Kaiser Foundation found that "25 had restricted eligibility for Medicaid, 18 reduced benefits, and 17 increased co-payments." Sixteen states said that prescription drug costs were the biggest factor in increased Medicaid spending.[91] According to the National Governors Association and the National Association of State Budget Officers:

> Thirty-seven states chopped a total of $14.5 billion off the current year's [2003] budgets, most cutting services across the board and nearly half laying off workers, . . . while governors in 29 states proposed a total of $17.5 billion in new taxes and fees for next year, the most since 1979 . . . Ray Scheppach, executive director of the governors' group . . . last year described the states' budget outlook as the bleakest since World War II and today extended that to the War of 1812. "It's clearly the worst since we've been keeping statistics."[92]

As of mid-2003, the states' deficits represented "between 14.5 and 18 percent of all state expenditures," according to the Center on Budget and Policy Priorities. And in fiscal 2004, the total deficit of all states was expected to be $70 billion to $85 billion, an increase of about 73 percent since 2002.[93] We should not overlook the fact that individuals and businesses are also suffering "deficits" to the point of widespread bankruptcy.

Bankruptcies

The onerous debt burden of Americans today is not surprising in view of the fact that the ratio of savings to disposable income in 2000 placed the United States *last* among the advanced industrial nations reporting this statistic, including Europe, Japan, and Canada. In fact, the United States was the only nation with a negative savings rate, namely, –0.1 percent.[94] This slump in savings has been a major source of America's growing dependency on foreign investment.

Here are some figures that pin down the consequences. In 2002, total household debt of $8 trillion surpassed total household disposable income.[95] A year earlier, the number of Americans who graduated from college was surpassed by the number who filed for bankruptcy.[96] From 2000 to 2001, personal bankruptcies increased 13 percent, from 35,472 to 40,099.[97] This situation has been growing worse since the '80s. The overuse of credit cards during the '90s boom was largely responsible for the record indebtedness of Americans today. Credit card debt tripled between 1989 and 2001;[98] in 2003 it amounted to $7,000 out of $18,700 of consumer debt per U.S. household. Moreover, many observers agree that the rising cost of health care has played a significant role in personal bankruptcy. (See chapter 3 on rising health costs.)

Brisk consumption might be important for short-term growth, but long-term growth is sustained by the capital for productive investment provided by savings.[99] In short, consumption is necessary but not sufficient. When it significantly exceeds the current financial means of consumers, it can be highly detrimental to aggregate savings, which can retard the economy to a significant degree. And savings will dwindle further when the Federal Reserve Board raises interest rates to control inflation.

Productivity, Job Stress, and Child Care for Working Parents

Until recently, productivity growth in America was sluggish, and in fact was slower than in Europe. Even as recently as 2001, several European countries had higher productivity growth than the United States, and a few others were not far behind.[100] Indeed, in 2001 in our country "output per hour shrank 1.2 percent in the first quarter—the biggest decline in eight years [and] labor costs rose at the fastest rate in nearly four years."[101] But productivity rose in the first quarter of 2002 by 9.1 percent in manufacturing and 9.3 percent in nonfarm business. In 2003 it rose an impressive 5.7 percent in nonfarm business.[102]

This suggested to many that the recession was itself receding, and that the comparatively poor comparison with Europe had turned into a quite favorable one. But since unemployment had not declined (as of early 2004), higher productivity meant that technological improvements or various means of squeezing more output from workers had occurred. Another possibility is that the number of hours spent on the job by American workers has been increasingly underestimated, so the measurement of productivity could be faulty. And if workers are spending more time on the job without their extra hours being reported, this would be one of the ways in which workers are being squeezed to produce more. Another means is to merge two jobs into one. The fact that more workers are not being hired (unemployment has remained at the same low level) suggests that "squeezing" might be the case. As one economist has remarked, "Companies don't need new labor when they can squeeze every last bit of productivity out of the operations they are already running."[103] Another means of increasing productivity is to outsource jobs that are being less efficiently done, which gives a false impression of the number of hours of work by employees.

These considerations remind us that productivity, which is measured by output per man-hour, is not the whole story of output, for if people work more hours, then output will be increased independently of productivity rates. And this seems to have been the case in America for a number of years. We have simply spent more time on the job than in Europe. Thus, one analyst has noted that, in spite of lower productivity in the recent past, the United States was doing better than Europe in overall output. "This is because more Americans work; the state takes less from their wages (and provides less in return); they work longer hours—28 percent more than Germans, 43 percent more than the French, and they take shorter vacations or none at all."[104] Overall, Americans work 350 hours longer each year than their European counterparts, which comes to about nine additional weeks of work.[105] (Another analyst has estimated that Americans actually spend 15 more weeks on the job than workers do in Europe.) In any case, "the average American is working longer hours for lower wages than was the case 30 years ago."[106]

Whatever the true state of affairs regarding output per man-hour, the longer working hours of Americans compared with those of workers in other advanced countries is evidently a long-term fact of life; for it is the culmination of a trend that has been evident for a number of years and that has possibly taken a serious toll in declining job satisfaction, health, leisure time, and perhaps other areas such as marital difficulties and time spent with one's children, all of which are known to be related to mental health and general well-being. Thus, it is worthwhile looking at this problem in some detail. (For data on mental health in America, see chapter 3.) But first, let us note the lengths that some commentators will go in upholding the myth of American virtue in order to mask reality.

A recent op-ed piece in the *New York Times* by David Brooks[107] attributed our much longer working hours to America's superior "work ethic"—as if American workers had much if anything to say about the number of hours they are obliged to work, the vacation time they are denied, or the resulting job stress they must endure to maintain a satisfactory standard of living, especially in times of high unemployment. When we examine the widespread job stress of workers in America (see below), it is hard to believe that they are happy about the amount of time that they must expose themselves to so much tension and strain, "work ethic" notwithstanding.

According to a government study of job stress in 1999 by the American Institute of Stress:

> The number of hours worked increased 8% in one generation to an average 47 hrs/week with 20% working 49 hrs/week. U.S. workers put in more hours on the job than the labor force of any other industrial nation, where the trend has been just the opposite . . . In a 2001 survey, nearly 40% of workers described their office environment as "most like a real life survivor program." . . . An es-

timated 1 million workers are absent [from work] every day due to stress. The European Agency for Safety and Health at Work reported that over half of the 440 million working days lost annually in the U.S. from absenteeism are stress related and that one in five of all last minute no-shows are due to job stress . . . unanticipated absenteeism is estimated to cost American companies $602/worker/year and the price tag for large employers could approach $3.5 million annually . . .[108]

These findings are congruent with the results of other surveys among workers. According to a Gallup Poll, "80% of workers feel stress on the job . . . 25% have felt like screaming or shouting because of job stress . . . 10% are aware of an assault or violent act in their workplace . . ."[109] Another survey found that "19%, or almost one in five respondents, had quit a previous position because of job stress . . . 34% reported difficulty in sleeping because they were too stressed-out . . . 12% had called in sick because of job stress. . ."[110] Clearly, American employees are not whistling while they work.

Moreover, and not surprisingly, studies of the etiology of major health problems in America have pointed to the role of job stress, as reported in the *Boston Globe*: "Adding to a growing body of evidence that workplace stress is harmful, researchers have linked job strain with high rates of heart disease and other physical ailments . . ."[111] And comparisons with European countries reveal America's near preeminence with respect to poor working morale. Of five countries studied, "only UK workers have worse morale than U.S. employees. Almost one-fifth of UK businesses suffer from poor working morale; United States businesses trail closely at 15 percent."[112]

It seems likely that one reason for so much job stress in America is the decline in the number of workers who are represented by unions, which has increased the power of employers to determine wages, working hours and conditions, benefits, and layoffs. From 1945 to 1999, union membership in America declined from 35.5 percent to 13.9 percent of the labor force, bringing it to "the lowest percentage in the industrial world."[113]

Added to stress on the job in America is the burden of paying for child care when both parents are working, which has been a growing trend as families try harder to make ends meet and women seek to participate in society outside the home. Here again we find that America is outstandingly remiss in assisting families (in spite of hoopla about "family values"). As the *Atlantic Monthly* reported in a special issue devoted to the "real state of the union" in 2003:

> After-school-care programs are relatively scarce, and day-care standards are uneven . . . the expense of day care—which is often more than the tuition at a state college—is borne almost entirely by parents alone. In stark contrast, most European nations view child care as a national responsibility and publicly subsidize it . . .[114]

In spite of its travails, having a job is usually preferable to prolonged unemployment. But unemployment has been a sore point for the past few years.

Unemployment

In 2000 the unemployment rate in the United States (4%) was higher than that in several industrialized countries: Austria, Iceland, Luxembourg, the Netherlands, Switzerland, and Norway. However, rates considerably higher than that in the United States were experienced in 2000 in France (10%), Germany (7.9%), and Italy (10.5%), and the UK had a moderately higher rate (5.5%)[115] Three years later, however, the U.S. rate had risen to 6.4%, and this did not include those who had stopped looking for work, including about 5.5 million youth aged 16–24, according to one study. Moreover, the United States has an unusually large number of part-time workers, many of whom are looking for full-time work. If the latter were added to the measure of unemployment, the rate in the United States would be "not unlike the 10% figures of western Europe."[116] In December 2002, the mean number of weeks unemployed was 18.5, up from 14.5 in December 2001, and 12.6 in January 2001.[117]

In October 2002, the *New York Times* reported, "The nation employs fewer people than it has at any point since late 1999, its longest stretch without job growth in 20 years."[118] The persistently high unemployment rate (around 6%) in the fourth quarter of 2003 *in spite of* a spurt in economic growth was largely due to corporations having exported jobs to low-wage havens and implemented labor-saving technologies, and also to their wariness about the economic outlook.

A small unemployment drop of 1 percent in the third quarter of 2003 was mainly attributable to an increase in the number of self-employed and did not exceed new entrants to the labor market due to an increase in employment-aged individuals. Moreover, a household survey showed that 1.5 million persons were searching for work, but not in the five weeks prior to the survey and therefore were not included in the unemployment statistics; and that another 457,000 did not believe that a job was available and had given up looking. These figures add about two million unemployed to the number that is based on applications for unemployment compensation, which is the usual basis for media reports of unemployment rates.[119] As mentioned earlier, our unusually large number of part-timers who want full-time jobs should also be taken into consideration as representing *under*-employment. And perhaps most unsettling of all, the increase expected by economists of about 130,000 jobs during the 2003 holiday season turned out to be only 1,000! In short, the employment situation in America amounts to a major crisis regardless of how the economists predict it, the media report it, or the politicians spin it. Recent data (as of March 2004) suggest that job growth may be picking up at last; but it remains to be seen whether this trend will continue. It will take many months to overcome the loss of at least 2.2 million jobs (some say 3 million jobs) since the beginning of the George W. Bush administration, an unusual number of which have disappeared forever.

There are deficiencies in our measurement of unemployment that should be taken into account other than those mentioned above. The figure might be artificially inflated by applications for compensation by persons not actually looking for work but who apply just to receive the money. This tendency has been estimated to increase unemployment figures based on applications by about 1.5 percent in times when payments are more generous. Moreover, the rate of job change in society at large affects estimates based on payrolls, since workers might be counted more than once. Further, payroll records omit the self-employed. And then, changes in the age structure of society can mean that particular job-holding patterns or profiles become influential, such as the greater tendency of young workers to spend time looking for work, then switching jobs or even dropping out of the work force to gain more education. Telephone surveys of households, for their own part, are heir to all the weaknesses of telephone surveys in general, but in particular to the possibility that many of the poorer unemployed might have been unable to pay their phone bills and have had their phones disconnected. And finally, there are the government's changes in definition of employment from one time period to another, making it difficult to chart trends.

These pitfalls and potholes of measurement often lead to different results yielded by different methods and time periods—which is a serious problem because we need accurate numbers for *administrative* purposes. But these problems also affect our estimates of social well-being if we depend upon the results, as we tend to do, to give us an idea of how *well off* we are in general. As noted earlier, employment is a poor indicator of well-being, and indeed could be detrimental to well-being if jobs are stressful or demoralizing, if pay is inadequate, if health and pension benefits continue to decline, if worker organizations continue to wither, or if the number of required working hours or jobs held simultaneously deprives us of productive or gratifying leisure time, especially with family and friends. These issues are part of a larger constellation of "occupational" issues that are not included in our notion of sheer "employment." Having an income and the self-esteem of gainful employment are worthwhile benefits, but they are by no means the whole story of job satisfaction, the state of one's mental and physical health as affected by work, or sense of well-being in general. The absence of social reports in America, and the lack of a sociological perspective on the workplace in general, compels us to fall back on strictly economic indicators, however. Thus, we commit the fallacy of conflating economics with the ebb and flow of human happiness, a quintessentially American fallacy. Consequently, we seldom have the slightest idea of how well or poorly off we really are in spite of the reassurance of high employment figures.

Still, the rise in jobs measured in March through May 2004 (248,000 in May alone) is a hopeful sign, but by no means a harbinger of vigorous economic or social health. The unemployment rate of 5.6 percent has remained the same over this period; but that could be due to discouraged workers reentering the labor market. More immediately worrisome is the rise in the unemployment rate of teenagers to 17.2 percent. Further, a number of months of job growth will be necessary to overcome the loss of two to three million jobs since the Republicans took office in 2001. And one must not forget that 150,000 new jobs are needed each month just to keep pace with population growth. This means that the increase of 248,000 jobs in May 2004 amounted to only a 98,000 excess increase. Further, as emphasized above, while employment might be necessary to enhance the well-being of many Americans, it is not sufficient and could even be detrimental for some. In fact, it appears that, according to a new 2004 government study, more than half of workers are now returning to jobs that pay less than the jobs they formerly held, inducing a sense of downward mobility that could substantially erode the so-called joy of work. In general, our occupational crisis could continue into the indefinite future regardless of the venerable "employment outlook" of the government or prognostications of economists.

A final point to bear in mind is that America does less than most other nations to ease the economic impact on the unemployed by supplementing their buying power. As Joseph Stiglitz, one of the world's leading economists, has pointed out, "America has one of the poorest unemployment insurance schemes among the advanced industrial countries, with more limited coverage, and benefits that are both shorter (only twenty-six weeks) and lower."[120] And according to a Princeton economist who was referring to our current situation, "75 percent of those who lose jobs still haven't found new jobs when their unemployment benefits run out . . ."[121]

In other words, not only is poverty more prevalent and job stress greater, but being out of work in America is more financially stressful than in other advanced industrial countries. This remains true even when the stock market goes up, the total wealth and productivity of the nation increase, employment figures swell, or economists announce an economic nirvana. Here, then, is just one more telling mark of a second-rate nation.

Other Comparisons with Europe

Inflation and Deflation

The price increases between 1999 and 2000 found America tied with Spain for the highest rate of annual change in consumer prices among 11 nations (i.e.,

United States and Europe).[122] In 2002, our inflation was the third highest of seven OECD countries after the UK and Italy.[123]

The new worry, however, was not inflation but its opposite: deflation. It was feared that production overcapacity, debt burdens (with the possibility of consumers being unable to borrow more), and overpriced stock—problems inherited from the '90s boom and bust—might cause prices to drop with dire repercussions. As prices begin dropping, after an initial burst of consumption consumers would postpone purchases in anticipation of even lower prices, a classic case of a self-fulfilling prophecy. And this scenario could be exacerbated by price reductions in foreign countries, particularly as a response to China's low-wage output, which would put further pressure on prices to drop in America.[124] The pervasiveness of the negative multiplier effect of deflation makes it harder to deal with than inflation and means that deflation could last as long as a decade and even lead to a great depression like the one in the '30s. Thus, America had good reason to fear deflation.

Deflation had already struck Germany and seemed likely to spill over into other European countries, and it had struck Japan almost 10 years ago. If America joined the downward trend in prices, the world would be in considerable trouble. And the rate of inflation in America had been slowing. According to one Web source on the economy, InflationData.com, as of June 2003, "The annual inflation rate is on a definite downtrend." It had been 3.5 in late 2002, then fell and rose again to 3.0 a few months later, and then fell to a position below both its linear regression line and its moving average for the previous 12 months.[125]

When deflation strikes, one of its main victims is debtors, whose asset values will decline and who are already burdened with great debt and even bankruptcy in America with mortgage foreclosures already at a 50-year high. Thus, deflation would erode credit ratings and fall with special force on the indebted unemployed. The value of stocks, some municipal bonds, and corporate bonds would be eroded also, and, of course, many businesses would have to close their doors and lay off workers from a paucity of profit. The Federal Reserve has been deeply concerned about the prospect of deflation and unsure of its ability to fend it off.

In the winter of 2003, however, fears of deflation were allayed when inflation began to rear its less ugly head, and a spurt of 0.5 percent in March 2004 began to arouse serious concern. Interest rates began to rise in anticipation of a rate increase by the Federal Reserve Board, and the stock market faltered as economists began to fear an "overheated economy." Major sources of this rise in the Consumer Price Index were increased energy, education, and medical costs, all three of which sectors are discussed in later chapters as significant problem areas in America that sharply differentiate it from other advanced nations. In sum, the new fear is that inflation will rise in response to an economic recovery;

and as we saw at the beginning of this section, the late boom years of the '90s found America tied for the highest rate of inflation of 11 advanced nations. Are we beginning to climb the same slippery slope again? If so, rate increases by the Federal Reserve Board will exacerbate the debt burden of middle- and lower-income individuals.

Contribution of Employers to Social Security

In 1998, the contribution of employers to Social Security as a percentage of labor costs was next to the lowest of 19 nations (U.S. and Europe),[126] and this situation has not significantly improved. This has placed an additional financial burden on American workers that is not characteristic of other advanced countries.

Gross Domestic Product (GDP)

In 2001, the growth rate of GDP in the European Union was 4.6 times higher than in America (1.4% vs. 0.3%).[127] In 2002, however, it was half the American rate (1.1% vs. 2.2%).[128] And in the third quarter of 2003, the GDP in America suddenly rose by 8.2 percent (annualized), a development that was greeted with jubilation. (The first quarter of 2004 has been estimated as close to 5.0 percent.) If more Americans knew what the GDP measured, however, this joyous response might well have been tempered.

The GDP is America's favorite measure of economic vitality. Since the economy is the nation's lead institution, that is, the keystone of its unique prominence and allegedly the fountain of all the good things of life (including military muscle), its performance is avidly monitored. And in the absence of periodic "social reports," as are common in European nations (see chapter 1), the GDP has become the prime indicator of how well the nation is doing overall. In effect, the American Myth has fostered and preserved a means of measuring the economy that can be exploited to present it (and by implication the nation's well-being) in the best possible light by obscuring the true state of affairs. Exactly what does the GDP measure? (The following discussion of the GDP is based largely on Cobb, Halstead, and Rowe.[129])

Although GDP growth is taken for granted as a sign of national vitality and improved quality of life, it is nothing of the kind, for the GDP reflects only the value of all finished goods and services, including transactions that are clear-cut evidence of social or environmental breakdown. For example, it includes treatment of the victims of motor vehicle accidents and repairs of wrecked vehicles; treatment of preventable illness (about 70% of all illnesses); consumer debt; crime prevention and imprisonment; road repairs owing to unrelieved heavy traffic (some $800 million in California alone) and damage to vehicles by poor

roads ($1.2 billion in California alone); pollution controls and treatment of ill-
ness caused by pollution (e.g., treatment of asthma among seventh and eighth
graders in North Carolina alone costs $15 million a year); contracts generated by
terrorist destruction; military protection of our foreign petroleum sources in lieu
of conservation or alternative forms of energy at home; and all the costs of cigarettes, gambling, divorce, substance abuse, AIDS, child abuse ($258 million a
day), obesity ($117 billion a year), mental illness, care for the homeless, domes-
tic violence ($10 billion a year), job stress and its physical toll, telemarketing
fraud ($40 billion a year), and pornography (one of the largest industries in
America). The financial transactions entailed in such activities and products are
a large part of the GDP, and especially in America. Military spending alone accounted for 16 percent of the GDP growth of 4.2 percent in the first quarter of
2004.[130] (See subsequent chapters for comparisons with other advanced nations
on some of these dimensions.) Nevertheless, the GDP is embraced by the public
as a reflection of how well off we are as a nation.

A few more words should be said about the military's recent contribution to
the GDP because it drives home the lesson of how easily matters of dubious
nature are tucked away in the GDP. The increase in military spending was
mainly attributed to "base support equipment" for the Air Force. Since it has
been alleged that the United States is building 14 military bases in Iraq (the exact number is elusive), it is likely that this is what necessitated the greatly increased spending. The president, however, confidently attributed the GDP's rise
to his tax cuts. Concerning the dubious nature of this military expenditure, as I
pointed out in the Introduction, the Iraq war may well have been undertaken
precisely to achieve this "military presence" in the Middle East; and the construction of these bases will very probably *further* inflame the region against us.
This demonstrates how easy it is for politicians to sell GDP growth as a token of
enhanced well-being for citizens when in fact such growth could involve highly
questionable transactions that the people might well deplore if they had full
knowledge of them.

This point is worth emphasizing. In view of the narrow way that "growth"
is measured, it is perfectly possible for growth to occur while the well-being of
the people is declining. Indeed, that is what happened from the late '60s into the
'80s at least, as mentioned in chapter 1, when an independent measure of well-
being was utilized to plot the nation's true "social health" instead of just the
number of dollars that had changed hands.[131] Similar results, where social,
physical, or environmental well-being was unchanged or falling while GDP was
rising, have been obtained by other indices that compared these phenomena.[132]
The Genuine Progress Indicator (GPI) showed a flat trend from 1950 to 1999
while the GDP rose steeply; and in 2000 the GPI's measure of socially productive growth showed that the conventional GDP was 3.5 times higher than the
GPI.[133] This tremendous discrepancy reveals the extent to which the GDP is in-

flated by socially negative transactions. Loosely speaking, one might conclude that the true state of human affairs is roughly three times worse than the GDP would lead us to believe.

The results of such studies, however, are rarely, if ever, reported by the media, politicians, or officials. In noting the failure of the media to report profound social changes in America, Miringoff and Miringoff have pointed out that "it is as if the Vietnam War had been fought with no press coverage, no chance for the country to understand what was happening, and no opportunity to make a judgment about it."[134] The GDP, in particular, muscles social trends off the front page because the American Myth strives to preserve our basically complacent pride in the economy, and ergo the nation, by a resolute use of this measure. When the GDP is high (even when inflated by negative transactions), it glorifies the nation; when it is low, its decline can be attributed to short-term, inexorable "economic forces" instead of to poor government policy or further social deterioration. This may well be why efforts to reform or supplement the GDP index have been consistently rebuffed by government, economists, and financial interests. The last major effort to utilize a more meaningful measure of national accomplishment was quashed by the Reagan administration, which no doubt feared the consequences.

GDP growth no longer even guarantees more jobs or higher compensation, which takes some of the wind out of the argument that tax subsidies to corporations are critical for sustaining employment and spending power. The impressive 8.2 percent growth (annualized) in the third quarter of 2003 was not accompanied by an increase in employment that exceeded the number of new entrants to the labor market or in wages and salaries. At the same time, profits were rising 40 percent, which meant greater dividends to stockholders and payoffs to executives. (As mentioned earlier, 90 percent of shares are held by the wealthiest 10 percent of households.) Somebody profited from the GDP spike, but it wasn't the most needy, and only moderately was it true of the middle class. America's wealth distribution system was busily at work diverting ever *more* wealth to the wealthy. (For further discussion of these points, see Krugman.[135])

All of which is by way of saying that the spurt of GDP reported in the third quarter of 2003 could have been good, could have been bad, or could have been anything but an accurate reflection of the nation's "progress" *as a place to live.* Moreover, as shown earlier, the extreme degree of income inequality in America means that most of the real benefits of growth as measured by the GDP tend to flow disproportionately to the top tier in wealth, whereas the middle and lower tiers enjoy far less, if any, improvement in their lot. Even a reduction in the unemployment rate can be a Pyrrhic victory if job stress, job demotion, loss of leisure time because of long working hours, multiple job holding, or lack of sufficient compensation to maintain a decent standard of living are the consequences. These effects, and the allocation of disproportionate shares of the economic pie among levels of wealth, are neatly obscured by employing an indicator of "growth" that fails to distinguish between real benefits to everybody and the magnitude of mere financial transactions. In short, GDP, and also employment figures (as discussed earlier), are both spurious measures of well-being in the United States.

Consumer Confidence and Spending

In view of our economic woes during the year 2002 it was not surprising that consumer confidence in the latter part of the year was quite low, especially among the most needy:

> The public's rating of the U.S. economy swooned to the lowest in eight years last week [in September 2002] . . . Only 30 percent of Americans said the economy was in excellent or good shape . . . Rich Americans had a lot less to worry about . . . Among the wealthy, the index stood at +11 last week, whereas for the nation's poorest households, the gauge weighed in at a dismal –49 . . . The lifetime average in weekly polls since December 1985 is –8.[136]

In the summer of 2003, however, actual spending was picking up, owing to falling prices, low-interest financing, and tax rebates. (In spite of the president's having taken credit for the impact of his tax cuts on spending, economists asserted that the cuts did not play a major role because only one-third of the money was spent. Moreover, tax cuts will shrink over the following two years, which could cause a serious reversal in the economy as spending falls.)[137]

Adjusted for inflation, spending was up 2.7 percent [annualized] in the second quarter of 2003, compared to 2.0 percent in the first quarter.[138] But consumers' outlook for the next six months (August 2003–January 2004) was far from optimistic. In July, expectations of improved business conditions fell from 23.5 percent in June to 20.2 percent in July. Anticipation of a better job market and of higher personal income declined to the same extent.[139] In short, the image in the economists' crystal ball as of summer 2003 was not only murky, but was perceived by consumers to be foreboding. In November the tax cut benefits were dwindling, and a 5 percent dip in spending for Christmas in 2003 was considered possible.[140]

The dip did not materialize, however, and, in fact, the increase in sales was almost three times higher than the one in December 2002 (a 2003 increase of 6 percent versus a 2002 increase of 2.2 percent). This was largely due to late purchases and perhaps somewhat due to a huge percentage increase in online sales of 37 percent (online sales comprise about 5 percent of all sales).[141] One gets the impression that consumers were postponing purchases to the last minute because of financial stress. But they came through after all, bringing cheer to the retail industry. The downside was the spur to consumer debt, which, as we have seen, was already at a record high; and this, of course, was especially true of the obligatory credit card use entailed in online sales. And as also mentioned earlier, job growth was negligible during the holiday season.

Finally, the fact that luxury stores enjoyed much stronger sales than even discount stores, in spite of an aggressive expansion of seasonal discounting by the latter,[142] demonstrated a much greater relative improvement in the buying power of more *affluent* consumers. This was probably due to the skewed distribution of the administration's tax cuts as well as to the widespread unemployment and debt entanglement that continued to place a brake on spending by *nonaffluent* consumers. Thus, we can discern in this spending pattern in late 2003 the unequal distribution of wealth in America, particularly under the current conservative administration whose policies seem indifferent at best to the widening gap between rich and poor. We can also discern the reluctance of consumers to put themselves deeper into debt, especially under economic conditions that evidently cannot remedy unemployment in spite of "growth."

In the new year of 2004, spending increased 0.5 percent in January, but only 0.2 percent in February. Further, consumer confidence barely changed in March. These signs of stagnation may well have been due to higher energy costs that reduced discretionary spending. But more disturbing was a prediction by a leading research firm that consumer spending would slow down by fall 2004 "as the lingering effects of federal tax cuts wane."[143] Since consumer spending accounts for about two-thirds of the nation's economic activity, this prediction is far from encouraging. And there is the prospect that even when spending increases, consumers are going further into debt with credit purchases, thereby reducing savings and retarding long-term production fueled by investment.

Recent Federal Budgets

The foregoing summary of economic conditions has shown that America faces a variety of macroeconomic problems, especially widespread poverty. As we shall see in later chapters, the nation is also suffering from a number of severe deficiencies in education, health, crime control, environmental protection, and so on, which have been widely documented and which require substantially more federal spending. The prevention of domestic terrorism is a relatively new burden for the nation, one that has already run into widespread charges that we have dealt poorly with this scourge. Addressing all of these problems requires enormous resources. Which brings us to the question of how well our recent federal budgets have reflected a determination to meet these critical challenges. The answer to that question is dismaying. Having spent our time in the foregoing pages exploring the world of severe domestic problems, we are now suddenly and wrenchingly obliged to turn our attention to the world of military spending, which absorbs the bulk of America's discretionary federal budget.

In 2002, the military was allocated 56 percent of the discretionary budget (that is, omitting the trust fund). This sum dwarfed the percentages allotted to other major categories: education, training, employment, and social services (9%); health care and research (6%); administration of justice (4%); natural resources and environment (4%); international affairs (3%); general science, space, and technology (3%); community and regional development (2%); and all other (13%).[144] As reported on the evening news to the American people in March 2002: "The U.S. spends more on defense that the next nine nations combined."[145]

When one contemplates the sums routinely allocated to defense by Congress and the administration, it is hard to avoid an impression of a devil-may-care recklessness more characteristic of a bellicose national temperament than the equanimity commonly associated with world leadership in modern times. Here are some statistics that I have summarized in my own words and that contribute to this impression:

> On June 27, 2002, it was reported that the Senate appropriated $5.9 billion for missile defense, and $14.3 billion for missile defense and/or counter-terrorism at the discretion of the president.[146]
>
> Each F22 fighter jet costs $220 million. The cost of the war in Afghanistan was about $30 million a day, or almost $1 billion a month.[147]
>
> According to the Pentagon's inspector general, the Pentagon cannot account for 25 percent of the funds it spends, namely, $2.3 trillion in transactions. Thirteen billion dollars given to weapons contractors from 1985 to 1995 was "lost," according to a Senate hearing.[148]

When we compare defense spending with funds for socioeconomic and environmental purposes covered by the discretionary budget from year to year, the priorities of America become clear. To be more precise, in each of the years 2002 and 2003, the estimated outlays for defense were *five times* the estimated discretionary outlays for "education, training, employment, and social services."[149] With regard to health, in 2002 and 2003 the estimated outlays for defense were *eight* and *six times* higher, respectively.[150] The proposed 2004 budget presented virtually the same distribution of discretionary funding as the 2003 budget,[151] and so the imbalances between defense and socioeconomic spending were preserved. Indeed, as reported in the press in February 2003, "the largest actual increase in money would go to defense, which would get a $16.9 billion increase in funding for the Pentagon, missile defense and other programs."[152]

The defense budget absorbs not only resources that might have been spent on domestic programs, but money for foreign aid as well. When the U.N. Development Program looked at Washington's budget for defense in 2003, it observed that the American defense budget would provide for "the minimal conditions required for the flowering of human potential worldwide."[153]

At the same time as allocations for socioeconomic and environmental purposes were scanted in the 2003 proposed budget, more tax breaks that would tend to benefit higher-income earners were also proposed.[154] These tax breaks were estimated to enlarge the national deficit far beyond the once notorious deficit of $290 billion in 1992.[155]

The same level of funding for, or even cuts, in social and environmental programs were widely viewed with hand-wringing dismay by many members of Congress, local officials, and numerous other concerned citizens, but to little avail. As one senator succinctly expressed it, "The larger defense spending causes all other programs to fall $5.5 billion. This is below the amount needed to keep up with inflation in 2002, and $62 billion below the amount needed for the next 10 years."[156]

Since the passing months might have blunted our appreciation of the impact of these cuts on America's "human infrastructure," it is important to remind ourselves of some of the more egregious reductions in 2001–2003 and their impacts on our social institutions and the lives of millions of Americans. The following is an inventory of some of the cuts in social and environmental programs in the past two years (my own words are in brackets):

> [Federal outlays for education increased 13.4 percent a year from 1996 through 2002; the increase in the Bush budget for 2003 was only 2.8 percent.][157]
>
> [The 2003 budget] does little to support many essential elements and challenges to a healthy America . . . [according to the Coalition for Health Funding].[158] [And according to the American Dental Association] The proposed budget cuts deeply into discretionary health spending.[159] [The Coalition concludes:] The health needs of the people go beyond protection against terrorist attack . . .[160] [Later we shall assess the state of America's health care system in some detail and see that these complaints were not without justification.]
>
> [The increases in the estimated discretionary outlays for "natural resources and the environment" from 2001 to 2002, and from 2002 to 2003, were zero,[161] which has inflamed environmentalists. In particular, the 2003 budget called for cutting the toxic substances Hydrology Research Program, the National Streamflow Program (for predicting floods, etc.), the Water Resources Research Act, and other programs.[162] Also, deep funding cuts were authorized in the Superfund program] slowing or halting the cleanup process at 33 toxic waste sites in 18 states [according to the Natural Resources Defense Council].[163]
>
> A group of mayors and police chiefs across the country [came to Washington] to express their concern that further progress in reducing crime in our cit-

ies would be jeopardized by proposed cuts in federal programs that assist local law enforcement. [The budget entails a cut of nearly $600 million or 80 percent in the Community Oriented Policing (COPS) Program. A comprehensive study of COPS found that the program] is directly linked to the drop in crime since 1995, preventing tens of thousands of violent crimes and hundreds of thousands of property crimes. [In addition, the local Law Enforcement Block Grant program would be cut by $200 million.[164] As Mayor Morial of New Orleans said,] We cannot afford to cut funding that helps prevent street crime in order to finance needed efforts to prevent terrorism.[165]

Bush's new program slashed $545 million from job training programs around the country.[166]

A new analysis released by Families USA today shows that nearly one million enrollees in the State Children's Health Insurance Program (SCHIP) are in jeopardy of losing health coverage because of reduction in federal funding [167] . . .

The Administration's proposed cuts in social services affecting youth, as passed by the Senate in January [2003], included: $60.9 million cut from child-care . . . ; $29 million cut from after-school programs; $13 million cut from programs that help abused and neglected children; $3 million cut from children's mental health funding; $42 million cut from substance-abuse programs.[168]

These reductions in expenditures for needed social programs should be viewed against the background fact that in the '90s America's social expenditures already placed it *next to last* among 18 democratic countries.[169] More recent data indicate that direct social spending in America is only 17 percent of GDP, compared with about 30 percent in Germany, Sweden, Italy, the Netherlands, Denmark, and the UK. Indirect spending raises the American level to 25 percent, but European nations also spend indirectly on social needs.[170] Moreover, far from alleviating the problems induced by the 2003 budget, the 2004 budget presented to Congress seemed designed to exacerbate them. In particular, in a *New York Times* article titled "Spending Spree at the Pentagon," it was observed that "at next year's projected level, Washington will be spending nearly as much on defense as the rest of the world combined."[171] And the cuts in social programs were accelerated. Here are a few examples:

[Reductions in vocational training and after-school services, elimination of 45 education programs, reduction of aid for rural development, elimination of a program to demolish and replace dilapidated public housing, etc., were planned.][172]

[The 2004 budget] would also make outright cuts in some poverty programs, such as a reduction by a fourth in the amount the government devoted last year to "community service" grants for dispossessed neighborhoods.[173]

In addition, in spite of pledges in the president's 2002 State of the Union Address to *expand* AmeriCorps funding by 50 percent, it was actually *cut* by 58 percent.[174] And in August 2003, the Bush administration proposed cuts in funding for after-school programs, youth employment, and the No-Child-Left-Behind program. Further, it was proposed to turn the funding of Head Start over to the states in the form of block grants, thereby undermining the federal guidelines for this very successful program, and to turn vouchers for public housing into block grants also, which would undermine its emphasis on benefiting the poor.

Concurrently, tax cuts that were intentionally designed to benefit the wealthy were proposed (and later enacted) that further squeezed social spending. These cuts were pursued with zeal by the administration as a means of helping ordinary Americans, it was claimed; but according to the Associated Press, "half of all taxpayers will get less than $100 from the Bush tax cut. Those who make more than one million a year will get an average cut of $92,000."[175]

A number of economists were outspokenly opposed to the tax cuts, including the chairman of the Federal Reserve, who noted that "the economy probably does not need any short-term stimulus and [warned] that budget deficits could spiral out of control."[176] In fact, 10 Nobel Prize–winning economists were opposed, and 400 leading U.S. economists signed a statement that the tax cuts would foster chronic deficits and hardly any growth.[177]

Many observers have claimed that these tax cuts and the increased spending for defense have created a record national debt that could pose a crushing burden for our grandchildren and have already done the nation untold harm by hobbling or eliminating a host of social and environmental programs. As a well-known historian of the decline of great nations has pointed out, "An enhanced national prosperity ... may be damaged by excessive spending upon armaments."[178] How much more meaningful this warning would seem to be when the nation's economy is faltering, and social needs are rising.

The defense budget is not the only drain on discretionary resources that could be allocated to basic social needs that span the nation, for members of Congress are profligate in spending federal money for pet projects (or "pork") on behalf of highly specific interests among their constituencies. In fiscal 2002 there were 8,341 such projects, "an increase of 32 percent over last year's total of 6,333 projects," according to the Council for Citizens Against Government Waste. "The cost was $20.1 billion, or 9 percent more than last year." And in 2001, there had been a 46 percent increase over the previous year. The total cost since 1991 has been $141 billion.[179] The problem is not that these projects are worthless, although many seem rather whimsical (e.g., a Cowgirl Museum, ornamental fish culture, manure management, and the use of wood), but they are acquiesced to by other members of Congress without scrutiny or objection because they too wish to benefit politically from handouts to constituents without scrutiny or objection. In times of a mushrooming national debt one might think that such spending would be reined in. But evidently increases are unstoppable. And when there is a call for restraint in congressional spending, instead of cutting back on these politically beneficial projects conservatives seize the opportunity to demand cuts in needed social programs that would benefit the whole nation.

The outlook for the future, judging from the current administration's announced plans for fiscal year 2005 (beginning in October 2004), entail additional setbacks for social programs as well as more tax cuts. Thus, housing vouchers for the poor, health benefits for veterans, biomedical research, and job training and employment programs were slated for "more control" in the projected budget. It is uncanny how these cuts are focused on areas of greatest need, as if some perverse fate were in charge of affairs. Since the small increases in domestic programs in the previous two years did not even keep up with inflation, it was obviously the increases in defense, homeland security, pork, and international affairs that combined with tax cuts to make the deficit swell from $374 billion in 2003 to more than $450 billion projected for 2004. As summarized by the *New York Times* in January 2004:

> Total federal revenues have declined for three consecutive years, apparently the first time that has happened since the early 1920s. But in those years, from 2002 to 2003, total federal spending has increased slightly more than 20 percent to $2.16 trillion last year.[180]

In terms of both social spending and fiscal responsibility, therefore, America has moved resolutely backward while shifting the remaining largess of an inherited surplus to large-scale business and the military. The lineaments of a first-rate nation are hard to discern in this conjunction of self-destructive tendencies.

One suspects that there is a long-term policy behind these cuts in federal programs; and that even if the nation had not gone to war, means would have been found by the neoconservatives in Washington to pursue this policy. For the slow, steady demolition of the federal government means that the public will be obliged to turn more and more to the private sector for all kinds of services. In short, the government's legal monopoly will be destroyed, and private business will then be able to move in and expand its profits enormously. Deregulation is also part of this strategy because it makes it possible for corporations to reduce their bills for pollution and exploitation of basic resources, as well as a host of other operating costs, including work and benefit safeguards. Deregulation also makes it possible to create private monopolies, which are actually far preferable to a totally competitive market as far as capitalists are concerned, in spite of their rhetoric about competition. (The purpose of this rhetoric, of course, is to oppose those regulations that are not clearly beneficial to corporations.) In fact, concentration has increased markedly in the past 25 years in a number of industries. Finally, the benefits of tax cuts and tax havens to corporations are obvious. (For more thorough discussion of these points, see source note.[181])

But in spite of budget cuts, economic woes, and grave warning signs on the nation's horizon, Americans can console themselves with the thought that their increased consumption over the past 40–50 years has made their lives happier and happier. But then, has it really? A brief look at the research bearing on this question is revealing.

Consumption and Happiness

A review of many years of research on the happiness quotient of Americans has noted that "social scientists have found striking evidence that high-consuming societies, just as high-living individuals, consume ever more without achieving satisfaction ... studies on happiness indicate [that] the main determinants of happiness in life are not related to consumption at all—prominent among them are satisfaction with work, leisure to develop talents, and friendships . . ."[182]

A major reason for the failure of consumption to enhance happiness is that the enjoyment of getting and having derives from comparison with the consumption of others, or "relative gratification," as sociologists call it. As we gain more consumer benefits, our standard of comparison shifts upward, and this is especially likely to occur if new products and services are constantly being offered to replace old products and services. That these new consumer items might be only "marginally differentiated" (an economic term) from earlier products and services makes little difference when consumption is largely a matter of competing with one's peers or trying to emulate one's betters. (In fact, the *inherent* quality of a new product might be worse than its predecessor's quality, as many audiophiles claim is the case with CDs, compared with phonograph records.) This pattern of competition need not be overt, as in an American Indian potlatch ceremony, however. As long as the enhancement of consumption improves one's private self-assessment of up-to-dateness and belonging, it is gratifying to the consumer. But such gratification lasts only a short while in a society barraged with new products and services, a society also obsessed with upward status mobility in which the symbolic functions of products and services come into play. This dynamic is confirmed by the fact that the greater the *visibility* of the new product or service to others, the faster the turnover in models or styles (e.g., automobiles, clothing, home furnishings, and hair styles). In other words, the closer consumption behavior comes to the overt nature of a potlatch, the more it is driven by relative gratification. These sociological reasons for the failure of consumption as a source of happiness are reinforced, of course, by the psychological fact that consumer products and services tend to lose their novelty over a certain period of time. Thus, one tends to take for granted what was once very alluring or gratifying. Market experts and advertisers are well aware of the American mania for constant consumption and actually encourage it in the very process of exploiting it.

The failure of consumption to increase long-term happiness is cold comfort to those in our society who cannot afford the basic necessities of a comfortable, safe, healthy, and decent standard of living. Beyond that level, the failure of increased consumption, and especially luxuries, to enhance happiness points to the existence of widespread, vacuous self-indulgence—hardly the earmark of a superior society. Indeed, the data suggest a continuous striving for a level of happiness that never arrives, and *will* never arrive through the medium of conventional consumerism.

This assessment also suggests the possibility of an insatiable pursuit of wealth, luxury, and status at the upper reaches of the economy, or, as I call it in the following section, a "bonanza mentality" that tramples on legal and ethical standards to attain its ends. This pursuit can have damaging consequences not only for society at large but for capitalism as well. Which brings us to the subject of Enronesque corporate fraud, one of the most prominent features of American economic behavior at the dawn of the 21st century.

Enron and Beyond: Corporate Fraud, Regulatory Laxity, and Tax Evasion

The financial collapse of Enron Corporation in late November 2001, and the subsequent fall of its auditing firm and other major corporations after disclosures of fraud, struck the American public like a lightning bolt. Enron was one of the world's largest corporations, and its follow-up act, WorldCom, was even larger. Although several corporations were later caught in the regulatory net that was finally cast by the government, the focus here is on Enron as a prototype of the pathological pursuit of wealth.

"Enron used financial engineering as a kind of plastic surgery, to make itself look better than it was," as one professor of law put it.[183] The purpose was to create a false picture of profits and losses. As a result, $70 billion of shareholder value was obliterated, and creditors were denied billions of dollars of Enron debt.[184] The number of Enron's employees was 21,000, and the estimated loss to their 401 pensions from purchase of the company's stocks was reported to be $1.2 billion.[185]

Was Enron's behavior purely a product of its own creativity, or was it assisted, or at least encouraged, by lackadaisical regulation by government agencies? That the latter is largely the case is suggested by the fact that the derivatives markets had been largely unregulated, and had not even been recently audited by federal regulators of securities.[186] Felix Rohatyn has elaborated this point. "The derivatives market had been deregulated late in December 2000 by the Commodities Futures Modernization Act. Although Enron was in effect a financial institution, it had, for a considerable period, no legal obligation to submit some of its most important financial operations to regulators for scrutiny."[187]

The power of Enron itself to influence the regulatory process is demonstrated by the following events. On August 6, 2001, the Federal Energy Regulatory Commission (FERC) chairman announced that he would resign. The CEO of Enron, Kenneth Lay, later claimed that he had played a critical role in forcing out the chairman because of a disagreement with him about additional regulations. Subsequently, according to an account of this episode, "Lay was allowed to handpick a new chairman of FERC."[188]

This intrusion of Enron into the regulatory process raises the chilling prospect that laxity in the creation and enforcement of regulations is not only a product of incompetence or overwork on the part of government agencies but a deliberate act of complicity among Congress, the administration, and corporations. And the more we examine the facts, the more this hypothesis makes sense. Take, for example, a successful bill introduced by Senator Phil Gramm from the president's (and Enron's) state of Texas that reveals that the senator was literally in bed with Enron. According to an investigative Texas magazine, a bill introduced by Senator Gramm of Texas and made into law "contained a provision that congressional aides referred to as the 'Enron exemption.'" First utilized in 1993 by the Futures Trading Commission (FTC), this provision provided for a "regulatory exemption on derivatives contracts." The chairperson of the FTC was Senator Gramm's wife, who was also a member of the Enron Board of Directors. It was this provision that made it possible for Enron to bloat its financial statements, according to this account.[189]

Moreover, Enron made campaign contributions to 71 current senators and 188 current representatives in an amount close to $6 million.[190] And almost all the members (51of 56) of the House Energy and Commerce Committee, which had the duty of investigating Enron later on, had accepted money from the company or from its auditing firm; and the great majority of the members of the House Financial Services Committee had also gotten campaign funds from Enron, which shows the breadth of the quid pro quo system (or "legalized corruption," as some critics have called it).

With respect to the president, Enron and its executives were "the largest single source of financial support for Bush's gubernatorial and presidential campaigns." But this may be only the tip of the iceberg, with the submerged portion embodied in the executive branch. Six members of President Bush's administration worked for Enron as employees, board members, or consultants. They are: the Economic Adviser to the President, the U.S. Trade Representative, the Secretary of the Army, the Chief of Staff to the President, and the Commerce Secretary. Karl Rove, the President's chief political advisor, "was a major stockholder when he met with Ken Lay to discuss Enron's problems with federal regulators."[191] Finally, President Bush was a personal friend of Enron's CEO, Ken Lay, whom he called "Kenny Boy."

In other words, Enron was a major recruiting ground for the Bush administration. Nor has the president been an idle bystander in his relations with the regulatory process. In 2001 he tried to eliminate 57 regulatory positions in the Securities and Exchange Commission (SEC) in spite of its well-known shortage of manpower.[192] Because of the practical importance to society of the government's regulatory function, it is hard to decide whether complicity reflects a violation of a pragmatic standard or an ethical one. Perhaps both. At any rate, it does not speak well for a superior form of either government or society, but attests to a robust symbiosis between government and big business.

It would be a mistake to assume that the Enron accounting gimmicks were unprecedented, or that Enron was the only mammoth perpetrator of business fraud. "Long before Enron and off-balance-sheet accounting became part of the financial lexicon of average American investors," says an economic analyst, "creative accounting was an accepted way of doing business in Silicon Valley."[193] Indeed, over 1,000 companies have been required to "correct their financial statements."[194] And with reference to Enron's ploys to improve its financial image by accounting shenanigans, a professor of law has assured us that "many other companies do the same thing . . . accounting subterfuge using derivatives is widespread . . ."[195]

Manipulation of derivatives bookkeeping is not the only means whereby corporations defraud customers or the public. Widespread manipulation of energy supplies, for example, has been exposed, notably in recent times by an administrative judge who concluded that "the El Paso Corporation illegally helped to drive up prices for natural gas in California during the state's power crisis in 2001 and 2002."[196] And the role of the government in fostering fraud either by omission or commission should also not be forgotten. Forty percent of the fraud cases in the United States are not prosecuted, and 40 percent of the convictions for fraud do not involve jail time.[197]

After Enron, another mammoth company, Global Crossing, was similarly charged with doctoring its books. Specifically, the corporation had deliberately misstated $3.8 billion in their accounting. And like Enron, its bankruptcy obliterated the 401(k) funds of thousands of employees.[198] And then came World-Com.

The fraudulent practices and subsequent bankruptcy of WorldCom were disclosed in June 2002, and in the following month Congress belatedly passed a tough new law that set up a Public Accounting Oversight Board, which was given the authority to set new standards or adapt existing ones and to examine the audits of auditing firms. But when it was discovered that the chairman, who had been selected by the SEC chairman, had formerly headed the audit commit-tee of a company that was later accused of fraud (a fact that the SEC chairman apparently concealed), the SEC chairman was forced to resign. His designee for chairman of the new oversight board then decided to beat a hasty retreat himself, and so both the new board and the old SEC became bereft of leadership—not an auspicious beginning for a crusade against corporate misconduct.[199]

This Marx Brothers parody of officialdom, if you will, was only the climax of years of farcical neglect of the SEC. From 1991 to 2000 the workload of SEC's division of "market and corporate supervision" increased 137 percent, while staffing increased only 29 percent. And even before these workload in-creases, the agency was notoriously underfunded.[200]

The financial consequences of the enfeeblement of regulatory oversight and the advantages taken of it by firms like Enron, WorldCom, and Global Crossing have been staggering. A Brookings Institute report has estimated that the effect on the economy has been a loss of $28–39 billion.[201] As PBS reported on July 19, 2002, "Today was the seventh biggest drop in the stock market in the stock market's history." And as the BBC reported, "The loss in the American stock market this year has been greater than the GNP of Germany."[202]

Although the Bush administration vowed to clamp down on corporate crime and approved Congress's new antifraud legislation, the White House showed another side of its persona by "urging Congress to provide the Securities and Exchange Commission with 27 percent less money than the recently passed anti-fraud legislation authorized," according to the *New York Times*.[203] This cut in funding would have meant that Merrill Lynch, for example, had more lawyers concerned with regulation than the entire enforcement division of the SEC. A stepchild of federal support for years, the administration had resisted pressure to allow the SEC to become a full-fledged member of the federal regulatory fam-ily. The move to further emasculate the SEC provoked an outcry, however, and several months later the president reversed his decision to cut appropriations.

The feebleness of efforts to reform the SEC *after* the Enron scandal is evi-denced by the agency's failure to detect the egregious wrongdoings in the mu-tual fund industry, which came to light two years after Enron's collapse. (An informant had gone to the New York attorney general.) Not surprisingly, the industry had been granted *exemptions* from several key provisions of the reform law that followed the Enron-WorldCom scandal.

Remoteness from public concern with corporate wrongdoing seems to have been reflected in the president's earlier advice to the American people following the stock market's nose dive and the loss of millions of dollars in pensions: "Don't think about the stock market. Think about more important things like [pause] loving your neighbor."[204]

This bizarre response did not accurately reflect the mood of the American people, however. When asked in 2001, and then again several times in 2002, if there was "too much," the "right amount," or "too little" government regulation of business corporations, the upward trend in the "too little" response was marked. It rose from 17 percent in July 2001 to 30 percent in February 2002, 33 percent in June 2002, and 37 percent in July 2002, an overall shift in 12 months of 20 percent. And a favorable attitude toward big corporations declined at the same time.[205]

Other well-known ways in which corporations apparently evade responsibility for contributing their fair share to the public weal is by the pursuit of federal subsidies and tax havens. As for subsidies, according to Public Citizens' Congress Watch, "each year U.S. taxpayers subsidize U.S. businesses to the tune of almost $125 billion, the equivalent of all the income tax paid by 60 million individuals and families [through] special corporate tax cuts, direct subsidies for advertising, research and training costs, and incentives to pursue overseas production and sale."[206] Tax reductions are especially helpful. Oil and pipeline companies, for example, paid only 5.7 percent of their American profits in federal income tax in 1998, and one-half paid none at all.[207] And earlier, in 1989 to 1995, "nearly a third of large corporations operating in the United States with assets of at least $250 million or sales of at least $50 million paid no U.S. income tax . . ."[208] From 1950 to 2000, corporate taxes as a percentage of total receipts fell from 25.5 percent to 10.2 percent. In the same period, payroll taxes increased from 6.9 percent to 31.1 percent.[209] Clearly, the burden was shifted. Another analyst has noted that the subsidies paid for by the government amount to $800 billion lost in foregone tax revenues, or what might be called a "hidden budget" that is not even presented in the official budget figures.[210]

A large chunk of unpaid taxes are attributable to offshore tax havens: "It is estimated that at least $70 billion in taxes is evaded each year through offshore accounts . . . Today [June 2002] there are about sixty offshore zones. With 1.2 percent of the world's population, they hold 26 percent of the world's assets."[211] Tax avoidance is not new, of course, but has been a growing problem for years. Sixty years ago corporations paid half of all U.S. taxes; in 2000, they paid only 7.4 percent.[212]

Unable to benefit from the revenue that business is able to avoid paying, the federal government is obliged to forgo support for an array of needed efforts to improve living conditions and the development of its human resources. The question becomes unavoidable, then: How can a nation be considered "great" when the well-to-do and powerful withhold resources, such as tax payments, from citizens with the unstinting acquiescence of the government under the pretext of "preserving free enterprise"? Nor can this policy be justified by reference to our democratic arrangements for representing the people's will, thereby assuring us that it is what the public desires. Not only does the public feel that big business has too much influence, but America's system of government is unique in that it fails to represent the spectrum of public interests by rejection of proportional representation, violation of the one-man-one vote principle by the intercession of the electoral college and the Senate, and popular election of a single executive in a winner-take-all, majoritarian contest.[213] (Violations of democratic representation are discussed more fully in chapter 11.) In fact, the system seems tailor-made for the rise of a plutocracy, which is precisely what appears to be happening in America. And apart from the influence on government of wealthy patrons, 40 percent of our senators are millionaires, as mentioned earlier.

Tax avoidance and the rampant fraud that were unveiled by bankruptcies and government investigations subsequent to Enron's collapse are traceable to what might be called a *bonanza mentality* that seems to pervade big business in America. It is not confined to the present but is a phenomenon with deep historical roots.

It could be argued that the bonanza mentality of Americans was born of a marriage of vast resources and the energies opened up by a "classless" society liberated from the European social matrix of religious, state, and class constraints. These two circumstances gave rise to an attitude of venturesome optimism and confidence in success, later to become known as the American Dream. The most spectacular expressions of this outlook were the settlement of the West and the gold rush. But at least two basic conditions were necessary for it to be transformed into the big-business culture of the 19th and 20th centuries.

These conditions were the absence of a tradition of socialist struggle, on the one hand, and the absence of an aristocratic value system, on the other. The former entailed an emphasis on the social needs of the working class and the poor, and also restraints on capitalistic exploitation; the latter reflected a culture with a code of honor, preoccupation with status instead of sheer wealth, and a morality of noblesse oblige toward the disadvantaged. In sum, internalized humanitarian norms, a code of honor, and demands for effective constraints on free enterprise were common in Europe but weak or absent in America. Thus, the American Dream was transformed by the elite into vigorous, private-sector exploitation of men and women, of the political system, and of the nation's natural resources with the assistance of a complicit legal system. By the time that unionism emerged as a functional alternative to European socialism, and the state had begun to clamp down on the more egregious practices of corporate enterprise (helped by "muckraking" journalism), the values and style of big business had become set. And faith in "free markets" had become the mantra of self-enrichment. As Kenneth Lay, Enron's CEO, intoned (as noted earlier): "I believe in God and I believe in free markets."[214]

Consequently, the growing body of regulatory laws and regulations long ago became viewed as an obstruction to be forestalled, evaded, or eliminated. At the same time, however, certain of these laws could be used as protection against competition or as façades of legality that offered loopholes. Thus, intimate knowledge of the legal, financial, and political systems became essential for the bonanza mentality to flourish on behalf of shady enrichment. Some of the means by which Enron thrived included offshore tax havens, accounting tricks, compliant auditors, selective compliance with environmental rules, and so on.[215]

Such practices fall into what might be called the "semi-legal" zone or, as a humorist has put it, the "weasel" zone defined as a "gigantic gray area between good moral behavior and outright felonious activities [where] everything's misleading without actually being a lie."[216] The importance of this zone is its magnitude, which defies formal regulation of every cranny of wiggle space. Consequently, not even regulations can completely cure the malignant effects of the bonanza mentality. (For another discussion of the semi-legal zone, see the author's book *Fatal Remedies: The Ironies of Social Intervention* (New York and London: Plenum Press, 1981), 96–99.)

From the corruption of the Grant administration after the Civil War to the Teapot Dome Affair of the '20s to the FHA scandals of the '60s to Michael Milken's securities fraud in the '80s to the current parade of corporate malfeasances (fueled by the speculative binge of the '90s), America has demonstrated a unique capacity for rip-off at the highest levels of business and industry, abetted by collusive government agencies and a lack of media investigative initiative. (A research project more than a decade ago discovered that 62 percent of the Fortune 500 corporations had been found guilty of major illegalities between 1975 and 1984, and 42 percent had engaged in corrupt practices at least twice.[217])

Collusion among industry, the government, and the media are further abetted by public apathy and ignorance of the extent to which the problem pervades America's social system, thanks largely to the American Myth. After all, the public is itself imbued with the bonanza mentality, and therefore admiring of its virtuosi in high places—until the latter threaten their personal well-being.

As C. Wright Mills has observed:

> A society that narrows the meaning of "success" to the big money and in its terms condemns failure as the chief vice, raising money to the plane of absolute value, will produce the sharp operator and the shady deal. Blessed are the cynical, for only they have what it takes to succeed.[218]

This peculiar confluence of outlook and circumstances can have broad ramifications for the economic system that we call capitalism. For the system cannot succeed if the goal of accumulating wealth ignores or repudiates the foundational needs of the system. A highly respected former governor of the New York Stock Exchange, Felix Rohatyn, has identified certain of these needs with reference to Enron and other disclosures:

I believe that market capitalism is the best economic system invented for the creation of wealth; but it must be fair, it must be regulated, and it must be ethical. The excess of the last few years shows how the system has failed in all three respects.[219]

It would be ironic indeed if America, the preeminent land of capitalism, brought capitalism to its knees, not by a revolt of the proletariat, but by a revolt of the investors. Much of the irony derives from the nature of the beast called corporations. Let us therefore turn to a brief examination of that peculiar form of social organization and its preeminent place in the American scheme of things.

Corporations as Persons and Their Political Ascendancy

Given the deficiencies of America's educational system (see chapter 4), many readers will be surprised to learn that leading figures in American history have repeatedly sounded the alarm about the growing political and economic power of corporations. Jefferson and Madison wanted an amendment to the Constitution "banning them from giving money to politicians or trying to influence elections in any way . . . and requiring that the first purpose for which all corporations were created be 'to serve the public good.'"[220] John Marshall wanted a corporation to be limited "only to those properties which the charter of creation confers on it . . ."[221] Abraham Lincoln was especially wary of corporations and foretold disaster from their being unleashed on society. As Lincoln wrote:

[As a result of the war] corporations have been enthroned and an era of corruption in high places will follow, and the money power of the country will endeavor to prolong its reign by working upon the prejudices of the people until all wealth is aggregated in a few hands and the Republic is destroyed.[222]

And later presidents Grover Cleveland and Teddy Roosevelt sounded much the same note. Cleveland reiterated Jefferson's and Madison's declaration that corporations should be "the servants of the people," adding that they were "fast becoming the people's masters." And Teddy Roosevelt flatly declared that "there can be no effective control of corporations while their political activity remains."[223]

As for banning corporations from influencing legislation, funding campaigns, or having any rights except those granted as "privileges," there was a not-too-distant past when these safeguards were the law in virtually every state, and when the punishment for violations was imprisonment. Here, for example, was the law of Wisconsin:

No corporation doing business in this state shall pay or contribute, or offer consent or agree to pay or contribute, directly or indirectly, any money, property,
free service of its officers or employees or thing of value to any political party,
organization, committee or individual for any political purpose whatsoever, or
for the purpose of influencing legislation of any kind, or to promote or defeat
the candidacy of any person for nomination, appointment or election to any political office.[224]

What happened? Anyone who proposed such a law today would be deri-
sively laughed out of court with the help, of course, of corporate financing. And
one of the greatest boosts that corporations received in surmounting the scruples
of people like Jefferson and Lincoln, as well as the laws of the states, had its
roots in an alleged decision by the Supreme Court in 1886. This ruling proclaimed that corporations were "persons" and, therefore, deserved the "equal
protection of the laws" under the 14th Amendment (designed to ease the transition of blacks into civil society after the abolition of slavery). Not only did corporate interests ride the tattered coattails of emancipated slaves into a new era of
freedom, but the Supreme Court's 1886 decision is thought to be the lone doing
of the Court Reporter who embellished the published version of the Court's ruling with an assertion that the 14th Amendment had been extended to corporations as "persons." This proposal had been made earlier and had been rejected
by the Court, but now it adhered to the new ruling as published. The story of
what might have happened is fascinating:

[I]n writing up the case's headnote—a commentary that has no precedential
status—the Court's reporter, a former railroad president . . . opened the headnote with the sentence: 'The defendant Corporations are persons within the intent of the clause in section 1 of the Fourteenth Amendment to the Constitution
of the United States, which forbids a State to deny to any person within its jurisdiction the equal protection of the laws.' Nowhere in the decision itself does
the Court say corporations are persons . . . with the stroke of his pen, [the]
Court Reporter . . . moved [corporations] out of that 'privileges' category . . .
and moved them into the 'rights' category with humans . . .[225]

The fact that the Court asserted in its opinion proper that it had declined to
decide the Constitutional question at that time lends support to this account. But
there is also the fact that in the same year the Court struck down 230 state laws
that had been passed to regulate corporations.[226] Presumably if it had not favored
the Reporter's claim in the headnote, it would not have heard these cases. One
shocking possibility is that the judges—or at least some of them—did not want
to take personal responsibility for having agreed to this idea and reached an
agreement with the Court Reporter for him to handle it himself. But whatever
the explanation, the "ruling" became the law of the land.

Corporations were not shy about broadening their powers in accordance with their new "person" status by appealing to the Bill of Rights in particular cases to acquire the same protections as individuals under the Constitution. Between 1890 and 1910, they brought 288 cases to the Supreme Court citing the protection of the Fourteenth Amendment (whereas only 19 such cases were brought on behalf of blacks).[227] In 1893, the due process and other protections of the Fifth Amendment were bestowed on corporations. In 1906, the search and seizure protections of the Fourth Amendment were bestowed on them. In 1925, the freedoms of press and speech of the First Amendment were given. And in 1976, the donation of money for political purposes was ruled as "speech." Subsequently, drilling rights and mineral rights were protected, and liability laws made it actionable to accuse corporations of wrongdoing (i.e., subject to charges of libel, slander, or defamation).[228]

Another landmark decision of the Supreme Court in favor of corporations was the Lochner case of 1905. A New York State labor reform law was invalidated because it required safer working conditions and a 10-hour work day, thereby depriving the owners of the corporation (a bakery) their property rights. This ruling led to the invalidation of more than 300 state and federal laws involving minimum wages, health and safety codes, rights to organize, a progressive income tax, and so on. Finally, the Supreme Court reined in this assault on social rights in 1937 when, as it asserted, public necessities came before property rights.[229]

While protection under the 14th Amendment was marching forward into many realms of corporate activity, the Supreme Court was obviating the antitrust laws. Monopolies were exempted in the cases of sugar production (1895); U.S. Steel (1920); agricultural seller co-ops (1922); rail, water, and motor carriers (1948); baseball (1953); banks (1966); newspapers; and so on. In fact, the antitrust laws were used to fight unionization in numerous cases.[230]

Some contemporary examples of applying the personhood doctrine to corporations will indicate the scope of its impact (my own words are in brackets):

[S]tates and localities cannot favor small or local businesses over corporate chain stores or out-of-state businesses.[231] [Banning of cigarette ads or campaign contributions is a violation of free speech.[232] Aircraft of the Environmental Protection Agency cannot fly over factories to monitor compliance with environmental emission laws because of protections against unreasonable search and seizure.[233] Liability for industrial accidents (including nuclear) cannot be unlimited.[234] Fourth Amendment rights of privacy have been claimed to] prevent voters or public officials from examining the software that runs [a corporation's] voting machines.[235] A subpoena issued by a federal grand jury to the secretary of a corporation [amounts to] an unreasonable search and seizure.[236] [Surprise inspections of workplaces under the OSHA (Occupational Safety and Health Administration) Act were struck down by the Supreme Court.][237]

[Recently, NIKE lost a suit against it for deceptive advertising under a California law that forbids intentional deception by corporations. In a public announcement denying that it used sweatshop workers in China, the suit claimed that this published statement was advertising and was deceptive. NIKE in effect claimed that it had the same right to lie that is enjoyed by individuals in spite of the California law. NIKE appealed the ruling to the Supreme Court.][238]

The notion that corporations are persons is an oddity among the nations of the world. Perhaps there is no clearer testimony to America's wholehearted devotion to business than this privileged personification of commercial corpulence.

This discussion of corporations as persons, and the help of the courts in overriding antitrust and social rights laws, as well as the indispensable help of Congress in providing a wealth (literally) of subsidies and legal protections, makes it abundantly clear that the contemporary dominance of corporations is not just the result of natural market forces. Without the "unnatural" force of government (and the cooperation of the mainstream media, as we shall see later), the power of corporations would be much diminished, and also much less destructive in a number of respects, also to be detailed later. Hence the importance of scrutinizing the historical strengthening of relations between government and corporations that has made it possible for the latter to gain control of the former "unnatural force" on behalf of its own "natural" urges.

A number of socioeconomic factors as well as government policies contributed to the growing dominance of corporations in politics and society at large. Here only a few highlights will be noted by citing the work of two historians who have summarized the events bringing us to our present state of affairs.

The Civil War was the womb from which the modern symbiosis of government and corporations emerged. Inasmuch as the federal state became the major customer for everything (shoes, textiles, steel, food, medicine, etc.), these industries flourished, and names like Armour, Swift, J. Pierpont Morgan, and others became commonly known. Moreover, the federal government was responsible for creating the Union Pacific and Southern Pacific railroads,[239] including the giveaway of millions of acres surrounding the track that extended far beyond the needed right-of-way.

Gradually, the courts became more and more probusiness after the war as business and commercial law practices were regarded as suitable backgrounds for judges, and legal theory of property rights was developed, including the idea of corporate personhood.[240] Concurrently, labor organization efforts were overwhelmed by federal troops and state militias, as well as powerful private forces that specialized in intimidation and violence, such as the Pinkertons. Following Carnegie's breaking of the Homestead strike, one historian of the event insisted that "it was common knowledge that the monumental profits earned by Carnegie Steel in the 1890s grew directly from the defeat of unionism."[241]

Meanwhile, the corporations were taking over the state legislatures, which until 1913 had been responsible for choosing the members of the U.S. Senate.[242] A "state boss" system arose through which "key leaders brokered the relationships between the corporations on one side and the state legislatures, the U.S. Senate, and Washington officialdom on the other. Presidents . . . were often nominated by cabals of state bosses . . . The capture of the Senate by business and finance represented the crippling of any populist or progressive role for government . . . It also represented an extraordinary fusion of politics and American millionairedom."[243] One of the most beneficial outcomes for industry was the enactment of tariffs by Congress that permitted the creation of large trusts.[244] In particular, "the McKinley tariff of 1890 and the Dingley tariff of 1897 stood out not only for unusually high rates but for grand motivation. Greed in these situations took on a new dimension."[245]

The Senate, federal courts, U.S. Supreme Court, and even the U.S. Army all became the obedient servants of corporate interest in only two or three decades. Legislation was passed to curb the formation of trusts, but it was only "empty shells, legislation designed to appear to respond to public demands."[246] No wonder it was called the Gilded Age. And owing to campaign financing, lobbying, and swapping of personnel, government and industry have continued, and even expanded their mutually beneficial relations in the 21st century, especially under conservative governments. As in the Gilded Age, "huge levels of government support for industry and technology in research grants, subsidies, wartime expenditures, and policy commitment" are provided by the federal government.[247] One of these technological inventions was the brainchild of the Army Ballistics Research Laboratory during World War II: the Electronic Numerical Integrator and Computer, the first computer with a stored memory. And the Internet had its inception in a Defense Department project. As for the telecommunications boom, one chronicler of the growth and role of wealth in American government policies has observed: "The free distribution of the public-owned electromagnetic spectrum to U.S. radio and television companies has been one of the greatest gifts of public property in history, valued as high as $100 billion."[248]

To resume our brief history of relations between corporations and government, although unions made a comeback after the days of the Homestead strike and the ensuing period of vigorous antiunion action by corporations (with the acquiescence and support of government), even in the middle years of the 20th century legislation was enacted that impeded the growth of workers' organizations. In 1947 the Taft-Hartley Act was passed, and earlier there was the Smith-Connally Act of 1943. The latter law authorized the federal government to take over industries that were being struck and prohibited unions from making direct political contributions; the former law made secondary boycotts illegal, required that union officials take anticommunist oaths, and supported right-to-work laws. Also, by the mid-1940s the prolabor members of the National Labor Relations Board had been eliminated; and the board obstructed efforts of unions to recruit new members, although it was supposed to protect them. These measures interfered with organizing drives in the South. Moreover, unions failed to gain political power sufficient to acquire the social benefits that were common in Europe, which we have seen to be conspicuously absent in America. Further, corporate battles with unions have escalated in recent years. Three-fourths of employers hire consultants to help resist organizing campaigns, according to a study by the AFL-CIO.[249]

The post–World War II decades enjoyed a period of prosperity and business-labor accommodation. But this rapprochement sputtered to a halt with the decline in corporate profits in the '60s. Moreover, restraints on corporate power began to be undermined by a decline in voter turnout among the less privileged and a breakdown of the New Deal solidarity of the Democratic Party. Both of these trends were largely the result of the decline in unionism, which in turn stemmed from union-busting efforts of industry, the changing composition of the work force (from manufacturing to service and to part-timers, owing to the influx of women), and the flight of industry to the Sunbelt. The migration of blacks to the North (when the promise of urban housing failed to satisfy the demand, destroyed black neighborhoods, and enriched developers) was also a factor in the decline of the Democratic Party. (The foregoing account is a much condensed version of the discussion by Piven and Cloward.[250])

In sum, the counterweight of a strong, widely based Democratic Party to the Republican tradition of conservatism with its "war chest" of millions was unable to sustain itself. And to a large degree its weakness was self-inflicted by local and state politicians who were apprehensive about the threat of new, potential voters being registered to vote by agents of the war on poverty (a threat imposed by the federal government through Democratic presidents who desperately needed the underprivileged urban vote). This apprehension provoked strong resistance of these politicians to allowing voter registration though federal poverty programs. The continuing weakness of the Democratic Party is attested by the fact that even though it won the popular vote in the 2000 presidential election (but lost the electoral vote), it was hesitant to mount a vigorous campaign of opposition to the conservative juggernaut of the current Bush administration until the appearance of Howard Dean.

Today (2004) we are riding the crest of the corporate political wave that began building up in the '70s. As Piven and Cloward point out, "beginning in the 1970s and continuing into the 1980s, American corporations mobilized for politics with a focus and determination rare in the American experience . . . calling for tax and regulatory rollbacks, cuts in spending on social programs, a tougher stance toward unions and increases in military spending."[251]

One of the most significant manifestations of this surge of corporate influence was the loophole exploited by the Federal Election Commission in 1978 to allow the contribution of "soft money" to political campaigns. (This development and its effects are discussed in chapter 11, "Democracy," under the heading of "Filling the Electoral Power Vacuum with Special-Interest Wealth and Influence.")

While many benefits have flowed to corporations from the swashbuckling mood of neoconservatism in Washington, as detailed throughout this book, one in particular has special significance: the decline in the corporate tax rate. Here are some figures that demonstrate this increasing giveaway to corporations under the present administration. The following corporations enjoyed major reductions in their tax rates: General Electric, from 31.2 percent in 1999 to 20.5 percent in the third quarter of 2002; Bristol-Myers Squibb, from 25.2 percent in 2000 to 15.4 percent in 2001; Procter and Gamble, from 36.7 percent in 2000 to 31.8 percent in 2001.[252] Meanwhile, audits of the large corporations have fallen from 1 in 4 to 1 in 6 since 1999.[253] (As previously noted, the working poor are now more likely to be audited than the wealthy.)

It would be naïve to assume that the tax-rate reductions for corporations have been the result of rational economic policy, much less the will of the people. In 1996 a study found that the most popular issue among lobbyists in Washington was taxation. In the first half of the that year, "2,251 different special interests disclosed an interest in tax legislation . . . tax-related lobbying even edged out lobbying on budget and appropriations matters."[254]

In addition to federal reduction in tax rates, federal law permits multinational businesses to lower their taxes by shifting domestic profits to their overseas books. Here is how it's done.

> Corporations "buy" supplies and services from their overseas selves, grossly inflating the price they pay. These phony purchases move huge sums of corporate profits out of our country into the accounts for their foreign affiliates, thus escaping U.S. taxation . . .[255]

As suggested earlier, the ultimate outcome of the new wave of corporate political mobilization in the last three decades is the George W. Bush administration. But the close ties with corporations reflected in the personnel of the current Bush administration (documented above and below) date back to the early period following World War II. As C. Wright Mills noted in 1956:

> The long-term tendency of business and government to become more intricately and deeply involved with each other has [since World War II] reached a new point of explicitness. The two cannot now be seen clearly as two distinct worlds . . . The growth of the executive branch of the government, with its agencies that patrol the complex economy, does not mean merely the enlarge-

ment of government as some sort of autonomous bureaucracy: it has meant the ascendance of the corporation's man as a political eminence.[256]

While no one would quarrel with the benefits that have flowed from public-private cooperation in the industrial development of America, at the same time the public is threatened with limited control over possible abuses motivated by sheer self-interest, such as poor quality of goods or services; deceptive advertising; the forgoing of other, more publicly desirable outcomes and uses of technological developments; and the side effects on the environment and health. The elected representatives and officials who smooth the way for private developments are responsible for overseeing the public impacts of those developments, and so the money that obtains development rights, subsidies, and tax benefits also influences the creation of legal loopholes and the averting of one's eyes from the possible ravages of the bonanza mentality.

At the very least, citizens are obliged to pay three times for the benefits of industry: first, in taxes for government-funded R&D whose results are turned over to industry; second, for the cost of goods and services of industry, which are often marked up on behalf of spectacular profits without any government-imposed limits; and, finally, in forgone public services owing to corporations' tax evasions, tax cuts, and tax loopholes that are created by lobbying and campaign financing, or, alternatively, in increased taxes on citizens to pay for these services. In short, what has traditionally been called corruption has been legalized in the name of "free speech" to promote "business prosperity," "industrial development," "free enterprise," and "full employment." But it is all still a matter of *paying* the government to do one's bidding, regardless of the buzz words, with the consequence that the public is required to bear the costs, socially and financially, at a number of points in the obscure chain of causes, side effects, and "blowbacks."

*   *   *

Instead of summarizing the overall economic situation sketched in this chapter, it is more important to endeavor to answer two simple questions: do we have anything to worry about, and are we any worse off than other major industrial nations?

The answer to both questions is yes. It appears that we are *uniquely* at risk because of our trade deficit, national debt, and negative savings rate, as pointed out by numerous economists, as well as because of our socially debilitating gulf between upper- and lower-income classes, a gulf that continues to grow, and our painful occupational crisis. Thus, the long term looks ominous, economically and in terms of quality of life, even if the short term is able to take care of itself. Even the International Monetary Fund, usually considered to be an adjunct to the United States, has expressed alarm. As it stated in a report in early 2004, "Higher borrowing costs abroad would mean that the adverse effects of United States fiscal deficits would spill over into global investment and output."[257] Moreover, nothing that the current administration has been doing, even if successful, seems sufficient to deal with the onslaught of retiring baby boomers in the not-too-distant future, according to the IMF report. Indeed, the commitment to further tax cuts will seemingly gut the Social Security fund at a time when it will be most needed as the result of a demographic bulge in numbers of elderly citizens. Meanwhile, at our backs is the housing bubble, which could burst and flood the nation with more bankruptcies or even cause a recession.

In addition, we seem to be uniquely liable to be disserved and ripped off by large-scale corporations, as evidenced by the Enron complex, and increasingly to be denied the tax resources of corporations by tax breaks and evasions that flourish with the acquiescence of government. Further, our work force is more vulnerable than those in other nations as shown by the decline of unions, exceptionally long annual working hours, multiple job-holding, regressive taxation, part-time work, unrelieved job stress and poor working morale, high rents and low wages for the working poor, corporate exportation of jobs, lack of child-care support for working families, increasing cost of health coverage, and the dwindling of employer benefit programs. And the large and growing gap between rich and poor (abetted by the rising cost of higher education and the dropouts precipitated by "No Child Left Behind") with the consequence of the highest poverty rate among advanced nations, is another indicator of long-term trouble and social deterioration. And this is especially true under an archconservative government that simply dismisses complaints about the privileged allocation of resources as nothing more than mischievous "class warfare" even while it exacerbates class division to a degree beyond anything in 20th-century American history. In fact, at least one economist has observed that Europe and America have swapped positions in terms of being hierarchical and class-ridden.

Unfortunately, America's habit of taking the GDP and other purely economic indicators as representing the nation's well-being diverts attention from the real state of affairs—in quality of life, social health, happiness, genuine progress, or whatever one wishes to call it—and also diverts attention from the much greater proportional shares that accrue to upper-income levels. Moreover, our fixation on unemployment rates causes us to ignore the larger picture of an *occupational crisis* reflected in long working hours, downward wage rates, deunionization, multiple-job holding, and so forth. Thus, the magnitude of financial transactions, output, and unemployment figures take the place of *social reports* that might be, and have been, completely at odds with the standard economic indicators as a reflection of the people's well-being. Other advanced nations produce and heed annual social reports by the government, but the United States does not even produce one. And so, the American Myth continues to insulate us from the shocks of social reality that occur *regardless* of whether economic performance is deemed to be magnificent or wretched. If the latter, then the keepers of the flame of national greatness can always attribute it to the natural forces of a modern economy, similar to the inexorable course of past epidemics—that is, until *cures* were found and vigorously *enforced.*

Finally, the rampant and explicit collusion among government, corporate enterprise, and the mainstream media in America guarantees that all these short-comings will endure and even expand with the blessing of the great American Myth. If this is the best that the world's foremost exemplar of free enterprise can offer, then the American experience might be considered a withering commentary on capitalism.

Perhaps what needs to be revised is the deeply entrenched notion that one's economy is the sacrosanct mainspring of a society, something distinct and life-enhancing that obeys universal laws of momentum and can only be fine-tuned. In fact, economic mechanisms operate within a particular society and culture and gain their raison d'etre from that context. They emerge from, and are sustained and guided in specific directions by, social and cultural variables, including formal and informal power structures. Thus, economic forces are controllable by alterations of context, and can and *should* be basically reconfigured when they do harm. If rising GDP poisons the quality of life under certain conditions (e.g., extreme inequality of wealth), or if rising productivity poisons the work force with "squeezing" and job stress, then these components of economic growth should be detoxified by legal measures. And that goes for any other "natural" economic forces that are harmful to human beings or the environment. Accordingly, when one hears the objection that some new measure, such as the Kyoto Treaty on global warming, would be bad for the economy, one might well ask, "Ah, but would it be good for the people?"

3

Health, Health Care, and Costs

Laudable progress in health care and physical well-being has been one of the miraculous gifts bestowed on mankind by the 20th century. In advanced nations, at least, people are living much longer than a century ago and suffering far fewer ailments. But the consequences of technological progress of any kind are seldom, if ever, unalloyed blessings. And these consequences can even interfere with, or negate, the very blessings that were intended and are widely assumed to have occurred. A look at the health care field in America provides a good example of how matters can go awry.

Two questions commonly raised by improved medical care allude to the possibility of perverse outcomes: Who is benefiting and at what cost? If benefits are unevenly distributed because of traditional inequities in the distribution of resources in a society, or if their high cost limits the consumption of other good things in life, then the clear benefits of medical advancements to many citizens are diminished. Further, expenditures for breakthroughs in medical therapy can sap the resources that might be used for *prevention* of illnesses in the first place (a major portion of which are actually preventable), thereby lowering the level of physical well-being or off-setting to some degree the achievements of therapy. And the modern popularity of high-tech innovations can divert attention from low-tech therapies that might be even more beneficial. In light of these trade-offs, it becomes advisable to refer to the *net* benefits of improved care, regardless of technological promise. As an economist would put it, the "opportunity costs" need to be kept sharply in focus.

Moreover, if longer life or improved physical well-being collides with the traditional level and distribution of resources among different interest groups in society, many adjustments might need to be made, such as increased provisions for the growing number of elderly, which could cause a drain on other resources and lead to aggressive competition among these groups. And then, it needs to be recognized that all technological innovations have a certain *lulling* effect that can give us a false sense of security, whether it be an implicit faith in the O-rings of a space shuttle, in the material used for breast implants, or in the expertise of one's physician. With regard to medical technologies, their increased *complexity* invites errors of professional judgment in their application, a possi-

75

bility that tends to be overlooked in the groundswell of confidence that these technologies arouse. In fact, the inadequate dissemination of up-to-date medical information among physicians is regarded by experts as a major stumbling block in our health care system today (as discussed below). Or again, overweening confidence in health care in general can foster an assumption that illnesses and disabilities have diminished in the population to levels that no longer warrant our grave concern, and especially with respect to less "popular" illnesses or disabilities.

Finally, we come to the problem of exploitation for profit by the developers and distributors of new medical technologies and by insurance companies, exploitation that often proceeds with the protection of state authority on grounds of preserving "free enterprise." Such exploitation becomes especially troublesome when a new technology is not just a matter of convenience or enjoyment but of life and death. In other words, many consumers of expensive medical technologies are presented with a stark choice between "your money or your life," a phrase more suited to the underworld of street thugs. Thus, exploitation by developers, middlemen, and insurers adds a whole new dimension to the equation of unanticipated consequences, one that aggravates some of the problems already mentioned—such as over-confidence in drugs (fostered by advertising and by many physicians), the diversion of resources from preventive care or from expenditures for other consumer goods or services that make life worthwhile or endurable, or the growing complexity and confusing alternatives of therapy that have arisen because of intense competition for the medical-care dollar and aggressive marketing

All these problems have emerged in the wake of our 20th-century revolution in medical science. How successful America has been in dealing with them is problematic at best. As a matter of fact, there is evidence that it has dealt with them less adroitly than most other advanced nations. But first, let us look at the overall level of well-being in America in case we have been lulled into neglect or denial of our continuing high level of suffering and of the prevalence of life-threatening conditions. Then we shall move on to prevention, costs, quality, and the profit-enhancing exploitation of medical technology by developers and middlemen, with many references to the vexing role of government in all these matters. Comparisons with other nations will be made where possible, and a concluding section will summarize our findings.

Leading Causes of Death, Major Illnesses, and Disabilities

As inhabitants of a nation that values youthfulness and puts great stock in physical prowess, zest, and attractiveness, Americans tend to shun the realities of enfeeblement, disease, mental disorder, and death that beset so many, especially the elderly. And owing to our confidence in the contemporary miracles of medical science, as noted above, we may assume that suffering is being eradicated and that death is being outstandingly deferred in America. It is worthwhile, therefore, to inform ourselves about the facts of illness and death by perusing some statistics on their prevalence and leading causes.

In 2001, the number one cause of death in America for both men and women was heart disease, and it occurred 26 percent more frequently than the second most frequent cause, which was cancer. And cancer occurred 239 percent more frequently than the next highest cause, which was stroke. These three causes of death accounted for the demise of 1.4 million Americans, which was 0.5 percent of the total population and 59 percent of all deaths.[1]

Other health-related causes of death among the top 10 are: chronic lower respiratory tract disease, diabetes, pneumonia/influenza, Alzheimer's disease, nephritis, and septicemia, in descending order of frequency.[2]

In addition to health-related causes of death, there were 101,537 fatal accidents, which made this cause number five among all causes.[3] About half of fatal accidents are caused by motor vehicles (43,458 in 1997),[4] and about a third of these vehicular deaths are caused by falling asleep at the wheel.[5]

The 11th leading cause of death in 2001 was suicide (30,622 cases); and among males it was the 8th leading cause of death.[6] This points to the importance of including mental health in our study of health problems. (See below.)

Although a great deal of attention has been focused on the risk of breast cancer, it accounts for only 1–4 percent of female deaths, whereas heart disease or stroke accounts for 50 percent of deaths among women.[7] However, women who have heart attacks are given different treatments than men in hospitals, which might account for the fact that they are more likely to die within one year.[8] (See below on "Distribution of Health Costs—Hospitals.") Half of all heart attacks, incidentally, occur within normal cholesterol range, in spite of the tendency of physicians to focus on this measure of risk.[9]

Another illness to which women are more prone than men is rheumatoid arthritis. About 75 percent of patients with this disease are female. Including men and women, there are 2.1 million cases in the United States each year, and it can strike fairly young in life. In all, there are 42 million cases of arthritis in the country, or 23 out of every 100 Americans.[10]

Another commonly disabling disease, one that can lead to death, is asthma. In 1996, 10.2 million adults were afflicted with this health problem. Direct and indirect costs for treating asthma were estimated at $12.7 billion in 1998.[11] Interestingly enough, costs of asthma have increased greatly since the mid-1980s,[12] which suggests the role played by the pollution of America's air. (See also below.)

A major source of lung disease, the only leading cause of death in America that is still rising, is pollution consisting of "fine particle matter," or "particulate matter" (PM), according to testimony before a Senate subcommittee by the former head of the Environmental Protection Agency of the federal government, Carol Browner. And according to Dr. Clay Ballentine of Ashville, North Carolina, who also testified at these hearings, 4 percent of all U.S. deaths are due to air pollution exposure, and 20–30 percent of children have symptoms of asthma (which has resulted in 2,000 hospitalizations in North Carolina). In fact, asthma in children is the number one cause of lost school days in North Carolina, according to Dr. Ballentine; and, as mentioned in chapter 2, the cost of hospitalization of seventh-eighth graders has been $15 million in that state alone.[13] (For more on pollution in America, see chapter 6.)

Concerning diabetes, the sixth major killer in America, 17 million are sufferers of type 2, and 6 million have it and do not know it. In the past four years, health care costs for this disease have doubled.[14]

Nephritis, killer number nine in 2000, is an inflammation of the kidneys caused by a variety of factors. As one source says of chronic nephritis, "Its course is long and its prognosis is poor . . . No treatment is available in most cases." It could require kidney transplantation. Acute nephritis may be caused by several infections in the body, including strep throat, pneumonia, chicken pox, infectious hepatitis, scarlet fever, syphilis, and malaria. Allergic reaction to certain drugs or side effects of drugs can also cause interstitial nephritis. These effects, of course, can be avoided; and prevention of the diseases that are often the root causes of nephritis is also possible with the acute variety.[15, 16]

Septicemia, or blood poisoning, the 10th highest in frequency of fatal diseases in 2001, is a serious infection of the bloodstream. Appropriate treatment of localized infections, especially meningococcus (which can also cause meningitis), and a vaccine that is commonly included in childhood vaccination schedules can prevent the disease from occurring. Fatality rates of the disease are around 20 percent.[17]

Although not the major cause of fatal cancer, it is worth noting that one American dies every hour from skin cancer,[18] the vast majority of which cases are preventable.

Moving on to AIDS, we find that 800,000 cases have been reported since the epidemic began in America. The number of cases in Washington, D.C., alone has increased threefold since 1991.[19] For the country as a whole, there are 40,000 new cases annually, and the biggest increase lately has been among heterosexuals and young women.[20] Again, the great majority of these cases are probably avoidable.

Although AIDS has received preeminent attention as a disease that only death can ultimately cure, it is by no means the only incurable condition that afflicts million of Americans. As Senator Joseph Lieberman has reported, "Almost half of our U.S. population is living with a condition for which we cannot yet offer the hope of a cure."[21]

Behind several of the death statistics reported above is overweight: " . . . three in five adults aged 20–74 are overweight. One in four Americans is considered obese." It is not surprising, then, that about 300,000 fat-related deaths occur each year.[22] The health costs of obesity each year are estimated to be $117 billion. An estimated $50 billion a year are spent on diet products.[23] With respect to youths 6–17 years of age, annual obesity-related hospital costs increased threefold [from 1979 to 2000] . . . from $35 million to $127 million.[24]

Moving the search for causation another step backward, one of the causes of overweight (as well as of heart disease that proves fatal and possibly other ailments mentioned above) is the extremely low level of physical activity among Americans: "Seven in ten adults are not active regularly in their leisure time— including four in ten who are not active at all."[25] Consequently, the obesity rate was higher in the United States than in 15 European countries out of the 20 nations reporting in a study conducted in the '90s.[26]

Another prevalent factor lying behind death statistics with respect to a host of illnesses, such as cancer and cardiac and lung disorders, is cigarette smoking. Four hundred thousand Americans die from cigarette smoking each year, yet cigarettes continue to be manufactured legally.[27]

But whatever the proximate causes of these diseases and ailments, one must not forget that "for all health indicators considered, each increase in either income or education increased the likelihood of being in good health," which reminds us of the significance of poverty.[28] Thus, the causes of death need to embrace something not usually regarded as a health risk, and that something is being poor. Indeed, an astounding fact is that the leading cause of death among young black men, and also the second leading cause among Hispanic men, is murder.[29] Few events affect one's physical condition with greater certainty than being shot.

Homicide is a specialty of America when compared with the rates of other advanced nations. From 1980 to 2000, the homicide rate in America was triple the rate in Canada,[30] and in 1998 it was six times higher than in the UK. For white victims only, it was twice the rate in Europe as a whole.[31] Despite a drop in homicides in the '90s, violent crime in major cities increased 40 percent from 1969 to 1999,[32] and homicides increased 3.1 percent from 2000 to 2001.[33]

Facilitating this comparatively high level of carnage in the United States is the widespread ownership of firearms. In 2000, 66 percent of murder victims were killed with firearms.[34] Indeed, gun ownership is far more common in America than in European countries, where the murder rate is much lower. The mean percentage of persons owning guns in eight European countries was 16 percent in 1991, compared with 49 percent in the United States. The mean murder rate in these same European countries in the '80s was 1.4 per 100,000, compared with 9 per 100,000 in the United States in 1991.[35] According to FBI statistics for 2000:

> Every year [in America], more than 30,000 people are shot to death in murders, suicides, and accidents. Another 65,000 suffer from gun injuries . . . firearms kill about 85 people every day in this country.[36]

One way to gain a perspective on the magnitude of the problem in America is to consider the following facts:

> More Americans died in non-military shootings than in war this century . . . In fact, more Americans were killed by non-military gun violence from 1979 through 1997 (651,697) than died in all wars since 1775 (650,858) . . . About 51 percent of the gun deaths were suicide, and the vast majority of the rest were murders.[37]

From 1994 to 1997 there was a sharp decline in homicides by juveniles, which has been attributed entirely to fewer homicides by firearms.[38]

Finally, we come to a social indicator that is generally construed to be a measure of a country's socioeconomic development: the infant mortality rate. Although the infant mortality rate has declined in recent years in the United States, it is still higher than that in 19 other countries, including the UK, Germany, France, Austria, Italy, Belgium, Australia, Japan, and Singapore. In fact, our infant mortality rate is the same as that of Guadeloupe, the Korean Republic, Malta, and New Caledonia.[39] (That infant mortality can be markedly reduced in America if the authorities try hard enough is evidenced by the case of Illinois, which reduced infant mortality by 22 percent in the '90s.[40]) This poor showing for America might reflect the large disparity in income distribution mentioned in the preceding chapter on the economy, inasmuch as resources are simply not reaching into the disadvantaged strata of society. For example, the infant mortality rate among blacks in 1999 was more than twice that of whites.[41]

At a number of places in the preceding presentation, as with references to overweight, cigarette smoking, and lack of physical activity, I have mentioned the possibility of preventing diseases or other potential sources of death or disablement. The subject of preventability should not be overlooked in any effort to evaluate the maturity of American society, for it reflects the readiness of Americans to participate in the reckless endangerment of their own lives by means of sedentary, self-indulgent lifestyles or other causes of injury and death that are controllable. Because of its significance as a social indicator, this topic will be taken up in detail later.

Another matter that requires attention is the vexing question of soaring health-care costs in "the only major nation on earth that does not have a national health care program that guarantees health care to all."[42] But first, we should consider mental or emotional illness, and then a few "health risks" that are extremely common, but are not viewed simply as medical matters because of their broader implications for social order and the norms of civilized behavior. These issues are: domestic violence, child abuse, and the consumption of alcohol and illicit substances. The question that must be asked is how does our mental-illness rate and our performance as wife beaters, child abusers, and drug consumers measure up to the idea of America as an exemplary nation, one worthy of the world's emulation?

Mental Illness

According to a 2001 report of the National Institutes of Health, "One in every five Americans experiences a mental disorder in any given year, and half of all Americans have such disorders at some time in their lives, but most of them never seek treatment."[43] And, according to a report in 2003, 5 to 9 percent of children (4 million) have serious emotional disturbances.[44]

If we define mental illness for the moment as including Alzheimer's disease, depression, attention-deficit/hyperactivity disorder, phobias, and suicide, then mental illness becomes the second cause of disability in America after heart disease. Yet, only 6.9 percent of the 14.8 million adults with serious mental illness (estimated at 7.3 percent of all adults) received treatment in the 12 months prior to a survey in 2001, and only 18.4 percent of youths did so. Forty-five percent of the youths said they "felt depressed."[45] As for severe depression, it appears that up to 2.5 percent of children and up to 8.3 percent of adolescents suffer from this affliction in America.[46]

Large numbers of mentally ill persons are among those found on the streets of America because of the deinstitutionalization policy of several decades ago that almost emptied the mental hospitals. It has been reported that the number of mentally ill "admitted" to U.S. jails each year is about 670,000, eight times the number admitted to our state mental institutions because of lack of capacity. Human Rights Watch has estimated that 25 percent of inmates nationwide are mentally ill.[47] And the police admit that they often arrest the mentally ill when other facilities are unavailable. A study by the Open Society Institute has revealed that "a shocking 29 percent of jails surveyed reported to have incarcerated mentally ill persons against whom no criminal charges were filed . . . suicide is the leading cause of death in jail."[48]

As already noted, in 2001 suicide was the 11th leading cause of death in the nation as a whole. In that year, the total number of suicide deaths was 30,622. In fact, suicides outnumbered homicides by 3 to 2. Among young people 15 to 24, suicide was the third leading cause of death,[49] and the rate almost tripled between 1950 and the late 1990s. For youths under 15 it quadrupled.[50] How do these rates compare with other advanced nations?

The U.S. rate [of suicide in 1996] for 15–24 year olds is higher than 14 other [industrial nations] for males, 6 other countries for females. For children under 15 the U.S. suicide rate was two times higher than that of all other 25 industrialized countries combined.[51]

Judging from the absence of suicide as a topic in the mainstream media, it is apparently verboten.

That this state of affairs with respect to mental illness is part of a larger constellation of personal loss of bearings and estrangement is suggested by the striking decline in the level of interpersonal trust in America in the past 50 years. In 1950, 55 percent of the public believed that "most people can be trusted," but by 2000 a downward trend over the years wound up with only about 33 percent feeling that most people could be trusted.[52] (And it is quite likely that threats of domestic terrorism since that time have further aggravated this attitudinal malady of America, at least with respect to certain ethnic groups and perhaps immigrants in general.) With regard to youth in particular, an international study of schoolchildren found that the Americans ranked virtually at the bottom of 28 countries in the frequency of saying that their "classmates are always or often kind and helpful," and in the bottom quartile in saying that they "spend time with friends after school."[53] (For other international comparisons regarding health, see a later section of this chapter.) These data imply that the nation is suffering a grave loss of capacity for social integration.

Perhaps the same factors that are conducive to suicide are operating in the broader area of mental illness, at least among adults. According to the National Institutes of Health, "The strongest risk factors for attempted suicide in adults are depression, alcohol abuse, cocaine use, and separation or divorce."[54]

Domestic Violence

Like mental illness, domestic violence is a problem that lies beneath the radar of most Americans' perceptions, owing largely to the media's blackout of this subject, even though it occurs with shocking frequency. Every 13 seconds in America a woman is battered, and 30 percent of female murder victims, according to the late Senator Wellstone, are killed by their intimate partners. In fact, injuries from domestic violence occur more frequently to women than those caused by automobile accidents and cancer deaths combined.[55] Nor is the cost in dollars negligible: The estimate is that gender violence costs the economy $10 billion per year. As for the efforts we have made to protect victims of domestic violence, America has more animal shelters than domestic violence shelters.[56]

Child Abuse

One of the most depressing trends in America has been the increase in the number of child abuse cases in the past 25 years. Each year more than 3 million children are reported abused or neglected, and more than 1 million of these reports are confirmed.[57] While it is possible that teachers, physicians, and others have become less reluctant to report such cases, it is unlikely that the increase in the rate from 10.1 per 1,000 in 1976 to 47.0 in 1996 can be attributed to this factor alone. (The Child Abuse Prevention and Treatment Act that required professionals to report suspected cases was passed in 1974.) An increase in the number of cases of serious injury reported suggest an authentic rise in abuse, inasmuch as one would expect serious injuries to have been reported almost routinely in the earliest years of the law. And yet, reports have steadily increased. Almost half of the cases are negligence, which includes malnutrition, failure to prevent accidents, lack of medical care, and other forms of endangerment. Finally, it appears that about 1,400 children die annually from negligence, abuse, or both, according to data collected in 2002.[58] (Sexual abuse accounts for about 11 percent of all abuse cases.)

In dollar terms, it is estimated that $258 million is spent each day as a result of abuse and neglect of children.[59] Seventeen million of this amount is spent on hospitalization ($6.2 billion annually). The annual cost of the child welfare system is estimated to be $39 million a day ($14.2 billion annually).[60]

Alcohol and the Use of Illicit Substances

Another cause for alarm on the health chart of America is the frequent abuse of alcohol and illicit drugs. About 1 out of every 13 American adults suffers from severe alcohol problems, according to a report of the Harvard Medical School. This comes to nearly 14 million adults. And 100,000 Americans die each year from causes related to alcohol.[61]

American teenagers are much more likely to use illicit drugs than European youths, while the latter more often drink alcohol and smoke cigarettes, according to a study of 31 nations in 2000. In other words, American youths are more willing to break the law to satisfy their desire for mood-altering substances. Moreover, the age of first use seems to have dropped considerably over the past 40 years. Today, 41 percent of American 10th graders have tried marijuana and 23 percent have used other illicit drugs, compared with 17 percent and 6 percent, respectively, among European 10th graders. Twenty-six percent of the American students smoke cigarettes at least once a day and 40 percent have used alcohol in the past month, compared with 37 percent and 61 percent, respectively, in

Europe.[62] It should be mentioned, incidentally, that the use of marijuana and other illicit drugs spread to Europe from America.

Although American youths are less likely to drink alcohol than their European counterparts, their drinking is by no means a casual affair. Of the 10.1 million 12- to 20-year-olds in the United States who used alcohol in 2001, 28.5 percent were underage, which meant that alcohol to them was an illicit substance. Of this latter category, nearly 6.8 million (19%) were binge drinkers and 2.1 million (6%) were heavy drinkers. A fact that should be of particular concern to the public at large is the frequency of driving under the influence. Almost one out of four persons aged 18–25 years (22.8%) had driven under the influence of alcohol in the previous 12 months. Of those 12 years or older, 16.6 million (7.3%) were either dependent on, or abusers of, alcohol or illicit drugs; and 2.4 million of the latter were also dependent on, or abusers of, *both* alcohol and illicit drugs. For the entire population, "the number of persons with substance dependence or abuse increased from . . . 6.5 percent of the population in 2000 to . . . 7.3 percent in 2001."[63]

Unfortunately, many who need treatment for illicit drug use do not recognize the problem. The total number needing treatment for an illicit drug problem is 4.7 million to 6.1 million. Yet the number in treatment in a special facility in 2001 was only 0 .8 million to 1.1 million. In other words, the number needing, but not receiving, treatment is 3.9 million to 5 million. And according to the 2001 study, 101,000 of these try to get treatment but are unsuccessful.[64] Thus, the number needing, but not receiving, treatment in 2001 was sufficient to populate a large city. It is hard to remember, though, when one last heard about America's alcohol problem in the mainstream media.

Prevention of Illness, Deferment of Death

To what extent can Americans avoid or minimize the main causes of death or disablement? Stated another way, how many lives could have been saved or illnesses averted by preventive measures that are well known today? As pointed out earlier, the answer can shed some light on the proneness of Americans to endanger their own lives by sedentary, self-indulgent, or reckless lifestyles, and even to do so knowingly. Are victims never to be blamed? What follows are a few pertinent examples of conclusions by research on the avoidability of illness or disability.

As one specialist has noted, "Heart disease is one of the most preventable of all diseases and yet it's America's number-one killer and has been every year since 1921."[65] Sources of advice on lifestyle changes that would enhance health and longevity are abundant these days, but how many Americans take them seriously? Judging from the high rates of obesity in America reported earlier, and the numerous other cases of poor health and death reported above in spite of the many instances of preventability, it would appear that the message has not yet gotten across. Diets that include fatty fish like salmon, swordfish, and rainbow trout to help reduce the risk of heart attacks,[66] folic acid, which protects adult nerve cells against diseases of old age like Parkinson's and is found in citrus fruits and juices, whole wheat bread, and dry beans,[67] and so on, are simple and affordable forms of prevention. Smoking, of course, is the main cause of "chronic obstructive pulmonary diseases."[68]

Even the big killers like pneumonia, heart problems, cancer, and diabetes can be prevented: Pneumococcal pneumonia by the pneumococcal vaccine;[69] high blood pressure by physical activity and reduced intake of food with or without medication;[70] prostate cancer by consumption of tomato sauce;[71] type 2 diabetes and stroke by whole-grain foods;[72] and cancer in general by diet changes.[73] (Regarding the last point, the American Cancer Society claims that "diet contributes to about one-third of cancer cases in the U.S."[74]) Walking or exercising vigorously on a regular basis is especially helpful in fending off coronary heart disease;[75] but only about a third of American adults engage in the recommended levels of activity.[76] One cannot help but wonder if disregard of preventive self-care, especially with respect to overeating, is related to the high levels of depression and job stress in America that were documented earlier.

Overall, the great majority of illnesses and disablements that Americans suffer could probably have been avoided by either personal or governmental action, the latter mainly to improve the quality of the environment. According to Surgeon General Koop of the Reagan administration, treatment of preventable illnesses accounted for 70 percent of the nation's medical costs.[77] Thus, enormous costs in productivity loss, suffering, and life itself, as well as massive sums of money for treatment, could be saved by effective measures of prevention.

This admonition is not new, of course. In fact, 28 years ago the *New York Times* bemoaned the waste of money caused by not following preventive measures, pointing out that black lung disease, an affliction of miners, could have been prevented 30 years earlier. Nevertheless, cost of treatment had risen to $1 billion. The *Times* also cited $20 billion a year spent on treatment of illnesses arising from cigarette smoking, and $15 billion for preventable circulatory illnesses.[78] Two years ago the Columbia University College of Physicians and Surgeons made the same point:

> Prevention of disease is the best investment a nation or person can make. Yet only a fraction of the annual federal budget is expended in disease prevention.[79]

At least one study has found that the United States has fallen behind other advanced nations in preventive treatment, with fatal consequences:

Potential years of life lost due to premature mortality [i.e., considered preventable if appropriate and timely medical treatment had been given] were significantly higher in the U.S. than the OECD median for both males and females in
1999.[80]

For example, studies have found that from 42 percent to 62 percent of heart
patients in America are not prescribed the appropriate drug (depending on the
heart condition), and that only one quarter of diabetic patients have regular
measures of blood level, among many other lapses.[81] This suggests the possibility that a quarter to at least a half of Americans cannot rely on their physicians to
know what he or she is doing at all times. That is a hard pill to swallow.

Accidents, the fifth leading killer in the United States, are almost all avoidable by simple precautions, such as not driving when drunk (as 23 percent of
persons aged 18–25 admit doing) or drowsy, and enforcing workplace safety
regulations. Even suicide can be prevented through someone's understanding
and compassion, by paying attention to the symptoms of severe depression in
oneself or others and seeking help, and by publicizing the availability of diagnostic and preventive resources. Homicide can be reduced by stricter gun control, improved law enforcement with community-oriented policing, antiviolence
campaigns, marital counseling, and probably many other measures.

To be sure, these measures cost money. Yet Americans seem willing to
spend vast sums on therapeutic treatment. And treatment is not only more costly
than prevention, but further undermines attention to prevention by lulling us into
a false sense of security about our health risks, inasmuch as we assume we can
depend on therapeutic medicine to save us. Finally, irony of ironies, as mentioned above, medical treatment can actually play a causative role in illness and
death. In fact, $68 million of the proposed 2003 federal budget was allocated for
dealing with "medical errors/patient safety."[82] Actually, at least 200,000 Americans are estimated to die each year from medical errors.[83] (Medical errors associated with hospitals and the failure of physicians to provide recommended care
are discussed later.)

But the most cogent argument on behalf of putting more money into prevention is the greater bang for the buck it provides over therapeutic medicine.
Medical costs are spiraling out of control, and have been doing so for years. This
domain of health care needs to be examined in detail, for if therapeutic care is
not affordable, what difference does it make if it's the best in the world?

The Cost of Health Care

No other domestic issue has risen so spectacularly to the fore in recent years as
the cost of health care. It has left far behind the traditional issues of quality and

quantity of caregivers (as serious as these are), and apparently baffled the nation's ability to deal with it politically, economically, and professionally in spite
of the many successful examples in other advanced nations (one being just
across the border in Canada). Demographic changes, a zealous commitment to
free enterprise and profit-taking, high levels of illness and premature death, an
emphasis on high-tech therapeutic care instead of prevention, and the continuing
or worsening maldistribution of wealth have created a farrago of viewpoints and
proposals with a bewildering array of options for those who can afford private
insurance. Thus, the conservative ideology of a government that rejects nationalized health care for all has condemned the system to a series of makeshift, over-
priced programs, particularly through privatization, that fail to serve some 40
million Americans. And yet America spends far more on health care per capita
or as a percentage of GDP than any other advanced country in the world.

Overall Costs

According to a five-nation survey of public attitudes toward health care in 2002:

> [T]he U.S. has the highest proportion of the public reporting problems paying
> their medical bills . . . a third of citizens with below average incomes said they
> did not fill a prescription, did not get recommended tests or treatment, and did
> not visit a doctor when they had a medical problem because of cost barriers.[84]

This reluctance to seek medical care is not surprising in view of the fact that
medical costs in America increased 75 percent between 1988 and 1998.[85] They
increased 10 percent in 2001 alone.[86] These increases have been much higher
than the rate of inflation and have been especially onerous for persons living on
fixed incomes, and particularly for those 41 million Americans who do not have
any form of health insurance (because of its cost). Not that somebody isn't paying for it: 14 cents of every dollar in the American economy is spent on some
kind of health care.[87] In fact, Americans were spending $1,300 more per capita
on health care than would be predicted on the basis of GDP per capita.[88] Here's
the bottom line:

> Americans spent $1.3 trillion on health care in 2000, or 13.2 percent of the
> gross national product, far more than any other nation.[89]

Distribution of Health Costs

The health-care dollar is distributed as follows: about 33 percent goes to hospitals, about 20 percent goes to physicians, and about 10 percent goes for prescription drugs.[90] The first two (hospitals and physicians) are predicted to increase
about 6.6 percent per year from 2000 to 2012, while drug spending will likely

increase 11.1 percent a year during the same period.[91] Drug costs rose 14.5 percent on average per year during 1997–2001, whereas the cost of physicians' services rose only 6.7 percent per year in that period.[92]

All of these increases, it should be noted, are considerably greater than the expected increase in inflation. This is largely because the demand for health care is "inelastic," that is to say, it strongly resists reduction inasmuch as it is a matter of life and death, or at least of physical well-being and the alleviation of suffering. The public is perforce tolerant, therefore, of higher prices.

Interestingly enough, the one participant in the provision of medical care that has enjoyed by far the greatest profit is the pharmaceutical industry. (See below.) Now let us look at each of these participants in brief.

Hospitals

The senior vice president for policy of the American Hospital Association has summed up the plight of hospitals with depressing candor:

> The shortage of nurses and other caregivers is driving up labor costs, prescription drug and technology costs are spiraling out of control, and the ranks of the nation's uninsured continue to swell. At the same time, hospital services are rising as the baby boomers age and medical advances allow us to cure more Americans.[93]

The rise of hospital costs by 12 percent in 2001, compared with only 3.7 percent in 2000, means that hospitalization accounted for half (51%) of the total health-care-spending increases of 10 percent in that year. In particular, the average wage increase in 2001 was nearly double the 2000 increase, owing to the severe shortage of nurses and other skilled personnel. These shortages also meant an increase of 2.4 percent in the total number of hours worked by employees.[94] These cost increases for patients occurred in spite of patients spending fewer days in the hospital.[95] Owing to the increased expense of treating high-cost medical conditions, and the incentives of HMOs to encourage homecare, a 26 percent decrease occurred from 1993 to 2000 in hospital days per patient for treatment of heart attack, for example.[96] Yet the cost of hospitalization has continued to climb and to outdistance by far that in other advanced countries. In 1999 the cost of one day of hospitalization in the United States was double the $788 per day in Canada, which was the next most expensive country, and it was almost three times the median of OECD countries.[97]

One would normally conclude from these comparisons that the United States offered more hospital facilities and staff than other nations, and therefore deserved the accolade of being number one among advanced countries. But anyone who drew that conclusion would be sadly disappointed. Hospitals have been closing their doors all over America—900 between 1980 and 2000. As the chairman of the emergency medical department of Emory University School of Medicine declared in 2001: "We don't have enough ER [emergency room] capacity in this country to get through tonight's 911 calls."[98] Under-capacity of hospital facilities, as well as understaffing, has been a problem also in earlier years. The number of hospital beds and physicians per 1,000 persons in the United States compared with other nations tells the story succinctly. In 1998 we had 3.9 beds per 1,000, which was one-half the average of 16 European countries. It was one-fifth of the number in Switzerland (18.3), a third of the number in Norway (14.7), and four-tenths of the number in Germany (9.4).[99] As for the ratio of physicians, in 1997 we had only 2.7 per 1,000 persons compared with 6.8 in Italy, 4.3 in Spain, 3.4 in Germany and Belgium, and so on.[100] In per capita terms, then, we are significantly behind in the availability of health-care facilities and physicians. (A recent news item on radio reported projections of a shortage of 50,000 physicians in 2010 and of 200,000 in 2020.)

Concerning health-care professionals other than physicians, "eighteen percent of jobs in the nation's public health labs are open . . . Fifteen percent of the nation's nursing jobs [are] unfilled . . ." As a consequence of the shortage of capacity and personnel in hospitals, "one out of eight urban hospitals diverts or turns away new emergency patients one-fifth of the time because of overcrowding," according to one study. And another study found the shocking circumstance that "in at least nine states, every hospital in a local area had diverted ambulances simultaneously on a number of occasions."[101]

One reason that medical facilities and staff are insufficient in our nation is probably the increased use of emergency services by persons without medical insurance, and therefore without their own doctors. In 2001 alone, visits to emergency rooms increased by 5 million, as mentioned earlier.[102] (See also the financial pressure on emergency physicians from rampant increases in medical insurance premiums discussed below.)

It is almost inconceivable that a crisis of these proportions could occur in a modern industrialized nation, much less in the richest country in the world, which spends far more per capita on health care than any other country. And in this post 9/11 era, our hospitals are expected to deal with bioterrorist emergencies when they cannot even handle patients on normal days or nights. (For the underfunding of our first response capacity, see chapter 11 on "Democracy" in America and the failure of the federal government to provide the resources even for needs that it itself has identified as being absolutely critical.) Severe shortages of clinics, hospitals and beds, nurses, public health personnel, and especially trauma physicians have already produced a crisis. But even admission to hospitals does not guarantee adequate care. In fact, it can kill you.

According to Sherwin Nuland, the prominent author-physician, two-thirds of the "complications" that patients have are due to errors in care, and 44,000 die in a year at least partly as a result of that care. The proportion of patients with complications resulting from care is 4 percent.[103] Another source has reported an estimated 75,000 deaths a year from unsanitary conditions in hospitals, and noted that this made these conditions the number four cause of death in hospitals.[104] Moreover, it has been reported that

> nearly $5 billion are added to U.S. health costs every year as a result of infections that patients get while they are hospitalized for other health problems . . . Nearly two million patients annually get an infection . . . and nearly 88,000 die as a direct or indirect [consequence] of their infection . . . Prolonged blood stream infection can top $50,000. [But] insurance companies and other players, such as Medicaid, may reimburse the hospitals [only] on the basis of the patient's original condition . . .[105]

A more recent report (fall 2003) based on a large number of hospitals estimated 2.4 million extra days hospitalized and $9 billion in extra health-care costs per year due to medical errors; and a survey in 2004 reported 195,000 deaths per year.[106] A 1999 study reported by the Institute of Medicine found that

> [drug] errors occurred in nearly one out of five doses in a typical, 300 bed hospital, which translates to almost two errors per patient daily. Seven percent of the errors were considered potentially harmful.[107]

Many of these errors might be traceable to the shortage of nurses, which is reported to be 28,000. A Harvard study concluded that the lack of nurses to deal with complications has resulted in deaths.[108] Persuasive support for this outcome of the nursing shortage is afforded by a study of a sample of registered nurses, practical nurses, and occupational therapists in 1998. More than half reported insufficient time to spend with patients, and more than a third said understaffing had caused a deterioration in patient care. Their most commonly expressed concern was the closing of hospitals and clinics, and their second was the expansion of managed care.[109]

Female patients might be especially prone to receive inadequate care, if one can generalize from their treatment for heart attack, for they receive less aggressive treatment, and they die more often than men die within one year (42 percent of women die within a year compared with 24 percent of men).[110] Nursing-home patients seem to be especially vulnerable to poor treatment. One study found that one-half of the patients in nursing homes have untreated pain;[111] and another found that 70 percent of the terminally ill die in a medical facility with pain, and without family or friends present. Only one out of seven hospices have "palliative care."[112]

Comparative international data on details of hospital care are very limited, but one study found that Japan had three times as many MRI machines per capita as America and more than six times as many CT scanners. The rate of use of dialysis in Japan is almost twice the U.S. rate.[113]

Physicians' Services and Liability Insurance

As already mentioned, the percentage cost increase in physicians' services was only about half that of hospitals and of prescription drugs. The increased cost of physicians' services accounts for 28 percent of the overall increase in health-care costs, compared with 51 percent for hospitals and 21 percent for prescription drugs. The greater contribution to overall costs than that of drugs (in spite of a smaller *percentage* increase) is due to physicians' services costing twice as much as drugs to begin with. The increase in the business receipts of American physicians in FY 2002 over the previous year was only 3.6 percent.[114] It is also noteworthy that the number of sole proprietors declined 5.5 percent, while partnerships increased 9.1 percent,[115] suggesting that economic hardship forced physicians to combine practices and use common facilities.

It is widely believed that increases in the cost of liability insurance have been a major force behind the inflation of health-care costs in the past 10 or 15 years.[116] But, as a matter of fact, less than 1 percent of our national health-care cost is due to liability insurance.[117] Further, while medical costs overall increased 75 percent between 1988 and 1998, malpractice premiums increased only 5.6 percent.[118] This situation has changed drastically in recent years, but mainly for emergency physicians and those who deal with high-risk cases. In 2002, 3.7 percent of the net operating costs of physicians in sole proprietorships, the largest category, was devoted to insurance, which was considerably less than for salary and wages (10.4%).[119] But for emergency physicians, "premiums had risen from about 10% to 300%," according to a survey by the American College of Emergency Physicians in 31 states, "[and] in some cases above $200,000,"[120] which suggests a substantial increase in net operating costs for these particular physicians.

Some effects of the foregoing have been fewer emergency departments, fewer medical students entering high-risk specialties, more physicians who limit or discontinue services, and higher costs for many patients.[121] And while emergency department visits were mushrooming, an 8 percent cut in Medicare payment was experienced by emergency physicians (in 2002).[122]

The reason customarily given by the insurance industry for skyrocketing malpractice rates, a reason echoed by the media and politicians, is an alleged horde of malpractice suits that suddenly sprang forth and sought exorbitant settlements. Thus, proposals have been made to rewrite the tort laws so that jury awards are capped at a reasonable level. Not surprisingly, in view of his corporate bias, President George W. Bush led the charge for tort reform as the primary means of reducing medical costs (that is, instead of doing anything about high drug prices or other corporate sources of increasing costs). It so happens, however, that this diagnosis has little evidence to back it up. Indeed, "only one out of every eight malpractice victims ever files a claim . . . Nationally, the average insurance payment to a medical negligence victim is $30,000. The amount has remained virtually flat for a decade, according to the Consumer Federation of America."[123] What happened in recent years is that the insurance companies began hiking up the rates after a decade of stability,[124] which occurred in spite of the absence of an alleged rise in costly claims. As an adviser to the American Association of Retired Persons has stated: "There are no indications of an upturn in the number of malpractice claims or major increases in the average amount of final malpractice judgments."[125]

It appears, therefore, that the investment losses of insurance companies when the economy's bubble burst prompted them to increase rates while at the same time reducing risk by aggressively extending coverage to physicians whose risk of being sued was low. The crisis of the companies is indicated by the fact that many of them merged and consolidated, while some went out of business.[126] Here once again we confront the power of corporations in a very business-friendly political climate to enrich themselves at the expense of their customers and the public. Enormous sums for lobbying paid off once again, and the media are almost nowhere to be found as an investigative counterweight. Indeed, they continue to reiterate the role of outrageously high settlements, which by and large are a fiction.

Another industry in the health-care business that apparently puts profit above the health needs of the public is not nearly so economically stressed as the insurance industry. At least the latter had the excuse of hard times, even if they passed the burden on to consumers. But not the drug industry, which has been booming while the cost increase in prescription drugs has been averaging 14–17 percent annually. And there is no end in view.

Prescription Drugs

An analysis of the profitability of the Fortune 500 in 2002 clearly shows the superior position of the drug industry, which "is still by far the most profitable in America on all three counts: return on revenue (18.5 percent), return on assets (16.3 percent), and return on shareholders' equity (33.2 percent). (These figures are three times the medians of all other industries.)"[127] And, to be sure, the federal government has played a significant role in this remarkable display of profit-taking.

First, the effective tax rate of the industry has been the lowest of almost all industries, in spite of its high profits.[128] Second, only the United States government among those of industrialized nations places no limits on drug prices.[129] Third, a series of federal laws have extended the life of patents in recent years.[130]

Fourth, in 1997 the Food and Drug Administration relaxed its rules governing TV advertising for prescription drugs, which caused an explosion of TV ads: from $220 million spent on TV ads in 1996 to $1.57 billion in 2000.[131] Fifth, "the U.S. and New Zealand are the only countries that allow direct-to-consumer advertising of prescription drugs."[132] And sixth, notices from the Food and Drug Administration to drug manufacturers about ad violations, according to a report in 2002, had dropped substantially.[133]

But why has the federal government been such a big booster of the drug industry? The short answer is that since 1990 the pharmaceutical industry has spent over $234 million on political campaigns and $80 million on lobbying.[134] The biggest contributor to campaigns has been Pfizer, which gave $355,991 from election day 2000 to roughly mid-2002.[135] And Pfizer earned more in profits in the same period "than all the Fortune 500 companies in the homebuilding, apparel, railroad and publishing industries combined."[136]

In 2003 it was estimated that in the year of 2004 the Pharmaceutical Research and Manufacturers of America (PhRMA) would spend at least $150 million on lobbying, which would be "a 23 percent increase over the 2003 budget," and would also increase its membership dues to pay for the expanded lobbying campaign. Included is "a standing network of economists and thought leaders to speak against federal price control regulations through articles and testimony."[137]

The consequences of this symbiotic relationship between government and industry are runaway prices and untold harm to million of Americans who cannot afford the escalating prices of drugs, particularly seniors and the poor.

With regard to seniors:

> [S]ome of the drugs used most by seniors have been on the market for over ten years, some over 20 years, and yet they still continue to increase in price—as much as four times the rate of inflation.[138] Overall prescription drug spending for the elderly has increased 132% since 1992.[139] Average retail prices for prescription drugs are growing more than twice as fast as Social Security benefits.[140]

And with regard to all Americans, the percentage of the uninsured who do not have prescriptions filled for financial reasons is 42 percent.[141] Roughly 65 million Americans have no insurance for prescription drugs.[142] (In late 2003, a controversial prescription bill was passed by Congress and signed into law by the president. For a brief analysis of the shortcomings of this measure, which is widely regarded even by its supporters as only a first step, see the Afterword to this chapter.)

One wonders about the efficacy of a medical system without affordable access to medicine, as occurs in all other advanced societies. But then perhaps one should be grateful for the superior research and development that assures us of

healthier and longer lives in spite of driving up cost—*if,* that is, R&D is indeed
the reason for higher prices. Unfortunately, there is no evidence that rising R&D
costs are responsible. From 1995 to 2000, drug company staff employed on research actually *declined* slightly (from 49,000 to 48,000), but the sales staff
grew from 55,000 to 87,000, a 58 percent increase in only five years.[143] And in
2001, "the Fortune 500 drug companies devoted nearly three times as much of
their revenue to marketing and administration (30.4 percent of revenue) than to
research and development."[144]

Moreover, much of the money recorded as being devoted to R&D is actually devoted to *market* research, according to the Senate Aging Committee's
investigations.[145] And if we make a comparison with European countries, we find
that R&D spending is equal or higher in those countries, and that more new
drugs were brought to market from 1990 to 1999 than in the United States.[146] As
one analyst has cogently put it: "The industry is pinning its growth hopes less on
new products and more on persuading people, including healthy ones, to buy the
pills already being sold."[147] According to the *Wall Street Journal,* the industry's
total promotional outlay in 2000 was about $15.7 billion.[148] If direct advertising
to consumers were banned, as is the case in all other advanced industrial nations
except New Zealand, a large portion of this immense sum could be saved, and
perhaps even devoted to true research and development.

One reason that the drug industry has been able to reduce the proportion of
revenues devoted to R&D is that the federal government itself did much of the
original research. And this research was paid for, of course, by taxpayers. Indeed, "11 of the 14 top medically significant drugs in the past 25 years had roots
in studies paid for by the government."[149]

But can we at least be confident that the drugs we are persuaded to purchase
are the best that money can buy? Again, the record is disappointing. Drugs kill
some 14,000 hospital patients and injure another 750,000 every year, according
to Consumer Reports.[150] And of all the drugs approved from 1981 to 1991, the
Food and Drug Administration characterized only 16 percent as important therapeutic gains.[151] About two-thirds of the drugs approved from 1989 to 2000 were
found to be "modified versions of existing drugs or even identical," according to
a study by the National Institute for Health Care Management Foundation. Yet,
most of the increased spending was on these and other drugs that "did not provide significant benefits over those already on the market . . ."[152]

The most popular drugs are known as "lifestyle" drugs, such as Vioxx and
Celebrex, which currently dominate TV advertising, and they are not cheap by
any means even though they might be no better than much less expensive substitutes that can be bought across the counter. The following data on these two
drugs demonstrate how the prescription industry makes its profits and allocates
its revenues for ever greater profits.

Although Vioxx and Celebrex totaled $3.5 billion in sales in 2000 [and Vioxx alone cost $160 million for promotion], they do not represent significant improvements over other drugs. They are not more effective than ibuprofen in reducing pain and inflammation, and only slightly less likely to cause ulcers.[153] [As for Celebrex, which is not notably more effective than Advil, according to the *British Medical Journal* and *Express Scripts*, 30 pills cost $97 vs. Advil's 24 pills for $4. And Vioxx costs $135 for 30 pills, while Advil is just as effective.[154]]

It has also recently been disclosed that large advertising companies are investing in companies that perform clinical trials of experimental drugs. According to a professor emeritus at Harvard Medical School, "You cannot separate their advertising and marketing from their science anymore. Doctors are led to prescribe drugs that may not be necessarily worth the money, may not be better than a generic that is already on the market and their patients don't need. It's clearly contributing to the high cost of prescription drugs and health care." Another medical professor has cited "numerous cases in which, he said, drug companies manipulated results of clinical trials by controlling a study's design or choosing to make public only positive data."[155]

It would appear, then, that American consumers are paying for the advertising that persuades them to buy drugs that often are no more effective than other, cheaper drugs. And so, the absence of advertising costs in foreign countries, where direct advertising to consumers is prohibited, makes drugs much cheaper than our own. In fact,

> Foreign drug prices are 35%–50% less than U.S. prices. With respect to the United Kingdom, 77 frequently dispensed drugs are 60% more expensive in the U.S.[156]

And, of course, the absence of direct advertising protects the consumer from being misled by corporate hype.

Health Insurance

As pointed out earlier, the United States is the only advanced country in the world that does not have a universal health insurance program.[157] And not surprisingly, health insurance coverage and costs follow the pattern of health care and costs in general, a pattern striking for its failure to provide universal accessibility. Forty-three and a half million Americans lack health insurance in spite of the many private plans on the market,[158] and as many as "nearly 60 million people lack health insurance at some point in the year . . ."[159] In 2001, 11.7 percent of American children did not have health coverage,[160] amounting to at least 8 million children, and 30.7 percent of all poor people had no health insurance for the year.[161] If one thinks that the employed are able to obtain insurance through their jobs, the fact is that 57 percent of those earning $7 or less an hour are not offered coverage by employers,[162] and coverage of workers at any wage level is being reduced drastically because of the sluggish economy (see also below). Past times were bad enough because of rising premium costs (a mean of 7.5 percent a year between 1996 and 2000).[163] Thus, the average annual health insurance premium in 2000 was $2,655 for single coverage and $6,772 for family coverage in private-sector companies.[164] In 2002, health insurance premiums increased an average of 12.7 percent, the largest increase in a decade.[165]

State-funded medical coverage (14 percent of total state general fund expenditures last biennium) is in no better shape. It required 37 percent of the increase in GF-S appropriations between 2002 and 2003. State costs per person were increasing 3 to 5 times faster than general inflation, according to the Senate Ways and Means Committee.[166]

In the midst of all this bad news, CNN reported that a 13 percent increase in health insurance was predicted for 2003,[167] which turned out to be accurate. And by 2031, it is expected that companies will be paying less than 10 percent of retirees' health expenses, whereas today at least large employers pay more than half.[168] As for the private insurance providers, "HMO's are dumping beneficiaries in record numbers. From 1999 through January 1, 2002, more than 2.1 million seniors were dropped by their Medicare HMOs, where they typically received some drug coverage."[169] National insurance corporations, as contrasted with those that are locally owned, have been two and a half times more likely to have withdrawn from Medicare+Choice. This difference between local and national companies demonstrates that the standard payment level of the government is not alone responsible for withdrawal.[170] In fact, the government has been losing large amounts of money by working through HMOs.

Amid current plans in Washington to expand the privatization of health insurance, the following facts should be borne in mind:

> From 1998 to 2000 federal payments to Medicare HMOs exceeded by 13.2 percent the cost the program would have incurred by paying providers directly for care.[171] [The reason that HMOs are not cost-efficient compared with the government seems simple:] HMOs spend an average of 20% on agents' fees, marketing, advertising, administration, and profits. Medicare spends only 2% on administrative costs and nothing on the other cost items.[172]

In spite of the lower cost to beneficiaries and other advantages of public payment, however, many physicians feel burdened by the paperwork and restrictions on bills for medical services imposed by Medicare. And in fact, 17 percent of family practice doctors no longer take Medicare patients.[173]

Finally, as mentioned earlier in connection with the budget cuts of the Bush administration, in 2002 "nearly one million enrollees in the State Children's Health Insurance Program (SCHIP) were in jeopardy of losing health coverage because of reductions in federal funding for the program."[174]

The consequences of all these trends are frightening to contemplate in view of the hardships already being suffered through inadequate insurance or none at all. Among all poor children under 6 years of age, for example, 21 percent of those without health insurance had no usual source of care in 1998, compared with 4 percent of poor children covered by insurance.[175] And among older Americans with congestive heart failure, 25 percent of those without drug coverage do not fill all their prescriptions because of the cost, compared with 14 percent of those with coverage. Even larger discrepancies occur with respect to diabetes (31 percent vs. 14 percent), and for those with high blood pressure (28 percent vs. 12 percent).[176]

As a matter of fact, late-middle-aged adults without health insurance are more likely to decline in overall health, according to data from 1992 to 1996: Those who were "continuously uninsured were 23 percent more likely to develop a new physical difficulty that affected walking or climbing stairs . . . The intermittently uninsured were 1.41 times more likely to experience a major health decline."[177] And according to an estimate by the National Institute of Medicine, 18,000 people die each year because of the lack of health insurance.[178]

The cost of making health insurance more accessible was a hotly debated subject in 2003, especially owing to the variety of programs that were proposed by Democratic candidates for the presidency. One such candidate had reported that "the cost of one-half of the President's tax cut [of 2001] could provide universal health insurance."[179] Whether this is the case remains to be seen, but it does suggest that the cost of universal health insurance is within the realm of fiscal feasibility. Indeed, it is doubtful that the cost in public funds is the major stumbling block at all. More important is the desire of corporations to profit from the unrelenting need for health insurance. A compromise, of course, is some form of private-public combination. But whether such a solution could afford to pass on the extra costs of privatization (advertising, administration, etc.) to the consumer or to public subsidies, and whether the erosion of quality care in the interest of profit enhancement by private industry (with the self-interested acquiescence of Congress and the administration) can be prevented, are large questions.

Considering the annual loss to the economy of possibly billions of dollars owing to illnesses and accidents that are untreated or improperly treated, and the diversion of personal resources from other consumption expenses, universal health insurance with federal or state funding and management would seem to be a good public investment at almost any price. But not, of course, to those who are ideologically opposed or, more to the point, who desire to profit financially from the public's "inelastic demand" for medical assistance. (The limitations of the new Medicare law of December 2003, which is to go into full effect in 2006, have been widely acknowledged, as mentioned earlier; and there is the possibility that it would be repealed before implementation. For a brief discussion of this law, see the Afterword at the end of this chapter.)

Now let us turn to the question of whether the vaunted wealth of America and its lavish expenditure for health care (far exceeding that of other nations on a per capita basis) have produced a superior medical system with regard to the paramount goal of maintaining the health of the nation.

The Quality of Health Care

That the quality of health care in America falls far short of being outstanding can be inferred from certain data that have already been presented. The reduction in the number of hospitals, the shortage of nurses, the high cost of liability insurance that has driven a number of physicians and medical students away from the field of emergency medicine, the overcrowding of emergency rooms, the high cost of medical care and insurance that discourages many citizens from having regular doctors, the inability to purchase drugs that are prescribed or even to seek treatment in the first place, the high rate of infection and errors of drug administration in hospitals, and the low priority given to prevention compared with therapeutic treatment—all point to shortcomings that belie the notion of a superior system of health care.

Before looking at the system from a comparative perspective, it is worthwhile to examine the findings of a major recent study reported in *The New England Journal of Medicine* in 2003[180] that raises further questions about quality.

This study sought to determine the extent to which recommended care was provided to patients. The main finding was that patients received the best care (that is, recommended by experts) only about 55 percent of the time; this percentage was about the same regardless of whether the care was for prevention or treatment of acute or chronic types of cases. This result prompted the investigators to conclude: "The deficits we have identified in adherence to recommended processes for basic care pose serious threats to the health of the American public," and to call for "a major overhaul of our current health information systems." Overall, *46 percent* of the patients did not receive the recommended care, and 11 percent received care that "was not recommended and was potentially harmful." The percentages of best care varied according to the medical condition. For example, only 24 percent of diabetes patients reported a blood sugar test during the previous year, but 65 percent of hypertension patients received the recommended care. The lowest percentage of best care occurred with patients who were alcohol-dependent.[181]

According to Senator Clinton in a *New York Times* article published in April 2004, "close to a third of the $1.6 trillion we now spend on health care goes to care that is duplicative, fails to improve patient health or may even make it worse." She also cites a study that found that "for two-thirds of the patients who received a $15,000 surgery to prevent stroke, there was no compelling evidence that the surgery worked."[182] In addition, a recent (2004) investigation of women's health care delivered a scathing report. It found that "of 27 measures [of screening and testing of women], the nation passes on only two." In fact, "not a single U.S. state meets basic federal goals for caring for women's health." And the report concluded: "The nation is so far from the Healthy People goals that it receives an overall grade of unsatisfactory."[183]

As for mental illness, a 2003 study by the National Institute of Mental Health found that only 20 percent of the persons who had sought treatment for depression received adequate treatment. In fact, the largest facility for treatment of mental illness in America is the Los Angeles County Jail, which spent $10 million on medication in 2002.[184] A more recent report (September 2003) by the President's Freedom Commission on Mental Health found that the mental health system of the nation was deficient in so many ways that it needed thorough revamping.[185]

One reason for the deficits in recommended care that have been pointed out is the lack of definitive evidence in the reports of clinical trials and as a result of physicians' diagnoses. Another is the slow publication process. One study found that it took a median of five and a half years between the beginning of a study and the publication of results. Still another problem is believed to reside in the sample populations used in the clinical trials, especially when there are inherent physiological differences, such as racial and gender variations, between the trial population and the ultimate patients. Health-care costs also play a role, of course, inasmuch as the desire to contain costs might reduce the use of better but more expensive procedures, and patients might be discouraged from purchasing prescribed drugs. With regard to expensive procedures, one-half the growth in real per capita health-care expenditures is due to new technology.[186] (See this article for further discussion of "hidden barriers.")

Whatever the explanation for why patients are failing to receive the best treatment, the health-care system in America is far from being foolproof or even deathproof when it *could* be. Now let us see what comparative data can tell us about America's standing compared with other countries.

The Health of Americans Compared with
That of Citizens of Other Advanced Nations

The 26th annual report of the Department of Health and Human Services (pre-sented in 2002) trumpeted the good news: "Americans' health has changed for the better over the past 50 years, with men and women both living longer, fewer babies dying in infancy and the gap between white and black life expectancy narrowing in the past decade."[187] And it goes on to give some other examples: "Infectious disease rates have declined. The syphilis rate in 2000 . . . was the lowest since national reporting began in 1941 . . . AIDS deaths dropped after 1995 . . . deaths from unintentional injuries, cancer and heart disease are down sharply."[188]

What the report did not say is that similar improvements in health have oc-curred in other economically advanced nations. If one truly wishes to evaluate the progress of Americans' health, therefore, one must compare it with the health of citizens of other countries at the present time. So let us examine com-parisons with respect to each of the improvements mentioned above.

According to United Nations statistics reported in the year 2002, America's rate of infant mortality was higher than that in 21 countries of the world. In fact, it tied the rate in Guadeloupe, Korea, Martinique, Malta, New Caledonia, and Cuba, a fact mentioned earlier. Fourteen countries of Europe had lower rates of death in the first year of life than America. And with respect to life expectancy, the United States ranks 26th for females and 29th for males among 202 coun-tries. People live longer in 10 European countries.[189] As the UN report points out, "Whilst non-specific, [life expectancy] does provide a useful indicator of environmental and other risk factors on health."[190]

As for the narrowing of life expectancy between whites and blacks, the seven-year gap in 1990 has been shaved to six years.[191] (Comparative figures are not available for Europe.) Since this improvement occurred in the past decade, at this rate it will take 60 more years to close the gap.

The rate of death from coronary heart disease places the United States 6th highest in incidence among 17 reporting countries. However, it is in last place (17th) with respect to deaths from stroke, which is the only statistic cited thus far that deserves to be applauded.[192]

The case of AIDS is extremely interesting. For it appears that the rate of this infectious disease is higher in the United States than in 22 countries of western Europe, 22 countries of eastern Europe and central Asia, and 15 countries of south and southeast Asia. Indeed, America's rate of AIDS is higher than that of 111 countries outside of sub-Saharan Africa and the Caribbean.[193] A related sta-tistic that appears not to be reported internationally is the rate of syphilis and gonorrhea. A study that compared Canada with the United States, however, found lower rates for both diseases in Canada.[194]

The rate of cancer, another disease mentioned by the Department of Health as having undergone a "dramatic" decline in 50 years, was higher in America in the late '90s than in five European countries, but lower than in 10 other European countries. Thus, the United States rate of 143.5 cancer deaths per 100,000 population fell at about the mid-point between Denmark's high of 173.6 and Sweden's low of only 122.6 in the same period. This is certainly not as bad as the showing for AIDS, but there is still a good deal of catching up to be done, either through prevention or therapy.[195]

Accidental injuries were also mentioned by the Department's annual report as having markedly declined in the United States. (The time span was not stipulated, however.) If we restrict our attention to child injuries, we encounter the remarkable fact that the United States had a higher rate of such injuries than any of the 20 countries reporting in Europe, according to a 2001 report of the Children's Fund.[196] Since motor vehicle accidents account for 41 percent of child deaths by injuries (in all of the reporting countries combined), it is worthwhile looking at the rate of child deaths due to motor vehicles alone. And here we find the disturbing fact that the United States has a higher rate of such deaths than 20 of the 26 OECD countries reporting.[197]

Of course, not only children are killed in motor accidents. When we compare the rates of death from such accidents in America and Europe, we find that America ranks 3rd among 19 advanced countries (OECD plus America). In other words, 88 percent of the OECD countries have a lower rate of death from motor vehicles than the United States.[198]

Suicide rates may be regarded as one measure of mental health in a nation, although it is not mentioned as a health statistic in the Department of Health's statement cited above. In fact, mental health is not mentioned at all in that recital of markedly improved rates, which is quite curious. With regard to suicide, we find that the American rate is higher than that of five European countries (based on data from the late '90s).[199] Some medical writers regard homicide as a health matter, and here we find that the United States' rate far exceeds that of Europe, as mentioned earlier. (Among whites only the rate was twice the European rate even after a decline in America in the '90s.) Also mentioned in an earlier section, a national survey revealed that almost half (45%) of American youth said they "felt depressed."[200] Comparative data have further revealed that schoolchildren in America (in each category of 11-, 13-, and 15-year-olds) more often admitted "feeling low at least once a week" than in the great majority of 27 other rich countries in the world. Among 11-year-olds, America ranked first, and among 13- and 15-year-olds it ranked fourth among the 27 countries.[201]

Perhaps the higher level of mental distress among American youth accounts for the striking statistic that the schoolchildren in America referred to above ranked first among the 27 countries in having reported stomachaches and backaches at least once a week, and second with respect to having reported headaches once a week. (Headaches, according to health-care professionals, are considered to be a sign of depression in adolescents.) The Americans also ranked third in feeling tired in the morning four or more times a week.[202]

One source of mental stress could be social tension with peers. As mentioned earlier, the American school students ranked virtually at the bottom of 28 countries in frequency of saying that their "classmates are always or often kind and helpful," and in the bottom quartile in saying they "spend time with friends after school."[203]

Still another source of stress could be relations with parents. The American students ranked second in the frequency with which they admitted that they "find it difficult or very difficult to talk to their mother."[204] There was less difficulty talking with fathers; but this could have been because the Americans were least likely to be living with both of their parents among the 28 countries surveyed.[205] Thus, the fathers who had remained with the mothers were a select population. This finding points to another possible effect on mental health of a broken family.

With regard to physical health, it is not reassuring that the American students *most* often said that they were on a diet or should be on a diet, and *least* often said that they ate fruit every day. Moreover, the Americans ranked 4th in drinking soft drinks every day, but 18th in exercising twice a week or more.[206] This, of course, reminds us again of the outstanding obesity rate of Americans.

Although the evidence is limited, it by no means suggests the picture of a comparatively robust, happy, socially integrated generation of youth rising to the challenge of managing the world's leading nation and being a model for the rest of the global community. On almost every indicator, American youth fall well behind their foreign peers physically and emotionally (and educationally, as will be shown in the following chapter). Nor is health in the population at large always at least equal to that of most other advanced countries, as shown by the rates of heart disease, AIDS, injuries, drug abuse, life expectancy, and infant mortality (not to mention the setback to one's health from being shot with a gun). And judging from the health gaps between rich and poor, and between white and black (discussed later), America's health-care system is highly unbalanced, or to put it more bluntly, institutionally discriminatory. In fact, only 6 to 8 percent of American doctors are from minorities, according to a Harvard professor of medicine,[207] whereas the combined population of blacks and Hispanics alone in our country is around 27 percent. In light of all these data, it is not surprising that a study in 2000 found that America was ranked second from the bottom among 13 developed countries in the health of its population. Moreover, the director of the study has claimed that the situation has gotten worse in the past four years.[208]

Yet, we keep coming back to the odd fact, mentioned earlier, that America spends far more per capita on health than any other nation on earth. In 1998, the expenditure per capita on health care in the United States was $4,090, while the median for OECD countries was $1,747. And that figure was reported *before* the recent explosion in drug prices in the United States. Obviously, there is reason to believe that our high-dollar medical system is not the answer to patients' prayers. In fact, a recent study indicates that higher costs in different parts of the country are not related to quality. Thus, more days in the hospital or more doctor visits raises costs in certain areas without necessarily improving care.[209] Profits in the health-care industry, like any other industry, depend upon consumer demand, which in the case of health care can easily be manipulated by health-care providers and drug companies. The consequences are higher cost and less availability of caregivers. Thus, not only are Americans sicker in some ways than residents of other countries, but they find it harder to get medical attention they can afford. According to a poll by the Commonwealth Fund in 1998, 25 percent of Americans said that "getting care when needed" was extremely, very, or somewhat difficult, compared with 21 percent of Canadians, 19 percent of New Zealanders, 15 percent of UK residents, and 15 percent of Australians.[210]

How can one escape the conclusion that the system is basically flawed? A major reason for this state of affairs might be that it is at the mercy of profit-making industry, as shown in the case of prescription drugs and insurance costs, particularly with respect to HMOs. And this possible source of trouble shows itself in many other ways. For example, as reported in September 2002: "There are shortages of five vaccines that protect against eight of eleven vaccine preventable diseases, such as measles, mumps, chicken pox, etc."[211] This shortage had already lasted for more than half a year, and had become a serious threat to public health. Why did it occur? The report continued: "Vaccine manufacturers [have been] leaving the market for business reasons. There were 26 manufacturers in the '90s, but now there are only 12."[212] Can America afford to let its supply of vital drugs for children or for anyone else be ruled by market forces alone?

A year later, a similar crisis arose with the supply of flu vaccine. Only *two* companies in America manufacture the vaccine, and both had shipped out all their supplies in mid-November in response to an unusually high demand prompted by widespread outbreaks. As the *New York Times* pointed out, "Ordinarily, the government does not track precisely how many doses have been given or how much inventory remains."[213] In other words, the availability of a drug during the season when it is needed most, a drug that can be a matter of life or death for certain vulnerable groups, is left up to two private firms without careful government oversight of supply. Although Europe was experiencing a similarly severe influenza season, shortages had not been reported there, according to the World Health Organization. Consequently, America turned to Europe for the needed vaccine.

It is doubtful that there is another nation in the free world in which its leaders have been as unresponsive to a major public crisis like the health-care debacle as in America. Meanwhile, the American public suffers uniquely, as shown by a recent five-country survey of attitudes toward health care: "In general, the survey found that the U.S. generally ranks at the bottom among the five countries on most indicators of patient view and experiences."[214]

*   *   *

The data I have presented indicate that in America the cost of health care is much higher than elsewhere in advanced nations; the frequency of certain health risks (e.g., pollution, hunger, crime, obesity, poverty, job stress, and drug abuse), and thus of certain illnesses, is higher than in other advanced nations; health care is often poor (judging from surveys, studies of the appropriateness of treatment for particular ailments, and the high rate of medical errors) *in spite of* its much higher cost than elsewhere; life-threatening shortages of doctors and nurses prevail; preventive measures are minimized relative to therapy, which (together with high cost) is probably responsible for the larger proportion of preventable deaths than elsewhere; most name-brand prescription drugs are very over-priced, and some of the best-selling drugs are no better than much cheaper, nonprescription drugs, while direct advertising runs rampant unlike elsewhere; the availability of life-saving vaccines is determined by business conditions; hospitals have been closing; emergency-room facilities are overcrowded to the point of frequently having to divert ambulances; physicians are at the mercy of the insurance liability industry; the federal government refuses to cap drug prices; and the nation lacks a universal health-care program, which means that 43.6 million Americans do not have health insurance, a situation that is unheard of elsewhere in the developed world. Here, then, is persuasive evidence of America's second- or even third-rate standing among advanced nations.

An Afterword on the Medicare Prescription Drug and Modernization Act of 2003

The Medicare Prescription Drug and Modernization Act of December 2003 can only be summarized as distressingly inadequate except for purposes of reelection. Although the American Association of Retired Persons (AARP) fully recognized its deficiencies, the organization claimed to have supported the bill on the grounds that it was better than nothing. But if the law enhances the domination by private industry of America's health-care policy, which it promises to do, or reduces coverage and increases premiums, deductibles, or co-payments, which it will definitely do for many, it could be worse than no change for those who are adversely affected.

Huge gaps in coverage and sharp increases in premiums projected over the next few years (e.g., 10 percent in the first year alone), and huge benefits for pharmaceutical and insurance companies (including a new $1.3 billion subsidy to HMOs), are indicative of industry's hand in writing the law. Indeed, HMOs will receive "25 percent more from the government than traditional Medicare costs for the same beneficiaries," according to a health-cost expert.[215] Further, drug companies will be protected from government negotiations for drug costs and the capping of costs as done in other countries; consumers will not have the right to buy drugs from abroad (unless the drug is explicitly approved by the government); and Medigap supplements cannot be used for drug purchases. Meanwhile, the poorest will suffer higher co-payments and a reduction in some drug benefits by being shifted from Medicaid to Medicare, middle- and high-income seniors could lose their employer benefits, and almost two million will receive no drug benefit at all. And because each company will carry only certain drugs, multidrug consumers would have to sign up with several companies. Moreover, the elimination of certain drugs in a plan will mean that consumers could suddenly be deprived of what they signed up for.[216] In addition, when the law was passed the range and complexity of the options offered by private insurers threatened confusion and chaos. This prediction has been borne out, according to the *New York Times.*[217] Restrictions on allowed clinical procedures will mean the closing of hundreds of clinics so that the savings can be used for the drug-coverage plan. (The touted benefits to rural hospitals will amount to a mere 1 to 1.5 percent a year nationwide.)[218] And, of course, private insurers are able to screen their applicants for the most able-bodied clients, which will leave the neediest to the traditional Medicare program, driving up costs for the non-private sector and threatening its survival.

All of these undesirable consequences could have been avoided if Congress and the president had simply heeded the express wishes of the public. A poll five months before passage of the bill found that "63 percent of seniors wanted a seamless benefit added to traditional Medicare, comparable to the best that retired workers get. *Eighty-nine* percent wanted the federal government to negotiate lower drug prices with pharmaceutical companies—and a majority continued to favor this even after researchers presented the counterargument that it could hurt research and development"[219] (emphasis added). As a matter of fact, *twenty years ago* two-thirds of Americans preferred the nationalized health care system of Canada.[220] Yet, the new law of 2003 did nothing to make affordable insurance available to the 43.6 million Americans who do not have it and has left many fundamental decisions up to private companies. As we shall see in chapter 11 on democracy, America's record of representing the wishes of its people is one of the worst in the democratic, industrial world, owing largely to the intervention of powerful economic interest groups and an outmoded system of representation.

As for AARP's endorsement of the 2003 law, it could afford to ignore public opinion and even the wishes of its members because its share of income from dues has dropped to only 30 percent in recent years while profits have been realized from sales of drugs and services under its name.[221] Clearly, the symbioses between industry and government, and between industry and the public, via a national association that ostensibly represents a large segment of the public but is dependent on the very industries it is supposed to be monitoring, are alive and well in the higgledy-piggledy health-care system of America.

4

Education

In today's world, education is the sine qua non of national prosperity. A contemporary advanced nation that cannot properly educate itself does not deserve the credentials of modernity, much less the laurels of greatness. Both on the world stage and at home it will stumble like an oaf and repeat the mistakes of history. Its democracy will falter, its workshops and farms will languish, its private life will be deprived of richness and cosmopolitanism, its economy will be bottom heavy with poverty and crime, and its leaders will behave like muttonheads.

Modern economies are based on copious abilities to produce, convey, interpret, and put to use both technical and social knowledge, and more so than ever before in history. But has America risen to this challenge? The preponderance of the evidence points to a diagnosis of "barely." And even well-intentioned efforts to improve education seem to be hamstrung by ignorance of the art of policy formation and intervention, which must be based upon hardheaded, research-validated knowledge of the knowledge industry of education itself. Common sense, conventional wisdom, quick fixes, gut feeling, and, least of all, political ideology cannot do the job.

This chapter will examine six topics: educational achievement in America compared with other advanced nations, spending on education, factors related to school achievement, innovation and organization, dropping out of secondary school and the negative role of the federal government, and access to higher education. And with respect to each topic we shall find cause for grave concern.

Educational Achievement Compared with Other Nations

First, let us look at math scores. In 1995, American students in grade four scored only in the middle of 26 reporting countries on math, according to the International Assessment of Educational Achievement. By grade eight they were in the bottom third; and by grade 12 they were nearly in last place.[1] This low ranking for the United States was confirmed by another study a few years later (1999) of 38 countries (the OECD nations and four others), which found that America's

15-year-olds ranked 19th in math. (Fifteen-year-olds were the only students in the study.)[2] Looking at the results of the 1995 assessment in another way, students of 19 European countries reporting did better at the 8th-grade level; students of 14 European countries reporting did better at the 12th-grade level; and, in fact, at this grade level America placed 3rd from the bottom among all 21 countries reporting. And even the "top students" among the 12th-grade Americans did worse than the students of all the European countries except one.[3]

In late 2003, the Education Department and the media boasted that the latest scores at grades 4 and 8 were the highest ever.[4] But at the same meager annual rate of increase (since 1996), it would take 166 years for 4th graders and 122 years for 8th graders in the United States to achieve a perfect score. Verbal scores remained about the same. No comparisons with other nations were given.

In science in the 1995 study mentioned above, the United States ranked 3rd at grade 4, but 17th at grade 6 and 16th at grade 12. And once again, even the "top students" among Americans in grade 12 did more poorly than students in all the European countries reporting.[5]

A study in 2000 of the "literacy/retrieval" achievement of 15-year-olds (from 31 OECD countries plus four other nations) found that the United States ranked 15th, that is, no better than mediocre.[6] It also found that only 8 percent of the American students read 1–2 hours a day for their own enjoyment, and 41 percent did not read "at all" for enjoyment. This placed the United States 23rd in rank with respect to reading outside of classroom requirements.[7]

According to the International Assessment survey of 17-year-olds in 1999, "53% said they did some reading for fun—not for school—at least once a week, a figure that was down from 64% in the mid-eighties." When asked whether they saw adults reading at home daily, only 34% said yes, which was down from 42% in the mid-'80s.[8]

Quite obviously, American students have been bringing up the rear in educational achievement compared with other countries, and their time spent reading is far behind the average of other countries. That only about a third of the students saw adults reading at home daily goes a long way in explaining their own behavior. To put it bluntly, Americans, both young and old, appear to be educationally handicapped. That Americans can be characterized as nonpracticing literates is indicated by a study of adults that found they devote 24 minutes a day on average to reading, but more than 4 hours to television and more than 3 hours to radio.[9]

While math, science, and literacy are certainly subjects that require at least a moderate level of competent mastery, one is struck by the muted interest of the public, politicians, and educators alike in social subjects like history, economics, anthropology, or sociology, both in the curriculum and in students' competence. It is a mark either of America's naïveté or its distrust of these subjects that they never receive the attention given to math or science in the schools. Instead, they are treated (if at all) as supplemental subjects for "infusion" into other curricula or as "elective" courses reserved for high school advanced placement students. Overall, therefore, only a very small minority of secondary students in America take social science courses. One might think that such subjects are too controversial or sensitive for secondary students, but then one must admit that sex education has been widely introduced into the schools. The paucity of courses in sociology, anthropology, and political science is a sign of an insistent provincialism.

An even clearer sign of provincialism in pre-college education is the fact that America offers foreign languages to the majority of students at a much older age than other advanced nations do: 14 years of age in America compared to 6 years in four nations, 8 to 9 years in six nations, and below 12 years in the remaining nine nations studied.[10] Since foreign language teaching cannot be accused of violating local pieties, as with the teaching of social science courses, its rarity among younger students cannot be attributed to anything but sheer cultural isolationism.

With respect to history, the results of a National Assessment test in 1994 revealed that only 17 percent of 4th graders achieved the Proficient level, 14 percent of 8th graders, and 11 percent of 12th graders. And these scores were much lower than those four years earlier. The percentages who scored below the Basic level were 36 percent, 39 percent, and 57 percent of 4th, 8th, and 12th graders, respectively.[11] As for "civics," the percentages of 4th, 8th, and 12th graders who performed at or above the Proficient level were as follows: only 23 percent, 22 percent, and 26 percent, respectively.[12]

If our young adults found themselves roaming the earth, some would not be able to find their way home. The National Geographic Society's survey of 18- to 24-year-olds in 2002 found that "one in 10 young Americans could not locate his country on a blank map of the world . . . 85% could not find Afghanistan, Iraq, or Israel" and "29% could not find the Pacific Ocean."[13] Compared with other nations, the United States did extremely poorly, receiving a grade of "D" with a score next to last. In fact, Americans were least likely to know the population category of the United States, and also least likely to know (post 9/11) that al Qaeda and the Taliban were both based in Afghanistan.[14]

In view of this dismal record of educational achievement among American students, which has placed the nation behind other advanced countries, it is not surprising that in 1996, "only 25% of adults have a great deal of confidence in the people running education . . . down from 49% in 1974."[15] As one authority has observed: "One would think that with our vastly superior resources and the level of educational spending which far exceeds these [foreign] competitors, we would outperform everyone—not so . . ."[16] To what degree is this criticism that we have failed to use our wealth wisely to enhance learning truly justified? The following section on educational spending suggests that it is well founded.

Spending on Education as a Measure of National Commitment

In 2000 the United States ranked ninth in expenditure on elementary-secondary education as a percentage of GDP and fifth in per pupil expenditure among 30 OECD countries.[17] But when we examine the association between per pupil expenditure and achievement on a combined index of reading, math, and science literacy (based on 1998 data), we find that the United States' score was 20 points below where it should have been according to statistical expectation, much lower than any other country except Mexico. A few countries did much better than expected. Korea, for example, spent $30,844 per pupil compared to America's $35,000, but was 50 score points *above* expectation (signified by a positive trend line showing the association between achievement and per pupil expenditure for all the nations) compared with America's 20 points *below* expectation.[18]

Evidently, America is not getting its money's worth. Seemingly, other strategies in addition to sheer financial effort are called for. At the same time, the need to overcome special hindrances to learning in America might require even a greater outlay of funds, but allocated in new ways. (One of these ways is suggested later.) An increased allocation to education would seem possible inasmuch as, in spite of our high per pupil expenditure, we rank ninth in the percentage of our GDP devoted to education. But past increases in funding for education in the federal budget were sharply reduced in the 2003 budget, namely, from an increase of 13.4 percent a year in 1996 to 2002 to an increase of only 2.8 percent in 2003. In sum, if our educational hindrances are indeed greater than those of other nations, which are apparently doing a much better job, it appears that we are unwilling to make the greater financial effort that is both needed and affordable. Indeed, it appears that we have been almost standing pat with respect to funding in spite of enormous publicity on behalf of the current administration's new initiative in raising achievement scores, which is discussed later.

It should also be noted that the near stagnation in funding for education in the 2003 budget has come at a time of "record growth in student enrollments; the increased proportion of students affected by poverty, special needs, and limited English proficiency; an enormous school facilities problem; a critical need for new, qualified teachers; rapidly changing educational technology needs; new testing and accountability requirements on states and school districts [see below] without a corresponding increase in the investment."[20] In short, an increase of federal funding well in excess of past years would seem to be called for. One cannot help but marvel at the discrepancy between the president's vow when he ran for office that education would be the top priority of his administration and the current state of disarray and underfunding. (See below for a program introduced by the administration that relies on state-mandated testing.)

Education funding in America, of course, is heavily dependent on local taxation of property, and the largest expense is staff salaries. Here once again we find evidence of a low level of commitment to education. For teachers' salaries have risen less than one-third of 1 percent annually for a number of years. The salary of accountants, in contrast, has doubled in the past 20 years and is now 20 percent more than that of teachers.[21] The monitoring of business accounts is evidently more important than the monitoring of the minds of young Americans.

Although America's expenditure per pupil has been one of the highest in the world, it has not been able to overcome its educational handicaps, according to the preceding data. The "No Child Left Behind" program that was signed into law in January 2002[22] offered hope of improvement in educational achievement to many Americans. But the $4 billion increase in federal spending in the 2003 budget over the previous year was only 2.8 percent, compared with a 13.4 percent increase per year from 1996 through 2002, as noted above. The amount for improving literacy amounted to the cost of only four F-22 fighters. Meanwhile, state budget deficits have made it necessary to reduce support for education at the state level. And, unfortunately, the new federal program suffers from a controversial feature: the augmentation of standardized testing in accordance with state-mandated standards. What has been the record of this intervention?

Within only seven months of the program's becoming law it was reported that schools in Texas, which had served as the model for the program, had engaged in a number of administrative practices aimed at beefing up the achievement scores, practices that might well be harmful to the basic goals of education, and even downright fraudulent, e.g., devoting weeks to teaching for the tests (leaving no time for teacher feedback after testing before the end of the semester), shifting borderline students into special education classes during the test period, asking parents to keep certain students home on test days, retaining poorly performing students in grade 9 so that the grade 10 test scores would be better, and so on.[23]

Moreover, steps have been taken more recently around the country to lower the states' performance bars in order to avoid federal financial sanctions and other deleterious consequences of failing the mandated tests. In Texas the lowering of the performance bar consisted of reducing the number of questions that must be answered correctly for passing. This practice was adopted by other states as well. Another ploy has been to reduce the required percentage of students who must pass the tests—in Michigan, for example, from 75 percent to 42 percent of high school students on English tests—to certify the schools as making sufficient progress. In Colorado, the grading system was changed so that students who had previously been classified as "partially proficient" became "proficient." As one educator warned: "The severe sanctions may hinder educational excellence because they implicitly encourage states to water down their content and performance standards in order to reduce the risk of sanctions."[24]

And here, once again, we find the possibility that a new policy that has not been thought through and objectively evaluated can make matters worse than before.

Still another consequence of this new federal program is higher dropout rates when poor test scores cause students to be retained a grade. This problem will be discussed later in terms of the dropout problem in general. But first, let us look at the factors that have been found to be related to educational achievement. In doing so, we shall see that the schools themselves play only a partial, and perhaps even a marginal, role in achievement.

Factors Related to School Achievement

The factors related to school achievement are of paramount importance because only by focusing on the barriers to educational performance can we remedy the problems that beset us.

In analyzing the data collected in the cross-national study of schoolchildren discussed above, both school factors and home background factors were found to be independently predictive of achievement in literacy.[25] The nine school factors were: percentage of teachers with university-level qualification; pupil/teacher ratio; teachers' expectations of student performance; teachers' morale and commitment; school autonomy; teacher-student relations; the disciplinary climate of the classroom; the extent to which teachers emphasize academic performance and place high demands on students; and the amount of homework that is done. Several of these factors run into the chicken-and-egg problem, however. That is, which of the school variables are causal and which are the consequences of poor student commitment or performance in the first place? For example, poor student performance could cause teachers to have lower expectations, and not vice versa; similarly with teacher morale and commitment, less emphasis on high standards of performance, less homework, and so on. In any case, it is reported that these nine factors together "explain" 31 percent of the variance among schools within countries, and 21 percent among countries. In short, in purely statistical terms this is a powerful brew of factors, although the chicken-and-egg problem would tend to call them into question as factors independent of the effect of prior student performance. In plain English, the so-called causes could be the consequences.

When we come to home background factors, however, such as income, education, and race of the parents, the effects are stronger and the direction of causality is clear. Adding these latter factors to the package of variables associated with achievement now explains 72 percent of the variance within countries, a substantial increase over the explanatory power of school factors alone. Specifically, background factors are about a third more important than school factors in explaining differences among schools within countries, and without any question of causality. (Among countries, school and environmental factors are about equally important.) In short, background factors probably far exceed the importance of school factors within a country.

The power of social background can be seen in another way. If we sort the students into the top one-quarter and the bottom one-quarter of parental educational attainment, we find a whopping 90 percent difference in the students' reading scores between these two groups in the United States. And only 8 other countries (or 26 percent) of the 31 countries in the study had a larger difference than this.[26] In short, social background is not only more influential in general, but seems to be especially so in America.

Once again we find that the fruit does not fall very far from the tree, and this might be especially true in America. In other words, social class might have an augmented influence on life-chances in America in spite of its ideology of equality and its perception of Europe as burdened with class differences. This, of course, is a large and portentous conclusion to draw from these limited data. Still, those who influence the distribution of opportunity and resources in America should take careful note. Because if we wish to live up to our notion of equal opportunity, the intergenerational cycle of inadequate education and lower socioeconomic status must be broken. And the federal government's mandated school testing program does nothing to attack this problem. Indeed, the comparatively low financial commitment to education (as a percentage of GDP) in America suggests that the social background problem, which would require large sums of money to overcome, is given short shrift. And no wonder, since it lies beyond the traditional realm of spending on education—like a man looking for his lost car keys at night under a street lamp, although it is more likely that he dropped them in a back alley.

Another implication of the importance of home background is that it might well nullify, or at least substantially limit, the possible benefits of transferring to a better school. This means that programs allowing parents to send their children to the school of their choice, including voucher programs, might be ineffectual. This outcome is especially likely if the parents' background influences their very choice of the school. Research shows that parents have been found to select schools that reflect their own ideas about how children should be raised, and these child-raising habits could be an integral part of the child's poor performance in school. Thus, working-class parents tend to choose schools that emphasize obedience and traditionally structured classrooms instead of more individually focused, intellectual performance.[27]

In short, giving parents the opportunity to match a school with their past child-raising values might only amplify the effect of these values. Although research on this issue has been available for many years, it seems to have been ignored. Note my mention at the outset of this chapter of "well-intentioned efforts that seem to be hamstrung by ignorance of the art of policy formation and intervention, which must be based upon hardheaded, research-validated knowledge of the knowledge industry of education itself." That definitely includes how the industry relates to its "market," and in particular to the social values and child-oriented practices of that market.

The long-term solution, of course, is to reduce poverty and other possible sources of educational disadvantage in the whole country. But there might be a short-term solution as well: to promote the joint participation of parents, local leaders and role models, youth workers, and even police and other resources in the neighborhood to overcome the educational barriers and disincentives in the community and family. Orientation sessions could be held in relaxed social settings with parents to encourage children to do homework, limit TV time, set an example of literacy and interest in current events at home by reading and discussing the news with children, and to stay in touch with the school on a regular basis to discuss a child's progress and problems (like a doctor insisting that a patient return for a checkup once a month and perhaps even calling the patient at home to remind him or her). Problem-solving sessions in which parents themselves share problems and possible solutions would be an extremely important part of the program. Supplemental programs of service organizations and field trips to work settings might also be included in a local effort. Information about the financial benefits of children finishing high school and applying to college, and counseling on college choice and sources of funds could also be offered. Even information about adult education opportunities for the parents themselves could be given. These local projects could, and should, be carried out under the auspices of PTAs, booster clubs, Rotary and Lions clubs, etc., with direct federal funding, guidelines, and technical assistance. In short, parents and other members of the community would themselves be in charge. And they could subcontract with tutors and schools if they chose to do so. Moreover, if the participants wanted to take up problems with the school systems and work for change, that would also be a possibility. But the core emphasis would be on improving community and home background factors that impinge on children in a particular locale.

The rationale for the program should be kept clearly in mind: what schoolchildren do, see, and hear outside of school can easily countervail the efforts of even the best of teachers and school administrators. And the sheer amount of time that students spend on homework can be eroded by their after-school activities. One international study found that 8th-grade students in the United States spent more time on sports per day than students in any other of the 38 countries surveyed.[28] And another study found that American 13-year-olds were the highest percentage watching TV for two or more hours daily in 17 countries with the exception of Scotland.[29] As for the cost of such a nationwide program: possibly another four F-22 fighter jets.

Innovation and the Organization of Education

One feature of American education that distinguishes it from most other advanced countries is the absence of a national ministry that regulates educational practice throughout the country. Does this distinction have an impact on educational practice? To explore this question we must realize that authority in the American system is not anarchic, but is distributed among four levels: the federal, state, district, and school levels. This distribution raises the question of which level has greatest authority. Moreover, if we are interested in the educational quality of service, then one must determine whether the predominant level of authority is the most appropriate for efforts at improvement. While this is a large and vexing question, certain data bear on it in a striking way.

First, we should realize that the federal and the state levels make only small percentages of educational decisions about such key issues as curriculum, staffing, and lay policies; furthermore, Americans would be opposed to any substantial increase in the authority of these levels because of our strong local control ideology. That leaves the district and the school levels as contenders for authority over these key issues. And we find that the large percentage of decisions made by the districts (72%) is far in excess of that in the same kinds of units in other countries, and far greater than the percentage of decisions made at the school level (25%) in America.[30] With regard to the school's autonomy, this is "less than in any other country except Switzerland."[31]

Now let's turn to the innovation rates of schools that have more or less autonomy within districts, that is, are more or less independent of the district bureaucracy. It turns out that the schools with more autonomy are more innovative. According to a study of 670 schools in 45 cities in 1968–69, the degree to which a school system is decentralized is related to the rate at which the principal innovates: 41 percent of the principals in centralized systems have high innovation rates in contrast to 56 percent of those in decentralized systems. "If all decisions have to go through the central office, the principals are less able to respond quickly and appropriately to their perceptions of what changes are needed in their schools."[32]

This contribution of the more autonomous schools to innovation is augmented when the principal has been serving in the job less than six years and is relatively young. Sixty-four percent of such principals were found to be more innovative compared with only 42 percent of the remainder,[33] a fairly substantial difference. This raises the possibility that placing poorly performing students in relatively autonomous schools led by "young Turks" would make a significant contribution to their education through the greater degree of innovativeness in these schools. And this possibility would be enhanced if the schools paid close attention to the R&D evidence supporting particular innovations. Finally, it is worth recalling that school autonomy was one of the nine school factors found related to educational achievement, and the direction of causality is clear.

Unfortunately, predominantly black districts tended to be more centralized than predominantly white ones, which might have prevented them from being more innovative. But decentralization remained a factor in innovativeness regardless of the racial balance of the school district.[34]

In light of these data at least, the answer to our earlier question is a qualified no: Dominant authority is not lodged at the appropriate level in the structure of American education. But misplaced authority is not the only problem with America's educational system. In the absence of a nationally mandated curriculum, as in most other countries, an array of functional substitutes has arisen.

The nation's professional network of R&D information, instructional materials, and training permeates schools in every part of the country, which lends a great deal of uniformity to the system. Some means whereby uniformity is fostered include: a federally operated system for retrieval of information, regional labs for educational R&D and dissemination, consultants and evaluation teams from all levels of the system, local schools of education that are interrelated nationally, regional and national accreditation agencies, preservice and in-service teacher training based on national resources and methods, testing services such as the College Entrance Examination Board, and, increasingly, mandated state tests with items borrowed from tests elsewhere—all of which contribute to a quasi-nationalized system.[35]

But probably the most influential player is the textbook industry. And once again we witness the role of corporate America in determining the quality, quantity, and cost of a basic human service. In fact, the two states with the largest public school enrollments—Texas and California—to a large degree determine by their adoptions what other states will do. Since a high volume of production is more profitable than production for small markets (unless the price is substantially raised), the ability to lower the cost of textbooks adopted by Texas and California makes these texts highly cost-competitive. The aura of market leadership shared by the two populous states also is highly persuasive. Further, as one expert has pointed out, "school systems do not like to change textbooks as long as the existing inventory is useable. Three- to five-year use of such materials seems to be common, and retention for much longer periods is not unusual."[36] Thus, the use of textbooks based on the decisions of two states tends to be locked in for a number of years across the nation. In short, America's educational system is national after all, but it is national to a large extent on the terms of private industry and on the basis of the desires of a very limited, unrepresentative portion of the market.

Dropping Out of Secondary Education and
the Negative Role of the Federal Government

It was reported in 2000 that the high-school-graduation rate in America was 74 percent, which placed the nation 23rd among 29 OECD countries.[37] Eleven percent of all 16- to 24-year-olds were not enrolled in high school and had not completed high school.[38] These figures do not suggest a high level of commitment to education in America, whereas other advanced countries seem to excel in this respect.

The income level of one's family is a major determinant of high-school-completion rates, just as it is for educational achievement on standardized tests, discussed earlier. In 2002:

> [C]hildren from families with incomes in the lowest 20% of all family incomes were six times as likely as their peers in the top 20% of income [not to complete high school.][39] [And] the completion rates for students of different racial or ethnic backgrounds were as follows: white, 92%: blacks, 84%; Hispanics, 64%. The overall rate was 86% of young adults. [About one-half million students drop out of high school annually.][40]

The last statistic means that in a five-year period, about two and a half million students drop out of high school. Not only are these nongraduates liable to earn less than graduates, but they are susceptible to higher rates of unemployment, and especially when the economy is sluggish. Thus, the jobless rate among nongraduates in 2000–2001 was 20.9 percent, which was more than five times the national average.[41] The nation, therefore, pays a high price for its comparatively high dropout rate, which clearly contributes to the unusually high rate of poverty in America when compared with other economically advanced nations. (See chapter 2.)

Besides contributing to a lower level of employability and income, and an increase in crime, as well as a lower level of cultural literacy and health, failing to finish high school precludes attendance at college, which is almost essential for realizing the American Dream (or even the idle reveries of a drowsy afternoon). This failure has three major economic consequences for the nation: a reduction in the technical-professional pool of workers (many companies now shop abroad for qualified personnel); a reduction in economic growth due to lower wages for consumption and investment; and a widening of the disparity between rich and poor. Concerning lower wages, male college graduates in 1990 had an income 57 percent higher than that of male high school graduates, and female college graduates made 75 percent more than female high school graduates.[42] Taxes, consumption, and welfare are all impacted by lower levels of wealth, not to mention crime, health, and one's sense of well-being and worth.

As for the increased gap between rich and poor, which was discussed in chapter 2, it is worth noting that "young children whose parents only completed high school had poverty rates [in 1997] ten times greater than those with parents who completed college."[43] This disparity is especially marked with respect to blacks and Hispanics, owing to their greater tendency than whites to drop out of high school. The difference between the percentages of blacks and whites who graduated is 8 percent, and between Hispanics and whites almost 30 percent. Hispanics now compose 13 percent of the U.S. population.[44]

The learning handicap suffered by high-school dropouts in America is more severe than in European countries for the following reason: Several subjects that are normally taught in the high-school years in other countries are taught only in college in the United States. Calculus is a good example. "In a sense," points out an America educator, "education in this country is a 16-year rather than a 12-year process."[45] This point means that the American high-school curriculum is less demanding than that in many other countries. This makes the comparatively low performance of U.S. secondary students in math and science understandable in terms of their simply not having been given equally advanced instruction in these subjects. But it is doubtful that it would explain their poor performance in literacy, which is not as dependent upon level of teaching.

The dropout rate reflects lack of enjoyment, or at least tolerance, of school, one would assume. And indeed, in the 1997–98 cross-national study of adolescents we find that only 27 percent of 11-year-olds, 20 percent of 13-year-olds, and 18 percent of 15-year-olds in America said they "like school a lot." These three age groups ranked 19th, 16th, and 9th, respectively, in the frequencies with which adolescents gave this response among the 28 countries in the study. Here are a few comparative figures among 11-year-olds in other countries: Germany, 66 percent; Portugal, 57 percent; Greece, 54 percent; France, 48 percent; and England, 41 percent. Since only 27 percent of the students in America said they "like school a lot," it seems fair to conclude that American students are simply less happy with their high-school experience. (Other age groups showed similar discrepancies between America and Europe.)[46]

A factor today that might well increase the dropout rate in the United States is the new federal requirement of standardized testing at certain grades in order to receive Title I money. (See the No-Child-Left-Behind program above.) Under the program, parents of students in failing schools will receive funding for transportation of their students to other schools. But no extra funding is provided to the low-scoring schools to help them overcome their deficiencies—for example, by reducing class size or providing reading specialists. Equally surprising is the lack of extra funds for those successful schools that are obliged to receive children from the failing schools. Thus, the New Hampshire School Administrators Association estimated that while the law adds $77 per transferring pupil in federal aid, it creates $575 per student in obligations.[47] This means that overcrowding in these receiving schools is inevitable. As the *New York Times* reported, ". . . state and local officials [say] the practical difficulties could prove overwhelming and undo years of progress toward reducing class size."[48]

But the more serious problem is the dropout incentive. The experience of Texas's aggressive testing program was a harbinger of things to come. The Houston Independent School District, for example, had a high-school-completion rate of only 47 percent in 2000, compared with a national rate of 86 percent.[49] And yet, what appeared to be huge gains in the scores on the Texas state test were the inspiration for the new federal emphasis on testing and the basis on which the former superintendent of the Houston district was appointed by President Bush as U.S. Commissioner of Education. That these test-score improvements were gained by de facto expulsion of poorly performing students seems not to have occurred to anyone. Although other large Texas cities also had unusually low graduate rates while emphasizing testing in compliance with the state's mandate, Houston's rate was the lowest. In fact, in the year 2000, Texas had a high-school-completion rate that ranked 21st out of the 25 largest states in the nation. It is hard to blame an organization for bad performance when its records of performance are fraudulent: Houston *reported* a dropout rate of 1.5 percent when it was actually closer to 40 percent.[50] This might well explain why its program was chosen by the Bush administration as the model for the nation. (Also, the president's home state is Texas.) Thus, it seems highly likely that whatever test gains occurred (and this in itself is a controversial issue) were the consequence of winnowing the chaff from the wheat by de facto expulsion.

One might think that it is only reasonable to retain students at a given level when they fail to pass a statewide, mandated test. But there is a downside to this assumption, an unintended consequence that could wipe out the benefits of testing for increasing the educational achievement level of American youth, namely, a large increase in dropouts for those older than the age of mandatory school attendance. Studies show that the chances of dropping out are increased 50 percent when a student is required to repeat one grade, and this probability is increased to 90 percent when the student is retained twice. And a research association in Texas found that "about 35,000 nine-year-olds could potentially fail the third grade under [the statewide testing program]. [And] when fifth and eight graders are added the number grows to 82,000."[51]

The experience in Texas has been confirmed by a survey of a number of states after the new testing program was put into effect nationwide. In 62 percent of the states studied, dropout rates worsened. As a *New York Times* article explained, "administrators held responsible for raising test scores at a school or in an entire district, occasionally pressured failing students to drop out . . . [Some students] were expelled en masse shortly before testing days, according to some educators who have filed lawsuits."[52]

Dropping out means not only that students no longer have the chance to improve their test scores by repeating a grade, but that they forgo the opportunity to learn in general. For it appears that improvements in performance on the tests is not related to improvements on other tests of academic achievement. As one observer put it, "students are being trained so narrowly because of [high stakes tests], they are having a hard time branching out and understanding general problem-solving . . . An independent panel of researchers has concluded that these findings are valid."[53] Evidently, the practice of teaching for the tests prepares students for making higher test scores without a concomitant increase in broader learning or the ability to think for themselves. (This reminds us that one can train a monkey how to type, but not how to express itself in words.)

It should be added, incidentally, that an additional criticism of the "No Child Left Behind" program concerns the jurisdiction within which parents have the right to shift their children from one school to another, namely, the jurisdiction of the school district. Some have pointed out that the disparity between districts is greater than that between schools within districts; therefore, unless this disparity is addressed, little will be gained by permitting parents to shift their children from one school to another within a district.[54]

Finally, there is the ethical question about the justice of determining the future life chances of an individual solely on the basis of a single criterion. The American Educational Research Association, the National Research Council, the American Psychological Association, and the National Academy of Sciences "all agree that total focus on a sole indicator with high-stakes consequences for children is unethical."[55]

These criticisms of the new federal program suggest that it is not the solution, or even a meaningful contribution to a solution, of the problem of educational deficiency in America. The root of the problem lies in the social context of the schools, and this is a target that the government seems reluctant to direct its attention to in a way that will overcome the inequities in background that are anathema to the American Dream and covered up by the American Myth.

It would be a mistake to assume, however, that graduation from high school means an automatic progression to higher education. While about 86 percent of young adults in America completed high school in 2000 (up from 83 percent in 1972), only 62 percent of these graduates attended college. And this figure was down from 67 percent in 1997 or only three years earlier.[56] A major reason that enrollment in college has not only failed to increase, but has declined is the astounding rise in cost.[57] And there is not a single government policy on the horizon at this writing (January 2004) that addresses this problem; in fact, the federal government has recently taken action to shift more of the financial burden to students (see below).

Access to Higher Education

The cost of higher education in 2000–2001 was more than double the cost in 1986–87 in both public and private institutions.[58] More recent statistics indicate that the cost of public college tuition rose 9.6 percent in 2002, and that of private college tuition rose 6 percent.[59] In New York State in 2000, the percentage of family income on average that was devoted to college tuition was 36 percent for public institutions and 85 percent for private institutions. These costs were 7.7 percent higher than those in the previous year for public institutions, and 5 percent higher for those in private institutions.[60]

One consequence of rising cost has been that "almost 70,000 high school graduates who were the brightest in their classes [will] have to forgo college [in the fall of 2003] because they can't afford rising tuitions and fees," according to a report issued by the Advisory Committee on Student Financial Assistance.[61] This, of course, is the most troubling aspect of the tuition explosion. And this discriminatory impact on lower-income students is a condition that has been growing more acute for a number of years, in spite of the "liberal" stints of the Clinton and Carter administrations. According to a report in late 2003, "in 1979 children from the richest 25 percent of American homes were only four times more likely to go to college than those from the poorest 25 percent of homes; but by 1994 they were *ten times* more likely"[62] (emphasis added). This amounts to a great victory for affirmative action on behalf of the rich who, thanks to higher tuition costs, have benefited from less competition for admission from brainy poor kids.

Another outcome of the tuition bulge was an increase of 85 percent in the number of Americans going to Canada for college in 2001.[63] Still another was an average of $17,000 in debt incurred by *two-thirds* of college graduates in 2001.[64] Overall, the percentage of graduates in 2002 who graduated in debt was *twice* what it was only eight years previously.[65]

Obviously, tuition has increased while assistance has remained relatively stagnant. And the cuts in state budgets and other shortfalls in the economy have only made the problem worse. "One reason that this issue may be overlooked by politicians," one critic speculates, "is that it is ignored in general"—that is, by the public who, of course, relies on the mainstream media to learn about what is happening in the nation. This lag in federal assistance is a clear indication, not just of a low level of commitment to education in America (in spite of the rhetoric of its politicians), but of a pragmatic failure to appreciate the long-term *economic* benefits of education. As the Educational Testing Service has reported, a $24,000 outlay by the state for a four-year public college education earns about $2 million dollars for the state during the work life of the graduate. The return is about $375,000 in higher taxes paid by each graduate to the state on average.[66] Indeed, if one looks at the economic benefits of the GI Bill following World

War II, one finds a $7 return on every dollar invested, according to a congressional study in 1988.[67] In other words, one might say that for every dollar *withheld* seven dollars are *lost*.

Today, however, federal assistance has not only remained stagnant, but has actually been reduced by a recent administrative ruling on eligibility in June 2003. This adjustment of an existing rule required neither congressional approval nor public comment of any kind, according to the *New York Times*.[68]

It is also interesting that in spite of higher tuition and fees, faculty salaries have not kept pace with inflation and more part-time faculty are being used. Yet, as a report of the National Commission on the Cost of Higher Education has pointed out, "student contact hours by faculty have been increasing, while the percentage of tenured faculty has declined."[69] In general, and over a longer period of time, the inflation rate of goods and services purchased by colleges and universities increased 154 percent from 1980 to 2000, while in the economy the Consumer Price Index increased only 118 percent. Institutions of higher education are being squeezed by business and government simultaneously, and the consequence might be not only unaffordability, but mediocrity. This is not a state of affairs that America needs to foster in parlous times of global competition.

The probability of an increasing number of dropouts from high school, together with a growing inability to afford the cost of higher education, has important implications for our already large and worsening inequality of income, or gulf between rich and poor where the middle class treads water for survival. Not only will a higher percentage of high school and college graduates hail from more affluent backgrounds, but the greater earning capacity of these graduates will increase the disparity between rich and poor. The failure to make higher education more affordable by assistance is an act of omission on the part of government, while the stimulus to dropping out provided by mandated, all-or-nothing tests is a commission of error. Although it is unlikely that the current administration in Washington is sufficiently astute to appreciate the effect of these outcomes on the class structure of America, it is possible that it would not be overly concerned if it were. For there is more than a hint of a "survival-of-the-fittest" social philosophy in radical conservatism, so that a growing gap between rich and poor can be safely regarded as nature's way. At any rate, the No-Child-Left-Behind legislation might be seen as a typical case of regressive intervention in which the goal is not only unachieved, but matters are actually made worse. (See the author's *Fatal Remedies: The Ironies of Social Intervention* (Plenum Press, 1981). Regarding mandated, all-or-nothing tests, the discussion of "Overload" on pages 73–76 is particularly germane.)

*   *   *

The educational tragedy that characterizes America today is startling in view of the current president's having placed educational reform at the top of his legislative agenda in his campaign for office, as mentioned earlier. Two and a half years after his assuming office, we find grossly underpaid schoolteachers, increased dropout rates, ever-increasing costs of higher education and indebtedness of graduates, the smallest rise in the education budget in five years (the School Renovation Program was completely eliminated, for example), diversion of funds for public education to privatization schemes, and a nationwide testing program that has been severely criticized by numerous education professionals and researchers. And all of these misguided actions and deliberate inactions have occurred at a time when the net enrollment of school-age children is rising and is projected to increase by *6 percent* between 2010 and 2020,[70] and when three-quarters of the nation's school buildings have been found by the American Society of Civil Engineers to need extensive repairs or replacement.[71]

One is led to wonder if these decisions of the current administration are related to an underlying ideology of ruthless competition applied to the educational realm. The apparent inclination to let students drop out who cannot compete on test scores, to let schools languish that cannot overcome the educational handicaps of its students and their communities with the available resources, to let school competition and parents determine the best place for their children to learn regardless of the parents' ability to make informed choices or overcome the influence of old habits of child rearing on their choice, to let schools that become overcrowded as a result of choice either increase their class size and suffer other consequences without assistance or close their doors, and to let school buildings tumble down if the community cannot find enough money to repair or replace them—all of these measures have in common a tendency to let things take their course while the weak drop by the wayside.

The place of professional research, evaluation, and dissemination of the best practices in this scheme of things is tenuous at best. For example, the centerpiece of the government's all-or-nothing tests was the program of a state (Texas) where achievement scores had actually *fallen* while dropout rates had *risen*, a state that ranked in the *bottom four* of all 50 states in SAT scores.[72] How much statistical sophistication would have been required to grasp the meaning of these simple facts? Here we witness the bitter fruit of a failure to heed the results of research and evaluation in deference to political ideology. Similarly, the evidence of the contribution of a higher education degree to the state treasury and economic vitality in general is a no-brainer for any rational policymaker. This reminds us that the world is seldom made a better place by the wishful thinking of ill-advised contenders for power, and could very well be made a worse one.

5

Crime and Punishment

One of the saddest commentaries on the state of American society is its singular and well-known penchant for crime; and America's failed efforts to deal with this scourge are almost as depressing as the scourge itself. One reason that our remedies do not work is that they are primarily introduced to gain momentary political advantage, a theme that will be touched on later. But first, let us look at the prevalence and incidence of crime.

Crime, Its Fluctuation, and Its Costs

In 2000 America had the highest rate of crime experienced by victims among 17 economically advanced nations. This statistic refers to the "incidence" of criminal acts, however, and not to the percentage of persons who were victims, which is called the "prevalence." With regard to prevalence, the United States ranked in the middle range (20%-24%) among the 18 nations. Thus, six countries had a higher percentage of victims than ours. In sum, more crimes per 100,000 were committed in the United States, meaning that we are the most prone to criminal behavior, but the percentage of victims was about average because many of our victims suffered *more than one* crime in a year.[1] As for violence, "the Department of Justice estimates that 83 percent of the population of America will be the victim of at least one violent crime at some point in their lives."[2]

Murder is a special scourge in America. In 1999, the nation ranked in the top quartile (9th) among 38 developed nations.[3] In 2001, the volume of murders increased 26.4 percent, which amounted to a 3.1 percent increase per 100,000.[4] Washington, D.C., had a rate of 46 killings per 100,000 in 1996–2000, which was the highest murder rate of 42 cities worldwide.[5]

Natural disasters account for fewer deaths, injuries, and loss of property than crime;[6] in 1999 the cost of crime (including correctional facilities, costs to criminals and victims, and prevention) exceeded $1 trillion, or $4,118 per American citizen.[7] In 1996, injury from a crime was more than twice as common as injury from a motor-vehicle accident. In addition, it should be noted that one police officer is killed every 53 hours; and in a year, 61,000 are assaulted and

19,000 are injured.[8] This is indeed carnage on a grand scale, and to a degree not experienced in other advanced nations.

I cited the crime rates for the current period at the outset of this chapter to correct an impression gained from the media and government spokesmen in recent years that the country is at last getting crime under control. This impression is clearly contradicted by the evidence. It is true, however, that crime rates fell in the '90s. According to victimization surveys, in 1995–96 violent crimes decreased 16 percent; in 1996–97, 7 percent; in 1997–98, 10 percent; and in 1999–2000, 15 percent. Similar decreases occurred for property crimes (with the exception of an insignificant decrease in 1998–99).[9] And crimes reported by the FBI based on police reports, as distinguished from those reported by victims in a survey, fell at about the same rate.[10]

While politicians and the police were quick to claim credit for these decreases, the major factor was a decline in the number of persons in the crime-prone age group. Men within the age bracket of 19 through 24 commit by far the majority of street crimes. Because the baby boomers were in the age group 35 to 52, and the second great wave of births placed men in the 17 or younger group, there was a slump in the crime-prone age. By the same token, juvenile crime began increasing again after the second baby boom came along,[11] and in fact, over the first decade of this century, youth crime is expected to increase *almost 30 percent.*[12]

In the late '70s, the drop in crime in subsequent decades was also predicted on the basis of birth statistics, and was borne out. As one analyst wrote: "With the passage of time, whatever the criminal justice policy, the incidence of crime will decrease as the members of these age groups grow older, and the size of new youth groups decline."[13] A new crime wave is expected in the present decade because ". . . by the year 2006, the number of teens aged 14 to 17 will be a fifth greater than it was in 1996, and the nation's teen cohort will be the largest since 1975."[14] If the current low rate of employment continues for the next several years (teenage unemployment in May 2004 was 17.2 percent), the combination of a youth bulge and the high unemployment rate among young people (and especially minorities) will produce a maelstrom of criminal behavior. But the chances of prolonged unemployment beyond the next year or so are slim— unless deflation sets in, in which case we can look forward to a perfect storm.

Although programs like Community Oriented Policing seem to have been effective in stemming a great deal of criminal behavior, the main response to crime in America has been incarceration. Recently, this response has overshadowed and displaced certain large-scale rehabilitation programs that had proven more cost-beneficial. In other words, in many cases "get tough" has replaced "get smart."

Imprisonment, Rehabilitation, and Parole

A major problem several decades ago was the lagging pace of prison construction. This lag was later reduced, but not sufficiently to keep pace with a rising tide of incarceration that reinvented undercapacity on a scale never experienced before, in spite of enormous sums spent on construction. In the 20 years from 1973 to 1993, spending on state correctional facilities increased 95 percent, a trend that continued in the '90s in spite of a decreasing crime rate.[15] What happened?

"Mandatory sentencing requirements and related court mandates are all contributing to this nearly unmanageable prison and jail population," according to a research agency in 1997 that focused on technological means of relieving overcrowding. "State prison systems [are] operating between 14% and 25% above their reported capacity."[16] Another source of increasing incarceration was the assault on drug crimes, to be discussed later.

The prison population increased over the past 11 years as follows:[17]

1992	1,295,150
1995	1,585,586
1998	1,816,931
2003	2,019,234

As a consequence of this splurge of imprisonment, by 2000 the United States had an incarceration rate that was eight times the European average. (It was 11.4 times the rate in Scandinavia and 5.5 times the rate in England/Wales.) The next highest rate, about half the U.S. rate, was found in South Africa.[18] And our longstanding reputation for having the highest rate of imprisonment of any nation in the world was impressively enhanced in the following year. In April 2003, the Justice Department announced that the prison and jail population had surpassed two million for the first time. The figure was 2,019,234, or 1 out of 104 persons 18 years of age or older living in the United States in 2000.[19] Who could deny that we live in the most "incapacitating" nation of all the advanced industrial countries? Moreover, it would be a mistake to assume that only the criminal is punished by incarceration. About 55 percent of male inmates and 60 percent of female inmates have children.

This mushrooming of the prison population has had several troublesome consequences. Most obviously, there is the price tag, which means that public funds are diverted from more productive or socially positive purposes. The cost of building and operating a prison cell is estimated to be $20,000 to $50,000 a year. This estimate does not include such costs as the lost labor-market productivity of inmates.[20] Over one-third of the $30 billion allocated in the Crime Act of 1996 was devoted to prison building, "the most expansive and costly [crime bill] in America's history."[21] This extravagance drained off funding from other state programs, such as education, which, as we have seen, is presently in dire straits along with other state services across the country. In fact, as early as the '80s, a 95 percent increase in state corrections spending occurred at a time when spending on higher education was decreasing 6 percent.[22]

Also resulting from overcrowding is more violence in prisons. A former secretary of corrections in two states who is a prison consultant has noted that in some places "there is a prison culture that tolerates violence, and it's been there a long time." And according to this expert, the problem has worsened with the need to hire guards who are inexperienced or undertrained to overcome the shortage of personnel. And since pay is low, turnover is high, and the rank-and-file who remain often rise quickly in the prison hierarchy to positions of author-ity, violence and other deprivations are more often tolerated and may even in-volve brutal treatment by guards.[23]

Another consequence of the pressure on state and federal budgets for build-ing and maintaining prisons and jails is reduced funds for prison educational programs, in spite of their proven cost-effectiveness. Reductions in these pro-grams have occurred in more than half of all state prisons since 1989, and virtu-ally all have eliminated post-secondary education. Yet, the higher the level of educational attainment among inmates, the lower the recidivism rate (that is, the rate of crimes committed after release), as indicated by the following figures:

> In Texas, the recidivism rate for those without college degrees was 60% . . . for degree holders a low 12% . . . In Ohio the respective figures were 40% vs. 18%; in New York state, 44.6% vs. 26.4% . . . A CURE-NY report . . . calcu-lates that post secondary correctional education alone would produce net na-tional average savings of hundreds of millions of dollars per year.[24]

A Rand study estimated that the Three-Strikes law (now found in a number of states in addition to California), which prescribes that felons found guilty of a third serious crime be locked up for 25 years to life, might reduce serious crime by 21 percent, but at a cost of $5.5 billion a year. A later study by Rand indi-cated that a combination of the graduation incentives and parent training could cut crime just as much for less than $1 billion.[25]

These findings of research show that the soaring expenditures for impris-onment have made alternative interventions more cost-effective, and yet, these programs are being cut back or ignored as either preventive or as supplemental programs. Given the high recidivism rates of released inmates who have not had the benefit of special programs, including programs that provide marketable skills, the benefit that society obtains from the warehousing of prisoners is mainly protection from predation during the term of their incarceration. But this gain comes at a far greater cost than if recidivism were reduced as well. For when a convict emerges from captivity, especially under our present economic conditions of high unemployment, the likelihood of his or her committing further offenses is quite high. The financial, social, psychological, and health costs of those offenses are also quite high.

As for becoming a repeat offender, according to the Department of Justice (2001), 67 percent of all those released in 1994 in 15 states were rearrested within three years.[26] Since only about 1 out of 100 violent offenders is arrested (which shows the inadequacy of law enforcement in general), it is quite likely that the crime rate of ex-convicts is much higher than rearrest statistics would indicate.

Nor is there a clear relationship between the sheer amount of time served in prison and recidivism, unless the term is long—which then makes going straight a function of the offender's having outgrown the crime-prone age. Witness, for example, a study in Florida which indicated that a term of more than five years was necessary to reduce the likelihood of repeat offenses.[27] Another Florida study found that a mere 4 percent improvement in recidivism is worth an estimated $65 million in savings to the criminal justice system and victims.[28]

Another consequence of overcrowding is that many who are sentenced will serve much less than their full term or be released on probation without any prison time served at all. And early release, of course, is not restricted to those who have been in educational or other effective rehabilitation programs. This rapidly-revolving-door policy undermines the credibility of the criminal justice system, which encourages additional violations of law, such as among ordinary recreational drug users. Moreover, we find that in 1998, felons sentenced to state prisons who received an average sentence of five years served on average only half their time.[29]

Are the problems of runaway costs for imprisonment and the burgeoning of the prison population insoluble? There are many who believe not, including virtually all the prison wardens of America.

A survey of prison wardens by Senator Paul Simon's subcommittee on the Constitution found that "92% believe that half of the offenders under their supervision could be released without endangering public safety." Moreover, "85% of the prison wardens . . . said that elected officials are not offering effective solutions to America's crime problem."[30] When, therefore, in the opening paragraph of this chapter I attributed the flaws of the system at least partly to "momentary political advantage" instead of rational design, I wasn't standing alone. It may gain votes to make laws that incarcerate more people, but it is hardly a rational form of policymaking when about half of those incarcerated do not pose a danger to society.

The wardens probably had in mind the huge population of nonviolent offenders, at least half of whom were drug offenders, for it has been this latter group that made the greatest contribution to the burgeoning prison population in the '80s and '90s. (Further, as we shall see below, their incarceration not only cost millions of dollars but had little or no effect on the illicit drug trade.) From 1986 to 1991, the population of drug offenders in prison rose nearly 300 percent.[31] In 1996, 61 percent of the commitments were for nonviolent offenses, of which 46 percent were for drug offenses.[32] From 1980 to 1997, there was an elevenfold increase in the number of imprisoned drug offenders.[33] Since 1996 the number arrested for drug offenses annually has been more than twice the number arrested for major violent crimes, and almost 80 percent of the drug arrests have been for simple possession. In all, as of March 2002, over 400,000 persons are in state and local prisons for drug offenses.[34]

As a consequence of this haul, in 2002: "the number in jail for drug offenses (about half a million) is greater than the entire jail population of western Europe."[35] The effect on the drug trade of this roundup of usual suspects seems to have been minimal. As the report of a cost-benefit analysis of imprisonment in three states (by the Manhattan Institute) has concluded: "The main effect of imprisoning drug sellers, we believe, is merely to open the market for another seller. Numerous studies of drug policy attest to the existence of this 'replacement' process . . . The imprisonment of a large number of drug offenders is not a cost-effective use of public resources."[36]

But don't drug offenders also commit other kinds of crimes, so that removing them from society reduces crime generally? This question is answered by a Rand Corporation study that found that, although drug offenders do commit other types of crime, they do so much less commonly than those arrested specifically for certain nondrug crimes. Thus, the arrest of drug offenders is not as effective in reducing other crimes as focusing on these other offenders would be. In view of the limited resources of the police and prison system, this would seem to be a powerful argument for paying less attention to drug offenders. As for reducing the use of drugs, the study also found that drug arrests had only a modest effect on consumption.[37]

Those who are imprisoned for drug offenses are not commonly exposed to treatment programs, and less so today than in the past. Projects in several states have shown a decrease in recidivism of as much as 65 percent for those who have completed a treatment program for addiction while imprisoned. As for savings in prison cost, a large-scale study in California found that each dollar spent for treatment saves seven dollars in future costs. A number of other studies have reached the same general conclusion.

However, according to the American Society of Addiction Medicine in 2001, information of this kind "does not seem to have received sufficient attention by legislators and other policy makers . . ." In addition, "many states have eliminated parole or other early-release options, so that a valuable way to induce prisoners to enter treatment programs has been lost."[38]

Although many states have found it necessary, on grounds of rapidly dwindling resources, to release prisoners early, parole and probation have been substantially reduced as a matter of present budgetary restrictions and past predetermined sentences: "Thirteen states and the federal government have gone as far as doing away with parole altogether, replacing it with a system of predetermined sentences and release times." According to the head of the Association of Paroling Authorities International: "A lot of this has been driven by legislation and political edict ... To eliminate [parole boards] from the criminal justice system is sort of foolhardy . . ."[39] The move away from parole started in the mid-1970s in reaction to rising crime rates. But the decline in these rates did not reverse the trend, quite possibly because money had to be diverted to prison construction and maintenance.

As for alternatives to imprisonment, such as community service or fines, studies have shown that they are just as effective as imprisonment in deterring certain kinds of crimes. But, as one criminologist has speculated, "the public is reluctant to accept fines or community service because those sanctions don't convey adequate moral condemnation of the criminal . . . Both liberal and conservative advocates have urged the use of alternative sentences for more than a decade, but progress has been slow."[40]

As a matter of fact, more professionally approved means of alternative treatment have been set aside in favor of popular notions about how to ensure that an offender will "go straight." For example, the notion of "shaming" the offender has led to a variety of new ways of dealing with offenders, including publication of their names in the newspapers or on billboards, requiring offenders to apologize on hands and knees, requiring them to wear a T-shirt emblazoned with his or her crime (like Hester Prynne?), and so on. These measures might gratify the righteousness of the public, but it is doubtful that they have much effect on offenders. One problem with this approach is that America is not a "shame culture," but a "guilt culture." To control deviant behavior by making a person feel that he or she has violated internalized values is the most effective means in such a culture—provided that the individual has actually internalized such values. Unfortunately, many have been "undersocialized," as sociologists call it.

In contrast to this internal source of normative control, the moral opinion of others, which is the mainspring of a "shame culture" (or, rather, a culture that stresses shame more than guilt, since all cultures feel guilt to some degree), is often utterly irrelevant to the mental universe of many persons who are alienated from their society or even in rebellion against it. And frequently the criminal justice system itself foments alienation and rebellion by enforcement of crimes without victims, such as involvement with drugs, or by patently racist behavior. If one feels abandoned by society, how can the opinions of that society toward one's behavior have any resonance?

Privatization of Prisons

A noteworthy part of the privatization trend in America has been played by corporations that have been awarded contracts by the government to take over the operation of prisons. In mid-2000, 86,625 inmates, or 6.1 percent of all federal and state inmates in some 30 states, were in private custody.[41] In 1998, revenues exceeded $1 billion. When for-profit prisons were resurrected in America by President Reagan in 1983 (they had been outlawed at the turn of the century), there were only 350 private inmates. What has been the impact of this trend over the past 20 years? In trying to answer this question, we need to step back and look at the larger picture of crime and punishment.

In the period 1980 to 1998, the overall prison population in America tripled. Since 1992 alone, it has increased 56 percent, as shown by the figures presented earlier. Earlier we saw that crime itself had decreased in the '90s. This odd divergence of incarceration and crime trends inspired the authors of a 2002 study to ask, "If crime is not on the rise, why are incarceration rates skyrocketing?"[42] The greatest increase in imprisonment has been for nonviolent crimes, and particularly drug offenses. (See the following section.) In other words, many offenses that formerly would not have been regarded as grounds for incarceration or, perhaps more importantly, grounds for lengthy sentences accounted for most of the imprisonment boom. Mandated sentencing, such as the Three-Strikes law, was largely responsible. But in the absence of a rise in crimes, why were mandated sentences implemented? One possible reason is the rise of privatization.

Could it be merely a coincidence that both prison privatization and the number of inmates increased together, in spite of a drop in the crime rate? One possible explanation for this correlation is that a third factor led to more imprisonment, which in turn led to privatization. One such factor could have been the rising tide of conservatism that prompted tougher laws with mandated sentences, which then inspired the privatizing of prisons to save money while also appealing to conservative sentiments. But in a period when the crime rate is falling, one would not expect even a conservative public to exercise strong initiative in demanding more stringent anti-crime laws (with the possible exception of California where the Three-Strikes law was invented). Politicians, however, can always improve their political chances by fanning the coals of public fear, thereby cultivating public pressure regardless of crime statistics or the cost of imprisonment. And this seems to have been the case in many instances. As the report of the Western Prison Project reminds us, "ever since the infamous Willy Horton ads were aired to discredit Democratic Presidential candidate Michael Dukakis in 1988, politicians from both political parties have had a morbid fear of appearing soft on crime."[43] And the report also notes that "contracting [with private firms to operate prisons] was not taken at the initiative of the correction agency, but was instead mandated by either the legislature or the chief executive of the jurisdiction, typically the governor,"[44] which points to a political motivation. Once having made a decision to swell the prison population for reasons of ideology or political benefit, a serious need for cost containment would arise because of increased construction and maintenance costs. And the main carrot held out to officials by proponents of privatization has been reduced cost.

The ascendancy of conservatism, however, might not be the only or even the main explanation for the simultaneous rise of privatization and the prison population. There is an alternative explanation, one that has the odor of a cynical exploitation of the opportunity to make a financial killing. And that explanation involves increased pressure on politicians by the private incarceration industry to enact laws that would swell the inmate population, thereby increasing profits. For it must not be overlooked that private operators elevate profits, first, by having a larger population of inmates and, second, by treating them more "efficiently," that is, in money-saving ways. The efficient processing of bulk resources is one of the chief means whereby manufacturing enterprises make a profit, and this economic imperative applies to the processing of humans as well as to the processing of physical resources. And although the percentage of private inmates in the nation is only 6.2 percent, changes in state or federal laws to accommodate the wishes of private operators or certain prisons would obviously apply to the entire prison system in a particular jurisdiction, including nonprivate facilities. Consequently, the population of inmates would expand *throughout* the state or nation.

Is there any evidence that private industry has aggressively promoted privatization (including the construction of new facilities) and, in particular, legislation that would incarcerate more persons? The answer is yes—substantial evidence. In fact, the industry banded together to promote the crafting of model legislation by the American Legislative Exchange Council (ALEC) whose Criminal Justice Task Force was chaired by the Director of Business Development for the largest private prison corporation in America. Substantial funds for ALEC came from several prison corporations. Subsequently, in the '90s, more than a thousand privatization bills were introduced in state legislatures, 22 percent of which became law. The two most frequently adopted bills were those that increased the incarceration rate, namely, Truth in Sentencing and Three Strikes, You're Out.[45]

Meanwhile, the corporate privatizers were endeavoring to influence candidates and officeholders by means of campaign contributions and lobbying. "In 1998," according to the Western Prison Project, "645 contributions to 361 candidates in 25 states (out of a total of 43 states surveyed) were made by prison corporations." And most of the contributions to lawmakers went to those "who would be considering corrections policy in the next legislative session." The amount contributed (more than half a million dollars) was almost as much as that given by the National Rifle Association. Moreover, 24 candidates for governorships received a total of $111,985, with winning candidates gaining 69 percent of this amount. Contributions to political party committees have been even more generous; more than $370,000 in Florida alone in 1998. Clearly, the industry has not been reluctant to promote its cause by urging passage of legislation favoring privatization and also more stringent laws that will swell the prison population.[46]

Unfortunately, there is no clear-cut evidence that private prisons have reduced either costs or recidivism. A comprehensive study by the General Accounting Office (GAO) in 1996, which reviewed the methodology and outcomes of a number of earlier studies, reported that one "could not conclude whether privatization saved money."[47] And there has been growing criticism of private prisons for resistance to unionization, increased escapes and inmate violence, cutting of costs in staffing and training (increasing the safety risk to personnel), reduction or loss of government oversight and accountability, violation of prisoners' rights with impunity, and standardization of inmate treatment and elimination of costly rehab programs.

Presumably as a consequence of these problems, some states have passed legislation that requires private prisons to meet the same standards as public ones, banned or suspended the construction of private prisons, and banned the export or import of prisoners. And substantial losses have been experienced by the industry on the stock market. Moreover, the private prison population declined by 6.1 percent in 2002 (mainly due to Texas).[48] And, finally, a survey in 1999 found that 60 percent agreed that "government is best suited to protect public safety—providing necessary security and preventing escape."[49]

Although the private prison boom might have peaked and begun a contraction, it is doubtful that pressure from the industry has evaporated. Moreover, the expected rise in crime over the coming years (see the earlier prediction based on demographic data) might rejuvenate enthusiasm for private industry to perform its cost-cutting magic in spite of an unproven record over a number of years. As long as the symbiosis between government and corporate enterprise is thriving in America, privatization will continue to be an attractive option in the minds of many politicians.

Since the problem of illegal drugs has played such a prominent part in the problem of coping with a burgeoning prison population, let us turn to this area for a brief look at current approaches, their side effects and reverse effects, and their popularity among the public. Reverse effects, by the way, are the hallmark of what have been called "regressive interventions," that is, interventions that make matters worse than before. The drug enforcement field seems to be a remarkably fertile hotbed for perverse consequences.

Drug Control: Enforcement or Prevention, Crime or Disease?

The preceding portrait of criminal justice in America suggests a system that has been suffering from overindulgence in regressive intervention for years, largely because of the priority of political interests over empirical research about the real state of affairs and the consequences of certain intervention efforts. To be honest, however, at the present time the government's true policy regarding illegal drugs is somewhat elusive, for its actions do not seem to coincide with its words. In addition to being shaped by considerations of political advantage, current government policy has a faint odor of corporatism, a factor that we have encountered at many points in earlier chapters. In fact, one might say quite literally that corporate business and the government of the United States are now joined at the head.

The drug strategy of the Bush administration has been stated quite clearly: "The President believes the most effective way to reduce the supply of drugs in America is to reduce demand for drugs in America by stopping drug use before it starts." This statement was released by the White House along with its 2003 budget request for "drug control." But when one examines the budget, one is struck by the fact that $45 million was slashed from the Center of Substance Abuse Prevention, and that, overall, more than two-thirds of the funds allocated for anti-drug efforts were devoted to law enforcement and interdiction.

One observer in the drug field clarified the apparent contradiction by pointing out that "when this administration thinks about prevention, all too often it means the $180 million anti-drug media campaign, an attempt to win hearts and minds through the power of advertising." For example, $3.5 million was spent for two advertisements during the Super Bowl.[50] This money, as well as the remaining funds for this ad campaign, goes to private advertising firms, of course. This might help explain why the ad campaign is funded at "three times the level of a program like Drug-Free Communities, which provides direct support to communities."[51]

Another reason that the administration might have adopted the rhetoric of prevention (and also rehabilitation) is the shift in public opinion from an emphasis on enforcement/punishment to an emphasis on prevention/rehabilitation in the past few years. "In 1994 . . . 48% favored addressing the causes of crime and 42% preferred the punitive approach. Since then there has been a significant movement toward the progressive view." In 2002, the combination of prevention and rehabilitation elicited support from 54 percent, whereas the approaches of punishment and enforcement won only 39 percent in a poll by Hart Associates. Further, 76 percent felt that too little emphasis was placed on prevention. These relative preferences were expressed by Republicans as well as Democrats. A similar shift occurred with regard to mandatory sentencing vs. leaving it to the discretion of judges. Even the majority of crime victims themselves (60 percent) believed that the top priority should be prevention and rehabilitation instead of the "warehousing" of nonviolent criminals.[52]

In terms of the federal budget, however, prevention and rehabilitation are by no means the top priorities of the administration. In its announcement of the drug control budget for 2003, the White House did underscore the budget's 6 percent growth for treatment, but then it also mentioned a 10 percent increase for border interdiction. In the final analysis, therefore, treatment wound up as only 20 percent of the $19.2 billion drug budget, or $3.8 billion. In contrast, the allocation for border interdiction and the Andean Initiative (in South America) alone added up to more than $3 billion, and there were many other enforcement expenses as well; together they amounted to more than *two-thirds* of the budget, compared with *one-fifth* for treatment.[53]

As for prevention, the White House announced a $15 million infusion of new money and highlighted the popular Drug-Free Communities Program, but said nothing about the ad campaign conducted by private industry, which received *three times* as much as the Drug-Free Communities Program.[54]

From this analysis of the budget, there appears to be a distinct disconnect between the wishes of the public and those of the Bush administration, a discrepancy that has been noted by others. While this discrepancy could be attributed to a "get tough" ideology on the part of conservatives in the administration, it is more easily explained by the bureaucratic momentum of the elaborate, highly costly efforts that were launched in the past, such as the Andean Initiative in South America (which includes protecting oil fields from the guerillas, who count the drug farmers among their constituents). And, of course, aggressive interdiction by the Coast Guard and Customs Service has been going on for years, not to mention the many other federal personnel involved in enforcement. Interventions of this kind and duration are extremely difficult to curtail, even when the public is expecting a shift of emphasis. Even when the strategy seems to be a failure, powerful constituencies and a mind-set that has prevailed for decades tend to keep it vigorously alive. To fully appreciate the force of this organizational momentum, one must confront the record with dispassion and evaluate the outcomes of a full-bore enforcement strategy.

The stunning failure of law enforcement to eradicate the illicit transport, sale, and consumption of proscribed drugs is underscored by the widespread trafficking and use of these drugs after some 60 years of aggressive enforcement effort. Apart from this failure, the side effects have been egregious and many, and include making the situation worse. They are well known by now: raising the price of drugs by lowering the supply with a consequent resort to crime and self-pauperization to support one's desire or addiction; the increase in court congestion by greater efforts to circumvent mandatory sentences; the criminogenic effect of undercover sellers and buyers of drugs who evoke illegal behavior from the public; the stimulus to corruption among police and other official personnel in drug enforcement; the fostering of an underground drug culture that is concealed from public health guardians and contributes to disease (e.g., from dirty needles); the alienation of drug-prone populations, including middle-class white youth, from the rule of law; the killings among drug gangs and their dealers; the alliance with unsavory leaders, including dictators abroad, and the violation of human rights on foreign soil; and on and on. And yet, the American people—in spite of their shift of support from enforcement to prevention and rehabilitation—are as far from legalizing and regulating drugs (which has been done in the Netherlands and Switzerland) as they are from the planet Mars, even though a majority (52%) feel that drug abuse should be treated "as a disease" instead of "as a crime" (32%).[55]

Finally, and by no means least in significance, it should be noted that prosecution of drug offenses falls disproportionately on blacks and Hispanics. Blacks make up 12 percent of the population and 13 percent of drug users; but they make up 38 percent of the arrests for drug offenses, 59 percent of those convicted for drug offenses, and 63 percent of those arrested for drug trafficking.[56] This selective enforcement of the drug laws of the United States has been a prominent feature of criminal justice for many years, and contributes to the shocking statistic that ". . . the chances of a black man being locked up some time in his life are one in four."[57]

A classical Marxist would view this instance of institutionalized discrimination as a means whereby the capitalists control the alienated *lumpenproletariat* by legal incapacitation. Although it is hard to believe that the "capitalists" have conspired to achieve this result, it does seem as though, willy-nilly, this is the way that things have worked out. In any event, it is quite clear that the criminal justice system of America is far from being color-blind, and perhaps even farther from being immune to the political dictates of legislators who are ignorant of, or indifferent to, the carefully compiled evidence of what is wrong with the system. As pointed out in chapter 1, America is far behind European nations in regular monitoring and reporting of critical facts in "social reports." The consequence is a crippled society, and law enforcement is one of the organs of the body politic that is most severely impacted. Nowhere is this crippling effect more in evidence than in our unique embrace of capital punishment.

Capital Punishment

In 1997, 40 countries carried out executions; in 2001, only 27 did so.[58] The trend has been definitely downward. Yet, the United States has maintained its unique standing as the *only* country in the industrialized world that executes anyone.[59] (In order to be accepted as a member of the European Union, a nation must not have the death penalty.) At the end of 2002 there were 3,557 persons on death row in America.[60] This represented an increase of 38 percent over 1992, and of 234 percent over 1982. Clearly, the number of persons facing execution increased enormously in the past 20 years. There was a decline of 1 percent since 2000, however, perhaps because of increased criticism and legal scrutiny of capital punishment cases. But this slight ebb is hardly a sign of imminent abolition.

We even execute juvenile offenders in America, a practice that is shared with only six countries: Iran, Pakistan, Nigeria, Saudi Arabia, Yemen, and the Democratic Republic of the Congo.[61] In 2002 there were 83 death row inmates in the United States sentenced as juveniles, or 2 percent of death row inmates.[62] This practice was abandoned in almost all other nations because of the U.N. Convention on the Rights of the Child and several other international treaties and agreements. Unfortunately, the United States is not fond of international agreements, as I make clear in chapter 7, and has refused to ratify the Convention on the Rights of the Child, which makes it one of only two nations that has so refused.[63]

The leader in executions in America is the state of Texas. Since reintroducing the death penalty in 1976, Texas has executed 271 men and women, which represents one-third of the state executions carried out in the nation.[64] The president, who was governor of Texas, has stated his personal support for execution of alleged capital offenders. In spite of the president's assertion that deterrence is the only reason for the death penalty, however, the overwhelming majority of criminologists and law enforcement officials say it has *no* deterrent value.

> [In a survey of 67 current and former presidents of the American Society of Criminology, Academy of Criminal Justice Sciences, and the Law and Society Association,] over 80 percent believe the existing research fails to support a deterrence justification for capital punishment. Over three-fourths believe that increasing the frequency of executions, or decreasing the time spent on death row before execution would not produce a general deterrent effect.[65]

Police chiefs and county sheriffs hold the same opinion: only 1 percent choose the death penalty as one of the primary ways to reduce crime, according to another survey.[66] Moreover, most of these professionals—specifically, 87 percent of the criminologists and 57 percent of the police chiefs—believe that it is accurate to say that "debates about the death penalty distract Congress and state legislatures from focusing on real solutions to crime problems."[67] The politicization of capital punishment, as well as of all other "get tough" policies, is a fact of American life that probably has more impact on the way we deal with capital offenders than all the conferences and books about crime and punishment by experts put together.

If the absence of a deterrent effect is not enough to undermine our faith in the death penalty, then we might ponder its unjust application among racial or ethnic groups. Although only 12 percent of Americans are blacks, 41 percent of the 3,122 people on death row in 1996 were blacks. This, of course, could be partly due to blacks more often committing murder. But when one looks at the color of the victim, one discovers that "those who killed whites were 4.3 times as likely to receive the death penalty as those who killed blacks. And blacks who killed whites were most likely of all to die."[68] Only racism can explain the skewed application of the ultimate penalty revealed by these data.

Even if execution had a deterrent effect, cost-benefit considerations demonstrate that it is cheaper just to lock up someone for life. Because of the costly court and appeal expenses that ensue from a sentence of death, "roughly it is costing us $2 million more to execute someone than it would be to keep them in jail for life."[69]

Finally, there is the fact that a shocking number of persons on death row have been found improperly tried or have been proven completely innocent. According to a Columbia University study, "68 percent of all death sentences reviewed by appellate courts between 1973 and 1995 were reversed because of serious error."[70] In recent years, 112 persons on death row have been released, and 60 percent of all cases have been found to contain seriously reversible errors. At least 12 were found innocent on the basis of DNA tests.[71] Even Texas has had to admit error! Seven people who had spent between 7 and 15 years on death row have been released on grounds that they were innocent.[72]

President Bush's opinion about the deterrent value of capital punishment notwithstanding, Americans have begun to shift their position on the issue. The news of releases from death row and of the unfairness of the process (often due to sheer legal ineptitude on the part of attorneys for the defendants) have been responsible for this change of attitude. In February 2000, 64 percent of Americans supported a moratorium on executions pending a resolution of questions about fairness,[73] and two bills have been introduced in Congress for a national moratorium. In June 2002, the Supreme Court weighed in by banning the death penalty for the mentally retarded.[74] Executions declined 13 percent in 2000, but the number of 85 still made that year the second highest since reinstatement of the penalty in 1976.[75]

As for the execution of juveniles, five courts have outlawed this practice for persons under 18, and the Supreme Court has rejected an appeal challenging the death penalty for such persons as unconstitutional. The decision was a close call of five to four,[76] however. Indeed, abolition of the penalty for all does not seem to be a near-term prospect. In spite of favoring a moratorium to study the whole question of capital punishment in 2000, the public was still inclined to favor it. At that time it was found that 51 percent believed that the penalty was applied fairly,[77] and in 2001, 67 percent believed in the penalty in general and only 7 percent opposed it.[78]

But perhaps the most challenging trend for anti-death advocates will be the revelations that might come out of moratorium hearings. Clemency hearings in Illinois have disclosed the gruesome details of several murders, and those revelations sparked an outburst of public support for the death penalty. A law professor who had led the attack on the Illinois law characterized the outcry as follows: "The pain and passion of these families [of the victims] is deafening. It's so overwhelming that people are forgetting all the problems that got us here." In fact, two major papers urged that the hearings be terminated.[79] If future hearings take the same turn, the campaign to abolish capital punishment could backfire.

But not even the public furor in Illinois, which was fanned by the local media, deterred the out-going governor from taking a historic step. Only a short time before leaving office, Illinois Governor Ryan commuted the death sentence of 167 persons, and he freed four others on grounds of their having been physically abused to extract a confession. As the governor explained, "Our capital system is haunted by error," and he referred in particular to the possible effects of race and poverty on one's receiving the ultimate penalty.[80]

Neither this action nor the anti-death penalty activism of many Americans, however, has dissuaded the federal government from promoting the penalty. Only three weeks after the governor's action, for example, the U.S. Attorney General took the following action, as reported by the *New York Times*:

> Attorney General Ashcroft has ordered U.S. attorneys in New York and Connecticut to seek the death penalty for a dozen defendants in cases in which prosecutors had recommended against or did not ask for capital punishment
> . . .[81]

By February 2003 the Attorney General had overruled 28 attorneys who had sought a lesser penalty in capital cases.[82]

As much as one might disagree with the policy of capital punishment and its appeal to the American people, it is not fair to assert that insistence on the death penalty is a mere matter of "vengeance" and therefore deserving of contempt. The members of a society need a sense that norms of "justice" suited to the crime are being observed in order to preserve their commitment to society's institutions. What is overlooked is that this particular means of applying justice is seriously flawed, not only morally but pragmatically. First, it is irreversible, so that any mistakes cannot be corrected. Second, it has been shown to be subject to deficiencies in the justice system, such as racism and inept attorneys or judges. Third, it is more costly than life imprisonment. Fourth, it is not effective as a crime deterrent. And fifth, it is inhumane, which matches the inhumanity of the act that is being punished. There is nothing wrong with enforcing justice in such a way as to preserve the people's faith in society as a moral community, but this is not the way. On the contrary, those who are opposed to the penalty might well have *their* faith in their community shaken to its foundations because capital punishment is perpetuated in spite of overwhelming expert opinion and evidence in opposition to it.

The conclusion that the criminal justice system has been derelict when handling capital punishment cases has broader implications. If such high-stakes cases are sometimes legally deficient (two-thirds of appealed cases were reversed in a 22-year period), or racially motivated, what must be the state of affairs with respect to more ordinary crimes of property or violence? Surely race and poverty play as important a role in judicial proceedings in noncapital offenses as they do in capital offenses. And surely the legal insufficiencies that have been disclosed in capital cases also stalk other types of cases, and probably much more so, owing to the limited amount of time and attention given to more ordinary, lower-profile cases. Is it possible that to a significant degree America's criminal justice system, which is often held up to the world as a model, is really a charade of justice?

*   *   *

The clear impression that one gains from this portrait of crime and punishment in the United States is that time is moving backward. Much of this atavistic behavior is due to the expansion of imprisonment as a solution to crime, which preempts other ways of dealing with the problem. These other ways include alternatives to incarceration, rehabilitation and educational programs that have proven much more successful than sheer incarceration, an army of youth workers in the inner cities, a new war on poverty, more federal support for drug prevention and rehabilitation in the community as contrasted with enforcement, the outlawing of privatization, and the resuscitation of our probation and parole system. The elimination of capital punishment is, of course, another necessity in a society that ostensibly values impartial, humane, and rational justice and the decent opinion of mankind. At the present time America's record in endeavoring to realize these basic values in the preservation of law and order is abysmal, both pragmatically and morally.

6

The Environment, Energy, and Natural Resources

Energy Consumption, Pollution, and Global Warming

The wealth of America is nowhere better attested than in its extraordinarily high level of energy consumption. With only 4 percent of the world's population, it consumed 30 percent of the world's energy in 1998. In contrast, western Europe consumed only 17 percent, the Middle East 5 percent, and Africa 3 percent.[1] This historically unprecedented energy binge comes at a high price, however, and especially in a nation that is largely dependent on high-energy-consuming products from manufacturers who are themselves voracious consumers of power. The price to society is pollution of the air, water, and earth; chronic illness; premature death; and also possibly global cataclysm. This is the only conclusion that can be drawn from the hard data that follow.

As for the magnitude of pollution, there is no other way of putting it: The United States has been the filthiest nation on earth. And though its greater filth has not consisted so much of dirt and grime, it has emitted poisonous substances that have affected millions of people, both inside and outside its borders. Our country released more carbon dioxide emission per capita in 1998 than any other OECD nation, namely 20 tons.[2] In 2002, about half of all the carbon dioxide released by industrialized nations and a quarter of the global total was produced by the United States.[3] In comparison with the British, Germans, or Japanese, America accounts for twice as much gas emission.[4]

America has not only been the abode of more chemicals, but in the '90s the amount of debris inhaled per person a year was estimated at 81 pounds, more than three times the amount inhaled per person in all the European OECD countries combined.[5] Similarly, in the '90s, the amount of municipal waste per person per year in America was more than double the amounts in Japan, the UK, Germany, France, or Italy, and 37 percent more than in Canada, the next highest in waste per person.[6] But the more serious problem has been with chemical pollution, although it has lessened in the past decade.

The Environmental Protection Agency defines "nonattainment areas" as those that persistently fail to meet air quality standards. In 2002, the agency designated over 180 such areas in the United States, covering more than 100 million people, or more than a third of the entire population.[7] And as many as 142 million Americans live in areas where ozone levels could endanger their health.[8] On August 14, 2002, it was announced that "it has been unhealthy to breathe the air in the Washington, D.C., area on ten of the last fourteen days."[9] According to some estimates, NAFTA has "doubled the pollution along the Mexican border where the American factories have moved."[10]

But not only have we fouled the air. Rivers, lakes, and shorelines have also been contaminated with our waste. According to the Natural Resources Defense Council in 2002, "one-half of our nation's lakes and one-third of our rivers are too polluted to be completely safe for swimming or fishing ... Raw sewage, poison run-off and other pollution have caused more than 22,000 beach closings or advisories since 1988 ..."[11] In addition to these sources of pollutants, radioactive waste is said by the Council to be "mistakenly thrown away 45 times a year in America";[12] and 70 million computers, which contain lead, mercury, and other hazardous substances, have been deposited in landfills.[13] Cellphones, too, are hazardous inasmuch as they contain "persistent and bioaccumulative toxic chemicals, or PBTs, which have been associated with cancer or other reproductive, neurological and developmental disorders," and these also have been sent to landfills.[14] As many as 91 industrial compounds and pollutants are found in the blood and urine of the average American.[15] Yet far from posing a financial burden, the economic benefits of pollution control over the past 10 years have exceeded the costs of compliance by a factor of five to seven times, according to a 2003 study by the Office of Management and the Budget.[16]

These facts about the health hazards of pollution and cost of control suggest that all the activism, environmental laws, and money necessary to bring it under control are well worth it. So let's look more closely and comprehensively at certain common pollutants and their health effects.

Ozone. [R]epeated exposure to high levels of ozone over several months or more can produce permanent structural damage in the lungs ... Ozone is also responsible for several billion dollars of agricultural crop yield loss in the U.S. each year.[17]

[Nitrogen oxide, which is important in forming ozone,] can irritate lungs and lower resistance to respiratory infections such as influenza ... [increase the] incidence of acute respiratory illness in children ... Acid rain ... [destroys] fish and plant life.[18]

[Sulfur dioxide can cause] respiratory illnesses, alterations in pulmonary defenses, aggravation of existing cardiovascular disease ... [and] chronic lung disease. [It can also damage trees and crops, and cause acidification of lakes and streams, and corrosion of buildings and monuments.][19]

Lead can affect kidneys, liver, nervous system . . . [cause] anemia, kidney disease, reproductive disorders . . . seizures, mental retardation . . . [and] osteoporosis.[20]

[Carbon monoxide is] most serious for those who suffer . . . cardiovascular disease . . . [and causes] visual impairment, reduced work capacity, reduced manual dexterity, poor learning ability, and difficulty in performing complex tasks.[21]

[Particulate matter (PM) causes] damage to lung tissue, cancer, or asthma . . . Thirty thousand die each year from fine particles pollution . . .[22] 20–30% of children have symptoms of asthma, which is the number one cause of lost school days.[23]

Overall, 4 percent of U.S. deaths are due to air pollution exposure, and two-thirds of Americans are at high risk of cancer from toxic chemicals.[24] Clearly, the degradation of health that is caused by pollution belies any notion that the issue is exaggerated.

Moreover, we need to recognize that it is not only the health of Americans that is at stake, but the health, wealth, happiness, and very existence of everyone in the world through the phenomenon known as "global warming." If the prediction is reliable, the world faces a future of increased flooding, severe storms, and droughts owing to the emission of "greenhouse gases." Here is the prediction in a nutshell: "global mean surface temperature will rise by between 1.4 and 5.8 degrees centigrade during the current century because of anthropogenic greenhouse gas emissions."[25]

Nor has this prediction been kept a secret from our government. In 1989, Dr. James Hansen, head of NASA's Goddard Institute for Space Studies, testified at congressional hearings, according to a summary by the National Academy of Science, and informed the representatives that "the probability of a hot summer has increased from 33% for the period 1950 through 1979 to 50% currently, and if current trends continue, the probability of a hot summer will reach 60% some time during the 1990s."[26]

A foretaste of what might unfold on a larger scale has been provided by Senator Ted Stevens of Alaska. Only a few years ago he reported the subsidence of Alaskan towns and crumbling of roads where permafrost used to serve as a foundation, the inundation of villages by seawater, the proliferation of beetles that have destroyed four million acres of spruce forest, and the infestation of mosquitoes in the northernmost city of Barrow. In addition, the possibility of catastrophic forest fires and the destabilization of the Alaskan pipeline have been reported by experts. These devastating effects are the result of a rise in temperature of about 5 degrees in summer and 10 degrees in winter over the past 30 years or so.[27]

The source of the "greenhouse effect" is the warming of the earth's atmosphere by the sun's radiation, which, after being absorbed by the earth and reradiated as infrared, is absorbed by the atmosphere and reflected *back* upon the earth by carbon dioxide and water vapor. Thus, the gas that mainly contributes to global warming is carbon dioxide. The United States accounts for 36.1 percent of all carbon dioxide emissions in the world.[28]

The major source of this dangerous pollutant is motor vehicles, which use two-thirds of the oil consumed in our country. This level of pollution is not an iron law of nature, however; it is the result of burning more fuel than necessary to power our vehicles. If the average mileage consumption in America of 20 miles per gallon were raised to 33 miles per gallon, America would no longer need to import oil from the Persian Gulf, according to the Natural Resources Defense Council.[29] The technology exists today (and has existed for some time) to meet this higher standard, but has not yet been applied. America's transportation system, therefore, is the chief culprit in the production of greenhouse gas, accounting for one-third of the emissions in the United States. Most of these emissions (60%), a large portion of which is unnecessary, are from cars and light trucks—reminding us once again of the ubiquitous role of American corporations in our national life.[30]

But why, one might ask, are carbon emissions such an urgent problem, apart from the slow warming of the earth by the greenhouse effect, a problem that our scientists will undoubtedly find a way to remedy?—or so we tell ourselves. In other words, why be alarmed about the problem today? Here is a partial answer [my summary]:

> It was estimated in 1991 that motor vehicle pollution caused roughly 50–70 million respiratory-related restricted activity days, 852 million headaches, approximately 20,000–46,000 cases of chronic respiratory illness, 530 cases of cancer from air toxins, and 40,000 premature deaths.[31]

Numerous other negative impacts on health have been documented since that time. See, for example, the effects of carbon monoxide on humans mentioned earlier in our list of major pollutants.

One possible solution, or at least one means of reducing the volume of auto pollution in America, is greater use of public transportation. Clearly, the fewer light trucks and cars on the road, the less the pollution. But America's romance with the auto and SUV, and the flimsy efforts of local, state, and national governments to improve public transportation (largely owing to the lobbyists and campaign funding of the auto industry) have rendered this approach utopian—but only in America. Europe and the Far East have left America far behind in the development of public transportation. Thus, "there is no frequent, reliable, super-fast connection between most of the metropolises of America," in the words of an Italian observer. "U.S. governments spend about 24% of their transportation money on public transportation (the rest was spent on roads), whereas Europeans spend 40% to 60% on public transportation."[32] Consequently, in the '90s America had the smallest percentage of travelers using public transportation of nine developed countries reporting, namely, only 1 percent. Japan reported 18 percent, Germany, 11 percent, and the UK, 8 percent. The mean percentage of the eight countries (aside from America) was 12.4 percent, or 12 times the percentage in America.[33] Thus, in 2000 the Texas Transportation Institute estimated that "congestion costs the drivers of seventy-five urban areas a combined total of almost $70 billion in wasted fuel and time."[34]

The possible savings in fuel consumption and pollution costs through constructing and using more public transportation are staggering. If only one in ten Americans used public transportation, according to the *American Public Transportation News,* "the U.S. would be able to reduce carbon dioxide emissions by more than 25% of the standard set by the Kyoto agreement [on global warming]." Further, if one in five Americans used public transportation for regular daily travel, they would cut carbon dioxide "by the equivalent of nearly 20 percent of the CO_2 emitted from fuel burned for residential uses and more than 20% of all CO_2 emitted by commercial enterprises." In the final analysis, "for every passenger mile traveled, public transportation is twice as fuel-efficient as private automobiles, sports utility vehicles (SUVs) and light trucks."[35]

While pollution comes from a number of sources, including factories and small businesses, motor vehicles take first place for their contribution to both health hazards and global warming by carbon emissions. What has our government done about this potentially fatal public nuisance?

The main effort by government was the 1975 Act of Congress establishing Corporate Average Fuel Economy standards (CAFE), which set goals for manufacturers of 27.5 miles per gallon for passenger cars and 20.7 miles per gallon for light trucks.[36] In order to evade the standard for passenger cars, the industry created the SUV and was able to exempt it from the 27.5-mpg requirement by having it classified as a light truck, thanks to the acquiescence of the government. Since that time, SUVs, together with minivans and pickups, have become increasingly popular; and in fact, in 2001 sales of these vehicles exceeded the sales of cars.[37] This increase in SUV sales, which augmented our dependence on foreign oil and worsened global warming, occurred in spite of existing technology that could lower the fuel consumption of SUVs. The crescendo of SUV sales, compared with the sales of other automobiles (an increase by a factor of seven), has meant that today "the average vehicle travels less on a gallon of gas than it did in 1980," according to the Union of Concerned Scientists.[38] Simply put, "SUVs . . . emit one-third more global-warming pollutants than cars."[39]

Meanwhile, the auto industry has devoted its attention to increasing horsepower, vehicle weight, and acceleration *instead* of fuel economy. In point of fact, auto manufacturers have spent 53 percent of new technology for power since the mid-1980s[40] while, as mentioned above, "fuel efficiency overall is no better than it was in 1980."[41] As for development of new, uninstalled technology for fuel efficiency, the auto companies have come up with experimental designs that can increase mileage to 100 miles per gallon.[42] According to the Natural Resources Defense Council, if fuel economy standards for new cars and light trucks were raised to just 40 miles per gallon by 2011 through such technology, "we would save 15 times more oil than the Arctic Refuge is likely to produce over the next 50 years."[43]

The importance of these facts can only be fully appreciated by our candidly recognizing that we have only 3 percent of the world's oil reserves, but consume 25 percent of the world's supply,[44] and that America's energy use has increased 30 percent since 1973, whereas our production of energy has increased only 13 percent.[45]

And what has Congress been doing recently to reduce energy consumption? In March 2002, the Senate defeated stricter gas-mileage standards, which had already been defeated in the House in 2001. After the defeat in the Senate, a new bill then authorized the National Highway Traffic Safety Administration to determine the appropriate standards.[46] Why were the stricter standards defeated? The answer would seem to be obvious. The average campaign contribution received from the auto industry by the 62 senators who opposed the bill was about $19,000, compared with $6,000 for those who supported the bill. Of those who received the most from the industry ($74,000 or more), 10 of the 11 senators opposed the bill. The one exception was John McCain, who, together with Senator Kerry, had prepared the bill.[47]

The explanation given for stalling on any effort to improve fuel efficiency—a measure that would reduce our dependency on foreign oil, protect the health of Americans, and possibly protect the world and its people from disaster—is threefold: to protect the jobs of auto workers, prevent more highway fatalities from the downsizing of cars, and preserve the "free market." Job loss and auto fatalities are the reasons voiced by President Bush and his party leaders in Congress for opposition to improvement in fuel efficiency. But it has been pointed out by the supporters of CAFE that jobs were not lost when the earlier standards were implemented. (See, for example, the statement of Congressman Sherwood Boehlert (R-NY) before the Senate Commerce Committee during hearings on CAFE reforms, December 6, 2001.) As for interfering with the free market, it is obvious that all consumer regulations interfere with the market, inasmuch as they restrict what consumers can buy, for reasons of health or safety, and yet the free market does not seem to have been defeated in America.

Concern over increased fatalities from the downsizing of vehicles is a more serious matter, especially since it is the most alarming objection to the average car buyer. This focus of attention on possible fatalities was engendered by a

National Academy of Science report which stated that 1,300 to 2,600 additional fatalities *might* have been caused by past downsizing.[48] This surmise was seized upon by supporters of the auto industry as grounds for rejecting any further raising of fuel standards. For example, a press release of the Competitive Enterprise Institute had the headline: "New Study Demonstrates Lethal Effects of Federal Auto Fuel Economy Standards;" and included in the text: "We support an appropriations freeze to prevent this deadly law from becoming any deadlier."[49]

The report of the National Academy contained a caveat: ". . . the actual effects [on safety] would be uncertain, and any adverse safety impact could be minimized or even reversed, if weight and size reduction were limited to heavier vehicles." Two scientists in the group that prepared the report persuasively refuted the idea that increased fatalities would automatically result, or had resulted in the past, from downsizing.[50] Nevertheless, the surmise about fatalities was cited as the basis for the Bush administration's resistance to higher standards. As the Senate Republican Conference said in a release: "The Administration is deeply concerned about [the Academy's] findings about the adverse impact the current CAFE program has on safety."[51]

This appeal to the specter of highway fatalities would seem to be especially obtuse in view of the following facts about SUVs reported in the *Washington Spectator*, vehicles that have all but crowded smaller cars off the market.

> SUVs are three times more likely to roll over in an accident, and emit one-third more global-warming pollutants than cars . . . [They are also] uniquely dangerous to other motorists, inflicting head, chest and leg injuries up to eight times as severe as those caused by other passenger vehicles.[52]

The obvious solution is to reduce the size, weight, or both of SUVs, as suggested by the National Academy's report (see above). This should be done in any case, regardless of the issue of fuel efficiency, owing to SUVs' danger to their occupants as well as other motorists. They are simply death traps for all concerned, it would seem. And smaller vehicles could be made somewhat larger without increasing fuel consumption. As the American Council for an Energy Efficient Economy has noted:

> Making heavier vehicles lighter (but not smaller) and making lighter cars larger (but not heavier) would not only increase safety but also increase fuel economy. We project a fuel economy increase of over 50% in association with these safety measures.[53]

Actually, since the time of the National Academy report, cars have been getting larger. But in reviewing this controversy, it is impossible to escape the conclusion that something besides safety is prompting the industry and its political allies to resist modifying the vehicles that they manufacture in the direction of more fuel economy. And the word for it is profit.

Profits per SUV sold are $10,000 to $20,000, and SUVs account for almost half of current sales.[54] Not surprisingly, then, $10 billion has been spent since 1990 on advertising to persuade Americans to buy SUVs instead of ordinary passenger cars.[55] It should also come as no surprise, therefore, that the auto industry had record profits in 2000.[56] As if these profits were not enough, the president has proposed tripling the tax deduction for small-business owners who purchase the largest SUVs and pickups.[57]

Nor is it a foregone conclusion that the price of cars would need to rise owing to compliance with improved efficiency standards. Although the industry claimed that complying with the 1993 fluorocarbon regulations would raise prices by $1,200, the industry admitted four years later that the costs were down to as little as $40.[58]

The industry is expert, however, at alarming consumers about the impact of compliance with higher fuel standards. Early in 2002 it mounted a multi-million-dollar ad campaign in rural areas to persuade consumers that they would lose their work vehicles if the new CAFE standards, introduced in the Senate by Kerry and McCain, were passed into law. Senators were deluged with protests from rural areas and the bill was defeated, as noted earlier.[59] But the most powerful inducement for support of the industry in Congress is campaign contributions, supplemented by lobbying.

The automotive sector contributed $4,832,322 to the 2001–2002 campaigns of the present incumbents of Congress, with 65 percent going to Republicans and 35 percent to Democrats.[60] And Congress is the target of massive lobbying by the industry, particularly on the issue of reducing fuel consumption by means of CAFE. In fact, 139 automotive companies have formed a Coalition for Energy Choice to oppose fuel economy regulation.[61]

Nor has the administration been forgotten by the industry. At least two of their crusaders have become members of the administration, not to mention those with past close ties to an oil industry that appreciates the auto industry's business. Contributions from the auto industry to the president's 1999–2000 campaign amounted to $1,272,497, and from the transportation sector as a whole, $2,381,474. In addition, Bush received more money from the oil and gas industry "than any other federal candidate for the last decade," according to the Center for Responsive Politics, an amount that came to $1.8 million.[62]

Concerning appointments of administration personnel with an auto industry background, one of Bush's three top advisers, Andrew Card, the White House Chief of Staff, was General Motors' chief lobbyist. Before working for GM, "Card had been the CEO of the industry's trade group, the American Automobile Manufacturers, which was the lead lobbying group against stricter fuel emission standards."[63] Moreover, Bush's Secretary of Energy, Spencer Abraham (who had served one term as a senator from Michigan, the nation's auto-manufacturing state), received more money from the auto industry when he ran for the Senate than any other candidate, namely $700,000. A top contributor to that campaign (Daimler-Chrysler) is currently introducing an extra large SUV "considered a 'military spin-off'" that is one foot longer than other SUVs with a mileage per gallon of about 10 miles. The coalition of auto manufacturers mentioned earlier that is fighting the fuel economy regulations donated $178,950 to Abraham's Senate campaign in 1999–2000.[64] In all, Abraham has received $994,650 from the transportation sector, 71 percent of which came from the automotive industry. Additionally, he has received $513,925 from the Energy/Natural Resources sector. Automotive was the second largest contributor to Abraham's campaign out of 20 industry sources listed for all candidates.[65]

In view of these ties to the industry, it is understandable that the deadline for issuing a new fuel economy standard for 2004 light trucks was ignored by the administration, which left the CAFE standard where it was in 1996, namely, 20.7 miles per gallon. And, of course, the industry has lobbied the administration not to increase the standard. As the director of the Natural Resource Defense Council's Climate Center has remarked, "The White House keeps insisting that America must reduce dependence on foreign oil, but it steadfastly resists raising fuel economy standards that would save billions of gallons of gas."[66] Several months after this statement, the administration announced that it had agreed to an increase in the standard for light trucks from 20.7 miles per gallon to 21.2, and that the industry would have until 2007 to make the change. In comparison with the change requested by critics, the urgency of taking drastic action, and the availability of appropriate technology, this new rule seems to be a petty token designed to undercut the administration's critics in the public mind.

What we appear to be witnessing is an extravaganza of legalized corruption at the behest of industry that has seemingly escaped the attention of the public, largely because of the mainstream media's lack of coverage. This lack of coverage is fairly common with regard to business issues that concern only a single industry, as contrasted with businesswide issues, such as the minimum wage. (See chapter 10 on the difference in treatment of "particularistic" vs. "unifying" issues.) Where does the public really stand on the question of greater fuel efficiency?

Public opinion surveys, interestingly enough, show strong support for improvements in fuel efficiency. For example, in March 2001, a Gallup poll found that 85 percent were in favor of mandates for more fuel-efficient cars, and an ABC News/*Washington Post* survey found that 89 percent favored government requirements to improve fuel efficiency.[67] While this would appear to highlight a fundamental divergence between industry and the public, one must accept the results of public opinion polls on this issue with caution. As one industry analyst has remarked: "There's no evidence that Americans in large numbers care about fuel economy. They always answer 'yes' on surveys, but then buy SUVs. It's like asking people if they want to lose weight and they say 'yes,' but then they go out and buy chicken-fried steak and potatoes."[68] The purchase of SUVs is not a physical addiction like eating food with high amounts of sugar or trans fat, but it does seem to reflect a strong desire based on a greater sense of security behind the wheel of a large vehicle and also on considerations of social status. If all of one's neighbors have SUVs sitting in their driveways, it would take a true maverick to buy an ordinary car. In fact, gas mileage ranks 20th among 35 features that Americans consider when purchasing a new car or truck.[69] As already mentioned, the sales of SUVs, minivans, and pickups in 2001 surpassed the sales of traditional, more fuel-efficient vehicles.[70]

This state of affairs attests to a serious, recurrent problem in America: The shaping and appeasement of public taste by an industry that cares little, if at all, about social costs, purchases the support of government and the indifference (or censorship) of the mainstream media, which depends on its ads for survival (see chapter 10 on the media), and then justifies its inertia by ringing appeals to free markets, employment, and flimsy evidence of the alarming side effects that would ensue from reforming its detrimental practices. Thus, all four partners—industry, the public, the media, and government—enter into symbiotic bondings that degrade the health, education, economic well-being, and quality of life of Americans.

This functional bonding of sectors is so cohesive that well-intentioned homilies are poignant cries in the wilderness—because not even a combination of science, common sense, and the self-interest of victims can dissolve it. One such voice in the wilderness had this to say: "Maximizing profits at the expense of human and environmental health is not a god-given right. Government's role is supposed to be to set standards that benefit all, not just a few powerful industries."[71]

Unfortunately, the American government at this historical moment disagrees with this particular definition of its role. Michael Smith, the Assistant Secretary of Energy for fossil energy, has explained his role as follows: "how best to utilize taxpayers' dollars to benefit industry."[72] This view of corporations as clients of government rather than servants of the public interest (the latter view having been expressed by President Grover Cleveland, among others), is the norm of the current conservative administration. To give another example of the official endorsement of this outlook: "During his first visit to Capitol Hill, Powell [chairman of the *regulatory* Federal Communications Commission] referred to media corporations simply as 'our clients.'"[73] Recent efforts by that commission to deregulate ownership of media outlets (see chapter 10) is a perfect reflection of this attitude.

The American people have not completely withdrawn, however, from the field of battle on the issue of automotive fuel emissions. In the absence of protection by the federal government, the states have begun to take action. A new law in California made it the first state to try to regulate greenhouse gases from automobiles in an effort to combat global warming by promoting hybrid-engine vehicles. This law, which was passed in spite of a multi-million-dollar advertising campaign mounted by the Alliance of Automobile Manufacturers, directed the California Air Resources Board to develop rules to achieve "maximum feasible and cost-effective" reductions in emissions by 2005 and to implement the rules starting with the 2009 models.[74] According to a statewide poll, 80 percent of Californians were willing to pay for the cost of antipollution measures limiting greenhouse gas emission from new autos.[75]

Thus, a major state with an enormous auto-pollution problem decided to take the initiative while the federal government stalled. But the latter was not asleep at the wheel. The Bush administration filed a friend-of-the-court brief on behalf of a lawsuit brought by Daimler-Chrysler and General Motors that sought to overturn the law. Its argument was that the aim of shifting to hybrid-engine vehicles overstepped the state's authority inasmuch as any issue concerning fuel economy is supposed to be determined solely by the federal government.[76] But California was soon followed by other states trying to reduce the pollution from vehicles produced by the auto industry. Of course, the industry was fighting these initiatives with all its legal and financial might. Finally, in the fall of 2003, the federal government ruled that the EPA does not have the authority to regulate greenhouse gas emission on the grounds that these gases are not "pollutants" under the law, which ruling can now be used to undercut a state's authority to regulate such emissions.[77]

Several years earlier, an international effort to limit greenhouse emissions was embodied in the Kyoto agreement of 1997. The treaty had been signed by 178 countries, including all the major industrialized countries *except one*: the United States, the world's chief polluter. The Senate had passed a motion opposing the Kyoto Climate Treaty by 95 to 0, which made it much easier for President Bush to reject it in April 2001. In announcing his rejection, he explained his action as follows: "We will not do anything to harm the economy." Earlier, in November 2000, delegates from over 160 countries had met at The Hague to discuss implementation of the treaty. But the talks failed because of the impossible demands of the United States, which included a plan "to increase its emission of greenhouse gases by 8 percent instead of cutting them by 7 percent by 2010, as required by the treaty."[78] It is irrelevant to ask what the American people thought about this turn of events at the time because the American press hardly covered the talks, and the TV newscasts not at all, and so the public had little comprehension of what was taking place. The contrasting headlines in

Europe and America tell the story of our mainstream media's bias or outright censorship with chilling simplicity:[79]

The London Times	"Pollution Pact Under Threat as America Is Accused of Con Trick"
The London Independent	"U.S. Blocks Attempts to Cut Global Warming."
Agence France Presse	"Gas-Guzzling U.S. Under Fire at Global Warming Talks"
The New York Times	"U.S. Move Improves Chance for Global Warming Treaty"

Once again we witness the symbiosis between the media, government, and industry, with the public cooperating as befuddled bystander. This Gordian knot of collusion would not be nearly so frustrating if feasible technical solutions did not exist that could actually result in billions of dollars saved. For example, the nonpartisan American Council for an Energy-Efficient Economy has issued a report that demonstrates how 10 policies could reduce energy consumption 18 percent by 2020. The total short-run investment would be $213 billion through 2010, while the savings to consumers would be $400 billion, for a net savings of about $200 billion. The net savings through 2020 would be $500 billion. And these estimates do not include the economic benefits from lower air pollution. Further, employment in companies concerned with energy efficiency and renewable energy would greatly increase. The net reduction in greenhouse gas emissions of the 10 policies would surpass the target set by the Kyoto treaty for the United States, which, as we have seen, has been rejected by the president because of its alleged harm to the economy.[80] The government's more recent ruling that the EPA does not even have the legal right to regulate greenhouse gas (see earlier) effectively put the kibosh on any efforts to do so—unless, of course, Congress rewrites the EPA-authorizing legislation. Thus, the administration has thrown this burning issue back into the lap of Congress.

Having faced the inevitable refusal of the United States to cooperate with any further proposals to cope with global warming, the international community has turned its attention to means of mitigating the expected catastrophes. As one report of the subsequent New Delhi conference explained:

> Instead of looking mostly at ways to reduce the level of heat-trapping gases . . . the 10-day conference [sponsored by the UN] will discuss how to build greater capacity, especially in developing countries, for minimizing vulnerabilities and preparing for worsening droughts, floods, storms, health emergencies, and other expected impacts.[81]

The cost of mainly weather-related natural disasters in 2002 alone has been estimated by the UN at $70 billion.[82]

The United States has also pressed for exemptions from the Ozone Treaty that would allow it to continue using a pesticide that is the chief destroyer of the ozone layer. This layer protects life on Earth from deadly radiation. When the Cambridge scientist who discovered the ozone hole over Antarctica heard about the Bush administration's efforts, he responded: "This is madness. We do not need this chemical. We do need the ozone. How stupid can people be?"[83]

So much for the threat of pollution to the world environment and America's refusal to abate the emission of its harmful chemicals because of industry's opposition. Let us now ask: What is happening to the environment within the boundary of the nation, and what has been the government's role in protecting our natural heritage for reasons of health, recreation, and the future survival of our animal, mineral, and vegetable kingdoms?

Actions of the Current Administration That Endanger the Nation's Environment

At the risk of appearing supercilious, I am compelled to answer the preceding question simply by saying "nothing." In fact, it can be argued that the current administration has substantially worsened the already vulnerable state of our environment. This is a very serious charge, so I shall cite the evidence in some detail, for the topic of how best to handle our natural resources, which belong to the public and not the government or industry, could hardly be more important to every man, woman, and child in the United States.

Here is a selection of evidence of the government's malfeasance concerning that which belongs to all of us.

[The head of the President's Office of Management and the Budget solicits input from industry lobbyists on] which federal regulations should be targeted for elimination.[84]

The Bush administration issued rules Tuesday to make it easier for industrial plants and refineries to modernize without having to buy expensive pollution controls—and immediately was sued by nine states charging that the changes undermine their efforts to protect public health . . . The more relaxed requirements "will bring more acid rain, more smog, more asthma, and more respiratory diseases to million of Americans," said New York Attorney General Eliot Spitzer . . . A wide range of industries lobbied heavily for an easing of the rules . . .[85]

[In spite of a National Academy of Science report that the risk of cancer from arsenic is many times worse than previously assumed by the Environmental Protection Agency] the EPA issues an arsenic-in-tap water standard higher than that recommended by public health advocates.[86] [This action was taken in spite of the public's desire for greater regulation of the quality of water in 2002, with 59 percent so indicating in a public opinion poll by RoperASW.]

[EPA's director general reveals that 33 Superfund, toxic cleanup sites had not received any federal funding. Further, the administration refused to reauthorize a corporate tax to pay for cleanups.[87] And yet,] one of four people in America lives within four miles of a Superfund site. Eighty-five percent of all Superfund sites have contaminated groundwater. Fifty percent of people, and virtually 100 percent in all rural areas, rely on groundwater for drinking water.[88]

[The administration appeals a federal judge's decision to ban drilling off California's coast.[89]]

[In spite of EPA's opposition, the Bureau of Land Management approves] the largest oil and gas exploration project ever in Utah [without conducting a full environmental study.[90]]

[A National Park official with 30 years of experience in the service resigns because the administration wants him to approve a 28-mile road through the largest undeveloped wilderness in the United States (the Great Smoky Mountains, already one of the most polluted areas in America) and allow development.[91]]

[The EPA deletes a whole chapter on global warming from its annual report on air pollution. Earlier the president had dismissed the State Department report to the UN that covers the harm of global warming, referring to it in a contemptuous tone and saying,] "I've seen the report put out by the bureaucracy."[92]

[The Interior Department loses its authority to deny permits for hard mining on federal lands if "substantial irreparable harm" is expected].[93]

The Bush administration proposed today [November 27, 2002] to give managers of the 155 national forests more discretion to approve logging and commercial activities with less evaluation of potential damage.[94] [It had already proposed to eliminate review by the public of plans for forest use.[95]]

[Throughout the Department of Health and Human Services, the administration has been replacing renowned scientists on toxic review panels with scientists who have ties to industry.[96]]

[The administration eases environment restrictions on logging on federal land in the Northwest.[97]]

[The EPA inspector general reveals that the EPA is nearly two years behind in developing standards required by law for 176 toxic air substances.[98]]

[Mining companies are allowed to buy public lands for less than $5 an acre—and they pay no royalties on the gold or other minerals they extract.[99]]

58.5 million acres of unblemished national forest lands are targeted for "asset management . . ."[100]

The Army Corps of Engineers has approved permits to turn 5,000 acres of the Florida Everglades into open-pit limestone mines.[101]

[The Department of Energy announces that the government no longer needs to prove that the rock formations under the Yucca Mountain nuclear waste site will prevent contamination of the environment.[102]]

[An Interior Department field office whose job was] to coordinate work on a 30-year, $8.4 billion recovery plan for the Everglades [is shut down.[103]]

[The ban on snowmobiles in Yellowstone and Grand Teton national parks is deferred. The ban on snowmobiles in Minnesota's Voyageurs National Park is reversed.[104] About 90 percent of the dense hydrocarbon haze in Yellowstone in the winter of 2001 was caused by about 67,000 snowmobiles in the park. Park employees had to strap on respirators.]

[Deep cuts are announced in proposed environmental spending by the Office of Management and Budget in order to] shift its budgetary emphasis toward military defense and homeland security.[105]

One might argue that national security in these perilous times justifies slashing the funds for environmental protection. But much of this protection costs nothing except an enforcement effort or rejection of industrial intrusions. It is not easy to understand how lifting bans on snowmobiles, permitting more arsenic in drinking water, allowing logging and mining on federal lands (with virtually no compensation to the government), and making taxpayers clean up toxic wastes of industry (instead of charging the polluters) advances national security. A far more likely source of the assault on environmental protections is the corporate bias of the Bush administration, particularly in the Department of the Interior, headed by Secretary Gale Norton, a bias that no one bothers to conceal. The roster of top personnel in the Department makes it clear why. The vice president of the United Mining Company became Norton's Deputy Secretary. A lawyer for the gas, timber, and oil industries became her Assistant Secretary for Land and Minerals Management. And a lobbyist for the water industry who had opposed the Clean Water Act became her Assistant Secretary for Water and Science.[106]

Other Crises of the Global Environment and America's Response

It is one thing for our nation to expose its own citizens to toxic substances and accelerate the destruction of its own natural assets, but it is quite another to ignore our obligation to help prevent destruction of the rest of the planet or to mitigate the known threats to human life in the rest of the world due to environmental rape. Here are a few of the global disasters that are slowly but surely overtaking us.

[Within 50 years all the ice in the Arctic ocean will disappear. Sea level might rise 18 inches in this century.[107] According to NASA scientists in 2003,

as reported by the Natural Resources Defense Council,] the Arctic polar ice cap
has shrunk nearly 20 percent over the past 20 years due to warmer tempera-
tures.[108]

[In 20 years half of the world's forests will be gone.[109]]

One quarter of all fish stocks [in the world] are listed as "depleted" or in
danger of being depleted; another 44% are being fished at the biological limit.[110]

[Almost one-half of the world's coast lines are too polluted for life.[111]]

[One thousand species are facing extinction.[112]]

Since the 1950s, 23% of all cropland, pastures, forests, and woodland have
been degraded . . .[113]

[About one billion people lack access to safe drinking water.[114]]

The World Bank predicts that the world will run short of adequate water in
the next 20 years.[115]

One sector of society that has not overlooked the water crisis is private enterprise. As the *Wall Street Journal* has pointed out: "water will be to the 21st
century what oil was to the 20th . . . the liquid everybody needs is going private,
creating one of the world's great business opportunities."[116] In the past few
years, as a matter of fact, the water systems of the following cities have been
taken over wholly or in part by transnational conglomerates: Atlanta, Berlin,
Buenos Aires, Casablanca, Charleston, Chattanooga, Houston, Jacksonville,
Jersey City, Lexington, New Orleans, Peoria, San Francisco, and many others.
And entire countries, such as Ghana and Bolivia, have also placed private companies in charge of providing water services.[117] Consequently, fees, rates, and
deterioration have increased in a number of locales, prompting greater regulation and even deprivatization.[118] The federal government of the United States is
not oblivious to the prospects for private corporations as they take the plunge
into the water business. A bill proposed by the current administration "would
make funding [for upgrading and expanding water facilities] conditional on
whether cities consider turning their water over to private corporations."[119] This
bill, submitted by the administration, was prompted by lobbying from the National Association of Water Companies, and is just one step removed from mandatory privatization.

The American government's response to the prospect of water shortages
can be generalized to all of its environmental policies both domestically and
internationally. This was made abundantly clear by the proposals and obstruc-
tionist tactics of the United States at the World Summit on Sustainable Development in Johannesburg, August/September 2002. As UN Secretary General
Kofi Annan pointed out at the summit, "Developed countries, in particular, have
not lived up to the promise they made either to protect the environment or to
help the developing world."[120] One of the 10 goals of the summit was to "increase U.S. assistance to developing countries to protect their environments and
the global environment."[121] Yet, a number of proposals set forth by the delegates

were repeatedly opposed by the United States, such as "to halt and reverse the current trend in loss of natural resources at the global and national levels by 2015," and "to halve by the year 2015 the proportion of people who are unable to reach, or to afford, safe drinking water."[122] As for global warming, the United States refused even to discuss the subject.[123] And, of course, the United States utterly balked at the proposal that "those who contribute most to causing environmental problems . . . take the lead in addressing them."[124]

For its own part the United States proposed that governments reduce tariffs, boost free trade, and encourage "voluntary initiatives to improve social and environmental performance." More concretely, the United States insisted on a series of "voluntary" partnerships with corporations to deal with water, sanitation, health, energy, agriculture, and biodiversity. No mention was made of regulatory mechanisms to ensure accountability of businesses. Thus, according to one observer at the conference, the United States proposed "Enron environmentalism." The U.S. State Department called the policy "shared accountability," a phrase that did not apply to the way in which corporations conducted themselves but only to relations between host countries and U.S. corporations in undertaking environmental projects.

The United States had begun to implement its policy before the summit by creating the Global Development Alliance in the USAID, founded on the principle that "public-private alliances . . . represent an important business model for USAID, and are applicable to many of the Agency's programs . . ." One of the strictures for aid, however, is that "partners are to bring at least as many resources to the table as those provided by the USAID."[125] In short, privatization on a global scale has been the aim, which can be achieved by breaking the monopoly of the government in providing foreign assistance. Interestingly enough, none of the program functions listed by the USAID in describing this policy entails regulatory oversight of corporate behavior, in spite of the flood of corporate scandals that had recently inundated America. The proposed 2003 budget for this new program of Global Development Alliance was $47 million to be used "for development programs, implemented through public-private alliances."[126] This amount, one-fifth the cost of a single F-22 fighter jet, was supposed to be America's answer to the developmental needs of the poor and developing world.

Inasmuch as the United States rejected in Johannesburg the principle that governments can take "precautionary, preventative action when a practice or product raises potentially significant threats of harm to human health or the environment," the host government not only has no recourse to financial regulatory mechanisms overseeing the behavior of corporations, and no means of protecting its own industries (by tariffs, for example), but no recourse if harmful side effects are suspected. Moreover, the countries must show earnest by improving governance, or "social performance," as the United States puts it, which means behaving more like the American system (the results of which we have been examining with some disappointment and will examine further in later sections).

Putting all these utterances together, we arrive at the following formula: The United States will pay for half the cost of hiring a U.S. corporation to conduct activities for up to about $47 million for all countries in 2003, provided the countries undertake initiatives to reform their government, eliminate practices that protect domestic industry, and ignore any suspected, potentially harmful side effects of a U.S. corporation's activities or products (including products from American biotech companies). Aside from the breathtaking hubris of this policy, will it work? Essential to answering this question is the adequacy of funding.

In addition to the $47 million mentioned above, another section of the USAID (namely, the Bureau of Economic Growth, Agriculture and Trade) requested $28.3 million from Congress in the 2003 budget for the environment.[127] Moreover, the administration pledged (August 2002) the sum of $125 million a year for four years to the Global Environment Facility (GEF), an international bank focusing on the environment, to which other nations have pledged $2,920,000; the actual request in the 2003 budget was even higher ($177 million).[128] Finally, the most generous gesture of all: "On March 14th the President announced the Administration's intention to increase assistance to developing countries by $5 billion annually [for all aid, not just environmental] over three years, beginning in 2004."[129]

These pledges and budget requests were quite heartening—which is perhaps all they were meant to be, for they were either totally rejected or substantially trimmed by the president's own party in the House of Representatives. Of the annual $177 million requested for the GEF, Congress approved $107.3 million.[130] And of the promised $5 billion over three years, the House Budget Committee announced: "The [2003] budget does not contain money for this initiative. Providing this funding would require reducing funding in other areas, increasing the deficit, or increasing revenues."[131]

This left a possible funding level of $182.6 million a year at best for the government's international environmental efforts, which is equivalent to about 80 percent of a single F-22 fighter jet. Thus, not only is the government's new policy toward the global environment fraught with loopholes for corporations and pitfalls for host countries, but its funding is a pittance of what is needed (and affordable) from the richest country in the world to stem the degradation of the planet. Meanwhile, America proceeds undeterred with its contribution to global warming and the untold disasters that are expected to ensue.

In the 1990s the United States ranked last among 19 advanced, democratic countries in its contribution to developing countries as a proportion of GNP. It is obvious that presently it has no plans to behave otherwise in the near future with regard to the environment of these countries. (For discussion of America's foreign assistance policies with regard to nonenvironmental issues, see the following chapter.)

7

Foreign Affairs—Selected Issues

Americans take pride in two alleged achievements in the domain of foreign affairs: their humanitarian assistance to poor countries, and their superior military power. This chapter will examine the record with regard to each of these achievements and take up some additional issues. In the case of the military, the Afghanistan and Iraq wars will occupy much of our attention. In both cases, we shall focus particularly on the unintended effects of the wars, including terrorism (or guerilla warfare) and civilian deaths. It will be argued that Americans have little grounds for assuming that their government's relations with foreign lands are either outstandingly generous or militarily outstanding beyond the ability to deliver overwhelming firepower, which feat is indebted to technology. Further, I will argue that high-tech weaponry has a number of negative side effects, some of which can override its military benefits. But first, let us look at the economic, social, and demographic plight of underdeveloped countries and add a few words to what has already been said about their environment and poverty in previous chapters.

Foreign Assistance to Poor and Developing Countries

Economic, Social, and Environmental Deprivation in the World

Poverty

A few facts about the poverty of the population in much of the world were given in chapter 2. These are gathered together here and supplemented with additional information. What emerges is a situation of squalor and endangerment that is unimaginable to Americans. Because the facts cited in this and subsequent sections reflecting the perilous conditions of life in much of the world need to be shouted from the rooftops, I have set them apart from my commentary to give them greater prominence.

[Of the 6.2 billion people in today's world, 1.2 billion [19%] live on less than $1 per day.[1]]

[Each person in the United States has, on average, 75 times the average annual income of each person in the world's lowest-income countries.[2]]

[The GDP per capita in South Asia is $440, and in sub-Saharan Africa it is $500 per annum. In the rich countries it is $25,730.[3]]

[Eighty percent of the population of Venezuela is at or below the poverty level.[4]]

[Africa attracts less than 1 percent of the world's investment.[5]]

[The gap between the average income in the richest and poorest countries is greater now than ever. The 35 to 1 ratio in 1950 expanded to a 72 to 1 ratio in 1992. Further, there has been growing inequality within countries. This has meant, according to the UN Development Program, that] strong economic growth has not always been translated into poverty reduction.[6]

Exploitation of Children

[A]bout 246 million children between the ages of 5 and 14 are involved in child labour . . . 1 out of every 6 children in the world today has to work . . . 61% of them in Asia, 7% in Latin America, and 32% in Africa, [according to the World Bank.[7]]

[E]very year more than 700,000 children are victims of trafficking [including] involvement in the child sex trade.[8]

[W]ith more than 300,000 [children] recruited as soldiers during the last decade, more than 2 million killed in civil wars, and more than one million orphaned or separated from their families . . .[9]

Health

[As of 1998, according to the UN's Human Development Report,] 2.6 billion people lack basic sanitation, 1.3 billion have no access to clean water, 1.1 billion lack adequate housing and nearly 900 billion have no access to modern health services of any kind.[10]

11 million children under the age of five die each year, which represents 30,000 a day, or one every 3 seconds.[11]

[I]n Uganda, or Ethiopia, or Masawi, neither men nor women can expect to live even to age forty-five . . . in Sierra Leone 28 percent of all children die before reaching their fifth birthday . . .[12]

In Bolivia, one out of 10 children die before the age of five.[13]

By the year 2010, the life expectancy in Africa might be less than 40 years of age.[14]

It is estimated that 68 million will have died from AIDS in the most affected countries by 2020, with 55 million having died from this disease in Africa alone.[15]

Africa has three-fourths of the cases of AIDS in the world.[16]

[Twenty percent of Zambians are HIV positive.[17] One-half of Zambians are expected to die of AIDS.[18]]

One-third of the people in Zimbabwe have AIDS.[19]

Twenty-one million children in the developing world will lose one parent with AIDS before the end of the decade.[20]

There will be 420 million orphans by 2010 in Africa due to AIDS.[21]

In Africa, one million children have lost their teachers because of AIDS.[22]

Dehydration from diarrheal diseases claims the lives of four children every minute.[23]

Measles kills 1 in 10 children every year.[24]

[Lymphatic filariasis (leading to elephantiasis) has afflicted 41 million in Africa, and 100 million Africans have been infected by schistosomiasis (120 million in the world). River blindness has infected 850,000 people in the world.[25]]

Hunger

At least 826 million people worldwide are undernourished . . .[26]

[Some 11,000 children in the world die of hunger every day, according to the UN World Food Program.[27]]

[An estimated 14.5 million southern Africans face death from hunger. The UN says only one-third of the money requested has been donated.[28]]

The UN World Food Program has just warned that over 12 million people in Ethiopia and Eritrea are threatened with starvation over the next months [announced on November 14, 2002] . . . Most of these crises [from drought in Africa] are related to erratic weather patterns . . . In Central America over 1.5 million people have seen their food supplies wither because of drought . . . Insufficient funding of World Food Program operations [in North Korea] has led to the suspension of food aid rations for 3 million hungry women, children and elderly people—with a further 1.5 million people likely to be cut off in January [of 2003].[29]

It is interesting to contrast these statistics with the state of affairs in America, where three-fifths of American adults 20–74 years of age are overweight, and one-quarter are obese,[30] and, as mentioned earlier, where about 300,000 fat-related deaths occur each year.[31] Moreover, $17 billion a year is spent in Europe and America on pet food. This exceeds by $4 billion the estimated yearly additional amount needed to provide everyone in the world with basic health and nutrition, according to a UN report.[32] Obviously, because of the spectacular inequality of wealth in the world, our greater solicitude for our dogs and cats than for human beings is not only unseemly but can allow millions to die who had the misfortune to be born in countries of poverty and disease and who fail to receive adequate support from the rich nations.

Education

As mentioned at the outset of the chapter on education in America, education is the sine qua non of prosperity. As the Academy for Educational Development has pointed out, "most industrialized nations did not achieve significant economic growth until countries attained universal primary education." And studies have found that 10–20 percent higher wages are enjoyed in underdeveloped countries for every additional year beyond grade four. At the national level, "increases in literacy of 20–30% have led to increases in gross domestic product of up to 16% . . ." Moreover, the International Food Policy and Research Institute has found that "the most important factor in reducing child malnutrition is female education."[33] And yet, according to a UN report, the number of children around the world without access to schools is in excess of 156 million,[34] and more than 60% of those who are out of school are girls.[35] Should the current trend continue, it is estimated that almost a third of the world's children by 2015 will not attend schools or learn how to read or write.[36]

Being physically present in a school facility, however, is not sufficient; adequate supplies, trained teachers, and classrooms with a reasonably low number of pupils are also needed. But as the Academy for Educational Development reports: "it is rare for classes to be less than 40 students except in remote locations . . . in Zambia, more that one-half of primary students do not have a notebook and one quarter do not have exercise books . . . Teachers are frequently poorly trained and poorly paid."[37]

Natural Resources and the Environment

We have already looked at some problems in the realm of natural resources and the environment, including the increasing scarcity of clean water, the degradation of forests and farmland, the depletion of fish stocks, and natural disasters expected to result from global warming (which have already begun, as mentioned in the previous chapter). The impossibility of poor countries dealing with these crises unaided is obvious in view of their extremely limited resources. Indeed, the livelihoods of over one billion people are severely affected due to land degradation alone, according to the World Bank.[38] Drought, exhausted soil, poor roads for marketing the produce of farms, and the unaffordable costs of pest-proof seeds are some of the basic problems that beset farmers in much of the world.

Population Growth

It is expected that populations will double in 30 years or less in 74 of the less developed countries, while populations are stabilizing in the 51 richest countries.

Methods of controlling family size have proven to be quite effective. The Population Institute, for example, has cited 10 countries where contraceptive use has reduced fertility rates since 1973.[39] Thus, it is not a question of not knowing what to do, but of doing it. But not all family-planning solutions are easy to implement when money from the rich countries is scarce and the United States refuses to contribute money to the UN for campaigns that provide information about certain family-planning practices.

The consequences of a world population explosion can be disastrous. According to Jared Diamond, a prominent ecological anthropologist, there are both long- and short-run impacts: "in the short term . . . it removes mothers from the workplace and increases the ratio of non-working children to working adults. It also spells disaster in the long run, because more people competing for fixed or shrinking resources is a recipe for civil war, as has already happened in Rwanda and Burundi, Africa's most densely populated nations . . ." Thus, citizens of overpopulated nations "are frustrated to know that means to limit family size exist but are unavailable or unaffordable."[40]

The U.S. Response to the Need for Assistance

First, it is important to understand that the problems mentioned here are not insurmountable if the industrialized nations play a greater role. To put the financial question in perspective: United Nations data demonstrate that just 10 percent of the originally requested amount of funds for the attack on Afghanistan (about $40 billion) could provide the necessities for life to everyone.[41] And yet, the U.S. government has been the most niggardly of all the industrial nations. As ex-president Jimmy Carter, a crusader for world betterment, has pointed out: "the United States gives only one-thousandth of its gross national product for international assistance, while the average European country gives four times as much."[42] This places the United States 20th among advanced nations in its contribution as a percentage of gross national product.[43] Japan, for instance, devotes twice the percentage of GNP to aid that America does, and Denmark devotes more than 10 times the percentage given by America. While the percentage recommended by the UN is .70 of GNP, the United States contributes only .09.[44] In fact, the United States currently spends one-tenth on foreign aid of what it spent during the Eisenhower administration.[45] Not surprisingly, then, according to a European economic news source, "European countries and certain non-governmental organizations have repeatedly chided the U.S., the world's richest country, for sharing so little of its official bounty with the poor."[46]

That this criticism has fallen on deaf ears in America is attested by the substantial decrease in foreign aid in the government's proposed 2003 budget. In the '80s, the percentage of the discretionary portion of the budget allocated for foreign economic aid was .92, whereas the percentage proposed for 2003 was

.55. Similarly, the percentage of the national product that was devoted to aid was .20 in the '80s, but proposed as .11 for 2003. In fact, the amount proposed by the Bush administration for 2003 was as small as any other year since the end of World War II.[47]

Earlier we saw the appalling lack of education in underdeveloped countries. We need now to consider the following astounding fact: While America spends $35,000 per pupil on its own children, it spends about $1.75 for every child out of school in all the developing countries. And according to UNICEF, basic education materials alone cost $2.50 per child in these countries.[48]

As for hunger, it has been noted that America spends 40 times more on its own farmers than it does to fight famine in the entire underdeveloped world.[49] And with respect to population control, the Bush administration's proposed budget for 2003 reduced the international family-planning budget by 11 percent.[50]

The administration's attitude toward UN requests for more funds is strikingly revealed by its response when the World Health Organization proposed a program to combat diseases in poor countries. "The U.S. share of the expenses would have been about $10 billion per year—a small fraction of what we will spend on war and occupation [in Iraq]," according to an editorial in the *New York Times.* "Yet the Bush administration contemptuously dismissed the proposal."[51]

One must be cautious, incidentally, when the government refers to its "foreign aid" expenditures, for more than a third of that amount is devoted to military and police activities.[52]

It should be borne in mind, also, that the United States has not only failed to increase its share of humanitarian assistance but has actually blocked such assistance from other countries, as suggested by its behavior at the Johannesburg Summit on Sustainable Development in 2002, described in chapter 6. And when the British Chancellor of the Exchequer called for a "Marshall Plan" that would double the assistance to poor countries by about $100 billion a year, he was opposed by the U.S. Secretary of the Treasury. And specific targets for increased aid proposed by Britain and others were thwarted by the United States at the Monterrey conference. Yet only one-fifth of 1 percent of the income of rich countries would have contributed an extra $50 billion for meeting these targets.[53]

It should be duly noted that America is not the only country that has failed to give its UN allotted share for assistance, even though it is the chief holdback. In the '90s, development aid from all nations declined by 45 percent. These, of course, were boom years for America.[54] Less than three-fifths of the $800 million requested by the UN for emergencies in sub-Saharan Africa was donated by the advanced countries; and the target had already been reduced a third from the previous year because of complaints from donor countries.[55] Further, emergency appeals for aid in Angola (for at least 600,000 displaced persons), and for four million in Congo, Burundi, and Rwanda, brought only lukewarm responses. East Asia and Latin America, rather than Africa, have been receiving private investment funds.[56] Thus, America is not alone in its reluctance; but this does not mitigate the fact that it has tended to be the least generous among a crowd of holdbacks.

The United States has sought to justify its recalcitrance by arguing that aid has not been sufficiently effective to justify the outlays.[57] Bush's former U.S. Secretary of the Treasury, for example, stated that, while huge sums have been spent, "I would submit to you that we have precious little to show for it."[58] And he expressed this opinion on other occasions. A sweeping indictment of this sort can be taken by the public as a signal to back off on aid, thereby reducing pressure on the government to try to alleviate the terrible conditions of the poor people of the world with contributions from our vast treasury. So we need to give some serious attention to this indictment. How have other experts and authorities in the government and elsewhere viewed the question of effectiveness?

According to the government's own premier aid agency, the USAID, "U.S. foreign assistance programs have a long and distinguished list of accomplishments." Here are just a few examples:

> More than 3 million lives are saved every year through USAID immunization programs . . . 43 of the top 50 consumer nations of American agricultural products were once U.S. foreign aid recipients . . . USAID provided democracy and governance assistance to 36 of the 57 nations that successfully made the transition to democratic government during this period . . . Agricultural research sparked the "Green Revolution" in India [that] resulted in the most dramatic increase in agricultural yields and production in the history of mankind, allowing nations like India and Bangladesh to become nearly food self-sufficient . . . Early USAID action in southern Africa in 1992 prevented massive famine in the region, saving millions of lives . . .[59]

The World Bank has confirmed these accomplishments of aid, stating that hundreds of millions have benefited from clean water, access to schools, electrical power, health clinics, and so forth.[60] These accomplishments, and many more that could be listed, testify to the salutary impact of aid, and raise the question of why the Bush administration has adopted such a skeptical attitude.

To be sure, the bestowal of aid does not guarantee that every country will benefit, since many national features (corruption, dictatorship, poor commitment to reform, etc.) shape its impact. As the World Bank admits, "in different times and different places [aid] has been highly effective, totally ineffective, and everything in between."[61] But this common-sense caveat is a far cry from the U.S. Treasury Secretary's conclusion that "we have precious little to show for it." It is hard to escape the conclusion, therefore, that the administration's disparagement of past assistance has been intended to clear the way for adoption of its own policy.

As shown in the earlier chapter on environmental assistance, the administration wishes to promote alliances between foreign countries and U.S. corporations, but only if the recipient country has the appropriate governmental and social resources regarded as necessary by the United States and can match American grants with equal resources. These strictures obviously limit eligibility to safe investment venues. Moreover, the administration was opposed to increasing assistance to sub-Saharan Africa (where AIDS thrives) in the 2003 budget and actually decreased it by $39 million in 2002. And when the Senate was ready to approve more than requested, the administration lobbied against it. In fact, the president himself called two key senators to ask them to slash the aid budget.[62] And then, in a dramatic move, the president reversed his position on AIDS funding because of pressure from evangelical groups with missions in Africa, which made a large impression on the public, judging from its coverage by the mainstream media. However, the amount requested in the 2004 budget for this initiative was only about 5 percent of the total announced, a sort of now-you-see-it now-you-don't sleight of hand. But worse, the president's budget cut by almost half the funding level authorized by Congress for the Global Fund to Fight AIDS, Tuberculosis and Malaria. This fund is capable of delivering assistance much more expeditiously than the new AIDS program, which would not be felt in Africa for at least two years. The Global Fund, in comparison, can deliver the assistance within months.[63]

The reason for America's going it alone in this instance comports with its policy of controlling the allocation and conditions of funding so that it can reap the greatest political and economic benefits for itself by stimulating private investment by its own corporations. This requires some elucidation.

Although the goal of stimulating private investment in developing and poor countries is a commendable one (e.g., if Africa had just a 1 percent share of the international market, it would gain $70 billion), the record shows that in the past "most U.S. aid went to middle-income countries that are predominantly of political interest to us," according to a Harvard economist.[64] If economic interests are added to the political ones, then countries that are unable to meet the eligibility requirements will be deprived of aid, regardless of need. In other words, leaders of poor countries who do not have the means or the will to meet America's conditions (such as a professional bureaucracy; a separate judiciary; an infrastructure of good ports, roads, etc.; and a government devoid of corruption) will be turned down, while their people expire from hunger or disease in the millions.

In short, how can the humanitarian part of the mission be protected from an imperative concern for safe investment? This question is not prompted by cynicism, but by informed realism. As the International Food Policy Research Institute has asserted, "donor governments inevitably evaluate their foreign aid programs not only as altruistic activities, but also as political and economic investments."[65] And according to a working paper by the World Bank, "any tendency for aid to reward good policies has been overwhelmed by donors' pursuit of their own strategic interests."[66]

USAID itself has confirmed this tendency, saying that "the principal beneficiary of America's foreign assistance has always been the U.S." Thus, 80 percent of USAID contracts have gone directly to American firms to create new markets for American goods and more jobs. Nor is this simply a matter of America's superior qualifications: "Keeping the money in American hands are laws that oblige both USAID and [contracting corporations] to use American companies and American subcontractors wherever possible, even if the cost is significantly higher than using foreign ones."[67]

This arrangement is known as "tied bilateral grants" in the jargon of foreign aid. Here is what the World Bank says about this arrangement: "Studies have shown that tied aid reduces the value of that assistance by about 25%, and there is widespread agreement that untying bilateral aid would make it more effective." OECD countries, in fact, have been moving away from this approach, with the consequence that only about a fifth of all aid remained as "tied bilateral" in 1995.[68] The exception, of course, is the United States, which once again seems to be bringing up the rear.

Why is tied aid so cost-ineffective? One reason is the contract-bidding process. A proposal that costs $50,000 to produce can be handled only by big companies, thus driving out the small nonprofit groups that would like to play a role on strictly humanitarian grounds.[69] According to research by Representative Jim McDermott: "53 cents of every dollar spent by the United States on tackling the AIDS crisis in Africa never left the Washington, D.C., area."[70] This is where the big consulting firms are located, firms that depend upon foreign aid for as much as 90 percent of their business. So the vision of millions of dollars being shipped off to the Congo or some other cash-strapped country to enable it to deal with its problems is wide of the mark. The money goes down the street from Congressional Hill, and half of it stays there. This arrangement is perfectly acceptable to the big firms, especially because they don't have to compete with foreign enterprises, thereby giving them a quasi-monopoly inasmuch as the laws protect them from this inconvenience. And that is precisely what Congress wants because it means that the benefits will redound to the United States. As the former director of USAID said in an interview, "In order to sell these programs to Congress and keep them sold, aid agencies must show that foreign assistance benefits the United States."[71] The fact that domestic firms are protected by law from having to compete with foreign firms is another reason why tied bilateral aid is more expensive.

Not only does Congress want U.S. aid to benefit American business regardless of possibly higher costs, but it wants its pet projects to receive "earmarked" status in USAID's budget. These projects have included everything from Armenia to gorillas, depending upon the amount of campaign contributions that has been received from a particular constituency by the congressperson. For example, when Senator Mitch McConnell became chairman of the Senate Appropriations Subcommittee for Foreign Operations, he "used that position to channel aid money to Kentucky contractors . . . and to favored environmental causes," according to the *Washington Post.* Armenia received $59 million because it donated "nearly $200,000 for him and the Republican Party in Kentucky, and contributed also to the National Senatorial Committee" of which McConnell was chairman. The gorillas benefited from a similar association with a politician.[72]

Clearly, the use of aid funding as a means to enrich American corporations and gain campaign funds has been a tradition for years. This tradition has been substantially augmented by the current administration, which has been urging other wealthy countries to adopt its business model. This enrichment of donor countries by means of foreign assistance programs, including the stipulation of conditions for loans or debt forgiveness that entail the recipient country's turning over its money-making assets (e.g., water service) to private corporations, is what the demonstrators at world trade and assistance conferences are worried about. Yet nothing in President Bush's proposed program of alliances with U.S. corporations is aimed at ensuring some balance between economic or political interest, on the one hand, and humanitarian interests, on the other, at monitoring possible abuses by private developers, or preventing the side effects of interventions (e.g., pollution). Indeed, the government is keen on the idea of companies being compensated for "takings" (a legal term) of private property by a country's legal restrictions, which increase the cost of a company's operations. Thus, the financial impact of antipollution laws in a recipient country would, under this legal theory, justify compensation. These matters are a long way from concern for humanitarian crises in the world and from what the public thinks of when it hears the term "foreign aid," but they loom large on the radar screen of corporations, and thus in the minds of the current administration.

This threat to a humanitarian mission by favoring countries that offer a safe investment climate regardless of human need evidently generated a dispute within the administration. Indications are that most of the criticism stemmed from the USAID and the State Department. To resolve the dispute, the president circumvented the USAID by creating a new agency called the Millennium Challenge Corporation that will spend the $5 billion annual account that the president has proposed to become effective in 2004. A small group of "high performing" countries are presently considered eligible, namely, "nations that embrace principles such as the rule of law, open markets, and allocation of budget resources to health and education . . . [and that] adopt sound economic policies and attack corruption . . ." This policy is obviously good for business investment but excludes many poor countries that presumably will be left to the more limited funding of the USAID and its "core humanitarian mission." Every corporation must have a board, of course, and this board will decide about recommendations to be given to the president. Although the secretary of state wanted the new fund to be under his exclusive oversight and control, he was reduced to being appointed chairman of the board—which is to consist of the other cabinet heads. Unlike the chairman, these individuals have predominantly big-business backgrounds; and it is the full board that will vote on the proposals to be given to the president, effectively undercutting the role of the secretary of state.[73] Thus has America privatized foreign aid while leaving the humanitarian mission (which probably will deal with the great majority of the poor, starving, and diseased) to the mercies of the underfunded USAID, and to the nonprofit agencies that had formerly played second fiddle to the big corporations under the old, pre-Millennium Challenge arrangement.

In the final analysis, the inherent conflict between self-interested and humanitarian goals has been resolved by supporting two separate agencies, with the far greater proportion of assistance funds bestowed on the self-interested agency. This latter agency will continue to employ the rhetoric of altruism for the public's benefit, both domestically and abroad, while it pursues its primary mission of making a profit for American firms and creating trade advantages for the future.

Then there is the matter referred to earlier: the absolute urgency of dealing with emerging catastrophes that cannot be dealt with by commitment to long-term economic development for specific purposes with niggardly funding. Here is a recent example: It was reported in November 2002 that 12 million Ethiopians and Eritreans were threatened with starvation. How can "patience and a focus on ideas," as a World Bank officer put it, or a U.S. aid budget that would not take effect until 2004,[74] or the imposition of conditions for receiving aid that are evaluated independently of sheer need, forestall catastrophes of this kind? It is doubtful that either of these countries could qualify for aid under the conditions set by the administration.[75] As a matter of fact, regarding Eritrea the *Washington Post* has quoted U.S. officials as saying that it hasn't moved fast enough toward democracy.[76] Does that mean that its people must perish? And Eritrea is not alone in being disqualified. As the *New York Times* has reported, "Few, if any, Middle Eastern countries will be eligible for Millennium Challenge money because of corruption, high income levels or lack of democratic rights, experts and administration officials say."[77] Nor can the world's eight richest countries (the G8) plead that the UN's appeal for funds to deal with the crises in Eritrea and Ethiopia came as a surprise. In June 2002, *five months* before the announcement of imminent starvation in Ethiopia and Eritrea, African leaders asked the leaders of the G8 countries to give them $55 billion in assistance for Africa. Instead, the

G8 gave them only $6 billion, and then turned around and gave $20 billion to Russia to dismantle its nuclear weapons, a priority, of course, of the United States.[78]

There are several other aspects of the current U.S. aid policy that raise serious concerns. In the first place, there is the emphasis on countries with democratic governments. Laudable as this may seem, does it have any bearing on economic development? A review of research by the Congressional Budget Office concluded: "No firm empirical link exists . . . between democracy and the rate of economic growth. Different regions tend to yield different results."[79] Indeed, the democratic nation of India recently allowed its people to starve in large numbers by hoarding grain to keep up the price of bread in order to appease the farm lobby.[80] Obviously, special interest groups and their lobbyists are part of a democratic government, and they have the power to manipulate prices or exploit aid relief for their purposes. These groups, in other words, are perfectly capable of undermining the goals of foreign assistance. As a matter of fact, the "green revolution" of India that made it possible to produce the large grain surplus that the government impounded was largely the result of American assistance, which was probably given because America favored India's democratic form of government. In short, democracy can play at least as important a role in undermining aid efforts as authoritarian leaders who act on their own.

Once again, it appears that the administration has proposed a policy on grounds that are not supported by the facts. Should people suffer from America's refusal to give aid because their leader wants to go on ruling without elections? And should a democratic country be given aid when it is possible that interest groups will legally interfere with its intended use to promote their own special interests?

With respect to recurrent crises, like the impending starvation of millions of Ethiopians and Eritreans, what role can the U.S. business model of private-public alliances possibly play in cases of sudden crises of huge proportions? Of course, it is difficult to make a profit off diseased and destitute human beings who are starving to death. As the director of international policy of the nonprofit Health Global Access Project has put it, "Free trade doesn't work for the dead. A modest expansion of trade will be of little comfort to millions of Africans who will die of treatable illnesses."[81]

Now let us revisit the idea of the recipient nation's matching the resources of the U.S. grant. Not only does a U.S. corporation obtain a monopoly in doing business with the recipient (often on behalf of campaign donors back in America), but half of the original "seed" money is paid for by the recipient. Even if the value of the assistance is reduced by 25 percent as compared with non-unilateral tied grants (as estimated by the World Bank and mentioned earlier), the United States will gain a new, monopolized market at only half the price. The political party that concocted this scheme will eventually be rewarded with more campaign contributions. (These rewards will flow notwithstanding the campaign finance reform law that was recently enacted, owing to cavernous loopholes, to be noted in chapter 11.)

If America seriously wants a viable market in Africa for its products and services, it should wipe out the sources of disease and starvation as fast as possible and relax its overweening dedication to commercial advantages without, however, totally abandoning the stimulus of investment. A viable market, after all, depends on viable humans, that is, the preservation of life. If this sounds hopelessly utopian, consider the statement by another former president: "For less than 20 percent of the increase in America's budget for defense, everything necessary could be done in Africa to fight AIDS."[82]

Public Attitudes toward Foreign Assistance

How does the American public feel about our level of contribution to foreign countries and the purposes of assistance? But perhaps we should ask a prior question: Does the public have any idea of how little the government contributes in comparison with other nations?

Here again we enter a domain of public befuddlement, presumably owing to the mainstream media's dereliction in informing people about the cost, extent, limitations, types, purposes, and effects of aid. And no doubt the government's shifting policies and deceptive, self-serving rhetoric are not much help in clarifying the issues. "That the public is not well versed on foreign aid," one writer concludes, "is demonstrated by the fact that opinion polls . . . have repeatedly shown that the public assumes that as much as 15 percent of the national budget is spent on foreign aid. The actual figure is only 1 percent."[83] In spite of the United States having spent less as a percentage of GNP than any other industrialized nation for several years, 81 percent of the public believe the opposite: that America has spent more than any other nation on foreign assistance. When told in the survey that only 1 percent of the budget was spent on foreign assistance, those who had wanted to cut the amount dropped from 64 percent to 35 percent.[84] If these figures can be trusted, they suggest that a comfortable majority believe that as much as 15 percent of the budget, which was mentioned above as the perceived level of funding, is an acceptable amount for foreign assistance, a level far above the actual level of less than 1 percent.

Some surveys, however, do not define "foreign aid" for respondents before asking questions about it, so it is impossible to know if the public includes military and police assistance in its understanding of the term. As one analyst has pointed out, "Americans define 'foreign aid' very broadly—including any defense spending that benefits other countries."[85] But a study that explicitly defined aid as only economic or social development found that the respondents believed that as much as 20 percent of the federal budget was being earmarked for foreign aid, and that they even believed that less was spent on Medicare than aid.[86] In other words, even when humanitarian or economic aid is what the public has in mind, it still overestimates the amount currently expended by the government by a factor of 20.

Another problem in interpreting the public's perception of America's contribution is that the absolute amount is impressive, namely, 16 percent of all the assistance given by the industrialized nations. It is the amount relative to the country's wealth that is extremely small. But the most confusing part of the foreign assistance puzzle is the policy and practices of the government. Here Americans are almost totally in the dark, again owing to the media's failure to inform them. Thus, while the policy of the Bush administration is devoted to creating investment alliances with corporations, the American people are mainly concerned with humanitarian goals. A review of public opinion research in the '90s found that "Americans want to give foreign aid to relieve pain and suffering, not to build trading partners . . . Surveys that have attempted to document a self-interest reason for support of many of these [foreign policy] issues have failed."[87] Moreover, since the government's program of "alliances" will ignore nations that might be especially needful of assistance because of their failure to meet certain criteria, and since millions of suffering people live in these countries, it would seem that the public's humanitarian view of aid is not well reflected in the government's endeavors. What is well reflected, however, is industry's desire for markets and Congress's desire for projects that reward campaign donors.

In addition to the public's emphasis on humanitarian goals, it also seems to have abandoned its earlier position that aid should be reduced. This shift has occurred over the past several years, till only a minority now believes that a reduction is desirable; meanwhile, there has been no lowering in the public's estimate of the percentage of the budget devoted to aid.[88] This suggests that the public and the government have drifted farther and farther apart.

Nevertheless, Americans were the least likely of five industrialized nations in a survey conducted in 2001 to approve of increased aid. The percentages of the public that approved an increase in these five countries were as follows: Italy, 95 percent; France, 90 percent; Great Britain, 90 percent; Germany, 86 percent; and the United States, 53 percent.[89] Thus, the United States was more than 40 percentage points below the country with the highest approval rate. While this low approval rate in America might well stem from misperception of how much is currently being spent, it could also result from preemption of public attention by the war on terrorism and its associated hostility to foreign countries. For of the five countries, the U.S. public was most in favor of the war in Afghanistan, namely, 83 percent vs. a mean for the other four countries of 64 percent.

An imbalance of public attention between foreign aid and foreign war is demonstrated by the coverage of the mainstream media. Although suffering in underdeveloped lands had not gone away, the advent of wars in Afghanistan and Iraq far overshadowed it in all the leading news outlets. Even when victims dying of starvation or of AIDS are shown on television, the media rarely interrogate officials about America's exact intentions in providing aid, and never raise doubts about the motives behind foreign assistance by the government. Nor do they try to draw the public's attention to the fact that among the advanced nations, America contributes the least portion of its GNP to assistance. In contrast to this reticence, America's military intentions are constantly in the minds of the media, and its commitment of resources is a source of pride. Where the priority lies is not difficult to discern.

The basic goodness of the American people, however, is revealed by the fact that private contributions have been about three times the amount contributed by the government ($30 billion vs. $10 billion). This is not an atypical division of labor between the people and government in America. While the government's assistance is mainly devoted to expanding opportunities for corporate investment with the public's tax dollars, the public is trying to help the needy with its personal contributions.

Finally, a few more words about the public's persistent overestimation of the percentage of the budget devoted to foreign aid: This tendency to inflate that amount might well reflect an inflated sense of global rectitude, which in turn derives from the notion of excellence and an exemplary status among nations, namely, the American Myth. Or, as the president has put it in a speech to the nation, "Our nation is the greatest force for good in history."[90] Thus, as the public might reasonably conclude, we are bound to be making a sacrifice for the good of the poor. This disconnect between a self-image of purity and solicitude, on the one hand, and the realities of foreign policy driven by considerations of profit and power, on the other, is obscured by the altruistic rhetoric of political leaders and the self-righteous tone that is used against skeptics and dissenters. The public is more than content to remain in the dark because the light might destroy the American Myth from which it draws its sustenance. And the mainstream media are only too happy to enforce the Myth as a means of reassuring advertisers and their corporate clients that controversy about America's iconic status will never taint their wares. In short, questioning of the alleged verities is squelched by a combination of the public's need for cultural self-confidence, placation of the public by politicians (especially those who court the goodwill of large corporations), and the media's compliance with the wishes of their corporate sponsors and consumers.

So it is with foreign assistance. Needing to believe that we are devoting a significant portion of our budget to alleviate suffering and premature death, we mythologize our contribution by exaggerating it 20-fold. Consequently, we are reluctant to increase the amount, since it is already perceived as quite large, even larger than that of any other nation. In the final analysis, our sense of unique rectitude, it would seem, permits our government to enrich the rich and to allow the continuing destitution of the poor in underdeveloped lands without media exposure or public outcry, much less demonstrations in the street against the possibly inhumane policies of a nation that is allegedly in the vanguard of humanitarianism.

The Afghanistan War: A Case Study of Military Mismanagement with Tragic Consequences

As reported earlier, America now spends more on military preparedness than all other countries of the world combined. Much of this cost is due to the development and deployment of weapons of great technological sophistication, which have reduced the likelihood of American casualties, promised to overwhelm any enemy who uses less sophisticated weapons, and raised the expectation that innocent civilians can be spared death by the use of "precision" armaments.

These benefits, however, can easily be cancelled by two counterdevelopments in warfare: terrorism and biological and chemical weapons. Thus, it is no coincidence that the two nations America has felt called upon to attack in force recently have each represented the use of one of these countermethods: Afghanistan for its terrorism and Iraq for its biological and chemical threats. The former chose terrorism because of its inability to afford the production of conventional weapons that could be a match for the sophisticated weaponry of the West; and the latter chose weapons of mass destruction (WMD) (at least in the past) because it had enough wealth to develop huge amounts of chemical and biological substances, but not enough to match the technical arsenal of the West. While some fear that the two countries could have supplemented their particular weapon of preference with the other method or, worse, with a more technically sophisticated weapon (such as an atomic bomb), thus bringing to bear on America an unbeatable combination, so far this has not happened. But it could happen in the future with respect to any enemy. Meanwhile, the two relatively low-tech counterweapons are what threaten America the most.

America's military superiority in terms of hardware and size of its military is not to be doubted. But there are consequences of technological superiority that threaten to undermine America's goal of security. Terrorism and the possession of chemical or biological WMD are two such consequences, methods of warfare that were developed to counter the West's possession of high-tech weapons. And it is also possible that nations that are able to afford high-tech weaponry like the United States will be provoked to develop a similar arsenal, in what used to be called an "arms race." Another consequence is an expectation that

America will use its might to gain global advantages apart from security (especially in light of its new preemptive stance), which has inflamed many people in the world against us.

There are many other conceivable consequences. Our military secrets may be stolen and used against us. The flaunting of our military strength may give a false sense of security to the American people and its leaders, prompting them to lower their guard. (This was a consequence that probably allowed the 9/11 disaster to occur.) The huge investments in the defense industry could cause the industry and its work force to resist cutbacks in weapons construction. The high cost could undermine the achievement of other national goals by the diversion of funds, thus reducing popular support for needed military ventures. The emphasis on high technology could distract attention from expanding our nontechnological capabilities, such as mobile, rapid-response, quasi-guerilla forces. Indeed, overconfidence in the inherent superiority of high-tech weaponry could make us overlook the possibility that low-tech weaponry might sometimes be superior (e.g., in the reported shooting down of a $25 million Apache helicopter by small arms fire in Iraq) and, therefore, make us fail to take necessary measures for protection.

Another possible consequence is the failure to pursue diplomatic efforts with a dedication at least equal to that of military preparation in dealing with a potentially dangerous enemy. Another is to assume that America is capable of dealing with its enemies without the assistance or moral support of allies. Another is a tendency to overlook the possible damage to the infrastructure of the enemy's country by powerful munitions so that postwar reconstruction is severely hampered. Another is to raise one's expectations of military victory so high that prudent preparations are not made, anything less than unconditional surrender will not be acceptable, or that unforeseen difficulties (such as failing to capture the enemy's leader or bungling the postwar recovery) will backfire on military and civilian morale or on political support for the military establishment; and a high-tech military system can raise expectations of the accuracy of its weapons to the point that the prospect of a large number of civilian casualties is not given the serious consideration that it deserves.

Finally, there is always the possibility that the empowerment of military leaders by giving them a vast arsenal and the autonomy to take vigorous action can be exploited to exert influence on government decision-making or to gain power for themselves. Military involvement in domestic governance is by no means a far-fetched concern in light of the military's expanding role in law enforcement and its proposal for a centralized surveillance information center. In fact, some Bush officials have wanted to make it the lead agency in homeland security in egregious violation of the Posse Comitatus Act of 1878.[91]

In short, a potent, high-tech military machine is not an unmixed blessing for a country, and could even backfire.

It seems safe to say that nothing in the typical training for government service prepares policymakers to ponder unintended consequences in the way I have done here, that is, systematically and almost exhaustively, regardless of the intervention and in terms of guidelines derived from a study of a large array of negative consequences of purposive action. The usual outcome of this lack of clear-cut analysis is a slew of consequences in which the unintended far outnumber the intended. (My book, *Fatal Remedies: The Ironies of Social Intervention*, provides a guide for identifying possible unintended consequences before they occur. Much more work in this critical area of policymaking needs to be done, however.)

One of the most disturbing of the unintended consequences of our recent wars has been civilian casualties. This consequence is well known, and belligerents today have no excuse for ignoring or downplaying it. As the UN Department of Public Information has bluntly put it: "The primary victims of today's war are civilian women and their children."[92] The killing of innocent civilians is not only grotesquely inhumane but provokes the enemy to do likewise, as with terrorist attacks. And yet downplaying is evident in the dismissal of civilian deaths as simply an unavoidable outcome of war, or in referring to them with the antiseptic term "collateral damage" without the least hint that perhaps war should be avoided altogether if the chance of civilian casualties is high. As mentioned above, one of the problems with high-tech warfare is that the prosecutors of the war feel justified in assuring us (and themselves) that casualties will be low because of breakthroughs in technology like precision bombing. This expectation justifies taking fewer alternative measures to reduce civilian casualties—which, of course, makes them higher still, as we shall see below. This seems to have been the case in Afghanistan, and then later in Iraq. But first, let me set the stage for the Afghanistan conflict.

The war came during the worst drought in decades as food and medical supplies were being distributed by a large number of aid workers who fled when the attack began. This brought an end to the distribution effort.[93] Thus, as one analyst of the situation has written with reference to the civilian population, "These were poor people to begin with, and, on top of that, they had absolutely nothing to do with the events of 9/11."[94] The average income was $280 a year, and there had been little money for development under the Taliban (the development budget was only $343,000) because the bulk of money went to the *madrasa* religious schools ($14 million, which was five times the amount budgeted for health).[95] Moreover, large numbers had fled the country because of civil war, war with Russia, and Taliban oppression. Afghans had composed the largest group of refugees in the world for 20 years; in 1999 the number of refugees was estimated at more than two million people.[96] In short, here was a country marked by destitution, social disruption, and oppression by armed, religious, antediluvian fanatics.

Americans, meanwhile, were sublimely indifferent to terrorism and oblivious to the conditions in Afghanistan. "When asked [in 1999] to list the two or three biggest foreign-policy problems facing the U.S. today," reported the Program on International Policy Attitudes, "the most common response (by 21%) was 'I don't know.'" Only 12 percent of the general public said terrorism, and the "leaders" in the survey did not even include terrorism among the five most frequently cited problems.[97] Not surprisingly, then, the shock to the nation when the terrorists struck in New York and Washington, D.C., churned up a tsunami of vengefulness that was reflected in the results of a *New York Times* poll following 9/11: 58 percent of Americans supported going to war against Afghanistan "even if it means many thousands of innocent civilians may be killed."[98]

The violence and shock of the attacks made it possible for the nation's leaders to instill in the public mind the idea that terrorism itself, a tactic of warfare, is the enemy (namely, we are "at war with terrorism"). It would be as though an enemy of America had declared war against "high-tech weaponism." Consequently, the *reasons* that certain humans use the tactic of terrorism are treated offhandedly. Thus, vague platitudes about terrorists' hatred of freedom, their religious extremism, and so forth have been proffered and accepted by the public as sufficient explanation for terrorism. This widespread notion that the enemy can be stripped down to a tactic of warfare called terrorism, which is simply a means of combat, effectively diverts attention from the tangled web of historical and cultural factors that actually motivate those who have resorted to this tactic—not a few of which factors consist of America's own actions, both past and present. It also obscures the fact that so-called terrorists do not form a homogeneous group, but represent a range of interests and backgrounds.

This displacement of emphasis from *motives* to *means* of warfare makes it possible for us to preserve our self-image of victimized innocence dictated by the American Myth. But our ignorance of, or indifference to, what lies behind terrorism makes us unable to understand and eradicate its roots, including those actions of our own that continually provoke it—such as our nearly unqualified backing of Israel, our apparent lack of hesitation in attacking and occupying Middle Eastern nations, and our killing of thousands of innocent civilians. In addition, we ignore the long and ugly history of Western powers attacking and disposing of formerly great and proud Middle Eastern realms in any way they saw fit, a history indelibly etched in the minds of Middle Easterners.

The poll of Americans mentioned above, which found widespread support for going to war against Afghanistan in spite of abject ignorance of the history, conditions, or location of Afghanistan, and regardless of the possible toll in civilian deaths, no doubt reinforced the apparently spontaneous decision of the Bush administration to go to war. The gesture of giving the Taliban a chance by demanding that they turn over Bin Laden to American justice was probably only a legalistic pretext for invasion. Resort to the UN or to political/diplomatic measures, or to preparations for a successor government, or to consideration of small-scale special forces as a military means of disabling the leadership were all ignored, dismissed, or put on hold while military partners were assembled and plans were put into effect for massive bombardment by America's high-tech weaponry. In fact, it appears that the attack on Afghanistan could well have been a violation of international law, according to legal experts.[99] In any event, haste was the order of the day. Little time was available to ponder the possible unintended consequences of a war in Afghanistan; and the usual grounds for reassurance that civilian casualties would be minimized, namely, precision delivery of bombs and missiles, was no doubt warmly embraced as alleviating the problem. But did it? Or was there so much faith in high-tech systems that the issue of civilian casualties was not given serious attention? The first step in dealing with this question is to find out how many civilians died as a consequence of the American-led attack.

Drawing on hundreds of journalistic and official sources, one researcher (a professor of economics) concluded that around 3,500 civilians had been killed by U.S. bombs and missiles by the end of 2001, just three months after the terrorists attacked the United States.[100] A subsequent study by a nonpartisan organization specializing in military affairs yielded an estimate of between 1,000 and 1,300 civilians killed in the same period. This lower estimate was said to have resulted from "a more stringent accounting criteria in order to correct for likely reporting bias." But what the new study did was omit a large number of journalistic sources from *non-Western* nations, such as India, Pakistan, and Singapore, which contributed many articles used by the earlier study. Because the lower estimates were broadly consistent with estimates by Human Rights Watch, the Reuters news agency, and British intelligence (extrapolated from the end of October), this later study accepted the new estimates as more accurate than those of the earlier study cited above.[101]

Whatever bias might have occurred in the journalistic sources, however, would seem to have been especially likely among the *Western* journalists whose compatriots were dropping the bombs and who therefore might have been inclined to minimize the massacre of civilians. Further, we would expect the excluded Middle Eastern journalists to have enjoyed greater access culturally and linguistically to Afghan informants than Western journalists. The issue could have been resolved simply by taking a sample of the two types of sources and comparing their casualty figures for the same events. But apparently this reliability check was not carried out by either study. If we take the mean of the two studies, we arrive at a figure of 2,325 innocent, slain civilians. A third study by a British journalistic source estimated 1,300 to 1,800 deaths of civilians,[102] which reinforces our sense that the most likely number exceeded the 1,300 estimated in the second study mentioned above. Should the figure of 2,325 be regarded as high, low, or moderate by moral standards? Only a comparative perspective can help us answer this question.

The number of civilians who were killed in the 9/11 attacks in America was 3,027. This means that we killed almost one innocent Afghan civilian with bombs and missiles for every person killed by the terrorists in America (the actual statistic is 0.76 per American death). We might momentarily regard this level of killing as a form of justice, until we realize that Afghan civilians were not the people who attacked us. It was their oppressors. By no stretch of the imagination did they deserve to die because of the 9/11 attacks, any more than the citizens of Australia, Iceland, or Zanzibar deserved to die.

Another way of assessing the level of carnage is to note that, according to the second study (which may have been somewhat low in its estimate), more than one civilian in Afghanistan was killed for every 12 bombs or missiles expended.[103] This is a rather shocking statistic. If we imagine that only one person was dropping the bombs and that every time this person got to the 12th bomb he or she thought, "Well, well, this one is going to kill an innocent person who is probably a woman or a child," it is a safe bet that pretty soon this soldier would feel like a serial killer on a scale dwarfing the best efforts of the Boston Strangler. But then, our military personnel are trained not to have such thoughts.

Bombs and missiles were not the only source of civilian deaths in Afghanistan. As the author of the second study reported, "a minimum of 3,000 more deaths are attributable to the impact of the bombing campaign and war on the nation's refugee and famine crisis."[104]

We now arrive at a total civilian death toll of approximately 5,325: the 2,325 mean mentioned above and the 3,000 due to aftermath. This approaches *twice* the number of persons killed on 9/11, persons who were just as innocent as the 9/11 victims in New York, Washington, and Pennsylvania.

Why hasn't this message reached the American public? Perhaps because the mainstream media were not keen on reporting the casualties among innocent people caused by our assault. As the researcher for the first study noted: "I was able to find some mention of casualties in the foreign press, but almost nothing in the U.S. press."[105] The researcher for the second study simply excluded U.S. press reports entirely because of their obvious tendency to minimize or distort the numbers: "[The non-U.S. sources] seemed more attuned to the issue of civilian casualties than were U.S. newspapers."[106] This minimizing bias, of course, was part of the attitudinal climate in America that forbade uttering discouraging words about the war. As a professor of international law and international affairs at Princeton observed, "the patriotic mood was so intense that questioning the wisdom of the White House was treated as tantamount to disloyalty, an impression strengthened by an astonishingly conformist media."[107] What the professor couldn't have known at the time is that this mood continues to this day more than two years later, and that the mainstream media are *still* observing a moratorium on the question of civilian deaths.

The apparently casual attitude toward civilian casualties on the part of the mainstream media was not without conscious design. As the chairman of CNN said, "It seems perverse to focus too much on the casualties or hardship in Afghanistan . . . We must talk about how the Taliban are using civilian shields . . ."[108] A still more callous attitude was evinced by Brit Hume, an anchorman on Fox TV News, when he was asked why so little attention had been paid to civilian casualties: "OK, war is hell, people are dying, is that really news? And is it to be treated in a semi-straight-faced way? I think not."[109] More often, the casualties were given some credence, but downplayed or underestimated in a way to reassure the audience. For example, in the midst of battles that were costing hundreds of civilian lives, a journalist working for the *L.A. Times* wrote: "although estimates are still largely guesses, some experts believe that more than 1,000 Taliban and opposition troops have probably died in the fighting along with at least dozens of civilians"[110] when the true civilian figures were in the thousands. Most tellingly, none of the nightly newscasts on the three major networks offered any estimates at all of civilian casualties. Amnesty International had demanded "an immediate and full investigation into what may have been violations of international and humanitarian law such as direct attack on civilian objects or indiscriminate attacks . . . ," but this demand was not even reported by the U.S. press, ABC, CBS, or NBC. If ever mentioned, civilian casualties were dismissed as "part of the propaganda war" or simply the fate of "human shields."[111] If journalists raised the question of civilian casualties with Pentagon officials, they were assured that "collateral damage" is just a fact of life, and that claims about casualties were not credible. Some typical responses were: "the claims could not be independently verified" and "high civilian casualties are inflated by air," along with assurances about "the humanity of the air war."[112] Secretary of Defense Donald Rumsfeld declared: " . . . let's be clear. No nation in human history has done more to avoid civilian casualties than the United States has in this conflict."[113]

Meanwhile, U.S. bombs were hitting homes, a mosque, a truck full of refugees, villages, a hospital, a fully loaded bus, a civilian radio station, a marketplace, and a UN food warehouse (twice). "In many instances," according to the professor who prepared the first study (mentioned earlier) of the number of civilian casualties and who had read hundreds of press reports, "U.S. bombs fell on spots without any military significance."[114] Because of the controversial nature of claims that American airmen were responsible for the deaths of civilians who were not even remotely human shields, a few cases are worth quoting in full:

On October 19, U.S. planes had circled over Tarin Kot in Uruzgan early in the evening, then returned after everyone went to bed and dropped their bombs on the residential area, instead of on the Taliban base 2 miles away ... Mud houses were flattened and families destroyed ... A villager [said]: "We pulled the baby out, the others were buried in the rubble. There were bodies with no legs. We could do nothing. We just fled."[115]

The Afghan Islamic Press, the Pakistan News Service, the *Frontier Post*, the *Guardian*, the *Times of India*, AFP and the UN all reported that an F-18 jet had dropped a 1,000-lb cluster bomb on the 200-bed military hospital and a neighboring mosque, missing the military barrack by 500–1,000 metres.[116]

A warplane hit the home of an associate of Osama bin Laden at the suggestion of Afghan commanders who knew he was not there. That attack in Pachir Agam killed 70 villagers.[117]

[After a cruise missile strike, a 16-year-old ice cream vendor said:] "There was just a roaring sound, and then I opened my eyes and I was in a hospital. I lost my leg and two fingers. There were other people hurt. People were running all over the place."[118]

Television photos taken by Britain's Sky News showed footage of [an] F-18 dropping bombs, hitting a mud and timber family home. The TV report said ten members of a family were missing under the rubble and another 20 injured. A five-year-old girl lay in a wheelbarrow with a bloodied face.[119]

"A 2,000-pound bomb, no matter where you drop it, is a significant emotional event for anyone within a square mile," said a U.S. officer on an aircraft carrier.[120] Moreover, a significant proportion (10–30%) of "bomblets" in cluster bombs do not explode upon impact and lie strewn everywhere. It was estimated that 14,000 unexploded cluster bombs lay on the ground in Afghanistan after the war. And since they were the same color and size as the food packets that were being dropped by the Air Force, many civilians were blown up by the best of intentions.[121] And yet, "United States food packets rained from the sky ... Hungry Afghans rush to gather them up ... an average of about 88 casualties a month were attributed to landmines and unexploded ordnance in Afghanistan," according to a newspaper report in the UK.[122] Afghan civilians wondered about the meaning of it all, since the United States was supposed to be saving them from oppression. Said Khawaja, who was 25 years old: "We see only our mothers and children dying. Why do you kill us? What have our civilians done to you?"[123]

The Pentagon's reaction, when asked about this carnage, was predictable. When queried about actual reports of civilian casualties, Defense Secretary Rumsfeld gave a disingenuous reply: "Everyone knows that the United States of America does not target civilians."[124] The spokesperson for the Defense Department, Victoria Clark, wrote, "We take great care in our targeting process to avoid civilian casualties."[125] But a reply that can only be characterized as patently outrageous was given by General Franks, the commander in charge of prosecuting the Afghanistan War: "I can't imagine there's been a conflict in history where there has been less collateral damage, less unintended consequences."[126] In light of indisputable evidence supplied by the Pentagon itself, General Franks was either deceiving his audience of journalists or he had not seen the statistics on the Balkans war only two years earlier. In that war, there were .02 civilian deaths per weapon and .04 per sortie. In the Afghanistan war, the comparable figures were .11 and .28 civilian deaths per weapon and sortie, respectively, or five times and seven times as high a rate. Thus, there was a clear escalation from the Balkans war to the Afghanistan war in the "kill ratio" of munitions. In the Balkans war there were 13,000 sorties, 23,000 weapons, and 500 civilian deaths; in the Afghanistan war there were only 4,700 sorties, only 12,000 weapons, but about 2,300 civilian deaths (see calculations below) or, about four and a half times as many deaths in spite of far fewer sorties and weapons.[127] One can only conclude that the general misspoke.

We have seen thus far that the death toll among civilians was far higher than most Americans had envisioned, was repudiated by Pentagon officials, and squeamishly censored by the American mainstream media. What has yet to be shown is the shocking statistic that there were estimated to be 3,000 to 4,000 Taliban deaths in the same period, compared with 5,325 civilian deaths. In other words, we seem to have killed *more innocent civilians than enemy combatants.*

It is very important to be clear on this point. So here are the calculations of civilian deaths in tabular form:

First study (Herold)	3,500
Second study (PDA, Conetta)	(1,000 to 1,300)
or a mean of:	1,150
Total of two studies	4,650
Mean of the first and second studies	2,325
Deaths from refugee and famine crisis	3,000
Total civilian deaths	**5,325**

The apparent finding that civilian deaths exceeded enemy deaths by 52 percent is redolent of a baby-and-bathwater scenario.

Which raises three sensitive questions: Could civilian casualties of this magnitude have been avoided, and if so, did the military know how to avoid them? If the answers are in the affirmative, why did they not avoid them? Before exploring these questions, a few words need to be said about the refugee crisis caused by the war and also the worsening drought.

According to the U.S. Committee for Refugees, hundreds of thousands fled their homes when the war began; it was estimated that they included 40–70 percent of the residents of the larger cities. And conditions were described as "grossly inadequate" in two camps with 11,000 refugees. Further, "relief efforts were hampered by the Taliban's seizure of two UN food warehouses, looting by Taliban and armed gangs, and the United States' reported bombing of ICRC [i.e., Red Cross] food warehouses." As for the U.S. food drops, "the amount of food dropped was insignificant compared to the scale of the need."[128]

In all, one million persons were displaced by the war, an increase of 60 percent over the previous year when Afghanistan already had the largest refugee population in the world.[129] Moreover, because of continuing drought conditions, it was announced in October 2002 that four million Afghans would need food aid in the next 12 months.[130]

Approximately 3,000 civilian deaths were caused by the famine and refugee conditions, as mentioned earlier. And relatively little was done to alleviate the suffering in this early period of intense, aerial bombardment, as attested by the overcrowding in available refugee camps and the negligible effort of the United States to feed the starving by food drops—which in any case were potentially lethal because of their resemblance to unexploded munitions. Whether incompetence or moral insensibility was more to blame is hard to tell. The same could be said of the way in which war was waged by the overpowering might of the United States, a manner that produced two-thirds as many civilian deaths as enemy deaths from bombardment alone in the early, intense period of war. Why was this so? We saw earlier that the Balkans suffered relatively light civilian deaths. What was different about Afghanistan?

In the first place, in the Balkans the United States had guided its bombs and missiles by laser, while in Afghanistan it used Joint Direct Attack Munitions (JDAMs) that were guided by the Global Positioning System (GPS). As a report of the Joint Project on Defense Alternatives (PDA) points out: "Under test conditions, the JDAMs are simply less accurate than laser-guided bombs. Indeed, GPS-directed weapons are not routinely called 'precision' weapons at all, but 'accurate' or 'near precision' ones. [Under test conditions] 50 percent of the JDAMs dropped will hit within 32–42 feet of their programmed coordinates. By comparison, laser-guided bombs routinely achieve 3–8 meters [or 10–25 feet] ... Should an intended target sit among a cluster of buildings, the difference between these two circular areas is significant. And, of course, in either case 50 percent of the weapons fall outside the circles."[131] Why, then, did the military use the global positioning system in Afghanistan, especially since these "smart" bombs fell outside the intended target radius half of the time anyway? (Later, in the war against Iraq, the accuracy of JDAMS was increased to a radius of 15 feet.[132] But this had no effect on the blast area, of course.)

The answer is that the GPS-directed weapons are cheaper and usable in all kinds of weather and "can be launched from much greater distances and, because their targets need not be designated while the weapons are in flight, they can be dispensed in large batches . . . the aggregate effect will be a reduction in the average accuracy of the smart weapon mix."[133] One could reduce this account to a set of two simple statements: large batches plus less accuracy equals more civilian deaths; but cheaper cost and all-weather capability add up to the military superiority of a GPS-directed weapons system—which, in other words, trumps the possibility of saving civilian lives. Thus, it seems very likely that technical military imperatives took priority over the deaths of innocent people.

A word needs to be inserted here to underscore the questionable advantage of so-called pinpoint bombing in the saving of civilian lives. Everyone seems to believe that the accuracy of the bomb or missile is the sole determinant of the destruction of unintended targets. But it is the *blast area,* and not the exact point where munitions strike, that is critical. The military is not trying to knock somebody on the head, but to blow them to bits with overwhelming force. Whether one hits the area of a dime, a card table, or a swimming pool is irrelevant if the blast area is the same. Nevertheless, the military and the media keep referring to "precision" accuracy within a small circle as the way to evaluate the danger to innocent civilians.

Another component of the "weapons mix" was the cluster bomb, which constituted a higher percentage of munitions in Afghanistan than in the Balkans. According to the PDA-Conetta study, "In some cases cluster bombs had been used near civilian areas, leaving sub-munitions scattered among residences." Typically, these bomblets covered an area about 328 by 164 feet.[134]

Still another difference in weaponry between the Balkans and Afghanistan was the much greater use in Afghanistan of B-1 and B-52 bombers rather than B-2s, which are superior in both accuracy and flexibility—for example, in attacking targets of opportunity. In fact, the B-1 and B-52 bombers' capability for flexible bombing was something they "gained and began practicing only 18 months before the war began." Additionally, the decision to engage targets of opportunity in Afghanistan led to the more frequent use of "dumb" bombs, that is, bombs that were not guided by either laser or GPS.[135]

Another decision with potentially deadly results for civilians was reliance on the intelligence reports and advice of local leaders who were hostile to one another or even possibly sympathetic to the Taliban. One could destroy the residencies of one's own enemies by telling the U.S. military that they were occupied by Taliban or al Qaeda leaders without any regard for civilian casualties either in the residences or in the vicinity; this reportedly occurred.

Finally, it should be mentioned that the goal of the Afghanistan war, unlike that in the Balkans, was to destroy the Taliban/al Qaeda regime, not to force the enemy to negotiate. This meant that the residences of Taliban and al Qaeda leaders were fair game for bombing, and residences are usually located among other residences.[136]

If each of these decisions was looked upon as a "decision point," that is, an opportunity to weigh the implications for civilian casualties against military dictates, one would have to conclude that not a single one of these decision points was resolved in favor of lessening civilian casualties. In fact, the military in all its briefings and assurances that everything was being done to prevent civilian casualties did not, to my knowledge, say what these steps consisted of. And the media, again to my knowledge, never asked. If they did, an issue was not made out of it at all. (As shown earlier, the American media had little interest in civilian casualties.)

The apparent failure to modify tactics to protect civilians becomes especially puzzling when one realizes that, in Afghanistan, military targets were often set in civilian areas, not because civilians were being used as shields, as charged by the Pentagon, but because of historical and defensive reasons. In other words, civilian areas suffered from a special vulnerability to military action in Afghanistan that needed to be taken into account. The Soviet-backed government had placed garrisons and other military facilities in urbanized areas where they could be more easily protected from the rural mujahideen. Antiaircraft are usually found near important facilities that need protection, such as ministries of government, radio stations, power plants, and so on. These are areas occupied by civilians.[137]

These facts were no doubt common knowledge to U.S. intelligence and army commanders, and probably also to the secretary of defense. Yet decisions were apparently made without regard to this information, just as they were made about guidance systems, tactics of regime change, types of aircraft to be employed, and so forth. And then there was the fateful decision not to send ground troops, in the interest of keeping down the number of casualties among our military personnel, although their deployment might have spared many civilian lives from errant bombs and missiles. This *might* have been the seminal tactical decision that initiated the tilt toward large numbers of Afghan civilian deaths from bomb and missile blasts, or allegedly "precision" munitions.

It is hard to reconcile these facts and considerations with the defense secretary's assurance that "no nation in human history has done more to avoid civilian casualties than the United States has in this conflict." If the United States' bombardment from the air had had its intended effect of smashing the enemy in a short period of days or weeks, one might be more inclined to accept collateral damage. But only a few weeks after the war had been launched, it became clear that it was not going to be a cakewalk. As early as November 9, 2001, reports were surfacing of the allies' frustration with the U.S. prosecution of the war. British ministers, in particular, were aggravated by the course of events, and a news report revealed that "an air of stagnation has settled over the conflict." The

Pentagon became defensive toward criticism and, finally, unleashed the hounds of the Northern Alliance. Clearly, a *ground force was needed after all.*[138] U.S. air power had fallen short of its goal of trouncing the enemy with aerial, electronic battering alone (aside from a very limited number of special forces troops). And according to a book based on the author's presence during critical discussions of the president with his chief advisers, the latter had grave doubts about the course of the war; and the author concluded that it was essentially the Northern Alliance that had brought about the Taliban's defeat.[139]

How did the United States ensure the effective support of the Alliance in finishing the war that it had started? By having the CIA pay them millions of dollars (in hundred-dollar bills, by the way). Presumably, this sum was well worth the lives of American soldiers, which no doubt was given priority over the saving of civilian lives. Alternatively, the aerial bombardment could have been substantially moderated and American ground troops committed from the beginning. (It is true that there were certain practical obstacles to the deployment of ground troops, such as the distances involved, the lack of large, secure bases in the general area, and the difficulty of extracting troops quickly if necessary; but these might well have been overcome with more planning and a postponement of the war. In particular, if civilian casualties had been uppermost in the minds of the military planners, it is possible that a special, Herculean effort could have been made to overcome these problems.) In the final analysis, what the American military had failed to do with high-tech bombardment, the hardy Northern Alliance desperadoes were able to do by providing a "ground fulcrum" in return for millions of U.S. dollars. This is hardly the picture of a band of heroic, conquering American doughboys.

It was (and still is) presumed that the United States can afford its reluctance to commit ground forces because its high-tech arsenal of aerial weaponry can do the job with far less loss of *American* lives. The publicity for America's "precision" bombing in the Gulf War in the early '90s seemed to confirm this presumption. As noted above, however, the chance of hitting the target was only 50–50 even on the test range. (This probability was confirmed by the chairman of the Joint Chiefs of Staff in a Senate hearing in 2002.) Moreover, many of the bombs were not really "precision" in the technical lingo of the military, but "accurate." However, that was not the impression conveyed to the American people in the films of the bombardment that showed munitions going through windows in the Gulf War.

Neither in the Gulf War of 1991 nor in the Afghanistan war did the Defense Department provide the media with film showing bombs or missiles hitting a village, a truckload of refugees, or an open field; and it is doubtful that the media inquired about the representativeness of the small sample of films shown to them, that is, whether the specimens shown were a random sample of what had really occurred. (One reason that journalists can be manipulated by government briefings is their ignorance of basic statistics.) Thus, the American public gained a distorted image of the military's ability to inflict "surgical strikes." Here as elsewhere the media did its duty as the military's compliant propaganda arm. (This point will be elaborated in chapter 10.) In other words, the average American is simply unable to evaluate the truthfulness of the military's claims about its superior, high-tech weapons.

This brief survey of military decision-making in the prosecution of the Afghanistan war points to miscalculations by the American military, the adverse consequences of which are still playing out and may disable the country for years. (See below on the role of the warlords after the war.) In the case of Afghanistan, at least, it is possible that the vaunted puissance of America's military is not matched by either its strategic or tactical sagacity; and its humanitarian record during the war appeared to be atrocious. But to some extent these flaws were the fault of political considerations. The aversion of the U.S. military to casualties among its personnel, owing to the possible effect on public opinion, set constraints.[140] But no one from the government pointed out to the American people that aerial bombing was bound to kill thousands of innocent Afghan civilians, and that this toll might be reduced by committing some ground troops. Would it have made a difference? No one knows. The point is that it simply was not even tried, perhaps because it would have been an admission that "precision" bombing would not be able to save civilian lives after all, or that high tech might really mean low morality.

In any discussion of the costs of the Afghanistan war, one should not overlook the impact on the fragile environment of the drought-wracked country. "Losses of natural resources are beyond estimation," said a spokesman for the Society for Afghanistan's Viable Environment. "After a few years the forests will be gone." The writer continued: "In their place, the nearly barren land seeded with mines and unexploded bombs ... With many power plants and electrical lines destroyed ... millions of daily cooking fires are devouring the last vestige of the forests that once covered millions of acres of country." Cutting trees had become a profitable business, with the consequence that the top soil was blown away or washed into water courses, destroying farmland.[141]

And then, finally, there was the matter of cost in the bookkeeper's sense. The estimated cost per month was $500 million to $1 billion. A dumb bomb cost $600–$1400; a JDAM (smart, but not precision) cost $25,000; a daisy cutter, $27,000; a bunker buster, $231,000; a Black Hawk helicopter, $11 million; and a Pave Low helicopter, $40 million. The hourly cost of flying a Navy FA-18 was $5,000.[142] These are only a few of the costs, but they convey some idea of the immense sums that were expended in a war that eventually killed more civilians than enemy combatants, a war in which almost half of the civilian deaths were due to aerial bombardment.

As for reconstruction costs, no one knows. But the estimate that the "reconstruction of Afghanistan over the next several years could cost as much or more than the war to defeat the Taliban and destroy al Qaeda"[143] (which, as we now know, was not destroyed) is not unreasonable. Encouragingly, a press release by the U.S. Department of Defense in December 2002 assured us that "much of the immediate potential for humanitarian disaster has passed, and much of the country is more secure than it's been in decades."[144] But the first part of this reassuring statement was apparently contradicted by an announcement on CNN only two months earlier that "4 million Afghans will need food aid in the following 12 months." Still earlier in the year, a USAID official testified before a Senate committee as follows:

> Half the country lives in absolute poverty. Average life expectancy is 46 years. Malnutrition is widespread. The child mortality rate is among the highest in the world. Unemployment is running about 50%, and 70% of the people are illiterate. Virtually all the institutions have been destroyed and much of its infrastructure has been destroyed . . . The widespread famine we feared has not occurred. . . The drought has lasted four years.[145]

Thus, even if the famine had been avoided, many humanitarian problems must have persisted. And only two weeks after the Defense Department's assurance that a humanitarian disaster had not occurred, the *New York Times* reported:

> Half a million people—returning refugees who do not have a house to rebuild, those displaced by years of war and still unable to go home, and the urban poor made homeless by war and rising cost—have fallen through the aid net in the past year, and face the freezing winter with completely inadequate shelter in Afghanistan cities . . . Some 200,000 of them will need food aid . . .[146]

One cannot but wonder if the Defense Department's press release about the passing of the humanitarian crisis and these contemporaneous, on-the-scene reports were referring to the same country.

But the real test of America's commitment to assistance, still terribly needed one and a half years after the end of the war, was its level of funding to do the job of reconstruction. The president clearly expressed his dedication to the task: "In Afghanistan we helped to liberate an oppressed people," he said in his State of the Union address. "And we will continue helping them secure their country, rebuild their society and educate their children: boys and girls." And how much money was requested in President Bush's budget for this mission? The answer is none. The White House included nothing for reconstruction or humanitarian aid in Afghanistan when it sent its budget to Congress.[147] Was this due to clerical error or to distraction by other matters, such as preparations for the Iraq war?

The issue of security, the second part of the Defense Department's reassuring press release in December 2002, will be dealt with later. First, it is necessary to examine the outcomes of the war in terms of its goals, for only in this way can we determine whether all the cost in human lives, money for munitions, and environmental destruction was worth the effort.

To begin with, 3,000 to 4,000 Taliban coalition troops were counted as casualties, and 7,000 Taliban and foreign troops were taken prisoner. Only 75 U.S. military personnel were injured and few died.[148] However, it has been reported that "most of the top Taliban leadership survived the war and eluded capture." Of the three dozen or so most "wanted" Talibans, somewhat more than 12 were injured, killed, or defected. This amounts to a success rate of approximately 33 percent of the leadership; the top leader, Osama bin Laden, has still not been found.

The Acting Director of the FBI's counterterrorism division has estimated that, as a result of the war, "al-Qaeda's capability to commit 'horrific' acts has been reduced by 30%."[149] Unfortunately, it takes only a handful of persons to pull off a horrific act, or even just one person. Only a quarter to a third of the network, according to the CIA, was killed or captured, and "al-Qaeda retains cells in some 50 countries, few susceptible to military solutions."[150] According to U.S. intelligence officials as reported by *USA Today* in September 2002: "al-Qaeda's operatives are regrouping, recruiting, changing their tactics, and planning more terror missions against the west . . . Officials fear that up to 20,000 men who have attended bin Laden's terrorist camps in Afghanistan, Pakistan, Somalia and Sudan since the 1990s are still potential martyrs in his crusade." Sixty-five countries are estimated to contain terrorist cells, and "al-Qaeda also reportedly sent several shipments of gold to Sudan for safe-keeping."[151] And, of course, it is possible that terrorists of all stripes have become more motivated to engage in terrorist attacks.[152] As for ridding Afghanistan of al Qaeda, a UN report, released on December 17, 2002, asserted that the organization has activated training camps in the east of the country.[153]

These outcomes of the Afghanistan war provide an apt example of America's disinclination to seek or heed the lessons of other advanced countries, as noted in chapter 1. As a Spanish journalist has pointed out with respect to Spain's 30-year war against terrorism: "Using the army turned out to be a disaster. We were trying to kill mosquitoes with bombs. Innocents were killed, democracy suffered and we were no safer."[154]

As for Afghanistan's former involvement in production of drugs, according to the UN drug control agency:

> Afghanistan has again established itself as the world's largest opium poppy
> producer this year, with growers taking advantage of the power vacuum during
> the US-led war and the collapse of the Taliban regime . . . the Northern Alli-
> ance has been more clearly associated with narcotics than the Taliban.[155]

Which brings us to the question of the warlords, known during the war as
the Northern Alliance, a question that resumes our discussion of the war's effectiveness. The reader will recall that the U.S. government paid them handsomely
to come to our aid in fighting the Taliban. To what extent can we depend on
their cooperation, or at least their willingness to allow the Karzai government to
pursue its course unhindered in Kabul? And how have they been conducting
themselves in their own parts of the country? The answer to the first question is
that they will comply with U.S. wishes as long as the United States plies them
with millions of dollars in cash. According to the *London Observer*, "bin bags
full of US dollars have been flown to Afghanistan, sometimes on RAF planes, to
be given to key regional power brokers who could cause trouble for the Prime
Minister Hamid Karzai's administration . . ."[156] In short, the United States still
seems to be paying for its decision not to commit its own ground troops in Afghanistan, and paying in hard currency. According to some reports, the warlords
have not been averse to raising the ante from time to time.

What about the behavior of the warlords? Have these "allies" embraced the
principles for which the United States claims to have, at least in part, waged the
war, namely, the promotion of democracy and human rights, and especially with
regard to religious freedom and women's emancipation? We should recall that
the Northern Alliance was "a symbol of massacre, systematic rape and pillage"
in years past, according to a UK news source, and that this was precisely the
reason that the United States itself welcomed the Taliban to power in the mid-
1990s as the lesser of two evils. In fact, when the Northern Alliance left Kabul
in 1996, "it left the city with 50,000 dead behind it."[157]

Is it any wonder, then, that a number of months after the cessation of the
U.S.-led war against the Taliban, Human Rights Watch observed that immediate
steps were necessary to counteract the growing power of the warlords? Some of
the practices that were identified and condemned by this watchdog organization
were "local commanders corrupting the election process through use of threats,
beatings, imprisonments and other tactics of intimidation . . . generalized violence and criminality . . . reemergence of figures associated with the Taliban as
well as the extremist Islamist movement . . ."[158] And after citing the refusal of
the U.S.-led coalition and the UN Security Council to increase the security force
beyond the city of Kabul, Human Rights Watch observed that "US forces seem
to be doing little if anything to address the insecurity experienced by ordinary
Afghans." In fact, cooperation with the warlords seemed to be making matters
worse.[159] Even the religious police and school curriculum of the Taliban were

retained in some places. Here is an account of one incident by an election commissioner:

> Three boys, each about 8 or 9 years old, were killed when they were on their way to school. They were wearing turbans, and the police, army men, stop the three guys and ask them "why have you put on turbans?" And then they shot them. Two were killed, and one was not. We confirmed this.[160]

These reports by Human Rights Watch were issued about five months before the Defense Department's press release reassuring us that "the country is more secure than it's been in decades." Could conditions have improved so rapidly? Here is a press report that appeared the same month as the Defense Department's statement.

> Turf wars flare up frequently in the north, southeast and east as warlords tussle for power, land and money . . . the media-friendly Karzai does not yet control his country, despite enjoying the backing of the mighty U.S. military . . . Karzai's plans for a national army of up to 70,000 soldiers has got off to a painfully slow start. The force numbers between 1,000 and 1,500 a year after Karzai came to power.[161]

Meanwhile, the United States was staunchly opposed to expanding the peacekeeping force outside Kabul, "despite the repeated requests of Karzai, his ministers, and the people of Afghanistan."[162] As if more proof were needed of the stark discrepancy between the press release of the U.S. Department of Defense and the facts on the ground in Afghanistan, only a month or so before the Defense Department's statement, a story in the *San Francisco Chronicle* asserted that "outside the capital, Kabul, and large, once-cosmopolitan cities like Mazar-e-Sharif, parents continue to sell their daughters to future husbands, women are not allowed to run shops . . . widespread women's rights violations are partly to blame for the high maternal mortality rates . . . the second highest in the world . . ."[163] And early in 2003, an Afghan building contractor asked, "Why are they [i.e., the U.S.] going to war against Iraq when they have not sorted out problems here, like lack of security, the most important thing for us?"[164]

To deal with this devil's brew of warfare, religious savagery, violence against women and children, election fraud, police brutality, and opium trafficking, the State Department and USAID officials announced in December 2002 that "the United States will be deploying 8–10 joint regional teams throughout the country [that] will consist of about 60 people, including Special Forces, civil affairs, State Department and USAID representatives, and individuals from other coalition militaries."[165] If this statement meant that each team would consist of 60 people, then only about 550 people were going to try to drag this antediluvian country, wracked with devastation, death, and homelessness, into the 21st century, a country that has not even experienced the 18th century's Enlightenment. In doing so, they would be obliged to deal with tribal chieftains who care only for dollars and the perpetuation or expansion of power, are well armed, and to whom America is beholden for having saved it from ignominious defeat. If the statement meant that only 60 people total were to be involved, then the plan was utterly ludicrous.

This situation has arisen because of America's refusal to commit its own soldiers to fight the Taliban on the ground; this decision stalled the air assault in its tracks until the Northern Alliance could be persuaded to do the job for cash. The American media and the public, of course, to this day perceive the war as a triumph of military prowess and diplomacy. After all, almost no Americans died! And yet, the aftermath of the war will be felt for many years, and its failure to do more than dent the worldwide apparatus of terror has probably emboldened and invigorated its practitioners. Americans may have learned little from the war, but the terrorists probably learned a valuable lesson: Don't concentrate your forces in one country.

An Afterword on Civilian Casualties

One might have a just reason for going to war, but not necessarily a just manner of prosecuting the war. And simply to affirm that "war is hell" does not absolve one from failing to take precautions to avoid killing innocent people. Finally, simply to avow that one has done or will do everything feasible to prevent civilian casualties does not mean that one has done or will do anything whatsoever, especially when such measures are not made known. Even if these avowals are heartfelt and true, it is still possible that the precautions are inadequate or incompetently carried out. If this had not been the case in Afghanistan, then the record would not show such an egregious loss of civilian lives in the war. Because of the reputation for omission and deception earned by the Defense Department concerning postwar conditions in Afghanistan, it is hard to believe anything that the Department might say about civilians.

Protocol 1 to the 1949 Geneva Convention, disregard of which is deemed a war crime, reads as follows:

> States have a legal obligation under Article 51(5)(b) to refrain from attacks "which may be expected to cause incidental loss of civilian life, injury to civilians, damage to civilian objects or a combination thereof, which would be excessive in relation to the concrete and direct military advantage anticipated."[166]

Finally, there is the issue of international moral advantage. Before America's slaughter of Afghan civilians, the nation occupied the moral high ground as the wronged party owing to al Qaeda's 9/11 massacre of innocent people. But following the war, Islamic extremists, and perhaps a growing number of moderates, could point to America's massacre of thousands of unarmed civilians in Afghanistan as grounds for jihad. In short, the United States might have been seduced into the same cycle of vengeful bloodletting as the historically wronged Jews, who have been struggling with Palestinian terrorism, a struggle seemingly made endless by the infinite escalation of moral outrage. The American people will never know why the terrorists might have redoubled their hatred, because the American media have not told them nor given them the facts to draw their own conclusions.

Afghanistan was neither the first nor the last Middle Eastern nation to feel the wrath of Uncle Sam. Although the Gulf War against Iraq in 1990 is still widely believed by Americans to have been an extraordinarily "clean" war with pinpoint bombing and few civilian casualties, the facts are quite the contrary: "Most estimates of the civilian death toll [in the Gulf War] are approximately 15,000," according to a watchdog organization concerned with the American media.[167] In the second Iraq war of 2003–2004, current figures for civilian deaths are an estimated minimum of 8,930 and a maximum of 10,781 as of April 27, 2004.[168] This yields a figure of about 9,255 civilian deaths identified as of spring 2004. If we add to this figure the estimated number of civilian deaths caused by bombardment and the refugee crisis in the Afghanistan War two and a half years earlier (5,325), we arrive at a total of 14,580 civilian deaths caused by the American invasions of two Middle Eastern nations in the recent past. This figure is almost *five times* the number of victims in the 9/11 attacks, or about 4.8 civilians killed in Iraq and Afghanistan for every victim of 9/11. It also belies the notion that only "some" collateral damage is to be expected from war. Some day it may more aptly be called mass murder.

Now let us turn our full attention to the Iraq war and examine its prosecution and consequences in more detail.

The Iraq War of 2003 and More Military Mismanagement

As mentioned in the Introduction, top defense planners in our government proposed "regime change" in Iraq as early as 1991, following the Gulf War that left Saddam Hussein in charge of Iraq. It is possible, as some have asserted, that reluctance to further downsize the mammoth defense establishment after the Cold War and a desire to regenerate a waning conservatism were dominant factors in identifying a new enemy and focusing on Iraq. (Defense contracts accounted for about one-fifth of the manufacturing output of America and more than half a million jobs at the time.) But in the final analysis, it seems likely that the felt imperatives of protecting access to Middle Eastern oil, instigating stable democracies in the region, and gaining security benefits for both Israel and the United States by eliminating a hostile power in the area that possessed deadly unconventional weapons played more important roles in the Defense Department's proposal to uproot the regime of the Iraqi dictator.

The only problem was enlisting the support of the American people in this endeavor. This was achieved 10 years later (after the intervening administration of President Clinton), first, by the terrorist attacks on American soil on 9/11, and, second, by citing Iraq's possession of weapons of mass destruction and its record for destabilizing the Middle East. Underlying all these proximate causes was the American yearning to restore its credibility and self-respect as the greatest nation on earth. (See the Introduction.) Unfortunately, the war with Iraq revealed even more clearly than the Afghanistan war that America lacked a basic maturity in foreign affairs, which hobbled its efforts to assume the role of world leadership. It also raised further questions about the capabilities of our military machine, in spite of its reputation as second to none in the history of the world.

Immaturity in foreign affairs was revealed particularly in the failure of the U.S. government to foresee the impact of its preemptive aggression on the credibility of the United Nations, relations with its traditional allies, a paranoid dictator of a nuclear nation (North Korea) that the United States had menacingly criticized, world public opinion and terrorism, the support of its own people, the drain on its treasury, and postwar mayhem in Iraq. Afghanistan had been more or less left to its own devices (with help from NATO) in dealing with security problems outside Kabul, and the possible resurgence of both the Taliban and terrorism in general seemed to have been downgraded in the administration's agenda. Now, in 2003, the consequences of America's reckless handling of foreign affairs were coming home to roost. Iraq was engulfed in looting, sabotage, and guerrilla warfare, thousands of innocent people were slain during the war, UN principles were subverted by the preemptive attack, Americans began to lose trust in their leaders, North Korea expelled UN monitors, America's reputation in the world plunged to its lowest level ever, and terrorism seemed to be reinvigorated even in Iraq and Afghanistan.

These events, apparently unanticipated by the American government, exacerbated the American people's sense that world affairs were once again slipping out of their control. And in Iraq the specter of another quagmire—owing to the extremely unsettled conditions there—began to stalk the land, a development that America's leaders seemed not to have prepared for or even anticipated (and which they had dismissed when the possibility had been raised before the war). This lack of foresight prevailed in spite of a special report prepared by the State Department that predicted the postwar turmoil. Clearly, the prediction was not heeded by the president or the Defense Department in any practical way.[169] Owing to the flux of events in Iraq at this writing, I will focus here on just a few aspects of the conduct and aftereffects of the war.

In regard to the conduct of the war: It is difficult to detect an exceptionally able military machine in the experience of Task Force 1-64 Armor "Desert Rogues," according to the Pentagon's own After Action Report.[170] While several successes were mentioned, owing mostly to improvisation by individuals, the lion's share of the report was highly critical. On the assumption that the problems of this unit were not wholly unique, and that they indicate the managerial shortfalls of our military, it is well worth looking at some of the report's highlights.

In general, it was concluded that training manuals were inadequate for dealing with an enemy in an urban (or even semi-urban) setting. Thus, long before United States troops reached Baghdad, many problems were experienced. Owing to the ubiquity of bridge overpasses, low trees, and buildings on narrow streets, hidden tanks and vehicles "were not seen until they were only meters away." And aside from the endangerments of a city environment, the armor on the flanks of tank turrets and hulls was penetrated by rifles and grenade rounds. Armor that was available was not issued, and better armor needed to be made available. Tank commanders had to expose themselves in order to see the enemy and control movement. Tank radios and phones for communication with their infantry squads were either unusable or insecure. Personnel loading ammunition on tanks were outside and had little protection from enemy fire. Antipersonnel munitions to deal with the large number of enemy infantry were lacking. Night vision technology was "seriously flawed" and "proved all but worthless"; consequently, several vehicles crashed into berms and wadis. Global Positioning and TIS sights "could not provide positive identification of small arms, RPGs [grenade launchers] or mortars beyond 800m." Spare parts were not available except from wrecked vehicles, which "made maintenance operations difficult if not impossible for long periods of time."

Regarding air cover, "from the crossing of the line of departure to the cessation of hostilities in Baghdad, the task force did not have any attack aviation support . . . the aviators were not willing to fly to support the troops on the ground." Consequently, the report concludes that aviation simply should not be counted on in future conflicts because "the aviators are unreliable at best." Yet the report is emphatic about the critical importance of air cover: "As the brigade and division *main* effort, attack aviation should have been available *at all times* during combat operations or when enemy contact was likely" (emphasis added).

Special operations forces were totally useless to this unit—for example, in bringing special information of any value. In fact, "the special forces hid or moved behind the protection of armored forces *throughout the operation*" (emphasis added).

Units were required to operate *both* combat and "stability and support operations" (SASO, i.e., peacekeeping operations) at the same time in lieu of specialized personnel. Thus, the "radical and swift change from combat operations to SASO and back to combat operations over and over again causes many points of friction for the soldiers and their leaders." In particular, no training was given on checkpoint operations or dealing with civilians; and at no time was an interpreter available. Moreover, the unit ran out of "force protection" materials before reaching Baghdad. "In the meantime, the units utilized destroyed cars, flower posts, bicycle racks, and whatever else was available for force protection."

Nor did these problems end with the invasion phase. According to a number of news reports during the insurgency that occurred in early 2004, there were still inadequacies in protective armor, equipment maintenance, supplies, dealing with citizens, and preparation for urban warfare. According to an article in *Newsweek* in spring 2004, "The military is 1,800 armored Humvees short of its own stated requirement for Iraq. Despite desperate attempts to supply bolt-on armor, many soldiers still ride around in light-skinned Humvees . . . soldiers are rushing to jury-rig their Humvees with anything hard they can find . . . sandbags, even plywood panels . . ."[171] American civilians have been sending supplies to their relatives and friends who are fighting in Iraq. As for the numbers of personnel, military experts and members of Congress have noted a shortage of personnel to do the jobs of sealing the borders, protecting installations, policing, rebuilding, and combating the enemy.

This brief recital of deficiencies in the preparedness of one task force during the invasion and of the occupational forces more than a year later raises serious questions about the Defense Department's readiness for the Iraq war at the outset and its ability to learn from its early mistakes. For the picture that emerges is that of prolonged, slapdash mayhem, especially during the invasion phase, instead of the behavior of a modern, well-trained and well-equipped army led by planners and commanders of vision who are responsive to the needs of an invading or occupying army. In fact, it suggests that the reputation of the American military might be closer to myth than reality; or rather, that its main advantage by far is simply *overwhelming firepower*. (Some battlefield observers reported that the horrific noise of weaponry alone prompted many enemy combatants to drop their weapons and run.) None of the early problems, by the way, was conveyed to the American public by the media during the invasion, which leads one to question either the alertness of our embedded journalists or the integrity of our stateside American editors. If the problems mentioned in the after-action report quoted above had been conveyed to the public early in the war, perhaps they would not have persisted into the occupation phase for so many months.

It is noteworthy that the American government has not released figures about civilian deaths in Iraq, and indeed may never do so. At one point it was briefly mentioned in the media that the Pentagon had instructed our troops not to keep a record of such deaths. Such a policy, of course, would be the most effective means of preventing leaks and fending off questions at press conferences. Thus, one of the paramount reasons for the worldwide demonstrations against the war—the death of innocent civilians—will probably never be *officially* confirmed or disconfirmed. The best way to handle embarrassing accusations is not to have the data whereby anyone can prove innocence or guilt. This lack of information is not regarded as obstruction of justice on the part of the Defense Department, however, because the department has never been required by law (which means by Congress) to keep a record of civilian deaths.

It is also noteworthy that in spite of the unusual degree of access accorded the media, there was virtually no coverage of civilian casualties inflicted by Americans, especially during the invasion, or at least very little that was conveyed to the American people. Since it has been estimated by various sources that (as of April 2004) close to 10,000 civilians have perished in the war, this nonreporting has suggested a remarkable display of blindness, forbearance, or squeamishness by the media, and perhaps a combination of all three. (And it should be borne in mind that 40 percent of Iraqi citizens are estimated to be children.) During the invasion in particular, what monopolized the TV screen were soldiers fighting with modern weapons, bombs and missiles exploding at a great distance, sandstorms, and retired military brass musing about strategy and tactics. The only things missing were anguish, mutilation, pain, and death, which is what warfare is usually about. Whether the media's inattention was due to indifference on the part of journalists in the field, the blurring of the distinction between civilians and combatants (as with strikes against civilian vehicles in open country), control by the military, or censorship by editors in the States is unknown. But it is clear that little or nothing had changed since the coverage of the Afghanistan war, when the media essentially blacked out any evidence or discussion of civilian deaths. Evidently, the much applauded practice of "embedding" journalists in military units during the Iraq conflict gave a false impression of the latter's access to events—to put the best possible face on it.

Coverage by Middle Eastern and even European news organizations was in stark contrast to the de facto censorship by the American media. Here, for example, is a vignette from BBC News World Edition that would never have appeared in the mainstream American media during the invasion:

> A father was fleeing with his family from the fierce fighting in Nasiriya when an American bomb struck and "he lost his wife, six children, his father, his mother, and two brothers." The man said: "God take revenge on America."[172]

Only one congressman, to my knowledge, has personally requested the Department of Defense to supply any casualty figures in its possession. As Congressman Dennis Kucinich wrote to the Secretary: "The United States owes it to the people of Iraq and the world community to make this information public."[173] Why the government withholds such information (if it has it) is not known, since one would think that it would wish to demonstrate that prewar predictions in the tens of thousands of civilian casualties were exaggerated and, thus, to be able to take credit for its precision bombing as a lifesaver—unless it does not want the public to even think about civilian casualties high or low.

Equally puzzling is the banning of aid agencies from ministering to the population for a considerable time after the danger had subsided. This problem relates to the earlier discussion of the military's competence in the prosecution of the war, for (as shown below) the military insisted on controlling the dispensing of aid. And the confusion that ensued after the phase of conventional combat ended was mentioned in the after-action report referred to earlier. Here is what the Pentagon report had to say:

> Weeks after occupying Baghdad in force, the unit is still unable to direct the civilian populace to humanitarian agencies other than the Red Crescent. We have no way to direct people to places to receive food and water, to search for loved ones, to locate deceased personnel. The unit did not have the ability to answer any questions simply because of the unsynchronized and unplanned operations of the Civil Affairs community and other non-governmental organizations.[174]

The aid agencies were well aware of these failures and attributed them to the military's assertion of control without allowing them to take timely action. As one aid worker in Iraq said after the war, "I think people are right to be surprised that there are not more aid agencies in Iraq, but we cannot go to places like Basra without military agreement."[175] And that agreement was slow to come. Some agencies said that they were being told that areas passed hours before by convoys of journalists were still hostile. And there was widespread suspicion among the workers that they were being kept out "in order to undermine the role of the UN in post-war Iraq." Some agencies refused to work with the U.S. interim government because of this suspicion.[176] The preceding report of the frustrating delay in authorization to give aid was filed on April 14, 2003, five days after control of Baghdad was gained, eight days after resistance was quelled in Basra, eleven days after the Baghdad airport was seized, and eighteen days after the first humanitarian relief shipments began arriving in the port of Um Basr. (For dates, refer to source note 176.) During this period of time, Doctors Without Borders, the international medical agency, had only four physicians in Baghdad, a city of more than four million inhabitants where many were dying and needed immediate attention.

The reason for the delay in providing relief was the time it took for Washington to resolve the issue of who would be in charge of assistance. Evidently, this had not been part of the postwar planning. The president did not decide the matter until the second week of April, when the job was finally handed to the Department of Defense instead of the State Department, over the strenuous objections of the secretary of state.[177] There was never any question of giving it to the UN because of the Security Council's refusal to endorse the attack on Iraq. This decision not only endangered aid workers because of their association with the military but gave the military the authority to decide who should get aid, why, and with how much money.

"It is a disastrous decision," said a leading advocate of a human rights organization. And a vice president of Refugees International said that "instead of an objective assessment, which is best done by the State Department or the United Nations, we have a person in charge [General Jay Garner] who has a political past." Another leader of a relief effort predicted that "there will be a big debate about whether we can continue to work with the military. If they have veto power, then we may have to come home."[178]

What exactly were the challenges faced by the military in its unaccustomed role of managing a relief effort?—widespread blackouts and shortages of water, physical destruction, understaffed hospitals and lack of medicine to handle the casualties of war and the cases of illness and malnutrition owing to past deprivations, unexploded bombs, people searching for their loved ones, losses of property and government records to looters, hordes of children out of school, and pockets of hostility toward the occupying forces. (See the article cited in note 179 for a grim report on the situation.) One observer predicted that "long after the military has gone from Iraq, international relief organizations will still be on the ground trying to resolve the problems that it [i.e., the U.S. military] caused."[180] All of which raises a question about the wisdom of trying to kill a rat by burning down a house filled with people.

Casualties among innocent civilians will always be troubling to civilized aggressors in spite of the justice of a particular war. But when a major, professed goal of war is to *improve the lot* of civilians, the gap between intentions and outcomes becomes more than merely troubling. There were no dead among the few cheering bands of civilians shown on TV; and even the cheers of the living soon turned into massive demonstrations of hatred against the occupying forces for failing to restore basic services like water and electricity, killing the innocent, destroying essential infrastructure (such as radio stations and transmission lines), failing to protect government facilities and toxic depots from looting, firing all Baath government employees and army personnel (which swelled the number of unemployed by about 400,000 and created idle people filled with resentment), failing to communicate with Iraqis if only with a few, simple words in their own language, and so on. And then, suddenly, there appeared on television screens a painfully familiar image of hundreds of Middle Easterners surging down the street of a dusty town shrieking and cursing while carrying coffins on their shoulders filled with the victims of soldiers who had fired into an angry crowd. Palestine under Israeli occupation? No. Iraq under American occupation.

The administration's decision to prosecute the war in spite of widespread opposition is especially puzzling in light of the prescient view of the president's father when the latter was president. In his memoirs, written a few years after leaving office, he explained his decision not to eliminate the Saddam regime in the Gulf War as follows: "Trying to eliminate Saddam . . . would have incurred incalculable human and political costs . . . there was no exit strategy . . . Had we gone the invasion route, the United States could conceivably still be an occupying power in a bitterly hostile land." This was written several years, of course, before his son declared war against Iraq once again, this time with the intention of doing exactly what his father had rejected as a course of action 10 years earlier.

As for military prowess, it seems that the richest nation on earth had put its money into creating a monstrous war machine in lieu of ministering to the needs of people at home or elsewhere. It was then capable of overwhelming a third-rate military power weakened by years of harsh sanctions, and did so over the strenuous objections of millions around the world and their United Nations representatives, who feared the consequences for innocent Iraqis and the fomenting of terrorism, and doubted the motives of the aggressor. The consequences have been amply demonstrated, although the true motives still remain to be disclosed. (Concerning a possible economic motive, it is worth noting that reconstruction was initially limited to American companies, and that Paul Bremer, who became the U.S. Chief Administrator in Iraq, announced at a meeting of the World Economic Forum that 40 government-owned firms will be privatized and the laws rewritten to encourage investment in Iraq, all of which sounds suspiciously like an American effort to corporatize the country for American profit.) Does this victory, then, warrant acclaim? The secretary of defense has shown intense public chagrin over the attention that was given to the shambles in Iraq and the demonstrations by Iraqis instead of to the speedy military victory and disposal of a dictatorship. Moreover, it is the full array of consequences that needs to be kept under scrutiny, not just the intended ones, and this applies to any human action whatsoever. Failure to anticipate and prepare for unintended consequences that are undesirable must be fully weighed in the balance when evaluating the success of any action, whether it is attacking a nation militarily or building a chicken coop. America's apparent failure to do this is made all the more alarming by the recent lesson of Afghanistan, where thousands of innocent civilians were killed by more or less the same wayward munitions.

As for the American media, they performed remarkably well as propaganda organs in stark contrast to the coverage by other nations.[181] True, journalists were held at bay by the press briefings at Central Command, and limited in coverage by embedment in field units, but they did not try to protest these arrangements (at least not on camera) and managed to ignore the carnage while embracing the standard military euphemisms for slaughter like "degrading" the enemy, "collateral damage," and "softening up" the bunkers. Meanwhile, back in the stateside studios, anchorpersons gave what appeared to be stellar performances as cheerleaders for "our" side.[182] As one observer bluntly summed it up, "The coverage of this war in the press and on television has been disgusting. North American reporting, and in particular on the U.S. television stations, has been cravenly submissive to the Pentagon and the White House."[183]

But the mainstream media knew their audience, an audience whose tastes and informational needs they had largely shaped themselves. Thus, when telecasting to an overseas audience, CNN was quite capable of modifying its style. To be specific, the "most trusted name in news" divided its coverage between a domestic market and an international market, even to the extent of assigning different teams to the two markets; according to reports, the international coverage was "far more serious and informed than the American version."[184] In short, CNN gave the home market what it had taught them to expect and what the government preferred them to expect: war as a diversion from the daily affairs of life and the fulfillment of the American Myth of invincibility. In this regard, as well as in others, the American media performed much as they had in Afghanistan.

A noteworthy way in which the Iraq war did differ from its predecessor was the justification for the assault. The Afghanistan government had supported and sympathized with the perpetrators of the 9/11 attacks, whose headquarters and training facilities were located in that country. In contrast, it seems that the rationale for attacking Iraq had to be at least partially fabricated by the United States in the absence of an overt threat to the nation while being vouchsafed to the American people as the authentic coin of the realm. The incompetence of American intelligence agencies in general, and particularly with regard to Iraq's weapons of mass destruction (WMD), will be dealt with later (especially in chapter 11 on the performance of federal bureaucracies). But here it should be pointed out that the Iraq war was undertaken mainly on the basis of intelligence estimates of the probability of some future attack involving WMD and Iraq's cooperation with al Qaeda. Claims that such weapons were possessed by Iraq and, in addition, that the regime was linked to the 9/11 perpetrators, were reiterated on a number of occasions by the president and his associates. And these references were not vague generalities, or limited to the bogus claim in the president's State of the Union speech that Saddam had tried to buy uranium from Libya, but concrete and specific citations of WMD production and capacity in Iraq. For example, in the words of the president: "Right now, Iraq is expanding and improving facilities that were used for the production of biological weapons." Or again: "We now know that the regime has produced thousands of tons of chemical weapons . . . ," and "We've discovered through intelligence that Iraq has a growing fleet of manned and unmanned aerial vehicles that could be used to disperse chemical or biological weapons across broad areas . . . [including] missions targeting the United States." And also: "Iraq has stockpiled biological and chemical weapons and is rebuilding the facilities used to make more of those weapons."[185] Such specificity (and some other statements were even more detailed) does not suggest just liberal interpretations of intelligence reports or exaggerations of fact. They are full-bodied facts themselves, not just heightened rhetoric, and therefore could only have come from the intelligence gatherers or their higher-ups, it would appear.

As we now know (as of January 2004), the search for WMD in Iraq has been virtually abandoned as a fruitless enterprise. And it seems reasonable to say the same about the alleged linkage with al Qaeda terrorists. Indeed, a debriefing report of an interview with two top-ranking leaders of al Qaeda in American custody, carried out by the CIA, denied any such connection, but was not disclosed to the public before the war commenced.[186]

The administration's fall-back position has been that the elimination of Saddam was sufficient justification for the war. This face-saving maneuver has a certain appeal because of Saddam's heinous character and acts; and indeed, his ousting had, in fact, been cited as a supplementary reason to prosecute the war. But in the absence of an imminent threat to strike the United States with aerial vehicles laden with WMD, and so on, it sidesteps the question of whether the removal of an odious regime was worth the costs that were incurred, including the death of some 10,000 innocent Iraqi civilians, casualties of Americans amounting to 3,392 by the end of 2003 (including about 500 fatalities), the chaos of Iraqi society, the stimulation of terrorism, the setting of a worldwide precedent for preemptive war, the flouting of the UN by the world's most powerful leader, the sacrifice of much needed social and technical assistance in America and elsewhere in the world owing to the diversion of resources to the war, and the fomenting of more hatred and even a nuclear threat (namely, from North Korea or Iran) against America.

In particular, a huge cost in world opinion was revealed by international polls. As one pollster observed: "The rift between Americans and Western Europeans has widened and the bottom has fallen out in support of the U.S. in most of the Muslim world . . . Most of the respondents named Bush as the main source of their mistrust of America."[187] Percentage approval ratings of America dropped precipitously in a number of countries—for example, from 75 percent two years earlier to 15 percent in mid-2003 in the country of Indonesia. Also, regard of Muslims for Bin Laden actually improved in several places, and many inhabitants of foreign countries feared that the United States would invade their own lands. And these unflattering impressions of the United States extended beyond zones of conflict into Africa and the Far East.[188] In sum, unintended consequences that were highly undesirable extended far beyond the borders of Iraq.

Finally, there were the human rights violations of the occupying forces documented by Amnesty International and virtually blacked out by the American mainstream media. Eighteen detention camps held over 3,000 persons for months, many of whom had no access to lawyers or families. Prisoners reported being "hooded, forced to kneel or stand for prolonged periods of times, subjected to sleep deprivation for extended periods, exposed to loud music or bright lights—treatment which amounts to torture under international definitions." Of particular concern was the use of excessive force against civilians. As Amnesty International stated:

> We also investigated a number of incidents of the apparent use of excessive force, where Iraqis were shot dead by US/UK troops in non-combat situations when the troops were not in danger of life or serious injury. In response to demonstrations in the street or inside detention facilities, troops opened fire with live ammunition, without adequate (or any) warning . . . Compounding the frustration is the fact that the US has exempted all its military personnel from prosecution under Iraqi law for any act committed while in Iraq.[189]

This report was dated October 2003. But not until April 2004 were the abuses of Iraqi prisoners in Saddam Hussein's former torture chambers publicly admitted by the Pentagon and the president, and a full-scale investigation launched. This delay occurred notwithstanding the president's assertion in a television interview on May 5, 2004, that "when an issue of this magnitude is brought to our attention, we act."

In fact, the repercussions of the disclosures of abused detainees in Abu Ghraib prison were due not only to the abuses themselves but to the American government's having failed to share information about the abuses with Congress and the public for almost a year. If the photos had not finally been leaked to the press, it is very likely that these abuses would still be unknown to the public. Moreover, it is possible that few steps would have been taken to correct the situation because of the low priority given human rights abuses by the authorities. This judgment is supported by the fact that as early as June 2003 Amnesty International reported abuses that subjected detainees to "cruel, inhuman, or degrading" conditions, abuses that were characterized as violating international law. And the majority of these detainees had been mistakenly arrested. Amnesty International was assured by military lawyers and the office of the Coalition Provisional Authority that conditions would be "rapidly" improved.[190] Yet not until November (four months later) did individual military personnel submit reports of abuses to senior officers.

A report by the International Committee of the Red Cross was submitted on November 6, but the ground commander in Iraq did not learn about it until two months later. Also in November a report was filed by a major general who had been detailed to look into the matter; and Paul Bremer, the chief U.S. administrator in Iraq, brought the issue to the attention of the secretary of defense and other top leaders, urging that uncharged prisoners be released and conditions be improved. But not until January 2004 was the officer in charge of a military police brigade at the prison finally suspended. She promptly blamed intelligence officers, however. Also in January, leaked photos of abuse were shown to the secretary of defense, and later in the same month the president was informed of an ongoing investigation. Then, in February, a detailed 534-page report of "sadistic, blatant and wanton criminal abuses" was prepared by a major general and given to the Pentagon. Finally, in March (nine months after the Amnesty International report and the army's promise that conditions would be "rapidly" improved), six army personnel were charged with abuses of detainees.

Three weeks before the story broke in the American news media on April 28, the chairman of the Joint Chiefs of Staff called Dan Rather of CBS News and asked for a delay in airing the February report, even though he himself still had not read it. And in early May, top administration officials and the chairman had not read it. The secretary of defense said he had seen only a summary, but nevertheless told a television interviewer that he believed that the Geneva Convention "did not precisely apply." On May 3 the president's spokesman informed journalists that the president still had not seen the report that had been given to the Pentagon in February, and on the following day the military revealed that it had conducted 30 criminal investigations into the matter.

This thumbnail history of the investigation of prison abuse in Iraq suggests three conclusions: foot-dragging in the process of investigation, punishment, and reform (investigations of several of the major perpetrators got under way only in May 2004); denial or aloofness on the part of the nation's top military and civilian leaders; and the tip of an iceberg. As for the iceberg, it has been observed that the abuses in Iraq were transported from Guantanamo and Afghanistan and go back to 2002.[191] Thus, in both war zones abuses were extensive and systemic, reports by human rights organizations were ignored, and commanders professed ignorance of the situation. Nevertheless, on May 24, the president assured Americans that the abuses were the actions of "a few American troops."

Mistreatment of prisoners by Americans is not confined to Iraq and Afghanistan, but is also widespread in the States; and one reason that has been adduced for stateside abuses might apply to Iraq. As noted by a *New York Times* writer, "during the last quarter century, over 40 state prison systems were under some form of court order for brutality, crowding, poor food or lack of medical care . . ."[192] And what is particularly interesting is the attribution of abuse in the States to overcrowding (see chapter 5), which has led to the hiring of "large numbers of inexperienced and often undertrained guards." This problem seems to have loomed large in Iraq as well, as suggested by another article in the *New York Times*. As one prison guard in Iraq said, "You're a person working in

McDonald's one day; the next day you're standing in front of hundreds of prisoners . . . I don't think we were prepared."[193] And as an official report on the Iraq abuses by the military noted, the guards in Abu Ghraib had not received any training.

The pressures of the deadly insurgency in Iraq with an urgent need for intelligence may also have played a role. Indeed, there seems to be a strong tendency for American military personnel to commit atrocities when under severe stress. Americans have apparently forgotten that in past conflicts our soldiers have behaved like barbarians toward civilians and military suspects, even when the civilians posed no threat whatsoever. In fact, America probably has committed more war crimes since World War II than any other advanced democratic nation.

A case in point is the widespread commission of atrocities during the Korean War when the North Koreans were pressing down from the north and the Americans suddenly faced the prospect of a humiliating defeat. The most famous incident was the No Gun Ri massacre when American soldiers who were trying to evacuate a village in advance of the North Korean onslaught grew frustrated or enraged and began wantonly machine-gunning men, women, and children, even as they fled in panic. Nor was this an isolated incident. According to one report, "More that 30 percent of Americans had killed unarmed people in Korea and . . . more than 30 percent, in addition, had witnessed fellow Americans killing unarmed persons in Korea."[194] This criminal slaughter by Americans was confirmed by the Final Judgment of the Korea International War Crimes Tribunal: "The evidence of U.S. war crimes presented to this Tribunal included eyewitness testimony and documentary accounts of massacres of thousand of civilians in southern Korea by U.S. military forces during the war."[195]

American troops were confident that they could easily defeat the North Koreans because their commander had told them that the enemy would throw down their arms and flee when confronted by Americans. Later, when the American division had lost more than 3,000 troops and its commanding general had been captured, the division "fell apart" and Taejon fell. Accordingly, "commanders in Tokyo . . . suddenly realized that they might be humiliated by a gook army."[196] This is the typical context in which American massacres are spawned: the sudden, disorienting prospect of defeat at the hands of an enemy who was presumed to be inferior in every way to the American titan. The American Myth of invincibility does not take kindly to those who contravene it, especially when they are not regarded as worthy of respect because of their race or ethnicity.

Similar circumstances fostered the notorious massacre of civilians by American soldiers in My Lai at a time when the great American military was being savaged by an army of Asian peasants. Once again, civilians were indiscriminately murdered. And this incident, too, was not an isolated event. Much the same thing was happening all over the war zone.

Sadly, our haste to suppress the memory of these outbreaks of American savagery has allowed us to plead "shocked, shocked," and to deny that our troops could ever be capable of crimes against humanity. And thus we fail to heed the lessons of history. The Myth of American goodness wipes the slate clean every time. And so, today, the abuses in Abu Ghraib are characterized as isolated cases, rotten apples in a barrel full of Granny Smiths, and we are advised to put the whole thing behind us. It is precisely this attitude that guarantees the recurrence of war crimes, for it seems that when the American Myth of humaneness and coolness under stress confronts a resolute enemy who taunts us with the threat of defeat by an "inferior people," we are likely to be transformed into savages. This is especially likely to occur when the troops are not trained to deal with civilians or captives, as was clearly the case in Iraq—pointing to yet another instance of gross mismanagement by the military in the Iraqi theater of war. (A number of articles, other than those already cited, contributed to the writing of this section, especially regarding the historical portion of the Abu Ghraib cover-up. For these sources, see note 197.)

Was the removal of a dictator who did not have his finger on the trigger, and evidently did not even have a trigger, worth all of these lamentable consequences, most of which had been predicted by critics of the administration's policy—especially when the UN had offered a possible alternative to the war? In particular, were the consequences of the war less destabilizing and less potentially lethal than those of Saddam's odious regime, providing that UN monitoring could have continued? This question seems to lie beyond the comprehension of the American people, who have focused their attention almost solely on the credibility of their leaders, reflecting their greater interest in the possibility that their leaders deceived them than in the possibility of shocking consequences flowing from such deception.

Meanwhile, the embarrassed leaders have tried to exonerate themselves by citing Iraq's *past pattern* of WMD possession and use. But germane as that may be to an assessment of the probability of Iraq's using WMD, it is a far cry from concrete, detailed citations of the approximate number of tons of chemical weapons that Saddam currently had on hand, or a "growing fleet of aerial vehicles" that could possibly reach America. The latter type of information about contemporary realities was much more decisive in motivating the nation to go to war, and without a moment to lose, than were mere historical precedents. And it would have been impossible for Saddam to have smuggled such a huge arsenal out of the country without detection in anticipation of the announced U.S. attack. The facts cited by the president, then, can only be regarded either as unreliable data from intelligence agents (in the field or in Washington) or as testimony to a huge underground chamber somewhere in Iraq. But then again, there is a third possibility, namely, that the administration distorted the intelligence reports simply to gain public and congressional support. Presently, no one knows.

Here we need to pause and ask ourselves whether the reasons given for the Iraq war were the real reasons. If not, and if announcing the real reason would have caused consternation among Americans and the people of the world, then there was no alternative to deception of the public about WMD, the al Qaeda connection, and the admirable desire to free the Iraqi people from a brutal tyrant. And it so happens that this "real" reason has been lying out in the open ever since the publication in late 2000 of the Project for the New American Century that was prepared by candidate Bush's security advisors. Let us look at the key sentence once again: "While the unresolved conflict with Iraq provides the immediate justification, the need for a substantial American force presence in the Gulf transcends the issue of the regime of Saddam Hussein." This need is now being amply fulfilled while the public's attention is diverted by all sorts of other issues, such as the failure of our intelligence agencies.

In November 2003 it was reported that Paul Bremer, the U.S. Administrator in Iraq, was instructed by Washington about an arrangement with Britain that would give the two nations six permanent military bases in Iraq.[198] More recently it has been reported that 14 "enduring bases" are under construction.[199] This is probably why the United States is so adamantly opposed to any United Nations or NATO authority over military affairs in Iraq, and why it negotiated so vigorously with the Iraqi interim government to maintain control of military security. In short, we got what we really wanted, and nobody is going to take it away from us. Yet the inflammatory potential of this coup is enormous. Not only might Middle Easterners object to America's overthrowing a government in the region to gain a military stronghold, but the American people might wonder whether the death of its soldiers is worth 14 military bases just so the nation can become a vigilant overlord in the Middle East, not to mention the strong odor of empire building. The excuses of eliminating WMD, fighting terrorism, and overthrowing a tyrant were therefore necessary. And the choice of the most unpopular regime in the region as the target was a stroke of foreign policy genius. In the final analysis, regardless of all the suffering, embarrassment, expense, and protest, the goal of guarding America's main source of oil has been substantially accomplished, and without the least bit of telltale fanfare.

Corporate Influence on Military Preparedness

It is not clear that the particular high-tech weapons currently being manufactured are what the U.S. military really needs. In fact, there was much discussion at the outset of the Bush administration about shifting from outmoded weapon systems to new technologies more suited to the post–Cold War era. Has this goal been achieved or even begun to be achieved? Not according to a foreign policy analyst who has claimed that "the increases in defense spending have allowed the Pentagon to avoid reform and transformation. More than one third of the procurement budget for this year [2002] will go to big-ticket, Cold War–era weapons systems." The F-22 fighter jet, the F-35, and the Super-Hornet are three Cold War relics that had been scheduled for retirement and replacement, and yet were not only retained but given $14 billion for 2002 alone. And the analyst adds: "The failure of policymakers and defense officials to cancel unnecessary weapons programs is, in large part, due to the undue influence exerted by the top defense contractors."[200]

The Crusader program was criticized by both the president and the defense secretary for being outmoded, inasmuch as it was designed for dealing with the Soviet Union in a land war. But congressmen from a number of states where the Crusader's parts were made objected and evidently won. As Senator John McCain has pointed out, many "pork barrel projects" are added to the military budget every year.[201] Consequently, almost all the systems that were slated for review have been retained and refunded after a storm of lobbying.[202] As for contributions from the top six weapons companies, $6.5 million were contributed to candidates' campaigns and parties, while their lobbying expenses ran to $60 million in 2000.[203]

Congress is not the only branch of government that feels pressure from the weapons industry, for the administration has absorbed more than 30 former weapons contractors, consultants, and major shareholders among its major appointees.[204] These include the deputy administrator for defense, the transportation secretary, an assistant secretary of state, under secretary of the Air Force, the Pentagon comptroller, the director of NASA, the secretary of the Navy, and an under secretary of defense. The vice president's wife was on the Lockheed Martin Board from 1994 to 2001.

These facts not only suggest that America's quiver might hold a lot of outdated arrows but that much of the increased outlay for weapons production might have been due to donations and lobbying, as contrasted with technological or military need. (As noted in chapter 2, this increase has been a major source of the crises in social and environmental programs, since they are obliged to take a back seat in deference to funding for the war on terrorism.) Is there any merit in this indictment? Have we really needed the increased outlay for defense? According to the World Policy Institute's Arms Trade Center, in 1999 "arms spending of $276 billion a year [was] already more than twice as much as the combined military budgets of every conceivable U.S. adversary."[205] As for the suitability of high-tech weaponry to deal with our biggest security problem, terrorism, let us not forget that a CIA official (quoted earlier) has asserted that "Al-Qaeda retains cells in some 50 countries, few susceptible to military solutions."

An even more scandalous indictment is that we will be inclined to engage in wars against enemies more suited to our present arsenal, such as nations instead of terrorist cells. Thus, we might shy away from warfare that requires specially trained ground troops in favor of wars that allow the use of bombs and missiles. In other words, the means could dictate the ends, which is often the case when technology is involved And finally, could it be that one reason we seem always to be fighting the last war is because we are obliged by the defense industry and their proxies in Washington to employ the same weapons as the last war? But whatever the consequences of pressure from industry or Congress for production of certain weapons systems, it would seem that holding up the American military as a model of technological wizardry tailored to the task or mission at hand regardless of any other consideration might be ill-advised.

The overriding question, however, is that even when certain new weapons that are either under development or already part of the arsenal are technically praiseworthy, are they really needed, or do they mainly satisfy the defense industry's yearning for lucrative contracts? Clearly, the industry is highly energetic and generous in trying to gain the assent of Congress to the purchase of its products; and equally clearly, its paramount motivation is not patriotism but profit. What does this bode for the future, and particularly with regard to the current administration's revival of interest in nuclear weapons, an emphasis that reverses a 20-year trend? As the Arms Trade Research Center points out, "five of the top six donors to members of the House Armed Services Committee during the 1999/2000 election cycle were major nuclear weapons and missile defense contractors." And in the Senate, five of the top seven donors to the Armed Services Committee were the same contractors.[206] In any event, criticism of the high cost and possibly limited effectiveness of certain weapons systems by Congress or the public will no longer be a problem in the development of the missile defense system, which has already been the target of brickbats galore. For the secretary of defense has made a bold move:

> Defense Secretary Donald Rumsfeld has decided to exempt missile defense development from normal reporting procedures on costs and schedules . . . key tests will be conducted without oversight by the Pentagon's independent testing office.[207]

An especially odious arrangement between the Pentagon and a defense corporation is revealed in a recent deal to rent 100 aerial tankers from Boeing rather than purchase them, which gave Boeing an extra $29+ billion over the purchase price. One senator referred to the deal as follows: "I've seen a lot of rip-offs in my more than 20 years here. This is the most obscene."[208]

The Sanctions Alternative

As strange as it might sound, in spite of the death of more than 2,000 civilians during the American bombardment, the Afghan people were probably better off with bombs than with sanctions. Economic sanctions (or embargoes) have been America's preferred coercive alternative to military force; for sanctions are cheaper (although they involve losses to American manufacturers), do not entail the risk of American military casualties, and preclude the outcries of antiwar activists. But then, in the case of Iraq where sanctions were imposed in 1991 and continued until late 2003, antisanction advocates emerged, including many ordinary people in America and a host of international experts and officials. This movement, however, had little effect on the American government's determination to lead the UN Security Council in the continued imposition of sanctions on Iraq. What were the effects of these sanctions on the target population?

According to UNICEF, "If the substantial reduction in child mortality throughout Iraq in the 1980s had continued through the 1990s, there would have been half a million fewer deaths of children under five in the country as a whole during the eight-year period 1991 to 1998." In other words, half a million children died as a result of the sanctions in just eight years. And the spokesman goes on to say, "We are in the process of destroying an entire society. It is as simple and terrifying as that."[209] And the UN Human Rights Committee agreed with this assessment.[210]

Since America was the instigator and perpetuator of the sanctions, it is worth asking about its response to this information about the deaths of children. Here is part of an interview with the U.S. ambassador to the UN, Madeleine Albright, on television's *60 Minutes*:

Leslie Stahl	"We have heard that a half a million children have died. I mean, that's more children than died in Hiroshima. Is the price worth it?"
Albright	"I think this is a very hard choice, but the price—I think the price is worth it."[211]

The sanctions imposed on Iraq were multilateral, of course, which meant that the country could not compensate for the sanctions of any single country by increasing trade with others. But a large number of American sanctions have been unilateral. In fact, by 1997 there had been 75 countries that had been subjected to U.S. unilateral sanctions. What has been the success of these sanctions?

On the basis of five case studies (Cuba, Iran, Vietnam, Myanmar, and China), a researcher has concluded that "the economic impact of unilateral sanctions [is] usually not what we intend it to be . . . economic pain is easily passed on by an authoritarian regime to its people—usually the people we are trying to help." And judging by the five case studies, human rights and democratic objectives were not significantly enhanced. Finally, the researcher points out that U.S. sanction decisions tend to be made on a "weak information base,"[212] which reminds us of the weakness of our intelligence agencies. (See chapter 11 for numerous intelligence blunders of the U.S. government over the years.) This assessment suggests that the sanctions imposed on Iraq that killed half a million children were not only morally grotesque, but pragmatically worthless.

The conclusion that one draws from these cases is that sanctions are rarely smart, even when they are called "smart sanctions," that is, aimed at imports that contribute to military capability. For a good deal of equipment that is imported has *both* military and civilian utility, so that civilians are penalized as well. In sum, America has other ways of making innocent people suffer besides warfare; and in many cases the pragmatic value in terms of American goals is disputable or quite limited. Which reminds us that the line between being a superpower and being a rogue state is not impassable; and the path from one to the other is called "unilateralism," or, more colloquially, going it alone.

Unilateralism

In the words of a Princeton University professor of international affairs, "Unilateralism has emerged as the most contentious [post–Cold War] issue in US-European relations."[213] Europe seems to be unanimous in its rejection of unilateralism. As the German foreign minister has observed, "The international coalition against terror does not provide a basis for doing just anything against anybody—and certainly not by going it alone. This is the view of every European minister [of foreign affairs]."[214] But this solid phalanx of condemnation neither daunted nor swayed the United States. Although a tendency toward unilateral action was evident under the Clinton administration, the present administration has taken this policy to heights undreamed of by foreign policy analysts of the past. The following is a list of international treaties, conventions, protocols, and so forth, that the United States has rejected, abandoned, refused to ratify, or substantially weakened since 2000.

International Criminal Court
Kyoto Global Warming Treaty
Anti-Ballistic Missile Treaty
Comprehensive Nuclear Test Ban Treaty
Biological and Toxic Weapons Treaty
Land Mine Treaty
Small Arms Treaty

Convention on the Elimination of All Forms of Discrimination against
    Women
International Covenant on Economic, Social and Cultural Rights
Convention of Children's Rights
Vienna Convention on Law of Treaties
International Protocol on Involvement of Children in Armed Conflict
Air pollution—Persistent Organic Pollutants
Air pollution—Volatile Organic Compounds
Biodiversity agreement
Hazardous Waste agreement
With regard to preemptive military action: UN Charter Articles 1, 2(4), 24,
    34, 39, 41, and 51
With regard to treatment of prisoners of war: the Geneva Convention.

The administration has sought to explain its position with respect to several
of these actions. Thus, the Kyoto treaty has been described as inefficient, lacking in a mechanism for bringing in developing countries, and, most important of
all, according to the president, a threat to the U.S. economy.[215] The International
Criminal Court has been said to ignore the fact that U.S. military personnel are
prone to be singled out as targets of legal action because of America's prominent role in the world, and therefore the United States should enjoy certain exemptions. The Nuclear Test Ban and Anti-Ballistic Missile treaties have been
portrayed as Cold War relics. And so forth. Further, the basic UN principle that
preemptive military action in the absence of an imminent threat is forbidden is
said to be an anachronism in a world where terrorist states might possess weapons of mass destruction. Thus, seemingly to its credit, America has sought from
time to time to justify its renunciation of particular agreements.

    The fundamental meaning of America's repudiation of these agreements
will be discussed later. But first we need to look at America's latest unilateral
thrust: the enunciation of a doctrine of preemptive war. As stated by the president, "to forestall or prevent . . . hostile acts by adversaries, the United States
will, if necessary, act preemptively."[216] Supporters of the administration's policy
have pointed out that Article 51 of the UN Charter recognizes the right of self-
defense, and that the Charter also recognizes the sovereign equality and sanctity
of domestic jurisdiction and the right to enforce the UN's resolutions. But this
last-mentioned right is limited inasmuch as the Charter explicitly states that "regional arrangements or agencies" outside the UN are not precluded "provided
that their activities are consistent with the Purposes and Principles of the United
Nations" (Article 52).

    Opponents, on the other hand, point out that preemptive action violates sev-
eral articles of the Charter, and that the UN was founded expressly to limit na-

tional initiatives that threaten or harm other countries or ignore international protections of the environment, food safety, etc. As one legal analyst affirms:

> [I]n the absence of express Council authorization, [unilateral military action] remains an act of usurpation of Council powers and a resort to force prohibited under international law ... [which] represents a need to protect the diversity of cultures and claims ...[217]

America's reference to Article 51, in particular, as offering justification for preemptive action on grounds of self-defense is especially interesting, for the article explicitly rules out action that is not in response to an armed attack. Here is the article itself:

> Nothing in the present Charter shall impair the inherent right of individual or collective self-defense if an armed attack occurs against a Member of the United Nations until the Security Council has taken the measures necessary to maintain international peace and security.

The single condition under which military action by an individual member is permissible is the occurrence of an armed attack, according to this article. My dictionary says that "preemptive" means "marked by the seizing of the initiative: initiated by oneself." To cite being attacked as a justification for a preemptive attack is logically impossible. The administration is fully cognizant of this jarring disjunction between its interpretation of Article 51 and the actual words of the article, for it argues that the notion of an imminent attack is no longer sufficient as the sole justification for military action. In other words, it asserts that the article is flawed because it is out of date. As the president has declared, "We must adapt the concept of imminent threat to the capabilities and objectives of today's adversaries ... terrorists with concealed weapons of mass destruction."[218] What this reformulation amounts to is no less than an amendment to the UN Charter. So why refer to the article as it stands as a justification for preemptive action? Is it just because it employs the words "self-defense"?

The debate that has arisen among experts in international law regarding the justification for unilateralism indicates that the experts are at loggerheads on issues of definition, legality, and advisability. One distinction that needs to be made concerns the type of international issue that is at stake. Trade, environmental, and social issues are all regarded as best dealt with by multilateral decision-making, although unilateral action can be justified under certain conditions. But offensive warfare is almost universally frowned upon today as a matter for each nation to decide for itself. Any such doctrine, it is feared, could plunge the world into a chaos of belligerence—which is where it was before the UN was created.

As useful as it is to identify the conceptual, legal, and practical ramifications of the notion of unilateralism, one paramount fact about recent American behavior and policy remains: America has rejected binding, long-term, international agreements in a wholesale fashion, that is, virtually across the board without prejudice or discrimination. The similarity among the rejected agreements inheres solely in their being multilaterally binding, that is, that they set limits upon America's freedom of action. In other words, America desires an unconditional free hand in its foreign relations. And the caveat that America will still seek cooperative arrangements for certain purposes does not alter the fundamental character of this desire for a free hand, inasmuch as there is always the rider that "we reserve the right to act on our own," which negates any obligation under any agreement of any form directed to any issue. This rider simply means: "we will cooperate as long as other countries go along with what we want to do." This is not the ordinary definition of a treaty or even of a temporary coalition. It is the strategy of a free rider, a hitchhiker who will travel as far as he can go toward his destination and then get out and proceed on his own. In short, America subscribes to conditional multilateralism, the condition being that any agreement must not be binding. Which raises the question: why bother?

There is another feature of America's unilateralism that not surprisingly aggravates other nations: its contemptuous attitude. Vice President Cheney has expressed it in this way: "[The international landscape] is infested with weeds, rodents, and insects and the last administration did not do a good job of maintaining the grounds."[219] The national security adviser has been even more pointed in her comments: "[It is] not isolationist to suggest that the United States has a special role in the world and should not adhere to every international convention and agreement that someone thinks to propose. A Republican administration will proceed from the firm ground of the national interest, not from the interests of an illusory international community."[220]

This viewpoint implies that the treaties rejected by the United States were simply matters dreamed up by silly or hysterical people. And that not only are such people silly, but they are not us, so why should we pay them any heed? In other words, what do their interests have to do with ours? It also asserts the superiority of America over all nations of the world because of its exceptional nature in some unspecified way. And finally, it overlooks the possibility that acting in terms only of exigent national interest can have unintended consequences that, in the long term, can be extremely detrimental to national interest (as shown clearly in the cases of postwar Afghanistan and postwar Iraq).

More fundamentally, what the national security adviser seems to have overlooked is that the phrase "international community" is a metaphorical ideal that recognizes the existence of a host of common interests that can and must be dealt with by a common dedication to working together. It is the role of an ideal to focus aspiration, and it does not become "illusory" until something or someone stands in the way of its fulfillment. That seems to be precisely the part that is being played by the security adviser and her associates, namely, obstruction of a dream of universal concord and cooperation based on international treaties and other binding agreements.

This dream was born in 16th-century Europe and was known as irenism (also eirenism).[221] Much later, after numerous wars of unimaginable carnage, Western civilization revived and finally implemented the irenic ideal in an effective way with the founding of the United Nations. But the United States, the latest upstart superpower in a long Western line of upstart superpowers, will have no part of it—unless, of course, an irenic policy at a particular moment in time happens to coincide with the priorities of its ruling elite.

One possible beneficial outcome of America's regression to a pre-UN policy of jungle statesmanship is the awakening of Europe to its responsibility for world leadership. America's discreditable social disarray is well known abroad, where people decry its crime, capital punishment, guns, influence of money in politics, lack of social responsibility, and so forth. They would now be well advised, it seems, to realize that America might not even be reliable as an ally, and they should therefore earnestly pursue a leadership role in the world independently of America whenever feasible. As one European observer has put it: "the fight for security, prosperity and justice can no longer be won on any one nation's ground . . . America, for the moment, has disqualified itself from this task. It falls to Europe to undertake it . . ."[222]

Two circumstances are especially favorable for Europe's rise to preeminence: the greater appeal to developing countries of the socially responsible governments of Europe, and the worldwide distrust and even hatred of America fomented by its clumsy exercise of global influence. Another possible factor is the strong ties of Europe to its previous colonial possessions that speak its languages and have adopted its institutions. And some believe that Europe "will soon surpass the United States in all the measures of strength except the military."[223]

We have already seen evidence of the extremely negative impact of the Iraq war on world public opinion. And it is clear that "majorities in almost every country [among the 42 surveyed] said they disliked the spread of U.S. influence," according to a survey reported in the *International Herald Tribune* While many felt that the United States does not take their interests into account, "this was in stark contrast to Americans' solidly held view that the United States does take others' interests into account."[224] Clearly, the myth of America's solicitude for the rest of the world is alive and well among the American people. And not only is America perceived by the world as indifferent to the interests of others—it is believed to be the greatest *menace* in the world. *Time* magazine asked the following question in a poll of several hundred thousand people:

"Which country poses the greatest danger to world peace in 2003?" Only 7 percent cited North Korea; 8 percent, Iraq; and 84 percent, the United States.[225]

Topping off these highly unflattering notions of America is the widespread perception of our nation's sense of superiority, and not just based on strength or wealth, but on a superabundance of moral rectitude that Americans believe deserves the world's deference. As Jacques Rupnik, a former adviser to both French President Jacques Chirac and Czech President Vaclav Havel, put it, "Americans are fond of saying, 'the world changed on September 11.' What has changed is America. The extraordinary moral self-righteousness of this Administration is quite surprising and staggering to Europeans."[226]

The clash between American self-righteousness and its international performance for many years has gained it a reputation for monumental hypocrisy. In particular, America has unashamedly supported dictatorship while preaching the virtues of democracy. As recently noted in a leading British newspaper, the United States has supported Marcos in the Philippines, Suharto in Indonesia, the Shah in Iran, Somoza in Nicaragua, Batista in Cuba, Pinochet in Chile, and Mobutu in Congo/Zaire.[227] More recently it has given its support to Middle Eastern dictatorships such as in Pakistan, Saudi Arabia, and, most notably, Iraq under Saddam Hussein (whom we supplied with weapons of mass destruction!). The hypocrisy exhibited by this discrepancy between avowals of allegiance to democracy and active support for dictatorships—that is, until one of them discomforts us—has not escaped the attention of people in foreign lands, even though it seems to have escaped the attention of Americans. Further, it should be clearly noted that America's sales of arms to dictatorships like Kuwait, Ethiopia, Pakistan, Yemen, and Iraq go far beyond tacit approval of such regimes to providing them with the means of maintaining power and destabilizing their regions.

But if America arouses so much hostility, one might ask, how has it been able to line up allies for such foreign adventures as warfare in Afghanistan and Iraq? In the first place, dictators do not really care whether their populace loves or excoriates America. They will do pretty much as they wish. But they expect certain tangible benefits from becoming an ally of America. And even democratic countries are not ordinarily averse to receiving favors from the richest nation on earth, regardless of their people's opinions. And so, the answer to our question—how has America been able to line up allies?—is financial bribery.

We have already seen that the warlords of the Northern Alliance were given millions of dollars to make it possible for the coalition led by America to defeat the Taliban. In the case of our ally Pakistan, America pledged $1.2 billion in new economic aid and the rescheduling of a $4.5 billion debt.[228] Similarly, two-thirds of Egypt's debt was forgiven for help in the Gulf War, and Turkey received $3 billion.[229] For the later war with Iraq, Turkey received the promise of about $6 billion and up to $20 billion in loan guarantees.[230] Jordan has also been promised a largess ($1 billion in aid),[231] and Israel came to Washington in early 2003 to make final arrangements for $4 billion in military assistance and $8 billion in loan guarantees.[232] In all, since 1973, Israel has received $1.8 trillion, or more than twice the cost of the Vietnam War.[233] And so it goes.

Although "extraordinary statesmanship" usually receives the credit for gaining allies in war, a keynote of the American Myth, what really does the job is hard bargaining, or something more familiarly known as haggling. In effect, we rely on foreign armies from debtor nations to help us fight our wars, which makes them, in effect, our mercenaries. In the case of Afghanistan, payment to the warlords was evidently what tilted the balance against the Taliban. Sir Francis Bacon famously said that knowledge is power. But it doesn't hold a candle to the power of money.

*   *   *

The exploitative rules that America imbedded in Iraqi law before turning over power to the interim government nakedly exhibit all the strands of American imperialism that have been alluded to in this chapter. They include: privatization of all government-owned enterprises; allowance of foreign ownership of all businesses in reconstruction contracts with no requirement to invest any part of profits in Iraqi economy, and ownership of half of Iraqi banks, with 40-year ownership licenses; installation of U.S. auditors and inspectors general with authority over contracts, regulations, employees, etc.; suspension of all tariffs; non-preferential treatment of Iraqi businesses and hiring of Iraqis; reduction of corporate taxes; and immunity of foreign contractors from Iraqi law.[234] Thus, military oversight by virtue of enduring bases and economic control by virtue of law are conjoined.

It would require a heroic suspension of disbelief to assume that the Iraqi people on their own would ever have included these rules in their interim constitution, rules that essentially restrict their prosperity on behalf of foreign profits. That we compelled them to adopt these rules would seem to confirm the suspicion that America does not so much wish to foster democratic self-determination in Iraq as to create a façade of democracy that conceals and condones America's lust for economic advantage. If this is the face of globalization, its name is neo-imperialism.

America is by no means a novice as a colonial power, the foremost example today being Puerto Rico, the "oldest colony in the world." With more self-rule (endorsed by the UN) and curbing of U.S. corporations, this island could well enhance its economy and quality of life, and gain a host of democratic benefits. Time and again, however, America, the land of liberty and justice, has said no.

8

Racial, Ethnic, and Gender Inequality

Black Inequality

In spite of the rise of a so-called black middle class, research has revealed that blacks have benefited much less than their white peers during the same period of time. Blacks are more liable to be placed in positions that interface with other blacks and are dead-end jobs, to be concentrated disproportionately in the public sector (owing to affirmative action in employment), to earn less and to have less financial assets for hard times, and to fail to maintain the upper-income status of their parents (only 30 percent of blacks do so, compared with 60 percent of whites).[1] These findings make it necessary to look closely at the statistics that reflect current conditions overall for blacks in order to determine if and to what extent blacks have gained in the years since the civil rights movement. The results are not heartening.

While the percentage of black households with a personal income of less than $10,000 (in 2002 dollars) declined by 21 percent from 1970 to 1999, white households experienced an even greater decline in the same category (33 percent). In the final analysis, this brought black households to a median income of $27,910 in 1999, a figure that was 34 percent less than that of whites ($42,504). (Even in the midst of the boom years, the household income of blacks was 37 percent less than that of whites.) But most disturbing is the fact that the percentage of blacks in the under-$10,000 category was almost two and a half times that of whites in 1999, compared with only two times that of whites *thirty years earlier*.[2] Are we sliding backwards?

As for official poverty, in 2001 the percentage of blacks below the poverty line was 22.7 percent, compared with 9.9 percent of whites. Hispanics were 21.4 percent. Thus, the black and Hispanic poverty rates were more than twice that of whites.[3] Overall, however, there was a very small increase in black income as a percentage of white income. In 1991, black household income was 53.4 percent of white income, and in 2002 it was 54.1 percent of white income.[4]

223

This "progress of blacks" is hardly a matter for rejoicing, for it would appear that the discrepancy increased in the under-$10,000 category. One major reason for the consistently lower income of blacks is their propensity for being unemployed although looking for work. In 2000, the percentage of the white labor force that was unemployed was 3.5, while the same statistic for blacks was 7.6, or 2.2 times the rate of whites—that is, double the rate of white unemployment and then some.[5]

This discrepancy is somewhat enlarged when we compare young blacks and whites. The unemployment rate for blacks in the 20–24 age range was 2.6 times that of whites of the same age in 2000, and 20 years earlier (1980) it was 2.4 times that of whites. Indeed, while the rate of black unemployment was 15 percent among the 20- to 24-year-olds, and 24.7 percent among the 16- to 19-year-olds, for the nation as a whole it was only 4 percent in 2000.[6]

When blacks are obliged to compete with whites for jobs, as in the white suburbs, they search longer and more aggressively than whites, but are between 36–44 percent less likely to be hired—and this is true even when their experience and qualifications are equal to their white counterparts, according to a 2001 study by the Russell Sage Foundation.[7] It is very hard to argue that racial discrimination is not playing a role when looking at data like these.

Education, of course, is bound to be a structural factor in overall inequality of opportunity. But the role of educational level is not the complete answer, as suggested by the following data in addition to the Russell Sage study. In short, getting only a high-school education does not make a great difference in black unemployment. In 2000, the unemployment rate of blacks with a high-school education was 6.3 percent, whereas for whites it was 3.3 percent.[8] Thus, even with a high-school education, the unemployment rate among blacks is still almost twice that of whites. And even with a college education, the rate among blacks is almost twice that of whites, namely, 2.5 percent versus 1.4 percent, respectively. And getting a job does not guarantee equal treatment either. As research has found, "even when age, experience, education and other relevant factors are considered, blacks average at least 10 percent less pay than similar whites."[9]

Well-meaning white Americans have taken pride and consolation in the alleged progress of blacks in the years since the civil rights act of Congress in 1963. Nonetheless, the "underclass" or "acutely poor" still exist in large numbers, and not even education has been sufficient to expunge the inequality of opportunity that has plagued blacks ever since they were brought to America as chattel more than 200 years ago. In fact, education can sometimes be part of the problem. According to the head of the College Board testing agency, even when the potential of blacks and white children is equal, according to tests, "blacks are 40% less likely to be placed in advanced or accelerated classes . . . [and are] 2.5 times more likely to be placed in remedial or low-track classes, where they will typically be taught by the least qualified teachers, be given less challenging material to learn, and receive an average of nearly 40 hours less actual instruction annually."[10]

Even the increase in affluence among blacks has a cautionary lesson that seems to have been ignored. For this rise would probably not have occurred without the economic boom of the '90s in spite of programs like affirmative action in jobs and education. Only in the '90s did significant progress occur in the access of blacks to incomes above $75,000. While percentage increases in the '70s and '80s to this level of income were 1.6 and 2.6, respectively, in the '90s it was 5.0. Clearly, the latter decade played the most important role in boosting black income. But it played the same role in boosting white incomes, which also rose by 5 percent during those years.[11]

These data suggest that in the absence of a sustained boom period, blacks will fail to make progress in reducing the income gap relative to whites. And, indeed, as the economy became sluggish following the 1990s' boom, black unemployment rose faster than white unemployment, confirming the rule of "last hired, first fired." While the unemployment rate for whites held steady in September 2001, for example, the black rate increased to 9.1 percent. According to one analyst, this was because "[supplemental] positions appear to be drying up at the entry-level, and the low skilled and manual labor supplied disproportionately by blacks is gradually becoming a burden that small businesses and corporations can no longer carry."[12] A year later, as reported by the newspapers, "blacks were the group hit hardest by the rise in unemployment last month [November 2002]. Their jobless rate rose to 11 percent, a 1.2 percentage point average increase from October. In contrast, the rate for whites inched up a tenth of a point to 5.2 percent."[13] Not much support here for the notion that the poor bring it on themselves.

A joint project of MIT and the University of Chicago in 2002 employed a clever device for studying discrimination in hiring. They concocted and mailed 5,000 résumés in response to job ads, half of which had "black-sounding" names and half "white-sounding" names. The "white" names were favored with 50 percent more responses than the "black" names.[14] Another obstacle that blacks have suffered in seeking and holding jobs is their residential isolation. "No group in America is more isolated from job opportunities than African-Americans," one source points out (although the writer might have forgotten about native Americans on poverty-stricken reservations). "In every major city—except one—the distance between where people work and where they live is much greater for blacks than for whites."[15] And distance is more onerous for blacks because of the necessity of holding more than one job. As a street vendor in downtown Washington, D.C., has pointed out, "We may be able to get a job, but we need to work two or three of them to make ends meet . . . the question is what kinds of jobs are people getting?"[16]

So why don't blacks get mortgage loans, move to new neighborhoods, and so forth? Here again we find the door of opportunity only half open. According to the Boston Federal Reserve Bank, "blacks are 50 percent more likely than whites to be rejected for a mortgage loan, even after controlling for 38 factors that could explain higher rejection rates for blacks . . ."[17]

Earlier, in the chapter on crime and punishment, we saw that the crime rate is expected to rise substantially after the relatively quiescent years of the '90s owing to a demographic bulge in the crime-prone age. Having perused the statistics on black unemployment, we can now predict that the crisis in unemployment, and especially among younger blacks, will seriously inflate this tendency; for employment plays a powerful role in the reduction of crime among blacks. According to a prominent analyst of black society, the violent-crime ratio between male blacks and whites by the time they have reached their late 20s is 4 to 1. But when one controls for employment, no significant difference is discernible.[18] In plain English, unemployment accounts for almost all of the difference between the violent-crime rates of whites and blacks.

While whites may react with great trepidation to a prediction of increasing black crime because of unemployment, one should realize that blacks themselves are far more likely to be the victims. Half of the murder victims in the United States are blacks, who as a group have a rate seven times greater than whites.[19] As a matter of fact, there is a certain type of crime that is far more often perpetrated against blacks by whites than the other way around, namely, hate crimes.

In 1998, there were 500 hate groups operating in America, according to the Southern Poverty Law Center; and another agency, the Simon Wiesenthal Center in Los Angeles, has reported monitoring more than 2,000 hate sites on the Internet.[20] The FBI reported in 2000 that 36 percent of the 9,430 hate crimes reported to them were directed against blacks. This percentage was at least three times more than that directed against any other group victimized by hate crimes.[21]

But not only poverty, unemployment, poor education, and discrimination in housing threaten the well-being of blacks at a higher rate than whites. Lack of affordable health care also impacts the black community more than white communities. In 2001, 10.5 percent of blacks under the age of 18 years and 22.8 percent of older blacks did not have health insurance, compared with 7.2 percent and 14.5 percent of whites, respectively. While there was a slight improvement among younger blacks from 1998 to 2001, virtually no change occurred among older blacks.[22] This difference in access to health insurance, which makes it easier to afford a regular health-care provider, might account for the fact that in 2002 blacks used emergency facilities at hospitals at a rate 67 percent higher than whites, according to a survey by the National Center for Health Statistics.[23]

As for the health status of blacks, the facts are quite depressing. One in five children in Harlem has asthma[24] (8.7 percent nationally). The infant mortality rate was more than twice that of whites in 1998 (13.7 vs. 6.0 per 1,000 births).[25] The 1998 death rate from heart disease among black males was 22 percent higher than that of white males. And although the rate of heart disease among white males declined by 52 percent from 1950 to 1998, among black males it declined only 36 percent.[26] Black females were 34 percent more likely to die from heart disease than white females, and "black women are much less likely than men or white women to receive life-saving therapies for heart attack."[27]

In 1999, AIDS was the leading cause of death among black men aged 25–44, and the third leading cause of death among black women.[28] As already noted, homicide is the leading cause of death among black men under the age of 25. In short, if a black man can escape being murdered, then he can look forward to the possibility of contracting AIDS.

The average life expectancy for black Americans in 1999 was 71.4 years, compared with 77.3 years for whites.[29] In spite of the higher probabilities of illness and death among blacks even under medical supervision, only 6–8 percent of the doctors in America are from minorities of any kind, compared with a population of blacks of 12.3 percent as of 2000.[30]

In 2001, Congressman John Lewis obtained passage of a bill to "address health disparities in minority communities" with funding of $504 million over five years. If these funds were devoted to blacks only, the amount would have come to $2.90 per individual per year. But since they were supposed to be spent on all minorities (and the number of Hispanics is larger than that of blacks), the amount of money per individual black per year would have amounted to $2.12.[31] In view of the crisis in black health, this nonlargess is certainly a violation of the kind of moral standard that America is supposed to uphold.

The real need among minorities is universal health insurance, which would cost a good deal more than $2.90 per person, but which could be paid for by one-half the cost of President Bush's tax cut and cover all Americans and not just minorities.[32] Another fundamental need is the elimination of employment and wage gaps between blacks and whites to raise the socioeconomic level of blacks; for disparities in income are largely responsible for their deficits in health and health care. If we look only at black and white men in the highest and lowest economic brackets, the life expectancy of blacks in the highest bracket is 7.5 years longer than blacks in the lowest bracket. Among whites, the same disparity is 6.6 years. In other words, black and white health differences would be substantially reduced by greater income equality.[33]

In addition to the health disparities, we have already noted that "the chances of a black man being locked up sometime in his life are one in four."[34] And we have also seen that, although blacks make up only 13 percent of drug users, they account for 38 percent of the arrests for drug trafficking.[35] Finally, we recall from an earlier chapter that "blacks who killed whites were 4.3 times as likely to receive the death penalty as those who killed blacks."[36]

The most recent figures on incarceration of blacks, according to the Justice Department, are the following: "An estimated 12% of African-American men ages 20–24 are in jail or prison . . . By comparison, 1.6% of white men in the same age group are incarcerated."[37] The ratio, in other words, is 7.5 to 1. This means, incidentally, that about 800,000 black Americans, which is approximately the number of blacks in American prisons, are not allowed to vote. Most European nations, in contrast, do not disenfranchise felons.

Many Americans who view these dismal figures will console themselves with the thought that at least desegregation in education has helped blacks to achieve higher socioeconomic status. Earlier we saw, however, that graduation from high school or college still did not eliminate the difference in employment chances between blacks and whites. And now we need to confront the depressing fact that segregation in education has actually *increased* in the past decade. Because of the appalling implications of this turning back of the clock, a summary of the findings of a Harvard study that was released in 2001 deserves to be quoted in full:

> [S]egregation continued to intensify throughout the 1990s . . . much of the progress for black students since the 1960s was eliminated during a decade which brought three Supreme Court decisions limiting desegregation remedies . . . resegregation is contributing to a growing gap in quality between the schools being attended by white students and those serving a huge proportion of minority students. [And the segregation of Latinos surpasses that of blacks.] "This is ironic," said [the director of the study,] "considering that evidence exists that desegregated schools both improve test scores and positively change the lives of students, and that Americans increasingly express support for integrated schools." . . . Almost nine-tenths of segregated African-American and Latino schools experience concentrated poverty.[38]

Apart from segregation, many social and cultural variables combine to reduce the educational achievement of black students, although desegregation might reduce the impact of these variables. We have already noted that black students are more often placed in remedial or low-track classes regardless of their potential. Income level is another major factor. In fact, a recent summary and synthesis of racial differences in educational performance by Persell and Hendrie[39] cites research showing that "when blacks have comparable financial assets to those of whites, they graduate from high school at *higher* rates than whites and there are no racial differences in college completion rates or school expulsion rates" (my emphasis).

Especially noteworthy is the finding of research that a *context* of racial inequality, independently of individual characteristics, has a strong effect. As

summarized by Persell and Hendrie: "black educational disadvantage is exacerbated in areas of high racial inequality [measured by racial ratios of poverty,
income, and employment] over and above the effects of higher absolute poverty." This contextual effect highlights the importance of either overhauling the
socioeconomic and cultural environment itself or making it possible for blacks
to move to places with less racial inequality.

Another way in which context affects black student achievement is through
the level of financial resources in a community. As Persell and Hendrie observe:

> Because schools are supported by local property taxes and because there is so
> much housing segregation by social class and race in the United States, stu-
> dents who live in low-income areas are very likely to attend schools with lower
> per pupil expenditures. . . . [Also] schools with more low income and racial mi-
> nority students are more likely to have teachers who are not certified or are
> teaching out of their area of certification . . . and teachers with lower achieve-
> ment test scores. . . . Teachers' test scores are related to students' test
> scores. . . . [For citations of research on these points, see the publication by
> Persell and Hendrie.]

These statistics on the economic well-being, health, education, and treatment by the criminal justice system of blacks in America are among the most
shocking of advanced countries, and especially in America because it calls itself
the preeminent land of equal opportunity. And their plight persists in spite of
civil uprisings, marches in Washington, and a spate of sanctimonious legislation.
Not even the so-called Black Caucus of Congress seems to have made much of
an impression. Congressman Lewis's bill to address disparities in health care,
for example, asks for a dismal pittance of what is needed to improve the lives of
millions of suffering Americans.[40] Eliminating health disparities and supporting
health providers in underserved communities are measures that are desperately
needed, but if Congressman Lewis's bill is any indication of what Congress is
willing to do, nothing like the amount of money needed will be forthcoming.
Politicians without a large proportion of blacks in their states or districts will do
nothing; and that means that states with small populations, but which nevertheless have the same number of senators, will drag their feet while millions of
Americans (including Latinos and other minorities) continue to be mired in poverty, hunger, and ill health by racist institutions and individuals. As of 2003,
23.6 percent of blacks, or almost 1 in 4, lived below the poverty level.[41] Many
more who no longer live in poverty carry the scars of deprived and endangered
backgrounds, as well as of recurrent encounters with discrimination throughout
life.

The facts presented here have not escaped the attention of the federal government. In 2000, the Clinton administration prepared a report to the United
Nations on racism, a report submitted to the UN Committee on the Elimination

of Racial Discrimination. The following are some conditions cited in the report.[42]

> The persistence of attitudes, policies, and practices reflecting a legacy of segregation, ignorance, stereotyping, discrimination and disparities in opportunity and achievement;
> Inadequate enforcement of existing anti-discrimination laws;
> Economic disadvantage . . . Persons belonging to minority groups are disproportionately at the bottom of the income distribution curve;
> Continued segregation and discrimination in housing . . . , public accommodation and consumer goods;
> Lack of access to business capital and credit markets;
> Lack of access to technology and high-technology skills;
> Discrimination in the criminal justice system.

Blacks concur with this assessment. According to a survey conducted by the National Urban League in 2001 among 800 black adults nationwide, 70 percent believed that blacks were discriminated against in being paid lower wages, 74 percent believed that the criminal justice system was biased against blacks, 60 percent believed that the most important problem facing blacks was economic opportunity, and only 14 percent believed that the state of race relations today was excellent or good. As for their confidence in politicians to do the right thing, 64 percent answered in the negative. In particular, fully 81 percent believed that the Republican party was not committed to the issues that are most important to blacks. And these opinions were expressed by a sample in which 72 percent described themselves as financially better off than their parents.[43]

These views are definitely not shared by white Americans, however, who have ardently embraced the American Myth of equal racial opportunity. Eighty percent of whites say blacks enjoy equal educational opportunities, and 83 percent say they have equal housing opportunities. Only one-third of whites agree that "blacks face racial bias from police in their areas."[44] In a study in 1998, "64 percent of whites in the rigorous sample said blacks who can't get ahead are responsible for their own condition, while just 25 percent blamed racial discrimination."[45] Finally, the clash of black and white viewpoints is clearly reflected in the fact that 70 percent of whites say blacks are treated equally in their communities, while 50 percent of blacks say they have experienced discrimination in the past 30 days,[46] and an even larger percentage (80 percent) felt that there was widespread profiling in the country.[47]

Are blacks having paranoid fantasies? No—because the statistical evidence of disparities and discrimination, in spite of one's qualifications or efforts, confirms the black version of reality. Clearly, whites want to believe that blacks are not subject to unfair treatment (which is reminiscent of their unfounded belief that the government is contributing a sizeable portion of its budget to foreign assistance, mentioned earlier). Their isolation from black communities makes it possible for them to preserve this comfortable illusion, for 80 percent of whites live in virtually all-white neighborhoods.[48] So, once again, the American Myth is hard at work. The facts flatly contradict the notion of equality that is a key feature of the American Dream, but the Myth steps in to mitigate the discrepancy and reassure Americans that all is well in the land of opportunity.

Our dissidence-averse media have played a pivotal role in this charade with their failure to cover racism and discrimination or to resist spreading subliminal stereotypes of blacks as criminally inclined, vulgar, intellectually and politically irrelevant, and incapable or uninterested in, or just unworthy of, personal relationships with whites. Statistical data on these stereotypes in the media are presented by Entman and Rojecki.[49]

The ugliness of a persistent racist outlook in America and the complacent indifference of whites who are basically nonracist are the marks not of a superior nation that aspires to world leadership, but rather of a 19th-century colonial power. The refusal of mainstream politicians and the mainstream media to confront and examine openly this peculiar disease gnawing at the American psyche is indicative of an anemic democracy that lacks the nourishment of serious news gathering and reporting.

In addition to the see-no-evil media are the corporations that are fearful of a racial reform agenda in the South, because this agenda might foster a solidarity that could be translated into stronger labor unions. Nothing is better suited for keeping unions weak in the South than a white-based Republican Party of industrialists that opposes working-class solidarity by quashing appeals to genuine racial integration. A brief history of this politico-corporate resistance to civil rights in the South deserves to be presented here:

> [T]he 1948 Dixiecrat revolt—the Southern bolt from the Democratic Party in protest of Harry Truman's civil rights plank [was] carefully orchestrated by the corporate mandarins of the region or their lawyers, many of whom answered to parent companies in the North . . . The most persistent of the biracial movements bucking the established order was organized labor. Southern bosses had long used racist propaganda and vigilantes to foment strife between black and white workers, with the goal of keeping the unions weak and wages depressed. The aim of those powerful business interests was to roll back the New Deal . . . The same representatives of organized money who spearheaded the vicious campaign against Roosevelt became the brain trust of the Dixiecrat Party. . . . The main attraction the Republicans hold for the "regular people" who make up the bulk of their Southern constituency is that they are the party of the white man.[50]

Finally, one of the greatest insults to blacks in America has been precisely what I have been doing so far in this chapter—treating them purely as a social problem and neglecting their genius as a people. In the 300 years of its existence, America has made only two outstanding cultural contributions to the world: Broadway musicals and jazz (including blues). When jazz was combined with Broadway, it produced America's greatest composer, George Gershwin, who was the creator of the nation's most memorable and musically advanced opera of the times, *Porgy and Bess* (which, typical of American commercial values, was gutted by the producer for its original performance), set in a black neighborhood, performed by blacks, and based on black music and culture. It was a people who had risen from slavery who accomplished this and other astounding feats of cultural creation, including the Harlem Renaissance, and which in many instances transformed certain traditional European elements into a modern idiom. With regard to music alone, an historian has remarked:

> The genres of music that bear the marks of this [black] influence are legion. Let's name a few: gospel, spirituals, soul, rap, minstrel songs, Broadway musicals, ragtime, jazz, blues, R&B, rock, samba, reggae, salsa, cumbia, calypso, and even some contemporary operatic and symphonic music.[51]

This legacy has become a hallmark of American culture throughout the world. But here at home, we treat these cultural innovators as second- or third-class citizens. Indeed, for a number of years jazz artists had to go to Europe to be not only tolerated but warmly appreciated and embraced. The commercialized culture of white America simply could not absorb them, nor could the white hotels when they were on tour. And music is not the only cultural field in which blacks have excelled. Some of America's finest literature has come from black writers; and it should be frankly acknowledged that perhaps the greatest orators since Cicero have been black American preachers and activists.

Did the Romans treat the Greek artists of drama, epic, and so forth, as second-class citizens? On the contrary, they gave them full credit for cultural genius while paying them the respect of slavish imitation. In fact, Roman culture without Greek influence is unimaginable. And so it is with America.

America without black culture would be like New York City without Jewish culture. It simply would not be America.

Other Victims of Ethnic or Racial Prejudice and Discrimination

Although blacks have constituted the largest number of victims of intergroup prejudice and/or discrimination in the United States for many years and have been joined by Hispanics in the past 30 years, these groups are by no means the only targets of American bigotry. Jews in particular have shared much of the burden of victimization, and anti-Semitic attitudes are quite common.

According to the FBI Crime Reports of 2000, 12 percent of the reported hate crimes were directed against Jews;[52] and according to a survey of 1,000 adult Americans in 2002, "anti-Semitic propensities have increased in the U.S. since 1998, reversing a steady decline in anti-Jewish feeling in the U.S. over the past 10 years . . ." The percentage of Americans holding views about Jews that were unquestionably anti-Semitic was 17 percent, or about 35 million adults. The most anti-Semitic among them were "four times as likely to believe that American Jewish leaders have too much influence over U.S. foreign policy [as] Americans holding non-anti-Semitic beliefs." Forty-two percent of the former held this view, compared with 11 percent of the latter.[53]

That intolerance is a generic belief system is shown by the finding that those who hold negative attitudes toward Jews are also much more likely to feel the same way about immigrants, gays, and people of other racial, ethnic, and religious backgrounds than themselves.[54] This finding shows that events in the Israeli-Palestinian conflict are not significantly responsible for present-day anti-Semitism in America, for anti-Semitic attitudes are part of a larger constellation of intolerance that encompasses other groups as targets. Moreover, many Americans who disapprove of the Israeli government are not anti-Semitic. For example, 62 percent of faculty members and 51 percent of students "have an unfavorable impression of the Israeli government," but almost none fall into the category of the most anti-Semitic.[55]

As for the undue influence of Jews on foreign policy toward Israel, one would be well advised to consider the 40 million or so evangelicals who formed the backbone of President Bush's electoral support among whites, and who happen to view Israel as their own Holy Land. (It has been estimated that 25 percent of the president's electoral support came from the religious right.) By comparison, the 5.2 million Jews in America exercise scant influence.

From this perspective, the conflict between Israel and Palestine is indeed a religious war that affords a modern version of the Crusades of the Middle Ages in the minds of fundamentalist Americans. (In a famous slip of the tongue, President Bush as much as said so.) As far as top policymakers are concerned, however, public sentiment is probably viewed simply as a useful prop for preserving an American foothold in the Middle East as a means of protecting America's oil supply. This quid pro quo, or codependency, between government and the public plays a vital role in America's geopolitical staying power in the region despite all the horrible costs in lives, money, and regional reputation.

Then we come to that most neglected and historically wronged racial group in America—native American Indians. Marginalized to the point of near invisibility by the media (with the exception of the crazed, tomahawk-wielding savages of the movies) and the federal government, these original Americans hardly benefit at all from the spectacular affluence of the nation.

According to the National Congress of American Indians, "Indian reservations have a 31% poverty rate and 46% unemployment rate. Health, education
and income statistics are among the worst in the country."[56] In North Dakota,
where Indians had a 38 percent poverty rate in 2000,[57] the average rate of unemployment was 63 percent, compared with the U.S. rate of 4.3 percent at the
time.[58] Among Indians and indigenous Alaskans living in isolated communities,
the suicide rate is 50 percent higher than that of the general United States population.[59] And according to the American Indian Education Foundation, "62% of
American high school graduates attend college. Only 17% of American Indians
will go on to college."[60]

What has the federal government been doing about this morass of misery
and denied opportunity? In 1997, the Indian Health Service was funded at about
65 percent of the need for services. Whereas the health expenditure by the
agency was $1,132 per capita, the U.S. expenditure as a whole was $3,261, or
about three times the amount for Indians.[61] Moreover, according to an investigative report in the *Washington Post* in 2002, "The government's inability to keep
track of how much is owed to each of more than 300,000 Indians ranks as one of
the biggest accounting failures in government history." The total owed is re-
puted to be in the neighborhood of $10 billion.[62]

Finally, in spite of the rise of Indian gambling revenues (from $100 million
in 1988 to $8.3 billion a decade later), a computer analysis of federal unem-
ployment, poverty, and public assistance records "indicates the majority of
American Indians have benefited little."[63]

Gender Inequality

It seems almost uncharitable to chide America for its failure to have achieved
social, economic, and political parity between males and females by the turn of
the millennium. Commendable advances have been made in the past 35 years in
the liberation of women from roles strictly associated with the family and nurturance, from their subservience to males, and from discrimination in the workplace and in many noneconomic realms traditionally dominated by males, such
as politics, the military, and athletics. Today women form 47 percent of the
work force. Yet traditions and stereotypes that have prevailed for many centuries
die hard, and more so in some countries than in others. And among advanced
nations, America might be one of the diehards. In spite of its self-acclamations
of enlightened modernity, America still clings to many older beliefs and practices regarding gender. Indeed, there is even evidence that government policies
in the past four years have served to arrest or even reverse the progress of the
past 35 years. And in one vital respect, discussed below, America *continues* to
lag behind a number of other nations in female empowerment.

Before examining the evidence of lingering gender inequality, we need to note a condition that might go far in explaining the peculiar plight of women in America, namely, our failure to keep up with other advanced nations (and even with many developing nations) in the inclusion of women in our federal lower and upper parliaments, that is, our House of Representatives and Senate. One leading political scientist has cited the percentages of women in these bodies as an indirect proxy "of how well minorities are represented generally."[64] Similarly, another states, "What we know about women's representation should [also] be applicable to ethnoracial minorities."[65] But regardless of its serving as a marker of social equality at large, it is certainly a measure of women's political empowerment. And that's what makes the facts so disturbing.

As of April 2004, the United States ranks 58th among 194 countries of the world in the percentage of women in its lower chamber, namely, only 14.3 percent. Thus, 29 percent of the world's countries have a higher representation of women in that body. Compared with America's 14.3 percent representation, Sweden has 45.3 percent, Norway, 36.4 percent, Spain, 36 percent, Germany, 32.2 percent, and Switzerland, 25 percent. Indeed, every nation of Europe with the exceptions of Italy, Hungary, and France has a higher rate of female inclusion. Even Uganda, China, Botswana, and Angola excel the United States on this measure of equality.

As for the percentage of women in the upper chamber, the United States ranks 36th out of the 68 countries reporting, which means that 51 percent of other countries have a higher representation. Some of the nations that exceed the U.S. percentage in the upper chamber are Pakistan, Mexico, Burundi, Turkmenistan, Grenada, St. Lucia, Belarus, and the Congo. A number of nations, including developing nations, have even adopted *quotas* for female inclusion. Any notion, therefore, that America is in the vanguard of gender equality in the composition of its top representative bodies is a gross misapprehension.

Most startling of all, however, is the fact that the percentage of women in the lower chambers of Algeria, Jordan, Iran, Turkey, and Egypt, all Muslim nations, is only 10 percentage points below the percentage in the United States. If America has these states in mind when it preaches greater participation of women in the Muslim world, perhaps it should first reform its own backwardness.[66]

As suggested above, this imbalance in gender representation might help explain the continuing inequalities suffered by women in the workplace and labor market in America. For inequalities do indeed persist. First, we find that several traditionally female occupations still tend to be almost entirely filled by women (as of 2003). Occupations at least 90 percent female are: preschool and kindergarten teachers (98%); secretaries and administrative assistants (96%); childcare workers (95%); receptionists and information clerks (94%); teacher assistants (93%); registered nurses (93%); bookkeeping, accounting, and auditing clerks (92%); hairdressers and cosmeticians (91%); and nursing, psychiatric, and home health aides (90%). All of these fields have been traditional realms of female employment ever since women began working outside the home in America decades ago. In contrast to these figures, women held only 19 percent of executive management jobs in 2000. In fact, the percentage was higher in 1990, namely, 32 percent. Thus, there has been a significant *decline.*[67]

As for weekly earnings, in spite of a steady increase in women's pay relative to that of men since 1979—with the significant exception of a clear dip during the recent recession—women's earnings in 2002 were only 77.9 percent of men's earnings. This discrepancy tended to occur in every occupational category, and especially in sales (59.4%), precision production (67.1%), and executive, administrative, and managerial jobs (68%). Thus, in these occupations, which have been traditionally the preserves of men, the income discrepancies between males and females are greatest. This strongly suggests the role of powerful cultural norms, but also possibly discrimination in male-dominated occupations. Incidentally, inequality in pay occurs across all demographic groups, which means that the higher proportion of women than men with certain socio-economic backgrounds that might predispose them to lower pay does not explain the wage differential.[68] Moreover, the dip in relative pay in 1998–99, mentioned above, is probably an indication of discrimination insofar as it reflects a tendency to lay off higher-paid females more often than higher-paid men.

In light of these facts, it is unsurprising that a slightly higher percentage of women than men who are hourly-paid workers were found at or below minimum wage levels in 2002, namely, 3.7 percent vs. 2.2 percent. (The federal minimum wage is $5.15 per hour; only 11 states have higher levels.) This discrepancy was mainly due to women more often being part-time workers,[69] for in 2002, women were considerably more likely than men to be working part-time (7.5% vs. 1.5%). This factor, however, cannot entirely explain the discrepancy in weekly wages received by women and men in general. Even among only full-time workers in 1999, women's median weekly earnings ($473) were 76.5 percent of men's earnings ($618).[70] Nor can the lower earnings of women be explained by their more often holding multiple jobs. The percentages of men and women falling into this category are virtually the same.[71]

The status of being female in *combination* with other lower-status positions poses special problems. For example, the greatest advancement in the earnings of women has been among those with college degrees (a 22% increase in earnings 1979–98) compared with little or no improvement among those without a college education. Here we witness a strikingly unequal gain in women's income due to educational attainment, which signifies that the detrimental effect of our increasing barriers to college access (discussed in chapter 4) falls disproportionately on poorer females.

These data point to the conclusion that the greatest impact of wage inequality is on the working poor, which in turn directs our attention to the plight of former welfare recipients with dependent children who lost their benefits under the Clinton administration. A report released in 2003 noted that "as many as one in seven families who left welfare from 2000 through 2002 had no work, no spousal support and no other government benefits," according to the *New York Times.* (The reduction in the number of families on welfare from 1996 to 2003 was 2.4 million, a decrease of 54 percent.)[72] And these families had to confront a severe recession.

Even former welfare recipients who *could* find employment were burdened with incomes that were inadequate for self-support, much less for child-support. "The average woman coming off welfare since 1996 earns $7 an hour," writes Barbara Ehrenreich, a figure that comes to about $14,560 a year. With rent taking at least half of one's income in 14 million households (see chapter 2), that leaves $7,250 for everything else, including child care. As Ehrenreich says, "The math just doesn't add up."[73] A living wage in America two years ago was estimated to be about $30,000 a year for a single adult with two children, or about $14 an hour. "The shocking thing," as Ehrenreich points out in her book, *Nickel and Dimed,* "is that the majority of American workers, about 60 percent, earn less than $14 an hour."[74] With respect to women in particular, "In 1998, approximately 16 million women, or 39 percent of female wage and salary workers, were paid low wages" (i.e., defined as wages inadequate to support a family of four above the poverty level).[75]

Intermittent employment is characteristic of many part-time workers, and it might more often be necessary for women because of child-care responsibilities, limited education, or just the vagaries of the job market. But it is definitely no solution for poor working mothers. Intermittent workers cannot accumulate seniority, their job skills may lose marketability, they don't receive on-the-job training, they have a harder time being hired because of gaps in their employment record, and they are likely to be placed in lower-paying positions. Consequently, one finds that their wages are less than those of other women at the same point in their career.[76]

Related to intermittent work is the higher absenteeism rate of women when compared with men. In an average week in 1999, 5.1 percent of women, compared with 2.7 percent of men, failed to show up for work. Further, women were somewhat more likely than men to report reasons other than injury or illness as reasons for absenteeism.[77]

The pattern of part-time work, intermittent work, and absenteeism is probably attributable to the conflict between work and family roles, which is more characteristic of women. And not only are mothers under the pressure of child care and other domestic chores, but they are subjected to a culture that still believes that a woman's place is in the home. In 1998, polls showed that two-thirds of Americans believed that mothers should stay home and take care of their children, even if the family needed the mother's income and even if the children were teenagers.[78] (If the same question had been asked with reference to men staying home to take care of their children, no doubt these percentages would have approached zero. Nothing could reflect better the sexual stereotyping of women than the fact that the question was not even considered worth asking with respect to men.) This potent cultural expectation contributes to mothers' ambivalence about working and hence to absenteeism and intermittent employment.

While the outside world of work might be less rewarding to women when compared with the opportunities and financial rewards for men, domesticity offers its own special pitfall in the form of domestic violence regardless of whether one is employed. "Nearly one-third of American women report being physically or sexually abused by a husband or boyfriend at some point in their lives," writes an authority on women's issues.[79] And as mentioned in chapter 2, a woman is battered in America every 13 seconds. The Bureau of Justice has reported that "on average, more than three women are murdered by their husband or boyfriend in this country every day."[80] Finally, it should be noted that "683,000 women are raped per year in America, and 13 percent of college women say they had been forced to have sex in a dating situation."[81]

Moreover, without fear of sounding old-fashioned, we should bear in mind that women are indeed the weaker sex. Not only are they physically weaker than males, but they seem to be psychologically more vulnerable. As the chief psychiatrist at New York's Veterans Administration has noted, "Women are particularly susceptible to developing depression and anxiety disorder in response to stress compared to men." This is apparently because women under stress release more of the "trigger chemicals like CRF" than in the case of males.[82]

In sum, stress in both work and domestic affairs might have a uniquely debilitating effect on women. And looking back over the data, it would appear that women are more likely to be subjected to both sorts of stress than men because of their persistently unequal position in American society, their conflicting roles of work and homemaking (although mitigated by the benefits of getting outside the home and becoming a part of society at large), their physical inability to fend off domestic or other forms of violence, and their relative lack of power in the government to do anything about these and other problems. Finally, that a woman's body has become a battleground of religious and ideological warfare between opponents and proponents of abortion and family planning has not helped matters. In short, women are threatened with the loss of the most basic human right of all: the right to own one's body.

This last point reminds us of the role of the state in controlling the lives of women, which brings us to the record of the Bush administration. And the facts are dismaying. Not only has the current administration expressed its opposition to a woman's right to have an abortion, but programs of benefit to women and their children have suffered cuts in funding or been eliminated; enforcement of laws against discrimination has been relaxed; affirmative action in access to higher education has been opposed; measures that criminalize certain abortions, as well as antiabortion and anti-family-planning policies in general, have been embraced; and encouragement of recruitment to the military has been reduced. Among programs that have sustained funding cuts or been frozen are those for child care that would eliminate enrollment of 300,000 children by 2009; nutrition programs that would reduce the number of low-income children served by 450,000 by 2009; after-school programs; Title IX guidance for preventing sexual harassment in schools; and emergency shelters and domestic violence services. In addition, the Equal Pay Initiative has been eliminated, cases challenging sex discrimination in employment have been dropped, and a rule to facilitate paid leave for the birth or adoption of a child has been repealed. Finally, according to the Women's Law Center, "the Bush administration closed the White House Office for Women's Initiatives and Outreach, which used to monitor departments and agencies for policies impacting women."[83]

Once again we find a federal agenda devoted to obstructing or rolling back the nation's progress toward fundamental American goals. In this case, there are two goals: equality of opportunity and supplemental aid for the needy. Since women still suffer inequality after 35 years of female liberation, and still do not have sufficient representation in the House and Senate to remedy the situation, the tradition-oriented Bush administration has had a relatively free hand in undermining the human rights of women in America.

*   *   *

Many Americans are weary of hearing about the struggle of the nation's minorities and women to gain ground against prejudice, discrimination, and hate. They are prone to believe that the civil rights movement lies behind us and that blacks and women in particular have made great strides. They are content for the myth of America's progress toward equality to salve their social consciences while the facts remain buried in the statistical reports, unspoken by the mainstream media or by the people's own leaders. So, once again, in light of the data I have presented, we must ask whether America meets the moral standards of a people who proclaim themselves the most compassionate and egalitarian on the earth. This was the "promise" that Martin Luther King, Jr. referred to in his speech in Washington, D.C., in 1963; and the "dream" he professed to have had was simply the *fulfillment* of that promise, a promise enunciated in America's basic social contract. Yet that promise is *still* unfulfilled.

But no matter. The American Myth has *pronounced* it fulfilled and thereby consigned the realization of King's dream—which was the dream of the Declaration of Independence itself—either to oblivion or to a safely remote future.

9

Civil Liberties

America has long presented itself to the world as a bastion of civil liberties involving: freedom of expression, assembly, and petition; freedom from unreasonable or arbitrary searches and seizures of property; guarantees of grand-jury indictment, due process, and speedy public trials; and the right to information about accusations and to legal counsel. These rights, together with their implied "right to privacy," as it became known, are enunciated in the Bill of Rights of the Constitution and are guaranteed to "persons" and not just citizens. To what extent are these rights recognized in America today?

The Bill of Rights vs. the Patriot Act and Other Government Policies and Regulations

In its response to terrorism, the United States has enacted more legal measures that violate civil rights than any other country except India. Israel and Italy have each enacted one such measure, France two, and Germany and Spain three each, while the United States has enacted *nine*. India has enacted 10 such measures.[1]

Following the September 11 attacks, the government hastily drew up a lengthy (242 pages) law to deal with terrorism domestically. This law was passed on October 25, 2001, "with virtually no public hearing, and . . . accompanied by neither a conference nor a committee report," according to a report of the Center for Constitutional Rights.[2] The vote in the House was 356 to 66, and in the Senate it was 98 to 1. The law, known as the Patriot Act, was signed by the president on the following day. One analyst of the law characterized it in the following terms: "the United States intelligence community put together a laundry list of provisions designed to patch perceived holes in the pastiche of security laws in their arsenal and to grant to the FBI and Justice Department the same sorts of freewheeling intelligence gathering powers at home that the CIA has employed abroad for years."[3] According to once again to the Center for Constitutional Rights:

The War on Terror has seriously compromised the First, Fourth, Fifth and Sixth Amendment rights of citizens and non-citizens alike. From the USA Patriot Act's over-broad definition of domestic terrorism, to the FBI's new powers of search and surveillance, to the indefinite detention of both citizens and non-citizens without formal charges, the principles of free speech, due process, and equal protection under the law have been seriously undermined . . .[4]

Let us look at the law in relation to the amendments mentioned above and the right of privacy to see if these charges are justified.

First Amendment "Congress shall make no law . . . abridging the freedom of speech or of the press, or the right of the people peaceably to assemble, and to petition the Government for a redress of grievances."

The Patriot Act One of the four parts of the definition of domestic terror is "acts . . . that appear to be intended to influence the policy of a government by intimidation or coercion." As a civil rights attorney has reasonably noted:

Because this crime is couched in such vague and expansive terms, it may be read by federal law enforcement agencies as licensing the investigation and surveillance of political activists and organizations based on their opposition to government policies . . . Vigorous protest activities, by their very nature, could be construed as acts that "appear to be intended . . . to influence the policy of a government by intimidation or coercion." . . . Environmental activists, antiglobalization activists, and anti-abortion activists who use direct action to further their political agendas are particularly vulnerable to prosecution as "domestic terrorists."[5]

Moreover, the Patriot Act allows the government to bring charges of terrorism against anyone who provides support or assistance to an organization charged with terrorism. According to a journalist who interviewed the director of an immigration rights program, "She is especially concerned about those who have had any contact with the 46 organizations the State Department has labeled as terrorist organizations . . . People (not just detainees) may have supported these groups with the understanding that they were humanitarian or educational organizations. 'It is going back to the McCarthy era where it is guilt by association.'"[6] It should also be noted that this portion of the Patriot Act seems to violate the prohibition derived from the First Amendment against punishing a person for conduct that was not illegal at the time when it occurred.

In addition to subjecting protesters to possible charges of terrorism, freedom of assembly could be discouraged by the fear that an organization might have some relationship with terrorists, no matter how remote, and especially if it is affiliated with a Middle Eastern group or serving a Middle Eastern population. But not only organizations affiliated with foreign countries might be shunned, as pointed out by another observer:

[A] prudent immigrant—especially one who had fled his or her country for political reasons—will steer clear of all political activity, because it's simply too easy for any political group to be labeled "terrorist." The dream immigrants share of coming to America, a country in which people can speak and act without risk of punishment, no longer has a basis in reality.[7]

The Fourth Amendment "The right of the people to be secure in their persons, . . . against unreasonable searches and seizures, shall not be violated, and no Warrants shall issue but upon probable cause, supported by Oath or affirmation, and particularly describing the place to be searched, and the persons or things to be seized." The Right of Privacy (*Griswold v. Connecticut*, 381 U.S. 479, 1965): "The right of privacy is a fundamental personal right, emanating 'from the totality of the constitutional scheme under which we live.'"

The Patriot Act "[P]olice can now obtain court orders to conduct so-called 'sneak and peek' searches of homes and offices. This allows them to break in, examine and remove or alter items without immediately, if ever, presenting owners with a warrant detailing what they were entitled to do and where."[8] This provision is not subject to "sunset" in 2005 like some other provisions of the act.[9] (The House later voted to rescind this provision, but as of fall 2003 the Senate had not acted.)

Further, there are plans to implement "a new online wiretapping system that the FBI calls 'Carnivore.' The system forces Internet service providers to attach a black box to their networks— essentially a powerful computer running specialized software—through which all of their subscribers' communications flow . . . [for] scanning through tens of millions of emails and other communications from innocent Internet users as well as the targeted suspect."[10]

Nor has the Department of Defense been asleep. It wishes to implement a system "which includes an advanced form of data mining, would effectively provide government officials with immediate access to our personal information including: our communications (phone calls, emails, and web searches), financial records, purchases, prescriptions, school records, medical records and travel history . . ." The project is called Total Information Awareness or TIA.[11]

Libraries and bookstores are also susceptible to searches of their records. "Under the Act, investigators are authorized to seek a search warrant for 'any tangible things' in a library or bookstore . . . book circulation or purchase records, library papers, floppy disks and computer hard drives . . . [It] also enables the FBI to require libraries to turn over library circulation records, patron registration information and Internet use records . . . Formerly, an FBI agent was required to provide 'probable cause' . . . Most of the information regarding libraries and bookstores has been deemed 'confidential' and has not been supplied to Congress."[12]

Finally, "the new law compels any Internet provider or telephone company to turn over customer information, including phone numbers called, without a court order, if the FBI claims that the records are relevant to a terrorist investigation . . . The company is forbidden to disclose that the FBI is conducting an investigation . . ."[13]

While it is transparently clear that the Patriot Act increases violations of the Fourth Amendment, intrusions into private communications were becoming much more common even before 9/11. According to the American Civil Liberties Union, "in 1999, federal law enforcement conducted more wiretaps in one year than had ever been conducted before. And search warrants for online information from America Online subscribers doubled from 1998 to 1999."[14]

Even the doctor-patient and client-attorney relationships are not immune to government surveillance. Attorney General Ashcroft, for example, ordered the Drug Enforcement Administration to gain access to Oregon's state records of drug prescriptions, a record that was created to monitor compliance with Oregon's Death with Dignity Act.[15] And law enforcement agents are authorized to overhear telephone conversations between attorneys and clients, an action that violates entitlement to a fair and competent defense, owing to its intimidation effect. Thus, spying on attorney-client conversations violates due process as well as privacy.[16] Which brings us to the Fifth, Sixth, and Fourteenth Amendments.

Fifth Amendment "No person shall be . . . deprived of life, liberty, or property, without due process of law . . ." In its decision on *Zadvydas v. Davis*, 121 S. Ct. 2491, 2500 (2001), "the Supreme Court reminded us that the Due Process clause applies to all 'persons' within the United States, including aliens, whether their presence is lawful, unlawful, temporary, or permanent."[17] Or again, "the Supreme Court has repeatedly stated that the due process clause applies to all persons, aliens and citizens alike."[18]

Sixth Amendment "In all criminal prosecutions, the accused shall enjoy the right to a speedy and public trial, by an impartial jury of the State and district wherein the crime shall have been committed, which district shall have been previously ascertained by law, and to be informed of the nature and cause of the accusation; to be confronted with witnesses against him; to have compulsory process for obtaining witnesses in his favor, and to have the assistance of Counsel for his defense."

Fourteenth Amendment "No State shall make or enforce any law which shall abridge the privileges or immunities of citizens of the United States; nor shall any State deprive any person of life, liberty, or property, without due process of law; nor deny to any person within its jurisdiction the equal protection of the laws."

These are the fundamental laws of the land. Now, how well has the Bush administration observed them? The following excerpt from a 2002 statement by

Amnesty International suggests that our Justice Department leaves a great deal to be desired in its compliance with the Constitution.

> The Bush administration has launched a massive campaign of preventive deten-
> tion, based on little evidence of wrongdoing ... We don't even know how
> many people have been detained. In early November [2001], less than two
> months into the investigation, the Justice Department said the number was
> 1,147. But as criticism mounted over the scope of the roundup, the Justice De-
> partment responded by simply stopping its practice of announcing the running
> tally ... As of February [2002], despite the thousand-plus arrests, only one per-
> son had been charged with involvement in the 9/11 violence, Zacarias Mous-
> saoui. And he was picked up three weeks before the attacks. The Justice De-
> partment has been especially closed-mouthed about the largest group of
> detainees, the more than 725 people held on immigration charges. It refuses
> even to name them and has ordered them tried in secret ... Chief Immigration
> Judge Michael Creppy has instructed immigration judges not to list the cases on
> the public docket, and to refuse to confirm or deny that they even exist.[19]

The Patriot Act permits noncitizens to be held for periods up to 6 months if they cannot be deported.[20] According to the director of the Lawyers Committee for Human Rights, "Many innocent people are likely to be intimidated and, worse, picked up and lost in this new detention power without the ability to challenge it." She cited cases of calls from family members asking the where-abouts of their sons, brothers, and fathers; and said that "some significant num-ber of the [detainees] are having enormous difficulty contacting a lawyer."[21] Under the act, the attorney general has the "unilateral authority to detain aliens on his say-so, without a hearing and without any opportunity for the alien to respond to the charges."[22]

Another provision of the act allows the FBI to give its information to the CIA without prior judicial approval. This is a major departure from past prac-tice, which observed a strict boundary between police agencies and foreign intel-ligence agencies, according to the deputy director of the Center for Democracy and Technology, who added, "And it was done with very little debate."[23] The Center for Constitutional Rights has charged that the boundaries between the Executive branch, on the one hand, and both the Legislative and Judicial branches, on the other, have been violated by the Executive's usurpation of the other two branches' authority. These violations have been endorsed by interim agency regulations and executive orders[24] and by depriving the Judiciary of its role in deciding criminal cases.[25] Finally, it appears that the government has tar-geted persons of Middle Eastern descent and of the Muslim faith in violation of antidiscrimination laws written to protect minorities.[26]

It is clear from these reactions of legal professionals that the Patriot Act lends itself to widespread, serious abuse, which makes it imperative that Congress monitor its implementation. However, the chairman of the House Judiciary Committee has been unable to determine how well or poorly the act is working because "the Justice Department has classified as top-secret most of what it's doing under the Patriot Act," according to a report by the Associated Press.[27] In fact, there is no provision in the act to report to Congress, or even to judges, the implementation of key provisions for review. How Congress will be able to evaluate whether certain provisions should be continued or allowed to expire is an interesting question.[28]

This point reminds us that 13 of the 22 provisions in the act will expire on December 31, 2005, unless renewed by Congress. The remaining nine provisions need to be reviewed, but the act does not require any reporting to Congress about their implementation. Among those not expiring are the "sneak and peek" searches without warning or informing an individual that a search has taken place, the scope of subpoenas for records of electronic communications, and the overriding of the privacy provisions of the Cable Act.

Early in 2003 the public was made aware of a secret draft of the so-called Patriot Act II—more formally the Domestic Security Enhancement Act—which would augment the practices of the Patriot Act by expanding intelligence gathering, reducing judicial oversight, authorizing secret and undisclosed arrest, and setting new guidelines for prosecutors in seeking the death penalty.[29] It would also strip American citizens of citizenship for "support" of a terrorist organization. Inasmuch as the Constitution prohibits taking away citizenship, but allows voluntary relinquishment, the authors of the new act have explained that "an intent to relinquish nationality . . . can be inferred from conduct."[30] In other words, if found guilty, one's citizenship can be suspended regardless of whether or not one wished to relinquish it, which is possibly one of the most flagrant violations of the Constitution in its history.

Now let us proceed to a final comparison between fundamental laws and the administration's prerogatives, this time with reference to international law.

The International Covenant on Civil and Political Rights This covenant was ratified by the United States in 1992. "Article 14," according to the Lawyers' Committee for Human Rights, "requires, among other things, that defendants benefit from a presumption of innocence and that they have the right to appeal a conviction to a higher tribunal."[31] More generally, it calls for "compliance with transparency, fairness and due process in all courts and tribunals."[32] Further, Article 7 prohibits "torture and cruel, inhuman or degrading treatment or punishment, even in times of national emergency."[33]

President Bush's military order of November 13, 2001 This order "grants himself the power to turn any non-U.S. citizen whom he suspects is a terrorist, over to the secretary of defense to be tried by a 'military commission' under whatever rule the secretary of defense creates," once again in the words of the Lawyers' Committee. "No court would decide who goes before such a commission ... [and] the order's definition of 'terrorist' is so broad that, as written, it could include a person who harbored someone who aided someone in committing an act in preparation for an act of international terrorism that was designed to have an adverse effect on the U.S. economy ... None of the rights [found in Articles 7 and 14 of the International Covenant] is protected in the president's military order."[34] In particular, normal rules of evidence in civil cases do not apply; it is acceptable for the trial to be held in secret; judgments of guilt or innocence can be made by a two-thirds vote of a military panel; and no civilian judicial review is allowed, with the exception of the president or the secretary of defense.[35] This pretty much negates the International Covenant on Civil and Political Rights.

The Cardozo Professor of Jurisprudence at Columbia University's School of Law is emphatic about the illegality of this presidential order:

> There is no law available to support the proposed Bush tribunals. Leave aside whether the tribunals would be good or bad, kangaroo courts or simply streamlined procedure; the president has no authority to create them ... The prosecution of suspects for crimes committed on American soil must ... come before the federal courts. Neither the president nor Congress has the authority to suspend that constitutional guarantee.[36]

But, then, one might ask: Aren't these objections merely legalistic? What difference do they make to ordinary people? After all, only people who break the law have anything to worry about. One devoutly hopes that in most cases this is true. But "most" is not enough. To appreciate how easy it is to abuse the powers of the Patriot Act, let us look briefly at a few cases that depict the consequences of the Patriot Act and the climate of civil rights violations that it has fostered.

Anecdotal Evidence of Abuse

Here is what happened one night in an Indian restaurant in midtown Manhattan.

> All of a sudden, there was a terrible commotion and five NYPD in bulletproof vests stormed down the stairs. They had their guns drawn and were pointing them indiscriminately at the restaurant staff and at us ... [Three days later] I managed to ascertain that the whole thing has been one giant mistake. Loaded guns pointed in faces, people made to crawl on their hands and knees, police officers clearly exacerbating a tense situation by kicking in doors, taunting, keeping their fingers on the trigger and even after the situation was under control. A mistake. And according to the ACLU a perfectly legal one, thanks to the PATRIOT Act.[37]

The Patriot Act, in combination with widespread fear of terrorism, has set a tone of vigilance and intrusiveness in America that resembles the anti-Japanese hysteria that swept the country after Pearl Harbor. And it can penetrate anywhere. A peace and environmental activist was identified by a computer check at an airline counter, searched, and not allowed to travel to a conference in Chicago. An angry National Guardsman had a policeman escort her off the premises. Authorities admitted that she had been "singled out for added intensive screening."[38] A high school student was not permitted to wear an antiwar T-shirt, and was barred from trying to start a club promoting her views.[39] Nonviolent demonstrators against war were arrested at a march that did not have a permit, and were charged with felonies that could earn years in prison. According to the bail commissioner, the protesters had engaged in "serious crimes, given the times we live in."[40] A man carrying a novel with a cover showing a hand holding sticks of dynamite was interrogated for 45 minutes while police pored over the book. After his release, the airline would not allow him to fly.[41]

Even a highly esteemed international organization is not immune from becoming entangled in the dragnet. Here is what happened in Colorado.

> Most members of Amnesty International don't consider themselves part of a criminal extremist network. But that's how a Denver Police Department's intelligence database tracked [four members of the organization] . . . police blamed a secretary for inaccurately picking categories from Orion's drop-down lists. The secretary, when asked, was unable to define the term "criminal extremist" . . . a three-judge panel . . . recommended deleting information on 208 groups and 3,277 individuals for lack of evidence of criminal activity.[42]

And then there were the immigrants who were picked up and locked away with little opportunity to talk to a lawyer or even notify their families of their whereabouts, and who were kept in confinement for long periods of time. For example, an Egyptian sued the FBI agent who extracted a false confession from him for $20 million. The immigrant, a student, had been wrongly jailed for a month.[43] And the following is an excerpt from a brief for plaintiffs who had been locked up for months and allegedly abused:

> Although the government never asserted that there was evidence that any of the [Muslim, Pakistani, and Turkish] plaintiffs had links to terrorist groups and never charged them with commission of any crime, they were detained for over six months in tiny, windowless cells and were beaten and abused . . . they have . . . been subject to the severest degrading conditions, including being subjected to body cavity strip-searches and manacled and shackled whenever they were taken from their cells.[44]

These events were fully confirmed in a highly critical report by the Justice Department's Inspector General in June 2003.[45]

It is probable that our treatment of detainees who have violated immigration laws in any way, possibly including simple mistakes on forms or failure to meet a deadline, are mild compared with our treatment of Taliban prisoners of war at Guantanamo Bay, Cuba. Inasmuch as true prisoners of war are supposed to be released after the cessation of hostilities, these prisoners were redefined as "enemy combatants" under a special U.S. law, which for the most part means not wearing a uniform at the time of capture. And evidently a number of mistakes were made in their arrests. These mistakes were admitted by the government after these individuals had been held for a number of months in cages, according to a professor of law at the University of California. As the professor notes, "many prisoners were being held in Guantanamo by mistake because of inaccurate intelligence from foreign governments and because of arrests made in the heat of battle. Many [were] held in solitary confinement, some for as long as 15 months, with no charges filed against them and no end in sight. For a time, many were held in small cages." Some attempted suicide. They were also not allowed to speak to attorneys and "had virtually no outside contact. . . . This treatment violates basic principles of human rights law," the professor continues. In particular, he points out that the International Covenant on Civil and Political Rights provides that "no one shall be subjected to arbitrary arrest and detention."[46]

To vindicate his curtailment of legally protected civil liberties as a means of fighting terrorism, Attorney General Ashcroft has asserted that the United States is under attack by "fanatics who seek to extinguish freedom."[47] Since America is the archenemy of the terrorists, presumably this assertion extends to our *own* freedom. As the president himself has said, 'The Patriot Act defends our liberties." And Deputy Secretary of Defense Paul Wolfowitz said in an interview on the *Lehrer News Hour* on April 21, 2004, that our military personnel "are fighting [in Iraq] so we can have a free country." Is the "we" us? How can terrorists extinguish the freedom enjoyed by Americans? Is the administration afraid that al Qaeda is going to invade the United States, overwhelm its army, navy, air force, and National Guard, and seize the reins of power? There is no other way that it can extinguish our freedom in the United States. Or are these officials fabricating a threat to justify the way in which they are opposing terrorism? Our freedom cannot be extinguished by suicide bombing; so what rational sense do the assertions of the president, the attorney general, and the deputy defense secretary make? The might of the Nazi or Japanese military could conceivably have been a threat to our liberties. But the only current threat to America's liberties has come from the American government itself. Even supporters of the Patriot Act concede that it *curtails* liberty on behalf of security. So it seems disingenuous in the extreme to endeavor to arouse the people against al Qaeda by asserting, or even implying, that terrorists are jeopardizing our freedom when it is not only impossible for them to do so, but when it is *we ourselves* who are jeopardizing our freedom in our domestic fight against the terrorists. In sum, the administration's reasoning is flawed in two ways: its premise is false, and its solution is self-defeating. And, in fact, it is not inconceivable that one of the objectives of al Qaeda is to cause our government to drive the public into rebellion by abridging their liberties. If so, they've got a point.

The climate of restriction on civil liberties fostered by the Patriot Act, other measures of the Bush administration, and threatening statements by political leaders in general might well have emboldened local law enforcement agencies to adopt a hard line against any form of overtly unconventional behavior. This is suggested by some of the examples given earlier, but it is particularly germane to any form of mass political dissent in the streets of the cities. The possibility of a spillover of this kind from the fight against terrorism to routine local law enforcement might help to explain the gross violations of civil rights by the police in recent confrontations with anti–World Trade demonstrators. Thus, the "police riots" that erupted in Washington, D.C., in 2002 and in Miami in 2003 might well have been offshoots of the repressive policies of the current Bush administration and the related mood of apprehension among the American people. In fact, $8 million of the $87 billion approved by Congress for securing and rebuilding Iraq was allotted to the Miami police department for protection of the trade ministers who met in that city in November 2003. A connection with the war on terrorism, therefore, is more real than apparent. Since the episode in Miami was especially arresting, it deserves a brief summary here. (The Washington, D.C., episode will be depicted in the following chapter with reference to the mainstream media's censorship and distortion of public dissent and activism.)

Numerous eyewitness reports of police intimidation, interference with peaceful assembly, unwarranted arrests, and unprovoked brutality with injuries to both demonstrators and bystanders emanated from the melee that occurred in Miami on November 20, 2003.[48] About 2,000 demonstrators, the great majority of whom behaved peaceably (a very few threw rocks and tried to tear down a fence), gathered in Miami after having obtained all the requisite permits, met with the police to negotiate agreements beforehand, and provided their own security people to deal with troublemakers. Their purpose was to protest the Free Trade Area of America (FTAA) at a meeting of trade ministers in a local hotel. Sponsored and organized by a coalition of the AFL-CIO, Public Citizens, the Sierra Club, Oxfam America, the National Family Farm Coalition, and other concerned citizens who marched behind one of the Democratic candidates for the presidency, the participants were characterized by the police chief as "hardcore anarchists." ("If we don't lock 'em up tonight we'll lock 'em up tomorrow," he remarked.) Forty jurisdictions had contributed officers to the Miami police contingent that, according to the head of Miami's ACLU chapter, were "pumped up and primed for battle" in a show of overwhelming police presence. These officers used concussion grenades, tear gas, pepper spray, rubber bullets, batons, and electronic tasers against citizens who were trying to follow a designated route, gather in a designated place, exercise their right of free speech, and even obey the police when told to disperse.

Several labor unions called for a congressional investigation of the incidents. The president of the AFL-CIO sent a blistering letter to Attorney General Ashcroft demanding an investigation, prosecution of those responsible, determination of the extent to which federal funds were involved, the dropping of unlawful charges against peaceful protestors, the resignation of the Miami police chief, and measures to ensure that such behavior will not be repeated. A judge who presided over the cases of some of the protestors said that he had noted at least 20 felonies committed by police officers; and Amnesty International said that the Miami police might have broken international laws and covenants, and it specified civil rights violations in a letter to the governor of Florida. If this episode is typical of the way that American civil liberties are respected by authorities in the United States, then it would seem that the founders of the nation strove in vain to craft a blueprint of ordered liberty called the Constitution.

Now let us turn to the public's response to the curtailment of freedom by the U.S. government as a means of preventing others from allegedly trying to do the same thing.

Public Reaction to Curtailment of Civil Liberties

The nation's civil liberties and human rights organizations have launched recruitment and awareness campaigns, and also a series of lawsuits. And the membership of the American Civil Liberties Union has increased by 15 percent. Two Republican congressmen were so perturbed by the government's policies that they began working with the ACLU in a search for effective remedies. One of the two senators said that the Department of Justice was "out of control," and a Republican representative said, "I think we're on the verge of a very, very tough police state in this country."[49] More significantly, vociferous objection to the attorney general's plan to recruit tens of thousands of citizens to spy on their neighbors was responsible for waylaying this monstrosity before it could be turned loose on the public. But the government still has not given up the possibility of launching this neighborhood spying project.

A clear sign of citizens' discontent with the direction that affairs have taken has been the actions taken by communities across the country to indicate their displeasure with the Patriot Act. (Even before the Patriot Act, Portland, Oregon, refused to cooperate with the FBI in their investigation of Middle Eastern students in the city because of a state law that prevented questioning immigrants not suspected of a crime.[50]) The earliest resolutions against the act were mainly from university towns, but the movement soon swept the country. By 2004, according to the Bill of Rights Defense Committee, "4 states and 275 cities, towns, and counties have . . . passed resolutions, ordinances, or ballot initiatives to protect the civil liberties of their 48,986,173 residents."[51] In April 2003, however, after 151 communities had either passed resolutions or had committees working on them, only one community (Arcata, California) had passed an ordinance making it *illegal* to cooperate voluntarily with the Patriot Act.[52] Thus, it is not clear how far our communities are prepared to go in their effort to oppose the federal government's curtailment of civil liberties in America. A resolution declaring one's displeasure with a policy or law is not the same thing as defying that policy or law by some form of emphatic legal opposition.

Still, it is abundantly clear that the general public has pulled back from its rabid reaction to terrorism in the first months following the 9/11 attacks. Shortly after the attacks, according to national polls, "66 percent of Americans approved of stopping and searching people who are Arab or of Middle Eastern descent to see if they might be involved in potential terrorist activities . . . 38 percent favored allowing telephone conversations to be monitored, 77 percent favored video surveillance of public places, 62 percent approved of roadblock searches of vehicles, and 61 percent wanted to let the government monitor people's mail." Nine months later these percentages had dropped by 13 to 26 percent, with the exception of video surveillance of public places, which remained about the same. Further, in a later survey, "62% . . . said that government steps against terrorism should respect civil liberties—a significant increase from the 49% who endorsed that sentiment back in January," according to the report.[53]

While these shifts in public opinion suggest a growing inclination to protect our freedoms, it must be realized that large minorities of citizens who have been polled still believed in significant restraints. A third (35%) were still willing to let the government monitor the mail, and 49 percent still favored roadblock searches of vehicles. In sum, as the report points out, "The polls that reveal a growing resurgence in respect for civil liberties also measure continued willingness on the part of part of the population to let the government exercise extraordinary power to monitor and snoop."[54]

It should also be recognized that—shifts of public opinion and community resolutions notwithstanding—the laws that have compromised our traditional civil liberties are on the books. Further, they are subject to limited scrutiny (if any), while several are not even subject to conditional renewal by Congress, such as the "sneak and peek" searches.

It appears that the administration lunged with élan through a window of opportunity opened by the 9/11 attacks to gain the acquiescence of Congress to restrictions on civil liberties while the public's fear of terrorism was still high. The consequences, which are frighteningly unknowable at present, can only be chalked up to public hysteria and the government's failure or refusal to exert a calming influence of equanimity in all the actions it took after the attacks, including its punitive speeches and its draconian laws and executive edicts.

Indeed, the president's habit of arousing a sense of insecurity among citizens by reminding them continuously of the threat of terrorism, and especially weapons of mass destruction, has been pointed out by a clinical psychologist who specializes in the linguistic techniques of dominant personalities. As she notes in an article in *The Nation*: "Bush is a master at inducing learned helplessness in the electorate. He uses pessimistic language that creates fear and disables people from feeling they can solve their problems." To measure this tendency, she compared the ratio of negative to optimistic statements by Bush with that of other presidents, including those involved in a war (such as his father). She found that the ratio "in Bush's speeches and policy declarations is much higher, more pervasive and more long-lasting than that of any other President . . . [implying] that the crisis will last into the indeterminate future. There is also no specific plan of action . . . [leaving] the listener without hope that the crisis will ever end." The president, therefore, creates a "dependency dynamic between him and the electorate. . ." As she concludes in her short but provocative article, "people do not support Bush for the power of his ideas, but out of the despair and desperation in their hearts."[55]

This analysis shows how the defensive entrenchment of the American Myth has supplanted the courageous optimism of the American Dream, a transition that has relied on the public's fixation on the latest crisis as magnified by their leaders. Perhaps these magnifications, including the unsupported allegations of Iraq's ready-to-launch weapons of mass destruction, will backfire when they are exposed—but only if the public and media are not further deceived by those who manipulated the public in the first place.

10

The Media and Their Relationships with Corporations, the Government, and the Public

Media Mediocrity and Concentration

A short time after the president's State of the Union Address on January 29, 2003, a special issue of a major national magazine (the *Atlantic Monthly*) focused on a number of critical domestic issues under the headline "The Real State of the Union." These issues, it was noted by the magazine's editor, had been overlooked or downplayed by the government in general and by the president in particular. Thus a chasm had opened up between the conventional version of the nation's well-being and virtue, on the one hand, and the true state of affairs, on the other. "If one theme emerges from these essays, it is how disconnected our official politics has become from the real-world, fast-changing, interesting-in-their-details elements that constitute our national welfare."[1]

In chapter 1 of this book (written several months before the appearance of the special issue of the *Atlantic Monthly*), I similarly concluded that the shockingly poor performance of America had not crossed the threshold of American awareness. But instead of leaving the impression that only the government's failure to be forthcoming about the true state of affairs had been responsible for this adherence to beliefs that clashed with reality, I laid the blame on the mainstream media for failing to give Americans the information they needed to make sober judgments about the nation's socioeconomic and political record, both domestically and abroad. And in subsequent chapters we have seen numerous instances of the mainstream media's silence, distortion, selectivity, and propaganda.

Outright silence had been applied to the early antiwar protests until the worldwide demonstrations of 2002–3, which could hardly be ignored because they probably exceeded the magnitude of all previous demonstrations in history. Other topics that have been largely banished by silence include homelessness, job stress, civilian deaths from America's wars in the past decade or so, race

255

relations, corporate pollution, corporate influence on weapons adopted by the Defense Department, child poverty, the possible mental health deterioration of the population, and much more. And distortion and propaganda have been particularly noticeable in the coverage of politics and the military. Indeed, it has often seemed that any resemblance between American news coverage and the most critical conditions, events, and trends in the nation or world is not only purely coincidental, but often an intentional nonoccurrence. At best, the media seem irrelevant to American democracy.

Numerous articles and essays, and not a few books, have castigated the commercialized mainstream media for their unblushing commitment to a slanted version of reality. As one book by two experts on the media concluded:

> We quite agree with Chief Justice Hughes . . . on "the primary need of a vigilant and courageous press" if democratic processes are to function in a meaningful way. But the evidence we have reviewed indicates that this need is not met or even weakly approximated in actual practice.[2]

Another writer, a professor of communications research, directed attention to some of the fundamental sources of the American media's abdication of responsibility for public service as "ever-greater corporate concentration, media conglomeration, and hypercommercialism . . . The public is regarded not as a democratic polity but simply as a mass of consumers."[3]

To give the reader a taste of the arbitrary manner in which the mainstream media handle reality—in addition to examples already given in earlier chapters—the following are some cases that pertain to recent concerns about globalization and initiating war with Iraq.

Approximately 10,000 persons marched in Quito, Ecuador, in 2002 to protest the proposed Free Trade Area of the Americas proposal at a meeting of trade ministers. The protest was in opposition to the proposal's plan to "allow privatization of vital social services including water, energy, education, health care, and postal and financial services." But this demonstration was not reported in the following mainstream media outlets: *Time, Newsweek, U.S. News and World Report, USA Today*, or major TV programs.[4]

Certain African countries have been strongly criticized for refusing to import genetically modified produce, leaving the impression that their objections reflect some sort of primitive mentality. Only one media source (until very recently) mentioned that Europe had banned imports that are genetically modified. Thus Africans who planted seeds from this food, either deliberately or accidentally, would lose access to European markets.[5] Also, the media had not mentioned that genetically modified seeds cost a good deal more than ordinary seeds and that many African farmers cannot afford them in spite of their resistance to pests.

In September 2002, a large number of activists gathered in Washington, D.C., for the largest march against the World Bank since 9/11. Hundreds of nonviolent protesters were arrested en masse, including bystanders and journalists. Even journalists "were detained for 23 hours . . . the first 10 of those handcuffed on board a bus, the next 10 lying on the floor of a gymnasium with their right wrists shackled to their left ankles." These events were barely mentioned in the mainstream media. The comment evoked from Chris Matthews of MSNBC was: "Those people out in the streets, do they hate America?" Lou Dobbs on CNN's Moneyline said that mass arrests have simply become "part of the ritual." And *U.S. News* showed a picture of demonstrators wearing bandannas being surrounded by the police with the caption "Unmasked."[6] Those media that bothered to cover the demonstration focused on the issues of security and possible violence, with little if anything said about the reasons for the protests.[7] Especially troubling is the ignoring or exonerating of police brutality.[8] The ACLU filed suits against authorities for brutality, but the media's coverage gave the distinct impression that police violence was a necessary response to the marchers and bystanders.[9] When a guest journalist on Paula Zahn's CNN interview show described his unprovoked detention by police, she replied dismissively, "Well, that's not what the State Department said, but nevertheless we appreciate your side of the story."[10]

As for antiwar protest, some national TV networks, as well as local outlets, refused to sell advertising time to antiwar organizations.[11] At the same time, prominent TV news people made their support for military action unmistakable. Dan Rather, the CBS Evening News anchor, declared on a talk show: "George Bush is the president. He makes the decisions, and, you know, it's just one American, wherever he wants me to line up, just tell me where. And he'll make the call."[12] In the course of an interview with a congressman, Connie Chung of CNN aired a clip of President Bush saying that al Qaeda leaders had fled to Iraq where al Qaeda members were trained in bomb-making and the use of deadly gases and poisons. She then asked, "Congressman, doesn't that tell you that an invasion of Iraq is justified?" When the congressman tried to point out that "we haven't seen any proof that any of this has happened . . ." Chung interrupted, saying, "You don't believe what President Bush just said? With all due respect . . . you know . . . I mean, what . . . ." Later she said, "It sounds almost as if you're asking the American public, 'Believe Saddam Hussein, don't believe President Bush.'"[13] Later, of course, the American people discovered that the disavowals of Saddam Hussein were closer to the truth than the avowals of President Bush.

Immediately after airing a speech of the Iraqi ambassador to the UN in which he defended Iraq against the allegations of the U.S. secretary of state, Paula Zahn, anchorwoman of CNN, said huffily: "The UN expected to hear that kind of tirade from the Iraqi ambassador . . ."[14] This editorial comment was uttered in the midst of a straight news program, by no means an uncommon occurrence on CNN.

Fox TV dismissed the antiwar demonstrators in New York as "the usual protesters" or "serial protesters." And Fox's Web site read, "Antiwar rallies delight Iraq," and showed marchers in Baghdad instead of New York or London. Meanwhile, the media outside the United States were reporting the facts about the antiwar protests.[15] And when 19 Democrats held a press conference to raise questions about the administration's rush to war with Iraq, amidst cries across the country of "where are the Democrats?" the mainstream media tended to ignore both the event and the Democrats' position: "The *New York Times* buried the story inside the Saturday paper and denigrated the 19 members as being 'outside the mainstream.'"[16]

According to a media expert on CNN (May 13, 2004), although 47 percent of the public believes that some or all of our troops should be brought home from Iraq, not a single major newspaper has called for a pull-out. In fact, they are calling for *more* troops.

Perhaps the most shocking omission of our mainstream media, however, is coverage of major disasters in less developed countries that involve the death of tens of thousands, or even millions, of people, and the displacement, impoverishment, and orphaning of millions more. In 2003, AIDS killed more than two million humans in Africa and another million elsewhere in the world. But according to a study of the nightly news shows aired on the three major TV networks in America (ABC, CBS, and NBC), only 39 minutes in all were devoted to that catastrophe during the entire year.[17] It was as though the Black Death of the 14th century had been barely acknowledged by contemporary chronicles. Similarly, the civil wars in the Congo claimed an estimated three million victims in 2003, but this calamity netted only five minutes of the networks' attention. Refugee crises, civil wars, and outbreaks of killer epidemics, mass starvation, or genocide are rarely examined or even mentioned by our mainstream TV media, regardless of the human toll. The *top 10* crises of 2003 identified by Doctors Without Borders received a grand total of 30 minutes of coverage by the three networks over the entire year. The networks' attitude seems to be: if it isn't happening to Americans, it's not worth reporting.

We Americans may be a compassionate people, but one would never guess it from our media's aversion to the devastating eruptions of hopeless misery among masses of humans with whom we share a shrinking planet. This is not the way that a first-rate nation behaves. Indeed, the media's indifference to humanitarian crises might go a long way in explaining why the American government contributes the smallest amount of aid as a percentage of GNP among all the advanced nations. (See chapter 7.)

These are only a random handful of examples showing the media's handling of public information about significant events taking place in the nation and around the world, examples that show their violation of a people's right to receive objective information without censorship or political and chauvinistic embellishment. Other examples can be found on ProjectCensored.org, which recounts "the top 25 censored media stories" of a particular time period, or in any critical book or article on the American media. The top 25 censored stories of 2001–4 included the U.S. involvement in Colombia, the FCC's move to privatize the publicly owned airwaves, the U.S. nuclear revival, NAFTA's destruction of farming communities, the restrictions on access to abortion, the corporate exploitation of the Congo, and the failure of private prisons. But such exposures are of little avail in a media climate that pursues commercial entertainment above all other objectives.

One might try to mitigate the media's silence on so many vital issues, or its "suppression by omission," as one analyst has called it,[18] by arguing that they must be highly selective because of the torrent of significant news from within and without the nation. This would be a valid point if, in fact, it were significant news that was usually aired. But that is far from being the case. Indeed, the priorities are often just the reverse. As a professor of journalism and sociology at New York University has observed:

> [W]e are treated to ever more frequent rounds of 24/7 saturation: the month of the Nintendo Gulf War, the month of the death and transfiguration of Princess Diana, the year of Bill Clinton and Monica Lewinsky, the week of John F. Kennedy Jr.'s death, the months of the Elian Gonzales standoff . . . not to mention the hurricanes, air crashes, hijackings, hostage takings, rescues . . .[19]

Political campaigns, in particular, are upstaged by crime, which suggests a basic indifference to democracy on the part of the media. For example, while more than two hours were devoted to a sniper story by the nightly newscasts during October 21–25, 2002, only four minutes were devoted to the House elections.[20]

And the trend in coverage of violence seems to have been upward. In the first half of the '90s, there was a tripling of the number of stories about crime on the network TV news programs, and this occurred in a period when the crime rate was dropping. Some local stations devote more time to commercials than to news, and the news "tends to feature crime and violence, triviality, and celebrity," according to one observer of the media. In 1998, it was found that 40 percent of local news was on crime, disaster, war, or terrorism, and another 25 percent was called "fluff," including "stories about hair tattoos, beer baths, a dog returning home and a horse rescued from mud in California."[21]

Journalists sometimes refer to the difference between "hard" and "soft" news, according to Herbert Gans.[22] But each of these categories is so heterogeneous as to be almost useless for distinguishing between very worthwhile, somewhat worthwhile, and least worthwhile news. Thus, soft news includes both programs about health or disease and celebrity scandals or lifestyle information; hard news includes both political news involving top leaders and crime stories. (And how would one classify a crime story that is also a celebrity scandal?) In any case, Gans notes, over time, hard news has been partially replaced or supplemented by soft news in the media. This sounds like a greater effort to engage the audience in "human interest" concerns, but one can't be sure. At the present time, the coverage of news that is needed if one is to play a meaningful role in democracy seems so small that any diminution would obliterate it. A significant part of *past* diminution has been the reduction of foreign news through the cutting back or elimination of foreign news bureaus, another media trend on network television. As Gans points out, today a one-person bureau may cover a whole continent.[23]

A European journalist who had resided in the United States for a number of years noted a perverse trend in America's mass media. In the same period that "American thinkers vaulted forward—courageous, innovative and determined to talk in a public language . . . the mass media vaulted backward, thriving on increasingly simple stories and trivializing news into something indistinguishable from entertainment. As a result," this European journalist concluded, "a wealth of original and subtle thought—America's real wealth—was squandered."[24]

Finally, one cannot resist quoting a longtime script doctor at CBS who said in 2002: "Thirty years ago the newscasts were written for twelve year olds. Today they are written for seven year olds."[25]

The public cannot be accused of overlooking the media's default of their responsibilities, even though it rarely raises its voice about the problem, for the failure of the media to promote the common good by informing the public in a straightforward way has been reflected in the public's replies to pollsters. In 2002, the percentage who believed that "news organizations are highly professional" dropped from 73 percent to 49 percent just 10 months later. In fact, nearly 60 percent saw the media as an "obstacle" in helping society to solve its problems. Belief that news organizations are politically biased increased from 47 percent to 59 percent.[26] In short, most Americans believed that the media were failing to do their job, and in fact served as an obstruction in dealing with the nation's problems.

Gans[27] points out that public criticism of the media goes back at least to one of the earliest surveys of audience satisfaction, in 1939, when they were seen as too friendly toward the wealthy. Later studies have turned up the same perception. That the media are out of touch with average Americans has been another common criticism, as have been bias and inaccuracy. A poll in a 1985–1998 series of credibility studies found that nearly half agreed that journalists do not care about democracy, a response category that is far from being self-explanatory but nonetheless quite negative. (The foregoing studies are cited by

Gans in his searching and highly illuminating examination of the media.) These attitudes may have had real-life consequences for the media inasmuch as audience ratings of the network TV news programs have steadily declined since the '70s.[28]

To begin to understand the sources of the mainstream media's chronic failure to live up to their self-advertisements (and therefore, to put it bluntly, to justify their protection under the First Amendment), it is necessary to look at their codependent relationships with the three other power sectors: corporate business enterprise, government, and the public. For the media are by no means an autonomous player, self-righteous appeals to the "independence of the press" notwithstanding. They have little room to maneuver owing, first, to codependencies with each of their partners and, second, to their entanglement in the web of relationships between all four sectors. With regard to the latter, the linkage between any two of the power sectors is influenced by their linkages with the other power sectors. Then, too, one must bear in mind that the media themselves represent corporate society inasmuch as they are commercial enterprises in America. But it would require a doctoral dissertation to examine each of the primary linkages, their secondary influences on one another, and the role of the media's own corporate existence in their performance as gatherers and dispensers of the news. Here I can offer only highlights.

The Media and Corporate Enterprise

First, there is the symbiotic relationship between the media and other corporate enterprises. This linkage has been examined by a number of writers, and Herman and Chomsky[29] refer explicitly to the "reciprocal" or "symbiotic" nature of the linkage: "The mass media are drawn into a symbiotic relationship with powerful sources of information by economic necessity and reciprocity of interest."[30]

Corporations, in particular, offer four major benefits to the media: advertising revenue, packaged information, expert testimonials, and (in the absence of Enronesque scandals), enhanced power and prestige. The first benefit of advertising revenue is obvious because it constitutes the lifeblood of media outlets. The remaining three benefits require some clarification.

The second benefit, public relations (that is, packaged information for the media and others), constitutes a major business expenditure of corporations. As early as 20 years ago the U.S. Chamber of Commerce had a budget for research, communications, and political activities of $65 million. It published a business magazine called *Nation's Business* "with a circulation of 1.3 million and a weekly newspaper with 740,000 subscribers" and was producing "a weekly panel show distributed to 400 radio stations, as well as its own weekly panel-discussion programs carried by 128 commercial television stations." Advertising devoted to image and interests by corporate and trade associations "increased from $305 million in 1975 to $650 million in 1980 . . ." By 1984, outlays for political and grassroots efforts had increased to $1.6 billion.[31] All this output is welcomed by the media because it saves them the effort of routing out the "facts" themselves. Further, corporations not only offer precooked information to the media but behave like the media in their direct communications to the public independent of regular news organizations. This blurring of the boundary between the sectors is characteristic of all the sectoral linkages, a phenomenon that I referred to in the Introduction of this book as "transformative," and about which I shall say more later.

Moreover, the contribution of corporations in this regard is not limited to magazines and newspapers; it also includes facilitation of media access. McChesney refers to facilities in which media people can gather where they receive copies of speeches and forthcoming reports along with press releases. "In effect, the large bureaucracies of the powerful subsidize the mass media and gain special access by their contribution to reducing the media's costs of acquiring the raw materials of, and producing, news."[32]

As for the third benefit, in addition to disseminating material and facilitating media coverage by special arrangements, corporations have subsidized "think tanks" and taken other measures to co-opt experts and present them to the public through publications and personal appearances on talk shows. In other words, experts are bought, which is the first step in ensuring that the policy area "is awash with in-depth studies" that produce the right conclusions, according to Dr. Edwin Feulner of the Heritage Foundation.[33] This strategy, of course, is especially useful in neutralizing dissent from independent experts and academics.

In regard to the fourth benefit, the media's association (via advertisements, and so on) with leading corporations lends an aura of power and prestige, at least in periods when business scandals are not front-page news. To open a newspaper, for example, and see the half- or full-page ad of a corporate enterprise that dominates the locality or nation is to be subliminally impressed by the company that the paper keeps, so to speak. An upstanding reputation is therefore transferred to the news source itself.

In return for the benefits to the media that flow from the corporate sector, the media give regular exposure to business and economic news (especially if it is favorable or conducive to consumer confidence). The major newspapers and radio and TV programs regularly set aside space or time for the coverage of news helpful to financiers and investors, and also treat business leaders as heroes. The generous nature of this allotment is made all the more obvious when one contrasts it with the dearth of sections or segments primarily of interest to consumers, such as household finances, consumer fraud cases, or best buys that might discourage people from using the products of certain companies. The fact that everybody is a consumer, while only a small proportion are investors, makes little difference to the media's preoccupation with catering to corporations.[34]

The media also ensure that news that would reflect badly on certain companies, and especially advertisers, is dealt with discreetly or not at all. As Herman and Chomsky have pointed out: "Corporate advertisers on television will rarely sponsor programs that engage in serious criticisms of corporate activities, such as the problem of environmental degradation, the workings of the military-industrial complex, or corporate support of and benefits from Third World tyrannies."[35] And as Barbara Ehrenreich has shrewdly observed: "Corporate advertisers are concerned about placing ads in a 'good editorial environment.' They don't want their advertisements right across from an article on how workers of the world should unite and overthrow their capitalist bosses."[36]

As a general policy, it is important to avoid tainting the wares of advertisers with coverage of dissent or of suffering from certain social conditions—such as globalization protests, poverty, domestic or international atrocities committed by America, and so on. The psychological comfort of the American Myth that espouses the orderly arrangement of American society and its virtuous behavior toward the world is transferable to the objects or behaviors with which it is closely associated, including the commercial products of corporations—but only if evidence contrary to the mythology is banished from the frame of reference.

That corporations take these concerns very seriously is attested by their actions to ensure that media outlets and their products do not jeopardize their advertising message. Before some national advertisers will place ads, they insist on knowing the contents of certain issues. Some publishers have "corporate marketing departments" that try to make their magazines "an integral part of the [advertising] message . . . 'Let's be honest,' the president of Chanel confessed, 'I think you want to support those magazines which—from an editorial point of view—support you.'"[37] Two television reporters were fired in 1997 for refusing to "water down and create a misleading impression of their investigative report on Monsanto." Consequently, the report was not aired.[38] Many similar cases have been reported.

It is highly probable, moreover, that the sway of advertisers has increased with the rising proportion of ads on network television. In the '90s, all the networks increased their percentage of advertising time. Since 1989, for instance, ABC has increased its percentage of time devoted to commercials as much as 34 percent.[39] Even the Public Broadcasting System is no longer immune to the bacillus of corporate influence, owing, first, to its adoption of advertising some years ago and, second, to its reliance on federal and state legislatures that depend on corporate campaign contributions and that favor more of what is known euphemistically as "institutional advertising" on public media.[40]

A special relationship between the media and corporations arises when a news source is wholly owned by a national or international nonmedia business that is not conversant with the concept of press independence. GE, Disney, AT&T, and Sony now own major news outlets like NBC and ABC, and as one media expert has remarked, "Some of the new owners find it bizarre that any one would question the propriety of ordering their employee-journalists to promote the owner's corporation."[41] Furthermore, the parent organization is usually entangled in many parts of the military-industrial-political complex. GE, for example, which owns NBC, has heavy investments in military supplies, nuclear power, and finance, as well as playing a prominent role in supporting the Republican Party.[42] In fact, a former NBC correspondent resigned and wrote an expose of "GE's ongoing efforts to cheapen, degrade, and censor the news."[43] Not surprisingly, an Oregon ballot proposition to institute universal health care in the state was contemptuously dismissed by the *NBC Nightly News* with distortion of the proposal and total support of the criticisms made by insurance companies.[44] ABC News, which is owned by Disney, "rejected a report by its leading investigative correspondent exposing labor and safety practices at Disney World in Florida,"[45] and ABC has devoted considerable time to movies by Disney.[46] TCI, a "cable powerhouse with vast holdings in scores of other media enterprises," according to an historian of the media, has been purchased by AT&T.[47]

Whether or not a media source is owned by a large, traditionally nonmedia corporation, the media are denizens of corporate society and culture because they themselves are commercial, profit-seeking organizations. They are owned and often directly controlled by hardworking, astute businessmen who must be responsible to stockholders, and to customers who are looking for a profitable advertising platform. Their major policies are not controlled by creative thinkers, artists, cultural critics, political scientists, sociologists, foreign affairs experts, social researchers, or a host of other intellectual specialists, or even necessarily by journalists. That they are owned and tightly controlled by businessmen is a hard fact for the public to absorb; even harder to absorb are the implications for a high standard of journalism and up-to-date enlightenment about the world we live in. If, for example, the owners decide to cut the budget for foreign correspondents, then Americans simply will not be given news about a world that could explode in their faces (literally) any day. Prior to 9/11, this was precisely the case. And if business interests dictate a particular editorial policy or news coverage slant, including censorship, then so be it. Insofar as being well informed is an essential ingredient in the diet of a robust democracy, the implications for our form of government of a predominantly business-oriented public communications system are alarming.

Of particular concern is campaign coverage. During the 2002 election campaign, only 37 percent of 122 TV stations in the top 50 media markets aired any campaign coverage at all during five weeks in September-October. Instead, they published campaign ads, which is where the money was. In fact, for every election-related story, four campaign ads were aired. As a media watchdog organization has commented: ". . .the stations seem to have come to view covering local elections as akin to giving away free merchandise."[48] Russell Baker, a veteran journalist, has made this comment:

> The new [media] managerial class are balance sheet CEOs in the conventional business school style—eyes always peeled for a merger or acquisition, attention always focused on the stock market's quarterly report card. It is not even necessary that they know anything about journalism.[49]

A news director of a television station confirms this impression from his personal experience: "News division directors are not fired for putting on lousy news programs, they're fired for getting lower ratings than competitors—and in the television business they are fired regularly."[50]

Reporters may be thought of by the public as "independent, fair-minded professionals," but their hiring and firing, and their daily work, are controlled by corporations that can guide, censor, or squelch their output.[51] And today, according to a former NBC correspondent who covered the Gulf War, they "have less real influence on the daily news agenda than ever before, and they face harsh treatment from management if they speak out."[52] Although many journalists may not feel that the corporate owners have much or any influence at all on news organizations, their distance from the boardroom and acceptance of the traditional policies of their employers (such as not highlighting news of interest to a lower-income market, not reporting the number of civilian dead in American wars, not covering the reasons for antiglobalization protests, not providing regular "social reports" as contrasted with economic reports, not giving more coverage to foreign news because of its cost, and so forth) shield them from the facts of life about the influence of owners and advertisers.

One of the clearest signs of corporate bias in presentation of the news is the emphasis on "good demographics," namely, a market that is economically well off. Because the poor are poor consumers, advertisers are not interested in reaching them. Thus, news of importance to the poor, such as poverty or welfare programs, subsidized child health care, job discrimination, activism on behalf of the poor or unemployed, and so forth, are seldom given prominence or even coverage by the mainstream media. This means that major concerns of possibly 20 percent of the American population are downplayed or ignored.

In short, as a source quoted earlier put it: "The public is regarded not as a democratic polity, but as a mass of consumers." And consumers must be attracted, glad-handed, cajoled, placated, wooed, and seduced—in other words, manipulated into a sufficiently trusting and receptive mood to be persuaded to part with their money and, often, their common sense. They are not viewed as clients, wards, or citizens who need to be, and expect to be, educated, cured, assisted, or guided. Top managers of media corporations do not hold meetings to ponder how to improve the education, health, political or cultural sophistication, or social adjustment of their "target segment," but how to extract their money. Without this contextualization, the nature of mainstream media news in America cannot be understood. Furthermore, for a variety of reasons, television is more sensitive to its market imperatives than other media. Thus, it has become an electronic shopping mall. But unlike the dotcom bazaar, it offers periodic diversions to lure latent consumers into its precincts and hold them there hour after hour. One of these diversions is called the "news show."

One way not to mesmerize or seduce the TV audience is to expose it to negative features of their most cherished institutions: the Constitution, religion, heterosexual marriage, the military, the credibility of the president and other top officials charged with the public's well-being, free enterprise as an economic model, equality of opportunity, and the existing system of distributive justice. Thus, the latent cultural and political conservatism of a public that clings to the American Myth coalesces with the explicit economic conservatism of the corporate media and its advertisers. In effect, the media say to the public: "We'll let you have your brand of conservatism if you'll let us have ours." This amounts to a double acquiescence to a mythical version of social reality, which is hardly the state of mind envisaged by democratic theoreticians, including the founding fathers, who have advocated freedom of the press as essential to democracy. On the contrary, the way that our free press has been managed poses a grave threat to the democratic need for dissent, full disclosure, and untrammeled debate. The ultimate effects of this "unanticipated consequence" of the media in America have been amply documented in the pages of this book, where time and again we have seen the public misinformed and uninformed about the disastrous state of the nation.

One might object that the public has the right to switch to other media sources if they do not like what they are getting (or not getting). That is the glory of the free market, and competition will ultimately raise standards and improve the product. One thing wrong with this theory is that if there are fewer and fewer choices that the consumer can make among competing media sources, his or her exercise of taste or demand for reliable information is concomitantly constricted. This is precisely what has happened in America in the past 20 years, and on a titanic scale.

In 1983, more than half of all the media, including publishing and film, was controlled by about 50 conglomerates, but by 1986 the number had dropped to 29, by 1993 it had dropped to 20, and today it is fewer than 10. One large radio corporation, Clear Channel, now owns 1,200 stations, whereas in 1996 it owned only 40.[53] "Ordinary citizens," according to the late Senator Paul Wellstone, "don't stand a chance of having their voices heard against the power and influence of these corporate titans."[54] With regard to books, five conglomerates control 80 percent of all sales. As for radio, two corporate giants "control more than a third of all radio advertising revenue nationally, and up to 90 percent of some markets."[55] Ownership of individual radio stations has dropped 25 percent, and at least 70 percent of local market share is controlled by three or four broadcasters.[56]

The death of local stations means the death of in-depth local news coverage and the crowding out of innovative, experimentally creative shows of any kind, including popular music, that are needed to replenish American culture. A smattering of local news might be provided to give an appearance of localism, but by and large the cookie that is cut for consumers nationwide is what is also consumed locally. Were it not for the biases and omissions of large-scale, corporate-controlled advertising, this trend might be viewed as a boon for cosmopolitanism. But in reality it amounts to the homogenization of schlock.

With respect to popular music, for example:

[I]ndependent radio stations that once would have played edgy, political music have been gobbled up by corporations that control hundreds of stations and have no wish to rock the boat . . . With a few exceptions, the disc jockeys who once existed to discover provocative new music have long since been put out to pasture.[57]

And with regard to local television news, a study of the Project for Excellence in Journalism found that small companies with locally owned stations were "twice as likely to produce the highest quality news as were stations owned by the top 10 media groups."[58]

Moreover, local stations are no longer easily accessible to politicians or community groups for live coverage, or even to individuals who need to alert a community to an emergency. Representative Mark Foley of Florida related how he was having trouble getting air time to address his constituents since national companies had moved into his district and reduced five local stations to only one.[59] In Minot, North Dakota, the police tried to call the radio stations to alert the population to a potential disaster from the derailment of a freight train carrying a hazardous chemical. It took an hour and a half before anyone answered a phone. According to the *New York Times*, 300 people had to be hospitalized and some were partially blinded.[60]

Most significantly in terms of the damage to democracy: when a media corporation monopolizes a local market, it monopolizes the attention of the public regarding issues, information, and viewpoints, and thus forms the only picture of the nation or the world they are likely to obtain. It feeds the public with what the corporation's owners and managers want it to be fed, not what will provide it with the spectrum of viewpoints and data required to make "informed" judgments. To repeat: while today's media still have some educational or informational functions, they are primarily outlets for advertising. And a monopoly of

attention translates into a monopoly for products. The educational or informational functions could be abandoned without fatal consequences for the media as
money-making enterprises, and the owners know it. The same cannot be said of
the advertising function, which can be sustained by entertainment and trivial
news. Sadly, the constriction of the public's right to choose is occurring at the
same time as new technology is making it possible for TV viewers to access far
more channels. In spite of the diversification of technology, the homogeneity of
content is increasing.[61]

It is very doubtful that "freedom of the press" embraces freedom from the
responsibility to respect and satisfy the needs of the people for information
about current events. Surely it refers to protection from interference with the
fulfillment of that responsibility—a responsibility that is taken for granted by
Americans. Otherwise, freedom of the press would not have been guaranteed by
so august a document as the Constitution. The First Amendment is not cherished
because it endorses the freedom to get rich by peddling one's goods. In fact, the
freedom most urgently needed by the media today is freedom from its own corporate imperative of commercialism.

In recognition of the media's corporate and political power, one critic has
characterized media concentration as a "totalitarian tool."[62] And Americans cannot even be sure that the totalitarianism is homegrown, for the concentration that
has occurred, and is still occurring, is no less than global.[63] The global media
system, according to our media historian, "is dominated by fewer than ten global
TNC [transnational corporations], with another four or five dozen firms filling
out regional and niche markets." In fact, most of the revenues of United States
TV and film productions now come from outside the country.[64] Although the
United States currently dominates the globalization of media, eventually other
nations will establish a beachhead in America. Rupert Murdoch, who is based in
Australia and Britain, but holds 22 U.S. television stations that cover 40 percent
of the population, Twentieth Century Fox films, and over 130 daily newspapers,
in addition to book-publishing companies and other media assets, has moved far
beyond a beachhead and into the interior, and his incursion might be a harbinger
of things to come. As for his global reach, "by 1998 Murdoch claimed to have
TV networks and systems that reached more than 74 percent of the world's
population."[65]

To speak of today's media as "totalitarian tools" might be a slight exaggera-
tion, but one cannot argue with the proposition that owners of the major network
media are avatars of conservatism, and that today a conservative bias in news-
casting is pervasive.[66] Studies of the guests on news programs and talk shows
reveal this tilt toward the right wing "with scarcely anyone who would have
qualified as a liberal in the 1970s, let alone the 1940s."[67] A media watchdog organization has found that "of the 56 partisan guests on Special Report [Fox TV
news], 50 were Republicans and 6 were Democrats—a greater than 8 to 1 im-

balance."[68] According to another observer, "there are 80 hours per week, more than 4,000 hours per year, programmed for Republican and conservative talk shows, without a single second programmed for a Democratic or liberal perspective."[69] Most tellingly, out of the multitude of current affairs programs on TV, only one focuses on the media, CNN's Reliable Sources, and its guests are overwhelmingly white, male, employed by the mainstream media, and outspokenly conservative. Not a single representative of a citizens' group appeared on the program from December 1, 2001, to November 30, 2002.[70]

As for coverage of the Iraq war, the number of on-camera sources appearing on six top TV news programs during three weeks shortly after the bombing of Iraq began who were prowar far outweighed the number who were antiwar. The proportion of prowar sources appearing on the six programs was 64 percent of all sources and 71 percent of U.S. sources. Antiwar voices were only 10 percent of all sources and 3 percent of U.S. sources.[71] And this bias occurred only a few days after at least a million people around the world had risen in protest against the war, including tens of thousands in America.

How did America arrive at the present pass where corporations dominate programming and commerce wags the dog, and where concentration has led to homogenization and a national or international domination by large conglomerates?

A Brief History of Corporate Control of the Media

When radio broadcasting emerged in the 1920s, amateurs and nonprofit groups realized its potential for education and the flow of information well in advance of the business world's recognition of its potential for commerce. Colleges and universities, in particular, set up and ran their own stations throughout the country. As Robert McChesney, a media historian, has observed, "Educational institutions were arguably the 'true pioneers' of U.S. broadcasting, establishing over one hundred stations in the early 1920s." A survey in 1926 by American Telephone and Telegraph found that commercial broadcasters composed only 4.3 percent of all radio stations. Thus, the storm that would soon break was wholly unanticipated.[72]

When business interests finally recognized radio's profit-making possibilities (in 1927 to 1932), they managed to gain control of the Federal Radio Commission (FRC), which actually had been authorized to "favor those stations which best served the 'public interest, convenience, or necessity,' although the law did not attempt to define these terms."[73] The important players in the capture of the FRC were the newly created networks NBC (1926) and CBS (1927).

A reallocation of frequencies and broadcasting times by the FRC undercut the educational stations and gave priority to commercial interests, and did so

with scant publicity or oversight by Congress or the public.[74] To justify this pref-
erential shift toward commerce, the FRC asserted that advertising was "the only
form of material support that did not have ideological strings attached."[75] In
other words, raw commercial self-interest was not regarded as an ideology, presumably because in America it needed no justification. Overlooked was the fact
that unrestrained commitment to the pursuit of commercial interest is itself an
ideology—the ideology of the American bonanza mentality rooted in the sanctity of free enterprise.

As a consequence of the FRC's reallocation of frequencies and broadcasting
time, the number of college stations fell by half, and the remaining nonprofit
stations had to share frequencies with the new commercial stations. In 1932, as
an observer noted, "The amount of advertising on the air is beyond any expectation that could have existed five years ago." And by the early '30s, nonprofit
broadcasting was virtually absent from the air waves.[76]

This outcome was by no means welcomed by the public. In fact, it was almost universally scorned. In 1932, *Business Week* asserted: "Radio broadcasting
is threatened with a revolt of the listeners . . . Newspaper editors report more and
more letters of protest against irritating sales ballyhoo."[77] By then, however,
broadcasters had formed one of the strongest lobbies in Washington. They vigorously manipulated both public opinion and Congress and were able to mo-
nopolize the public's attention by their control of the airwaves, which were
made available at no charge to congressmen and federal officials at the discretion of the networks, a boon for politicians and broadcasters alike as their symbiotic relationship began to flourish.

A strong reform movement arose as a reaction to the commercial takeover
of the media, a movement composed of religious groups, organized labor, the
ACLU, and prominent educators (including John Dewey, America's leading
philosopher at the time). As one educational leader predicted:

> As a result of radio broadcasting, there will probably develop during the twen-
> tieth century either chaos or a world-order of civilization. Whether it be one or
> the other will depend upon whether broadcasting be used as a tool of education
> or an instrument of selfish greed.[78]

And many educators concurred. "Without freedom of speech," one wrote,
"without the honest presentation of facts by people whose primary interest is not
profits, there can be no intelligent basis for the determination of public policy."[79]
In other words, standards would plummet to the lowest common denominator:
"it is inevitable that a commercial concern catering to the public will present a
service as low in standard as the public will tolerate and will produce the most
profit."[80] It would be hard to argue that this prediction has not been borne out.

Britain, Canada, and other countries followed a different route without succumbing to government domination. But avoiding this trap was regarded as impossible in America. (Only much later, in the 1990s, did European media begin expanding their commercial advertising because of decreased subsidies.[81]) At least part of the reason for Europe's early rejection of the American model was its revulsion at the swamp waters of advertising that overflowed into the parlors of America day and night. Thus, when BBC's director visited America, he was shocked by the state of commercial broadcasting, noting that "the whole system of American broadcasting [lies] outside our comprehension . . ."[82]

Recognizing that the networks had become permanently entrenched, some prominent and well-funded reformers sought to work out arrangements with them to schedule a stipulated amount of public service or educational broadcasting. The networks were cool to the idea, however, and the relevant congressional committees were firmly in their grasp. Predictably, these efforts did not bear fruit.

In spite of overwhelming endorsement of broadcast reform by the Senate and House, the radio lobby was able to subvert the latter's commitment by gaining the support of certain key politicians. The political incompetence of the reformers also played a role. Moreover, public acceptance of commercial radio with its emphasis on entertainment had grown. But perhaps the most important stumbling block for the reformers was the difficulty of getting the newspapers to cover their arguments and efforts. A proposed bill to "set aside 25% of the channels for nonprofit broadcasters" was defeated because it was expected to be taken up by a newly formed agency called the Federal Communication Commission (1934). But the latter's hearings were overwhelmed by the networks' lobbyists and their well-crafted testimony. The opposition to commercial domination of the airwaves dissolved, and the CBS president admonished educators gathered in a meeting several years later that "he who attacks the American system [of broadcasting] attacks democracy itself."[83] By the late 1930s, only 30 educational stations were operating, and these were in deep financial trouble.[84]

The networks were responsible for some degree of obligation to have educational programs, however, and so they created something called "sustaining" programs that were able to survive in time slots that did not interest advertisers. But as advertisers expanded their purchase of time, the "sustaining" programs became limited to the most undesirable time slots. Their quality declined along with their audience, advertising was permitted, and the federal regulations were relaxed. By the 1990s, very little remained of the public service mission, and eventually even this pittance was diluted by ads about the networks' shows and the do-good character of the corporate sponsors. In 1996, the FCC required commercial networks to provide three hours a week of children's educational programming. This amounted to about 26 minutes a day, including advertisements aimed at children.

The Telecommunications Act of 1996 was billed as an instrument for in-creasing competition. In actuality, it made it possible "for the first time, for a single company to own more than one radio station in the same market; a single owner was now permitted to own both TV stations and cable systems in the same market."[85] At the same time, many regulations were eliminated on grounds that market competition would suffice to serve the public, the same rhetoric that we hear today about auto fuel efficiency, drug prices, health insurance, and every other activity of corporations with detrimental consequences. According to an analyst of media concentration, "the Telecommunications Act of 1996 swept away even the minimal consumer and diversity protection of the 1934 act that preceded it."[86] This protection was replaced with rules that made it much easier for broadcasters to concentrate ownership. And the pressure on the gov-ernment's regulatory authority to ease or eliminate even those rules remained very strong.

The pattern of mergers and the rise of market dominance by conglomerates can be seen in the history of the breakup of Bell Telephone and Telegraph by the government. After the breakup, a number of companies fought to make inroads on the turfs of the "baby Bells" that had been spawned. Although heavily fi-nanced, many began losing the battle and were bought by the survivors at low prices, which mergers led to much greater concentration in the market during the '90s. Thus, increased competition led to mergers, which led to far less diversi-fied competition or almost none at all. Moreover, this emergence of dominant telecommunication corporations in various markets facilitated the possibility of alliances and mergers with dominant computer and media companies, thereby paving the way in the future for "bundled services" that can draw on all three of these digital sectors. Meanwhile, the outcome of the emergence of concentrated local and national media has been token nods to local news coverage[87] along with an inevitable homogenization of the product and, consequently, the public's world view. "Needless to say," as McChesney observes, "the implications for democracy of this concentrated, conglomerated, and hypercommercialized me-dia are entirely negative."[88]

The paramount question for the FCC in the recent past has been how to re-vive the telecom industry after the spate of corporate scandals and the bust in the early 2000s.[89] Indeed, the future of the American economy might depend to some extent on the answer. The answer that the FCC has adopted (at least the chairman and a majority of members), however, has been the further relaxation or elimination of rules that had prevented an even greater degree of consolida-tion, both locally and nationally. These rules had prohibited ownership of local broadcast stations that served more than 35 percent of the market in the same community, prohibited ownership of cable TV systems and TV stations in the same community, and prohibited ownership of both newspapers and TV stations in the same community, among other things. The general expectation was that relaxation of these rules would greatly enhance concentration through mergers, and lead to domination of the media by only one or two firms in a number of cities.[90] The FCC was required to make its decision on these matters formal by June 2003. Meanwhile, Internet Web sites aroused the public to the impending relaxation or elimination of rules governing media concentration, and when this surge of protest had no effect on the FCC's expected decision to eviscerate the rules, certain members of Congress were aroused to override its decision.

This latest effort to satisfy the big media conglomerates reminds us that the FCC has long been "a classic example of what is called the 'captive' regulatory agency," in the words of McChesney. As he explains: "FCC members and officials sometimes come from the commercial broadcasting industry and often go there for lucrative employment after their stints in 'public service.'"[91] When, occasionally, the FCC has proposed changes that would help to redemocratize the media, it has come under intense opposition from powerful congressmen to cease and desist. The FCC majority and chairman, however, have been staunch supporters of the industry's opposition to regulations; and the chairman has stated clearly: "I start with the proposition that the rules are no longer necessary."[92] The FCC, therefore, stated its intention to hold only a single public hearing of an official nature on the matter.

Nevertheless, once again a strong reform movement has emerged to oppose the further deterioration of the media's obligation to serve the public instead of corporate owners. The recent protest included thousands of grassroots activists, the Newspaper Guild, Consumers Union, FAIR (Fairness and Accuracy in Reporting), and many other nonprofit, public-interest groups. But one should never underestimate the financial strength of the commercial media or the willingness of the FCC and Congress to comply with their wishes. This willingness, incidentally, has been well compensated. Viacom, for example, spent $1 million on candidates for office in Congress in 2002. And hundreds of all-expense-paid trips for members of Congress, their staff, and FCC employees were paid for by media corporations in the late '90s.[93]

Until the grassroots movement against the FCC rose to a crescendo, the mainstream media paid scant attention to the issue. By monopolizing mass communications, the media have gained as strong a stranglehold on the public as they have on Congress and the FCC. Before the movement hit its stride, thanks to an Internet activist group, a public opinion poll found that 72 percent of the public were unaware that the FCC was considering the abolition of media regulations. (For a report on FCC's embrace of further consolidation with regard to stimulating broadband connections, see John B. Judis, "Michael Powell v. the Economy," in the *New Republic*.[94]) A clear symptom of the commercial media's failure to serve the public is the growing chorus of "alternative" voices in the press, on television, and on the Web. (For news stories and information about the alternative media, search the following Web sites: Alternative Press Review, Alternative Press Center, and the Independent Press Association.)

The alternative media in America were invigorated by the Vietnam War's "underground press," as it was called, and have since taken root in more than 400 Web sites. Moreover, some interest groups that have been consistently ignored or downplayed by the commercial media have begun to create their own media. For example, poor people's groups have received training and advice from highly experienced media people and have launched their own media outlets. By becoming reporters, video producers, and radio hosts, they are endeavoring to circumvent the monopolies and the demographics-dominated mainstream press.[95] A development known as "blogging" has also caught the imagination of at least a million users of a Web site called Blogging.com that was started in 1999. "Badly researched or ideologically skewed reporting was being instantly skewered by the bloggers—as we saw recently when half-baked journalistic theories about the NASA shuttle disaster were effortlessly demolished by folks with serious aerospace expertise ... the blogging community refuses to accept the news 'agenda' as determined by mainstream media."[96]

It will be interesting to see how the giant corporate media make arrangements with Congress to block or take over these new "alternative" information resources in the service of the mainstream's commercial goals. Already a few large chains have absorbed certain performers in the alternative press. How commercialized, bland, and homogenized these sources will become remains to be seen.

With the two exceptions of protest against the Iraq war and the FCC's plans to deregulate rules governing ownership of the media in recent months, "people power" has sunk into utter desuetude in America in recent years. This loss of nerve has been attested by voter apathy and acquiescence to congressional and presidential attack on social programs, civil liberties, and nonconformist opinion. And the hold of the mainstream media on the public—owing to their symbiotic bonds with corporate advertisers and government—has placed huge hurdles in the way of any effort to amalgamate dissent. In effect, the alternative media today face the same challenge as the educational pioneers of radio 80 years ago, a challenge that turned out to be insurmountable. But there is a new weapon at hand, the Web, which permits rapid information-sharing, organizing, and fund-raising among scattered individuals, groups, and organizations that share common goals and yearn to vent their collective desires.

The Media and Government

No one would argue today that the mainstream media of America devote vigorous, self-conscious effort to scrutinizing the nation's dominant values and institutions for signs of frailty and, when such evidence is detected, unveiling and broadcasting it to the world with uncompromising documentation. And yet, this is the only means of divesting the American Myth of its powers of concealment and mollification. At present, the chief function of the mainstream media is not to reflect reality, but to uphold the nation's values and institutions, including the prevailing outlooks of representatives and officials.[97] This point seems so obvious that the great majority of Americans would simply shrug at its assertion. What this function provides are two of the chief benefits bestowed on government by the media: protection from close public scrutiny, skepticism, or opposition, and partisan support for its policies, especially in the military arena, providing that government personnel give the media the access they crave and the freedom to go on hawking their advertisers' wares. The ability to give or withhold these benefits is an impressive power, for a tool that serves the ostensible purpose of keeping the public informed can even more easily keep it uninformed, and people in government know that. Here are two indications of the power of the media in the eyes of government leaders:

> [M]any [members of Congress] regard the media companies in their districts as the single most terrifying category of interest group—you can cross the local bank president and live to tell the tale, but not the local broadcaster.[98]
>
> During the hard going in Vietnam, Lyndon Johnson confided to the editorial page [of the *Washington Post*] that the *Post*'s support for the war was worth two divisions.[99]

By its devotion to what Gans[100] calls "top down" news, a basic benefit of the media to government is that they allow officials or candidates to define the issues of the dialogue between themselves and the public. Even *criticisms* of policies are limited to the issues that officials or candidates have imposed on the public's consciousness with the acquiescence and assistance of the media, and usually officials and candidates are fully prepared to deflect, if not defuse, these criticisms as a result of cagey anticipation.

Many examples of social, environmental, economic, and political problems that have been ignored or given scant or biased coverage by the media have already been mentioned in the preceding chapters. They include the ramifications of poverty and unemployment, reasons for protests against globalization or war, the mental illness rate and the inadequacy of care, the price gouging of drug companies, the control of energy and antipollution policies by the oil and auto industries, tax evasion by major corporations, civilian deaths from recent American wars, the high cost of higher education, and, until much later, the absence of hard evidence that Iraq was ready to use WMD before the decision to attack, and numerous other "stories" that have been relegated either to the alternative media or to oblivion. (On the neglect of domestic issues, see also the discussion in chapter 1 of the critical need for a social well-being index that could be reported periodically by the media, and also an annual social report prepared by the federal government.) By suppressing or muting such stories, the commercial media protect government from criticism for its sins of both omission and commission and allow the nation to slump into a posture of ignorant indifference and flaccid democracy. The selection of events or facts for coverage, and the way those events or facts are handled in their presentation as news, are probably more powerful in shaping public opinion than dozens of editorials. The following are some additional examples of omission and distortion of facts in ways that have seriously compromised the truth and obviously redounded to the government's advantage.

In the preceding chapter we saw that half a million children were estimated by the UN to have died from the American-led sanctions during the '90s. Here is how Greta Van Susteren minimized these casualties on Fox News in early 2002: "The American sanctions, or the sanctions against Iraq, have caused the death of over 1,000 people."[101] To this day, the great majority of Americans are still unaware of the high death toll from the sanctions. In 1984, a priest in communist Poland was murdered by the police. According to a careful study, the American media devoted more attention to this single murder than to the police murders of about 100 priests in America's client states in Latin America.[102] In 1998, a reporter working for the *Washington Post* learned that UNSCOM [United Nations Special Commission] inspectors in Iraq were spying for the United States "in efforts to undermine the Iraqi regime." But a senior U.S. government official persuaded the *Post* not to publish the story "for reasons of national security." At the time, a critical debate was taking place in the UN about the inspectors' relations with Iraq that could have benefited greatly from this information, which had explosive implications. The story was not published until three months later.[103] In 1996, the *San Jose Mercury News* published a story revealing the CIA's involvement with drug dealers in the inner cities of America. The story was boycotted by other papers, and several even published attacks on it. The reporter was demoted and forced to resign, and a retraction of the story was duly printed. Later research and a report of the CIA itself confirmed the facts that the journalist had reported, but "the matter was ignored in toto in the commercial news media."[104]

As in the case of corporations, a symbiotic or codependent relationship between government and the media entails a number of quid pro quos that limit the media's freedom of action and thought. Protection and helping to define the preferred issues of public dialogue are just two of the benefits that the media bestow on government. Another benefit is simple exposure. Lack of exposure is almost as fatal to a politician as negative exposure, for any kind or amount of exposure tends to legitimize the politician or official as an important functionary or aspirant to office. The shift mentioned earlier from live coverage to paid campaign ads has made live coverage an even more precious commodity. This circumstance adds to the "terrifying" nature of the media in the eyes of politicians.

In order to curry favor with the media on behalf of live exposure, politicians eagerly bow to the media's "production values,"[105] or, more colloquially, tricks of the trade. One of these tricks is reliance on "sound bites," which invariably oversimplify complex issues. As a media researcher has pointed out, "speeches that have no pithy, lively, and very short 'sound bites' (usually under ten seconds long) that can be extracted are disfavored over those that do; consequently, speakers concerned about getting into the news have to craft their communications so as to be littered with sound bites."[106]

Some other production values are an emphasis on victims vs. villains, clear-cut failures and successes of policies, programs, or actions, colorful and dramatic events, the "constant present tense" (which creates episodic, ahistorical news), and, in the case of TV, the visually arresting image, preferably with action.[107] The outcomes, of course, are a marked degree of distortion and bias, and a tendency for the public to think and communicate about issues defined by the power elite themselves in clichés, platitudes, and buzz words.

Here we have a clear demonstration of the transformation referred to earlier when one dependent power sector takes on the values or style of another power sector. If political actors want the attention of the media, they must behave like the media to satisfy the latter's notion of correct or arresting verbal presentation to the public. Interestingly enough, the media reciprocate by absorbing the habits and outlooks of government personnel. As the preceding source notes with perspicacity:

> The temptation is . . . strong to "go native" and adopt the norms and values of the institution being covered. After all, reporters must try to figure out what makes the institutional actors tick, and selling the story to one's editors and producers means not only placing those individuals as their key protagonists but also adopting a vision of that institution as a crucial player. As a result, in Tuchman's words, newsbeat journalists "ask the question appropriate to their sources' world."[108]

This latter transformation, incidentally, has been both a hazard and a boon to field anthropologists for generations. The boon is twofold: gaining trust and access, and getting inside the heads of the subjects. The hazard is that the subjects' version of reality will color that of the anthropologist. This is especially a hazard for reporters who are dealing with persons of superior status and power. Identification and a sense of collegiality with high-status individuals is very ego-gratifying and elevates one in the eyes of others. Again, the outcome can be a pervasive bias.

An intriguing case of blurring the boundaries between power sectors in addressing the public is provided by "video news releases." These are public relations announcements in the guise of independent news stories, a tactic developed first by the corporate world and then adopted by government. A striking example is the Bush administration's video news release about the virtues of the controversial Medicare and drug insurance law, a law that was drawn up by the administration and that has met with widespread criticism. (See chapter 3, "An Afterword on the 2003 Medicare and Drug Insurance Law.") The "news" video touted the new law as a godsend, particularly for senior citizens without drug benefits, in the style of a straight news report.

When reporters identify with government officials and their activities, the boundary between the news sector and the governmental sector is blurred in another way. A striking example was the media's coverage of the Gulf War of 1991. According to one media watchdog, "many reporters for national media abandoned any pretense of neutrality or reportorial distance in favor of boosterism for the war effort. As Hodding Carter, who once served as a State Department spokesperson, put it: 'If I were the government, I'd be paying the press for the kind of coverage it is getting.'. . . The use by journalists of 'we' to mean U.S. military forces was constant."[109]

This identification with authorities as critical sources of news might account for the mainstream media's conservative slant under the present Bush administration, at least before the president's popularity began to slip in early 2004. The adoption of government's current ideology means that the one institution that could serve as an avenue for dissent has substantially abandoned that role. And the same is probably true of liberal administrations. In either case, liberal or conservative, the mainstream media are chronically guilty of a failure of nerve, owing at least in part to their dependence on government sources in order to fulfill their reportorial mission. Thus, because of *mutual* dependency, not only do the media behave like a political institution, as compellingly argued by a political scientist,[110] but political structures try to behave in large part like the media. At any rate, shared values and styles need to be addressed as a distinct aspect of the consolidation of power among the different primary sectors.

This is not to say that either government or the establishment media have seduced one another to the point of abandoning all semblance of their primary missions. In the first place, the range of quality and style among actors in each sector is extremely wide. In the second place, their relationship is more in the nature of a prolonged, romantic engagement fraught with ambivalence than that of a marriage, but an engagement that involves many episodes of intimacy and coconspiracy. Except in extreme cases of deliberate propagandizing by a particular media source, or of patent favoritism on the part of government in the release of breaking news, the media retain at least a small zone of autonomy that can be expanded or constricted at their discretion. What is important to note is that pressures on the media to constrict their freedom of vision to suit the government have seemingly gained the upper hand in the past few years, perhaps because of the president's popularity and/or the threat to national security that has evoked a "rally-round-the-flag" attitude. Under such conditions, typical efforts of manipulation by government officials tend to be quite successful.

Officials and politicians have a wide repertoire of tactics for manipulating the media, including staged press conferences (with carefully crafted introductions), managed leaks, outright lying and more subtle distortions of the facts, handouts that compel attention to particular facts and afford quotable material, and blocking or tightly controlling access to certain events or kinds of information. The media's dependency on government press releases is a major avenue of government control and extends even to ostensibly foolproof statistical reports. As Gans[111] points out, "in relying on news releases, [the media] unwittingly accept the government's indicators, and the ways these are measured. In this country as elsewhere, these tend to understate negative statistics, for example, about the actual rates of poverty and unemployment." The tight control of war correspondents is a striking example of blocking. In the Gulf War, "all interviews had to be monitored by military public affairs escorts. Every line of copy, every still photograph, every strip of film had to be approved—censored—before being filed. And these rules were ruthlessly enforced."[112]

One consequence of this control of access during the Gulf War was the journalistic myth that the war had few civilian casualties, when in fact a report by International Physicians for the Prevention of Nuclear War and the London-based Medact organization later concluded that "the total possible deaths on all sides during the conflict and the following three months range from 48,000 to over 260,000." In addition, deaths from the civil war and adverse health effects after the war could have added another 220,000 deaths.[113] If this information had been available to the American people in the months preceding the 2003 Iraq war, there might have been more understanding of the position taken by antiwar protesters who unavailingly took to the streets of the world in 2002–3. Further, more attention might have been paid by journalists to civilian casualties after the war commenced, the military might have tried harder to minimize civilian casualties, and military spokesmen might have felt under pressure to acknowledge and give estimates of these casualties. But access to information of any kind during the first Iraq war was meager. As Christiane Amanpour of CNN said at a forum on covering war and bio-terrorism, "We got essentially zip, nothing of value during that campaign."[114]

But then, even if journalists had been allowed to get the facts, stories of civilian casualties might not have gotten past the editors of the mainstream media. As an example of the explicit manner in which editors banish unpleasant realities, the following is a memo circulated among the staff of the *New Herald* (Panama City, Florida) newspaper during the Afghanistan war.

DO NOT use photos on Page 1a showing civilian casualties from the U.S. war on Afghanistan . . . DO NOT USE wire stories which lead with civilian casualties. . . If the story needs rewriting to play down the civilian casualties, DO IT. The only exception is if the U.S. hits an orphanage, school or similar facility and kills scores or hundreds of children.[115]

With regard to favoritism toward particular journalists on the part of government when a story is extremely timely, mentioned above as an occasion when the media tend to completely lower their guard against seduction, not even the president is above the temptation to use this device. When he wished to manipulate opinion about Iraq before his State of the Union speech in 2003, for example, "he invited only conservative columnists, who went from gushing about the president to gushing more about the president," according to the *New York Times*.[116]

The most serious form of interference with a free press, however, occurs when the justice system punishes journalists for doing their job, which includes offering anonymity to their sources as a means of gaining a story. This situation has become so serious in America that the nation has been found to have less freedom of press than other Western countries, with the exception of Italy. According to a study by Reporters Without Borders, the United States is far behind other countries in press freedom, which is due mainly to "the number of journalists arrested or imprisoned here . . . the imprisonment of journalists who refused to reveal their sources in court." The report also mentioned arrests of several journalists for crossing security lines at some government buildings.[117]

*   *   *

The weight of the facts and observations in this chapter point to the conclusion that failings of the mainstream media are hugely responsible for prolonging many of our national flaws and, consequently, for our second-rate standing among advanced industrial societies. The attention to violence, trivia, celebrityhood, government propaganda, and military might, and the downplaying of numerous major domestic problems, not only fail to shed light on the everyday realities of our lives, but shield Americans from the distress of fellow citizens and the people of the world. If just a fraction of the compassion that is devoted by the media to the occasional kidnapping of children were addressed to the poverty, homelessness, discrimination, and uncared-for health problems of millions of Americans, the nation would be a far better place and would be on the road to moral recovery. But the mainstream media cannot be found in this project; instead, they are devoted to the lowest common denominator of diversion for the simple reason that the lowest common denominator (for people with money, that is) represents the largest number of customers for satisfying their commercial goals. In addition, they strive to placate the dominant political authorities by steering clear of dissent, collective anger, and the clay feet of our revered institutions. In so doing, they preserve the American Myth of national superiority that comforts the insecure, disheartened, and stressed-out multitude, and palliates or even wholly obscures the great disparity between myth and reality.

As a consequence, the commercial media bear a large share of the blame for our social and economic naiveté, our political apathy, our puerile level of political discourse, our ignorance of the rest of the world and its history, our retreat to blind patriotism and religious devotion when stressed by international events, our educational failure, our bad taste in popular music and comedy and obliviousness to the arts, our cultural homogenization and conformism, and our addiction to crime, violence, war, and sex as entertainment. Above all, they are content to allow the richest nation on earth to ignore the poor, hungry, and ill, both at home and abroad. And not least, they allow the nation to remain oblivious to the increasing frailty of its vaunted democracy, which is the subject of the following chapter.

11

Democracy

The American Model

American politicians and public school teachers are fond of proclaiming that America has the best democratic system in the world, a system largely responsible for our greatness, and the average citizen has taken up the chant. Not surprisingly, then, our leaders believe that the best way to promote stability, alleviate suffering, and thwart repression and injustice is to bring democracy to nondemocratic nations. One hopes, however, that this fond wish does not conceal a desire to promote our own version, because there is grave doubt that our version is superior to that of others.

To clear the ground a little before examining this issue, let us begin with a conundrum posed by America's dean of political scientists, Professor Robert Dahl of Yale University:

> [I]f our constitution is as good as most Americans seem to think, why haven't other democratic countries copied it? . . . every other democratic country has adopted a constitutional system very different from ours.[1]

In what ways, exactly, is our constitutional system different from other democracies?

Aside from ourselves, of the 21 countries with democratic institutions that have functioned continuously for half a century, there are only six federal systems (that is, with territorial units) like our own;[2] only four with strongly bicameral legislatures;[3] only two with "strong judicial review of national legislation";[4] only three with a strong two-party system and a weak third party;[5] and none with a "single popularly elected chief executive with important constitutional powers."[6] In other words, our system is seldom found anywhere except in America.

But, one might object, this only proves that the administrative structure is subject to variation. What about the business of equal representation of each voter, that is, the electoral system, which is the core of democracy? According to Dahl, the major features of this system are also rarely found. In his own words, "the peculiarities of our electoral system . . . natural as it may seem to us, is of a species rare to the vanishing point."[7] And when we look closely at how our system has endeavored to represent the people's will, we can begin to understand why other democratic nations have shunned it. In the first place, our "one-vote margin plurality" (or "predominantly majoritarian" system) means that a party wins everything or loses everything in the outcome. There is no divvying up seats among parties in a legislature according to each party's proportion of the vote. (The writers of the Constitution did not anticipate political parties.) This means further that we have a two-party system, which forces accommodations among interests within each party to a single platform, ideology, or political philosophy. This two-party system not only discourages the emergence of a third party but guarantees a compromising of interests within each party to the point of making them almost indistinguishable from one another and, hence, offering little choice to the electorate, who then tend to fall back on traditional party affiliations in the family or community. An exception to this rule is when one of the two parties adopts an extremely radical course, as with the current neo-conservative Republican Party.

The alternative to this system is called "proportional representation" and is found in 18 of the 22 democracies accounted for on this dimension. (See Dahl, Appendix Table 3.) In short, the United States is one of only four democracies that does not have a system of proportional representation. Thus, in most other countries multiparty systems are the rule, while America has only two major parties. Our system would be fairer if there were run-off elections for federal office between the two top vote-getters, as in France, which is another one of the four countries without proportional representation. But even this arrangement has not been adopted in America. (If we had a run-off system for presidential elections, the outcome of the last presidential election would very probably have been different, since those who voted for Nader would have voted mainly for Gore instead of Bush, thus giving the former the presidency.) Moreover, Britain, which traditionally has also been one of the four countries without proportional representation, has shifted to a proportional-representation system in two of its large domains (Scotland and Wales), and a similar shift in its national House of Commons has been proposed by the Labor Party. Thus, America stands almost alone in its rejection of a proportional-representation system, and this recalcitrance has had a significant impact on American government inasmuch as political minorities have not been well represented. This could be one reason why minorities in America frequently suffer from a profound sense of disempowerment and, hence, alienation from mainstream society.

Obviously, the predominantly majoritarian system tends to discriminate against minorities, who will not win a share of the legislative pie unless they bury their interests in one of the two parties and accommodate to the majority. Thus, as Dahl has observed, "in the debate over the relative desirability of proportionality versus majoritarianism, virtually no one questions that proportionality is fairer to citizens than majoritarianism."[8] Nevertheless, the land that is supposed to be the beacon of democracy refuses even to consider the adoption of a proportional system, a system found among about 80 percent of democratic countries.

America has tried to compensate for the liability of majoritarianism by gerrymandering "to ensure fairer representation for minorities in state legislatures and Congress," according to Dahl. But gerrymandering has also been used to weaken the voting power of minorities, and it is increasingly being used by the majority party to gain more legislative seats for itself. Consequently, because the Republican Party has been more successful than its opposition at gerrymandering in recent years, it has gained a lead over Democrats in the House and given more power to incumbent candidates. In 2002, under Republican rule, fewer incumbents lost to challengers than at any other time in American history. The number of incumbent losers was only four.[9]

As for the argument that a two-party system is more stable and less contentious, and therefore more effective, the evidence of research does not support this claim. In fact, judging from measures of effective performance that have been applied to America, many of which have been discussed in this book (with more to come later in this chapter), the opposite seems to be the case. Over and over we have found that America has been less effective than other democratic nations. And as for preventing contentiousness, "a proportional system can sometimes help to maintain internal peace, provide opportunities for compromise among opponents, and produce a broad consensus in favor of not only government policies but the country's political arrangements as well," writes Dahl.[10] Indeed, one researcher refers to these systems as "consensus governments." As a matter of fact, divisiveness between our two major parties is a chronic problem today, having been increasing for a number of years. It is likely that proportional representation would have moderated this contentiousness. Finally, it is also sometimes argued that the dissolving of many partisan interests into just two party platforms in elections clarifies the issues, making it easier for voters to make up their minds. What this claim ignores is that it is precisely the avoidance of intraparty compromises that makes issues stand out in a multiparty election campaign. Obviously, they are bound to be expressed with greater vigor and clarity when they constitute the core interests of a party than when they are submerged in a medley of interests that often clash. And, in fact, this submergence could have a lot to do with voter apathy in America and confusion about what each of our two parties really stands for.

Turning to the presidency, we find another set of practices that accord poorly with democratic ideals of fair representation. Indeed, we are the only democratic nation possessing a "single popularly elected chief executive endowed with important constitutional powers . . ." as Dahl puts it.[11] Elsewhere, with the exception of Costa Rica, a prime minister is selected by the national legislature, and he or she can be removed by a vote of no confidence by the legislature without waiting for a set time for elections as in America. This is known as the parliamentary system. In mixed systems, there is both a prime minister and a president, the former wielding most of the powers of government.

In addition, America not only holds a popular election for the president, but possesses an electoral college that has the final say regardless of the popular vote. How did this oddity come about? If we look at the deliberations of the Constitutional Convention, we find that formal proposals for direct election by the people were rejected twice. One alternative that was considered was election by Congress. But this and all other alternatives, including election by electors, were also rejected. The delegates were running out of stamina and patience after weeks of closed-door sessions debating and cogitating and were understandably eager to adjourn and go home. Finally, still another committee came forth with still another proposal for a certain number of electors to be appointed by the state legislatures. After adding a provision for the national House of Representatives to break any tie in the electoral vote, the proposal was adopted. At that moment, all pretensions to having set up a truly democratic presidency were obliterated. Although a popular vote was adopted by Congress years later, the electoral college remained intact. The consequence has been that a candidate can win the popular vote but lose the electoral college vote; this has occurred in four presidential elections (including 2000).

The core deficiency of the electoral college is its unequal representation of voters among states. Since the number of electors in each state is based on the total number of federal representatives and senators, the unequal representation by senators (two per state regardless of population size) is reproduced in the number of electors. The degree of unequal representation is therefore enormous. A Wyoming resident, for example, has four times as much voting power in the electoral college as a California resident. "The ten smallest states each choose two to three times as many electors as they would if a state's electors were strictly in proportion to its population," Dahl points out.[12] Obviously, the most populous states tend to be the more urbanized and thus have populations with very different interests and problems from those of the smaller states. The electoral college could be abolished by Congress by means of a constitutional amendment, of course, and the House has voted overwhelmingly to do so. But the Senate, "the citadel of unequal representation," as Dahl calls it, has been adamantly opposed.

Another monkey wrench in the democratic machinery for electing the president was the adoption of a winner-take-all system that accepts a plurality-plus-one as designating the winner. In other words, a winner need not represent the majority of voters if the votes are spread among three parties. As noted earlier, this could be remedied by a run-off between the top two candidates, as in some other countries, but Americans seem to be opposed to this simple solution in federal elections. Thus, minority presidents have been fairly frequent, the latest being the current president. In fact, in *one out of every three* presidential elections, according to Dahl, the president has not represented a majority of the voters.[13]

Finally, the unequal representation imposed by electing neither more nor less than two senators per state, regardless of population size, leads to such bizarre results as the following: "in 2000 the vote of a Nevada resident for the U.S. Senate was, in effect, worth about seventeen times the vote of a California resident. Among all federal systems in the advanced democracies, the degree of unequal representation in the U.S. Senate is exceeded only by Brazil and Argentina."[14]

It is hard to detect a true democracy in this clutter of outmoded constitutional provisions and electoral arrangements. One can only pity the nation on which it is imposed without profound modification. But the tragedy for America is that, in spite of full recognition of these deficiencies, the American Myth will not allow us to make basic alterations in the Constitution, which is heralded as being without peer if not "sacred." And so, whom or what can we hold responsible for the ways in which our government is conducted on a day-to-day basis and, in particular, for its failures to meet our expectations, unless it be ourselves who revere that document as if it were the original tablets from Mount Sinai? And where do we begin to repair the machinery—that is, even if we shook off our thralldom to the myth of American democracy and wished to do something about it? As Dahl writes with a touch of exasperation: "I, for one, am inclined to think that compared with the political systems of the other advanced democratic countries, ours is among the most opaque, complex, confusing, and difficult to understand."[15]

This lack of transparency could be beneficial to those who profit from the system just as it is, which might well explain the passivity of our leaders in undertaking reform. Thus, another role of the American Myth in this instance, as in many others, might be to legitimize the power of those who benefit from current arrangements, such as senators from states with sparse populations, leaders of the two major parties, state legislators who select the electors (without the formal intrusion of citizens who might imagine they have a right to elect the president), and politicians wherever they may be who are apprehensive about enfranchising those segments of society, such as the poor or minorities, that do not now have a constitutional right to vote.

The reader might well interrupt and protest: Who says the poor and minorities don't have a constitutional right to vote? After all, they have the same right as everybody else. And that is exactly the point: *No* American has a constitutional right to vote. As noted by Alexander Keyssar:

[T]he United States Constitution does not contain an affirmative guarantee of the right to vote in any elections. Although most Americans think that the Con-

stitution does grant them the right to vote . . . , in fact it does no such thing . . .
As recently as 1963, Congress chose not to pass a Constitutional amendment
that would have positively affirmed the ability of all citizens to vote.[16]

Another little-known fact, also according to Keyssar, is that in 2000 the Re-
publican-dominated Florida legislature fully intended to proceed with selecting
electors to suit their partisan, Republican interest in the event that a recount of
the vote gave the Democrats a plurality. This extreme action was only precluded
by the decision of the Supreme Court in their favor, a decision that cited the
absence of a popular right to vote for electors unless the state legislature grants
that power. Clearly, the electoral college can legally trump the popular vote.

Before we leave our constitutional model, a point made earlier about the
American presidential system needs to be elaborated, namely, the absence of
two heads of state as in some other democracies, one the ceremonial head and
the other the true executive. This coalescence of two different roles is, in fact, an
anomaly among social groups in general, for two leaders tend to emerge: the
task-oriented or "instrumental" leader and the symbolic or "tension release"
leader. The former sets goals, structures the situation toward achieving goals,
monitors compliance, and doles out rewards and punishments for performance.
The latter provides emotional support, inspiration, humor, and so on, thereby
fostering group cohesion, pride, and loyalty apart from sheer technical effort.
Often the two leaders disagree about how to manage affairs, and conflict ensues.
(This is a familiar theme of fiction, especially in military units and aboard ship.)
If one leader tries to override the other, disagreement often grows sharper until
resolved by some sort of compromise. When a *single* leader is obliged to combine both roles, however, not only is role conflict enervating (for example, in the
teacher's classroom position, as any teacher will confirm), but the danger of one
role overriding the other is increased. And a demotion of either role could
threaten the group's survival, either by failure to maintain morale, loyalty, and
sacrifice, on the one hand, or by failure to stay on-task and to achieve the
group's goals when its efforts become stressful or when loyalty wanes without
the relief that could be offered by more nurturance.

Because presidents are not only task leaders but are also under great pressure to build and preserve a favorable political image that will create public confidence and commitment—by displays of trustworthiness, patriotism, courage,
and other charismatic qualities—the danger arises that the symbolic role will be
exploited to enhance the incumbent's power regardless of how well he or she is
performing the task. In particular, a highly personable president who needs to
conceal or distract attention from his doubtful abilities can manipulate public
opinion in ways that protect him from suspicion of incompetence or failures of
policy. One traditional means of doing this is to seize upon and demonize both
external and internal enemies, even to trigger a war. Another is to play the role

of "first among equals," that is, the role of an ordinary, good-natured person who just happens to be the most powerful human in the nation or, in the case of the United States, on earth. And, of course, both ploys could be used in tandem by the same president. Some observers believe that this description fits the current president. Whether or not that is the case, it is easy to see how a hybrid executive can use his "human qualities" to upstage his purely executive abilities in the public eye. This would be much more difficult to carry off in a double-executive system. But Americans like the system as it is, mainly because it provides them with a managerial mastermind, a super-celebrity, and a paternalistic good shepherd all wrapped up in one—a consummate hero who can overcome all odds, which is a favorite theme of America's achievement-oriented culture.

Another likely outcome of the fusion of the two kinds of leadership is the public's receptiveness to a "personality factor" in the election of the president. While all candidates for office gain a certain measure of support because of their personableness, the president's awesome power evokes a special need for reassurance that he (she?) will play a friendly, paternalistic (maternalistic?) role with the public. Few want a martinet, prig, legalist, policy technician, or issue wonk to control their fate. So the tendency is to gravitate toward a leader who best fulfills the "symbolic" leader role. Thus, elections of presidents have often turned on the personality that is presented to the public. Eisenhower, for example, won the election of 1952 almost solely on the basis of a "warm" personality. His opponent, derogated as an "egghead," was doomed from the outset of the campaign in spite of his superior government experience, literacy, and gifts of statesmanship. The point is not that one candidate was better than the other, but that his perceived worth was largely based on personality rather than competence to perform the technical, decision-making, issue-oriented aspects of the job. This preference for a highly personable candidate reinforces the tendency to exploit the symbolic role to enhance power or to conceal incompetence as a performer after gaining office.

To Vote or Not to Vote

Major impediments to democracy in America have been laws that limited the franchise and controlled voter registration. Besides legal barriers, there have been a myriad extralegal efforts at local intimidation of voters, manipulation of suffrage regulations and laws, and sheer bungling in the purging of voter registration rolls and the counting of votes. (For a compelling case study of the 2000 presidential election in Florida, in which the election results were shaped by these latter factors, see Palast.[17]) More recently, following the chaos of trying to recount the vote in Florida in the 2000 presidential election, there are the new paperless electronic voting machines, dubbed the "worst technology of 2003" by

Fortune magazine owing to their known defects. However, inasmuch as we are here primarily concerned with the formal aspects of America's voting system, our discussion will focus on legal barriers.

Voter registration laws have been used to fend off challenges to the elite and dominant social groups from the very beginning of the nation as a constitutional federation of states. As a historian of the right to vote in America has summed up these legal barriers:

> Most men did not want to enfranchise women until the twentieth century; most whites did not want to enfranchise blacks or other racial minorities in their own states; the native-born often were resistant to granting suffrage to immigrants; the wealthy at times sought to deny political citizenship to the poor; established community residents preferred to fence out new arrivals.[18]

And efforts to eliminate the barriers that were erected were strenuously resisted over two centuries of America's constitutional existence.

In the second half of the 20th century, the 24th Amendment of 1964 and the Voting Rights Act of 1965 were major breakthroughs in the elimination of discriminatory voter registration laws, including literacy tests, poll taxes, and registration barriers "that had kept blacks and many poor whites from the polls."[19] The momentum carried over into the '70s, but with few tangible results. Congress proposed several bills to permit mail-in registration, but these were defeated by a southern Democratic and Republican coalition. When President Carter proposed a National Uniform Registration Act in 1977, he was surprised by Congress's resolute opposition.[20] Since most of the new registrants would be the poor, members of minority groups, or the young, the Republicans resisted the idea because these were groups that ordinarily voted for Democratic candidates.[21] (The South, in particular, was apprehensive about making it easier for blacks to vote. Some states, however, adopted postal registration and registration in public facilities, such as libraries and license bureaus.) These proposals continued to be opposed by Republicans on a variety of grounds, but the real basis for their resistance was that the disadvantaged would gain strength and pose a challenge to the conservative, Reaganite hegemony. Finally, under President Clinton, a National Voters Registration Act was passed and made law.

The effect of this new law was rather stunning. Nine million more registrants were added to the electorate, or only slightly less than 20 percent of the unregistered.[22] Although this upsurge encouraged the Democrats because the new registrants were disproportionately from groups that tend to vote for their party, the actual turnout at elections was poorer than expected. "In 1996," reports Keyssar in *The Right to Vote*, "half of all potential voters stayed home: turnout was lower than it had been in any presidential election since 1924. The

1998 congressional elections were no better at sparking interest of voters . . . something else was ailing the body politic."[23]

Indeed, voter apathy seems to be a unique feature of American politics. Deliberately imposed barriers in other democratic nations have also been dismantled, but the resulting turnout has been much higher than in America. The facts are worth highlighting:

> [I]n recent years, only half of all eligible adults have voted in presidential elections, and fewer than 40 percent generally cast their ballots in other contests. Electoral turnout has declined significantly over the last century, and it is markedly lower in the United States than in most other nations.[24]

The contrast with other nations in terms of turnout is startling. The means of the percentages of voters in elections (with available data) from 1991 to 2000 were: Italy, 90 percent; Iceland, 89 percent; Greece, 85 percent; Belgium, 84 percent; Denmark, 83 percent; Argentina, 81 percent; Portugal, 79 percent; Austria, 78 percent; Brazil, 77 percent; UK, 72 percent; and so on. Over the same period in the United States, the mean percentage of eligible voters in elections for which the data were available was 45 percent.[25] According to the Center for Voting and Democracy, America's rank in voter turnout in the *world* is 59th.[26]

The history of the labor movements in Europe was probably responsible for the much higher turnout on that continent. When voting rights were won, according to Frances Fox Piven and Richard A. Cloward, two other historians of voting patterns in America, "the fledgling Socialist, Labor, and Social Democratic political parties that already existed became significant organizational instruments for political power." Consequently, unlike America, "there is no correlation between social class and the likelihood of voting or not voting."[27]

A political system in which persons who govern have been placed in office by only one-fourth of the eligible electorate whom they govern is a poor excuse for a democracy, apart from the unfair restrictions in the Constitution discussed earlier. It clearly is not a fully representative democracy that we have in the United States. Because it offers the possibility of becoming a representative democracy, it avoids characterization as a dictatorship, but not much more can be said for it. Perhaps it is best called a truncated or mock democracy.

This state of affairs is difficult to absorb as the operative reality of our political life when we witness the enormous power wielded by the president and the panoply of status symbols and the genuflection that attend his comings and goings. The truth is that he represents only a small minority of the nation. Even before the current president, Bill Clinton was elected with the support of fewer than a quarter of the eligible voters, and the Republicans received even fewer votes when they gained control of the House of Representatives.[28] Although the percentage of eligible voters who cast a vote in the 2000 election increased by

2.2 percent over 1996, George W. Bush was elected by only a quarter of those eligible to vote,[29] and even received fewer popular votes than his opponent, thanks to the electoral college.

In the words of Keyssar, one of our leading historians of American suffrage:

> Although the formal right to vote is now nearly universal, few observers would characterize the United States as a vibrant democracy, as a nation where the equality of political rights offers release to a host of engaged and diverse political voices.[30]

The same verdict was reached by Piven and Cloward in *Why Americans Still Don't Vote*: "the United States was not a democracy, in the elementary sense of an effective universal suffrage, during the twentieth century."[31]

A legal barrier to voting that is resolutely preserved in America, in contrast to most European countries, is the disenfranchisement of felons. This handicap falls disproportionately on blacks because of their much greater likelihood of being imprisoned (some 800,000 blacks are imprisoned and 46 states restrict voting), which means that it penalizes the Democratic Party and hampers social reform efforts. Conservatives, therefore, are especially supportive of the ban. And the same might be said about the prohibition against voting for a president by residents of Washington, D.C., a city that is held up to schoolchildren as the citadel of democracy in the world.

Recently, new hurdles have appeared from the least expected quarter: the Help America Vote Act of 2002, which was passed to remedy the kinds of embarrassing problems that arose in the 2000 presidential election. Although this act in general was a big step forward, it enacted certain provisions that pose disincentives to voting on the part of the less privileged strata or marginal members of conventional society. These provisions were included in the act ostensibly to prevent voter fraud. But the imposition of additional proof-of-residence requirements has been criticized for violating privacy rights and stipulating ID proof that might discriminate against certain types of persons, such as those who have had name changes (e.g., divorced women), or have an unusual name or a name entered erroneously in the records, or who may feel threatened by having to show IDs at the polls after they have registered by mail.[32]

The possibility of heavy-handed enforcement of the antifraud provisions by FBI agents, combined with the profiling associated with the new emphasis on national security, could intimidate many minority citizens. These deleterious effects have been foreseen by a number of organizations. In fact, 24 national organizations have signed a letter to the attorney general of the United States expressing their concern with the antifraud provisions. These organizations include the League of Women Voters, the Lawyers Committee for Civil Rights Under Law, the NAACP, the National Mental Health Association, Public Citizen, and Common Cause. The letter noted the targeting of voters on Native American reservations by the FBI, the disproportional attention given to historically disenfranchised groups in general, and the voting suppression of blacks that occurred after the 1994 election in Alabama. "Already we are hearing that voters in Arkansas, who are attempting to vote early," the letter asserts, "are being harassed and photographed at the polling site . . . "[33] In short, the FBI, the very department of government that played such a vital historical role in the enfranchisement of black Americans, is now engaged in intimidation that jeopardizes the gains of those watershed years.

Although a few procedural barriers to voting still remain in America, much more important are cultural and institutional factors. These factors go to the heart of much that is awry in America today, factors that have betrayed the American Dream and called forth an American Myth that boasts a degree of egalitarianism and democracy that does not exist. The following observations by Public Citizen are a good summary of these factors.

> The political institutions and culture that evolved during the era of restricted suffrage spawned a political system that offers few attractive choices to the nation's least well-off citizens. The two major political parties operate within a narrow, ideological spectrum; the programmatic differences between candidates often are difficult to discern; the core social and economic policies of both parties are shaped largely by the desire to foster economic growth and therefore to satisfy the business and financial communities. Ideas and proposals that might appeal to the poor and are commonplace in other nations—such as national health insurance or laws enhancing job security—have been beyond the pale of modern American discourse.[34]

One of the most alarming consequences of the public's lack of participation in their political system by voting is the leeway it affords to the wealthy, and particularly the corporate leaders of America, to control government. And this control leads in turn to an even greater sense of disempowerment and voter apathy. Thus, a vicious cycle is set in motion. Indeed, it is not even clear that a substantial increase in voter turnout could now counteract the entrenched influence of lobbyists and campaign financiers, and it certainly could not do so in the absence of a vigilant mainstream media. Let us take a candid look at the current state of affairs in Washington and in political campaigns across the nation.

Filling the Electoral Power Vacuum with Special-Interest Wealth and Influence

Numerous instances of campaign financing by wealthy sources and of influence peddling in Washington have been identified in earlier chapters. Prominent in this study have been the automobile, pharmaceutical, oil, foreign development, health insurance, financial, farming, communications, and military weapons industries. But some labor unions have been major contributors as well. While the electorate is barely informed about the issues pertaining to each of these special interests and, in fact, is lulled into a soporific state of mind by the mainstream media, the legal bribery profession is alert, bustling with energy, and profligate with money. And it is definitely heeded by Congress and the administration. Indeed, being responsive to popular wishes or needs has even tended to become old-fashioned or disreputable. Two analysts of political life in contemporary America have raised a cogent question and suggested an unsettling answer.

> [W]hy has the derogatory term "pandering" been pinned on politicians who respond to public opinion? The answer is revealing: the term is deliberately employed by politicians, pundits, and other elites to belittle government responsiveness to public opinion and reflects a longstanding fear, uneasiness, and hostility among elites toward popular consent and influence over affairs of government. It is surely odd in a democracy to consider responsiveness to public opinion as disreputable . . . [35]

In contrast, the accusation of pandering is less often directed toward those bent on satisfying the wishes of campaign donors or lobbyists. These activities are simply regarded as part of the respectable, everyday business of politics (or politics of business). Why doesn't the public raise its voice when government representatives allow their actions to be purchased by industry?

The answer is they do, but only with respect to certain *kinds* of issues. Note that the probusiness issues cited in earlier chapters as having been so successfully promoted by industry without public interference reflected the interests of *particular* industries or companies, such as emissions standards in automotives, manipulation of supply in the oil industry, extension of the life of patents in the pharmaceutical industry, and so on. They were not issues that encompassed *all* business, such as the minimum wage, overtime pay, or NAFTA. This distinction between "particularistic" and "unifying" issues has been made by Mark Smith[36] in his elaborate statistical analysis of the influence of business on government. And his data lead to the conclusion that it is the particularistic issues that are less often attended to by the public. The reasons for this, according to Smith, are partly their greater complexity and apparent lack of substantive interest. But, most interesting of all, the public's lack of attention to particularistic issues is attributable to the failure of the mainstream media to grapple with them and bring them to the public's attention. As Smith points out, " . . . unifying issues . . . are the high-profile issues, so they get covered by the media, get talked about during the elections. . . . A particularistic issue, on the other hand, is so obscure no one has ever heard of it, and there is no public opinion." And without the "watchful eye" of the public, he explains, legislators can pretty well do what they please, which makes it easier for lobbyists to gain their ends: "Where campaign money comes in is when you're getting something very specific."[37]

While it might seem that the unifying issues and their disposal by Congress or the administration would have greater impact on society, the larger number of particularistic issues and their greater chance of success outweigh the higher-profile "unifying" issues in influence. In short, it is partly their sheer multiplicity that makes them so important when unmonitored by the public. And so, once again, we witness the critical role of the media in ignoring or dismissing information that is vitally important if citizens are to exercise their democratic rights in a responsible fashion. It should be stressed that the conclusion about the media's influence with respect to the salience of the two types of issues is not a mere surmise but is based on extremely detailed statistical research by a leading political scientist.

The active ingredient in the influence of business on government, of course, is money—first, as fodder for politicians running for office and second, as compensation for lobbyists and their activities in courting legislators. Unlimited contributions from individuals, groups, and corporations to political campaigns are called "soft money." It did not exist for federal elections until 1978, when the Federal Election Commission exploited a loophole in the federal election laws. Otherwise, it was illegal for corporations and unions to spend money in connection with federal elections, and for individuals to spend more than $1,000 on a federal candidate or more than $20,000 on a party for influencing federal elections. (These limits were raised to $2,000 and $25,000, respectively, under the new law discussed below.) The federal prohibition on corporate spending had been in effect since 1907, and the same prohibition on unions since 1947. What the soft-money loophole did was to allow money to be spent for "party building." But since huge amounts are raised by federal candidates and officeholders, the donors expect something for their investments; and their spending is "controlled by or coordinated with federal candidates."[38] In other words, the candidates got the money for their campaigns anyway.

In 1992, soft money amounted to $86 million; by 1996, it had mushroomed to $260 million and was expected to increase threefold for the 2000 presidential campaign. As a former Democratic fundraiser said, ". . . the White House is like a subway—you have to put in coins to open the gates." And this simile applies equally to Congress.[39]

Not only does soft money rob the electorate of its constitutional power over their representatives, but it also robs all of us of our money. According to Common Cause, in 1996–97 generous favors to several industries were enacted into law. In the seven preceding years these industries had contributed a total of $65.9 million to congressional campaigns. The total costs to consumers of the laws created on behalf of these industries were the following: loss of access to generic drugs, $550 million; loss of fuel efficiency in vehicles, $59 billion; higher cable TV and pay phone rates, $2.8 billion; cost of peanut and sugar farm policies, $1.6 billion.[40] The total annual cost to consumers of government policies on behalf of these industries alone was $64 billion, or an average of $228 for each man, woman, and child in America.

After years of effort by national organizations, and extensive study and debate in Congress initiated by a group of courageous members, the Bipartisan Campaign Reform Act (McCain-Feingold Law) was finally passed and signed into law in early 2002. A major purpose of the law was to place new constraints on soft money in campaigns for federal office—that is, to close the loophole that had been opened by the Federal Election Commission in 1978. No sooner was the president's signature dry on the paper than the FEC set to work again, however. As part of its rule-making role, the FEC shifted the receipt of money from national parties to "independent committees," which could then funnel the money where it wished. These independent "shadow committees," as Public Citizen calls them, could be composed of party activists, provided they are not formally part of the party structure; further, they would not have to disclose the sources of their money.[41] Moreover, state and local parties were ruled exempt from the new law and could spend money on attack ads against their opposing parties, ads that identified the candidates, and salaries of pollsters, media consultants, and so forth.[42] Finally, officeholders could participate in state and local soft-money-fundraising activities in every way as long as they do not ask for money for themselves; and the officeholders' Political Action Committees can raise soft money for the activities mentioned so long as the PAC's expenditures are not made "on behalf of" the officeholder.[43] The reaction of the law's writers and sponsors was immediate. They filed a lawsuit against the FEC, claiming that the FEC's damage was significant and contrary to congressional intent.[44]

The new law was also booby-trapped by a provision that advertisements on the media that appeared within 60 days of the general election "are subject to contribution limits and disclosure requirements."[45] Being a possible violation of free speech, this provision was counted on by opponents of the reform law to tempt the courts to nullify the whole act.[46] The FEC could have dealt with this provision in a way that preserved its constitutionality, but chose not to do so. (To the surprise of many, the Supreme Court later upheld the provisions of the reform law. But the ban on advertisements paid for with soft money 30 days before the primary was widely circumvented in 2004.[47])

In sum, the FEC took pains to ensure that a whole series of loopholes compensated for the loss of the 1978 loophole, and might even have succeeded in scuttling the new law in its entirety. As an act of political legerdemain, the performance was impressive. As a safeguard of democracy, "it's beyond silly," as a dissenting member of the FEC put it.

It is sometimes argued that contributing money in support of particular candidates, like lobbying for one's position on a particular issue, is simple advocacy; and in a democracy, one has the right to advocate certain policies. This argument would have some value if everyone could contribute the same amount so that candidates could compete with equal amounts of resources. But that is transparently not the case. In the first place, only a tiny minority of the population contribute the lion's share of campaign money: ". . . less than one-tenth of 1 percent of the U.S. population gave 83 percent of all campaign contributions in the 2000 elections . . ."[48] This means that the opposing candidates of the two major parties represent only a tiny fraction of the public in terms of expenditure for advocacy, and the source of that advocacy is obviously the wealthier members of society. If it is money that makes our democracy go round, then it is a democracy especially for the better-off.

In the second place, not even those who contribute have equal weight in campaign influence because of the difference in wealth between the two major political parties, which stems from the association of big business with the Republicans. In the 2000 presidential campaign, for example, the Republicans raised $193,088,650, compared with the Democrats' $132,804,039.[49] The fact that the margin of wealth expended by the Republicans failed to overcome the preference for the Democratic candidate in the popular vote reflects not the futility of spending huge amounts of campaign money but, rather, the dedication of the Democrats to their candidate in spite of the greater campaign spending of their opponent. This makes the defeat of the Democratic candidate in the electoral college all the more poignant and especially indicative of a severely deficient system of representation.

As for the magnitude of the lobbying industry, in 1997 $1.25 billion was spent on lobbying in Washington, and by 1998 the amount had increased to $1.42 billion. In the latter year, there were 18,590 lobbyists in Washington, and one year later (June 1999) the number had increased to 20,512. This meant that there were 38 lobbyists for every member of the House and Senate.[50] And in the states, $570 million was spent on lobbyists at 34 state capitals in 2000. Nearly 40,000 organizations were registered to lobby in these states.[51]

The wealthier campaign and lobbying sources have an advocacy edge not only over most citizens' groups but also over less wealthy sources within their industries. For example, Congress has been considering a bill that would ensure faster access to cheaper generic drugs. But the smaller generic-drug companies have been outspent by the rest of the industry by a 42-to-1 margin in campaign financing and lobbying, namely, $423 million vs. $10 million, respectively. If this money is free speech, as ruled by the courts, then the voice of one party in this shouting match is 42 times louder than the voice of another. That is roughly the difference between a murmur and a high-powered loudspeaker in a football stadium.

Campaign funding and lobbying are not the only means whereby special interests, and especially wealthy corporations, obtain the help of elected and appointed officials. Lucrative business deals, both during and after their term in office, and business deals, jobs, and gifts to their family members are also highly persuasive means of gaining special treatment. The promise of a high-paying job after leaving office is also a powerful inducement, and these jobs often include lobbying. In the '90s, Senator John McCain revealed that "at least 140 former members of Congress . . . are currently lobbying their former colleagues."[52]

The case of one senator who is currently in office (Ted Stevens of Alaska) and who has been investigated by writers for the *Los Angeles Times* reveals the almost limitless possibilities for corruption under the cover of law. The investigators pointed to "an increasingly widespread pattern in Washington: Senior senators do favors for special interests that pay hundreds of thousands of dollars in lobbying and consulting fees to the senators' children, spouses and other relatives . . . The senate has few ethic rules governing such arrangements."[53] Obviously, the representation of broad public interests, which is the usual meaning of democracy, is ill-served by this craven submission to Mammon that fills the power vacuum left by an apathetic electorate.

There is another, less often appreciated downside to the more-than-equal influence of well-heeled special interests: the distraction of the people's representatives not only from the needs and wishes of their constituencies, but also from the performance of the agencies that they have created. For the role of oversight is at least as important as that of crafting and passing legislation, and often more so. This point will be elaborated in a later section on "Where the Rubber Hits the Road." But first, let us examine the consequences of a flawed democracy.

What Difference Does It Make If Democracy Is Weak?

So far we have looked only at how practices diverge from an ideal model of democracy. The question of whether it makes any difference is key because it can reveal the true dimensions of our quasi-democratic quagmire. To give a complete answer, four subquestions need to be posed. First, how well does the nation perform, that is, what is the true state of affairs with respect to comparative and absolute standards? Second, how well do the actions of the government reflect citizens' wishes, including those that are expressed explicitly and those that can be inferred from widespread criticism? Third, how well do the actions of government reflect the promises made by successful candidates for office? And fourth, how satisfied are citizens with government and its political leaders?

The first subquestion is purely objective; the second and third pertain to the match between subjective desires or promises and the objective responses of the government when candidates assume power; and the fourth is purely subjective, that is, evaluative. Thus, these subquestions cover the whole spectrum of objective and subjective bases for evaluation.

Concerning the first subquestion, the true state of affairs in America is fairly well represented by the conditions reported in this book where major weaknesses have been found in every area that we have surveyed. Economic conditions have been dismal with respect to deficits, poverty, unemployment, consumer confidence, job stress, bankruptcies, and so on (although there are currently some signs of improvement in a few economic indicators); health care is inaccessible to millions and even risky; income inequality is enormous and growing; crime rates, drug abuse, and alcoholism are higher than elsewhere; racial equality is still very problematic (and even decreasing in education); social services of all kinds are limited or nonexistent; and foreign relations are in a shambles. All these conditions have been documented by statistics, expert testimony, and firsthand reports in earlier chapters, leaving no doubt that America is a seriously impaired nation clinging to a myth of supremacy.

Still, the prevalence of social problems does not demonstrate conclusively that our flawed system of representation is the culprit. The people could be indifferent or blasé about problems or just uncomplaining; or their wishes could lie in a realm beyond the capacity of even the most democratic government to satisfy. Although it is highly doubtful that people who suffer from poverty, unemployment, untreated illness, discrimination, or national insecurity simply do not care about their plight, let us focus on those issues that we know they care about and see how well the government has responded. This pertains to our second subquestion.

The following are some policy preferences that a majority, plurality, near majority, or near plurality has expressed in the recent past, but on which the government either failed to act or did the opposite of the people's wishes.

Public's wishes or criticisms	Government's response
Give inspectors and UN more time in Iraq (59%).[54]	About one month later an invasion of Iraq was ordered.
Wait for allied support before attacking Iraq.[55]	America was able to acquire only one major military ally before it attacked.
Handle foreign affairs better (44% disapproved, 47% approved).	World opinion is still strongly against U.S., especially because of Iraq war.
Handle the economy better (53% disapproved, 47% approved).[56]	Not done, except for questionable tax cuts.
Pay more attention to al Qaeda than Iraq (51% said al Qaeda was the greater threat).[57]	Iraq continues to be given more attention than al Qaeda.

Give foreign aid for humanitarian reasons instead of for building trading partners (see chapter 7).	Criteria for aid exclude some of the most suffering nations on behalf of safe corporate investment and development of trading partners (see chapter 7).
Allocate much higher percentage of budget to foreign aid (public believed 20% was allocated whereas less than1% was allocated, and was satisfied with the imagined 20% level; see chapter 7).	Budget allocations for foreign aid are still far below 20%, and less than other nations in terms of percentage of GNP.
Limit or reduce profits of big corporations (51% strongly believed that big corporations' profits are too high).[58]	Measures are constantly taken to increase corporate profits by tax cuts, subsidies, etc.
Reduce influence of big business on administration (66% said big business has too much influence, and 61% said the administration looks out for the interests of corporations instead of the people's).[59]	Not done.
Use regulations to protect the public interest (54% said they are necessary for this purpose).[60]	Regulations are being eliminated or relaxed in environmental protection, media concentration, industrial pollution, etc.
Increase regulation of water quality.	Arsenic standards are set higher.
Reduce unemployment.	Not done.
Pay for defense by postponing tax cuts (40%) instead of by reducing domestic spending (21%).[61]	Tax cuts are pushed through by the president while domestic spending continues to be reduced.
Provide affordable health insurance for all, including 42 million without it (majority have favored Canadian system for all).	Not done.
Do not relax rules that regulate media ownership (about 700,000 citizens expressed their opposition to FCC's plans to deregulate).	FCC votes to relax rules (but its decision was overturned by Congress after widespread public protest).

| Modify or eliminate laws and rules that threaten civil liberties (per the resolutions, etc., of 275 jurisdictions) (see chapter 8). | Plans are made for more restrictions, in Patriot Act II. |
| Recognize Gore as the president based on the 2000 popular election. | Bush was recognized as president. |

An especially curious instance of flouting public expectations has been the failure of the government to take appropriate steps to fight domestic terrorism, a threat the administration itself has emphasized by constant reiteration. According to a report on terrorism preparedness by the Emergency Responders Task Force, fire, police, and public health agencies are unequivocally unprepared, and cities do not have plans to deal with terrorism. In particular, 80,000 police are being fired around the country owing to lack of funds. Specific needs are for protective gear, secure and reliable communications equipment, hospitals that can deal with large numbers of casualties, and diagnostic capabilities regarding the effects of chemical or biological weapons.[62] These are all in very short supply because of inadequate federal funding.

While much of this failure might have been due to poor congressional oversight, the president himself has played a role in blocking antiterrorist measures, according to a Brookings Institution report that appeared in 2003. As reported in *The Nation*, "President Bush vetoed several specific (and relatively cost-effective) measures proposed by Congress that would have addressed critical national vulnerabilities." In particular, nothing was being done by the administration to promote improved security in private-sector firms, including those that handle dangerous materials.[63]

In addition, according to a *New York Times* columnist, the nation's ports, which are quite vulnerable to terrorist attack as well as portals for the smuggling of explosives and weapons (including "suitcase" atomic bombs), have been scanted by the government in the appropriations process in spite of their having been a major concern from the outset. As of June 2003, port security had received only one-tenth as much money as the Coast Guard said was needed.[64]

The list could go on, but these examples suffice to make the point of a current, pervasive discrepancy between citizens' expectations and the actions of the government, including Congress, the Executive, and the Supreme Court. While this spurning of the electorate might have increased in recent years, it is by no means confined to the present administration or Congress. A useful reminder of senatorial snubbing of public opinion in the past century in spite of most of the public's wishes is afforded by an article in the *New Yorker* that mentions a number of failures to adopt measures that, for example, protected blacks from disenfranchisement or that punished lynching, lowered tariffs, provided universal health coverage or educational aid, and so on.[65] With regard to health coverage, polls in the '80s and early '90s indicated that a majority of Americans wanted a Canadian-type, publicly operated single-payer health-care system, a guarantee of food and shelter for the poor, an increase in the capital gains tax, and a surcharge on millionaires,[66] all of which desires have been utterly ignored by both political parties for more than a decade.

In sum, our second subquestion can be answered by saying that our present democratic system responds poorly to the wishes of the public.

Our third subquestion involves the expectations of citizens based on candidates' promises when campaigning for office. Our current president will serve as an example, not because his promises are less likely to be kept than former candidates for the presidency, but because they are more familiar to readers. Also, President Bush made a major point in the campaign of pledging to honor his commitments. Since these examples were collected in mid-2003, the president had had two and a half years to fulfill his promises. And it appears that he has not only done nothing with regard to several promises—he has done the opposite.

In early 2000, President Bush was asked if he would veto the McCain-Feingold campaign finance reform bill. "Yes, I would," was his reply in an interview on ABC News. Two years later, however, he signed the bill into law.[67] In 2000 he also said he would set up "free trade from northernmost Canada to the tip of Cape Horn." Later, however, duties were imposed on Canadian softwood lumber that averaged 29 percent.[68] In his memoir and again when announcing his candidacy, Bush vowed to "end tariffs and break down barriers everywhere" and explicitly said, "I do not support import fees." But he imposed tariffs on steel imports up to 30 percent.[69] During the campaign, Bush mocked Gore's proposed tax credit for buying hybrid-fuel vehicles, but promised the same tax credit after being elected.[70] Further, in a campaign debate he stated his reluctance to support nation-building, but has done so in Afghanistan and Iraq.[71] Again, in his campaign, he stated that "sound science, and not politics, must prevail" in the dispute over Yucca Mountain as the nation's main burial place for nuclear waste. But later, according to Nevada officials, "Bush ignored a study by the congressional General Accounting Office . . . that said scientific testing to determine the facility's viability would not be complete before 2006."[72] Bush's own aides have acknowledged that his promise to restrict carbon dioxide emission was violated when he urged Republicans in Congress to oppose any mandatory limits on emission.[73] A vow to erase the $5 billion maintenance backlog in the National Park system because the parks were "at the breaking point" was honored by cutting 40 percent of the repair budget, thereby increasing the maintenance backlog by $1 billion.[74]

Regarding Bush's "compassionate conservatism" pledge in the campaign, the person who coordinated his domestic policy agency has admitted that only one of the six commitments in this policy domain gained a victory in Congress in spite of both houses of Congress being controlled by President Bush's party.[75] A consultant to Bush's aides has noted, "The compassionates win a lot of rhetorical battles, but when you look where the budget is, it shows hardly a hint of the compassionate."[76] In fact, tighter eligibility requirements have been proposed for a number of benefits for low-income persons, including tax credits, school lunches, and housing aid,[77] and many cuts in federal programs across the nation have hurt the disadvantaged in particular, as shown in chapter 2.

This recital of broken campaign promises of the current administration must take into consideration the intrusion of unforeseen events like the 9/11 attacks, the war on terrorism, and the recession. But, as noted earlier, the public preferred to pay for defense by reducing the tax cuts instead of cutting domestic programs, a preference that was notably ignored. Thus, the cost of war cannot be blamed for all the failed promises of the administration.

In the absence of a thoroughgoing empirical study of the "integrity record" of past administrations, it is impossible to know whether the Bush administration has scored higher, lower, or average on unkept campaign promises. But two political scientists have expressed a belief that responsiveness to citizens has deteriorated over the years in America: "Public opinion is not propelling policy decisions as it did in the past. Instead, politicians' own policy goals are increasingly driving major policy decisions and public opinion research . . ."[78] It would not be surprising if this were the case in view of the growing influence of wealthy special interests on government through campaign finance, lobbying, and appointments to top government posts, combined with continuing voter apathy, the antidemocratic role of the Senate and electoral college, and the commercialization and concentration of media that are more attuned to the interests of their advertisers than to the informational needs of the public.

Finally, we come to our fourth subquestion. If it is true that the government has been remiss in performing its representative duties and keeping its promises, we should find that the public is dissatisfied with or distrustful of government, and more so in certain respects than in the past. And that is precisely what we do find. In 2001, only 9 percent of the public believed that the views of the majority of citizens had a great deal of influence, whereas 68 percent thought that the majority's view *should* have a great deal of influence.[79] In 2002, only 44 percent trusted the government "to do what is right most of the time or always";[80] and in 2003, only 38 percent trusted the government to handle social issues "like the economy, health care, social security, and education."[81] As for long-term trends, "trust in government has fallen about half since its peak in 1966."[82] Regarding Congress in particular, confidence fell from 42 percent in 1973 to 22 percent in 1997.[83] A review of poll results over almost 50 years led two political scientists to conclude in 1983 that "the results suggest that the American people feel increasingly powerless."[84]

It is highly interesting, however, that in early 2003, 68 percent did trust the government in matters of national security and terrorism.[85] Since much less is being done than needs to be done, as already shown, and our intelligence agencies have a dismal record of accomplishment, including their failure to forestall the 9/11 attacks, this level of trust might be a matter of whistling in the dark instead of an informed and considered opinion. Further, when it comes to handling a specific security situation, such as attacking Iraq without UN or substantial allied support, we find the public changing its tune, as indicated earlier with regard to the public's having preferred that the attack on Iraq be postponed. Also, in early 2003, the president's approval rating for his handling of foreign policy was only 47 percent, with 44 percent disapproving. (In terms of his re-election prospects incidentally, in early 2003 independent voters were more likely to disapprove than approve of his foreign policy performance, namely, 48 percent vs. 42 percent.) More significantly, however, in a 2004 poll, we find that only 38 percent agreed that the country was going in the right direction, compared with 58 percent who believed that "things have pretty seriously gotten off on the wrong track." This latter question covered both foreign and domestic affairs.[86]

In sum, in the past two years, more than half of the public believed that matters had gotten out of hand, and only a little more than a third believed that the government could handle social issues. Thus, the evidence points once again to the failure of our democracy to function in a way that pays due respect to the vox populi.

Where the Rubber Hits the Road:
The Elusive Realm of Bureaucratic Performance

Another failure of our representative government lies in the domain of Congress's oversight responsibility. It is difficult to hold our representatives to account for failing to monitor the government's operations because oversight is seldom tied to specific party issues or campaign promises. The public takes this congressional role for granted; and it is often exploited by Congress to gain media coverage for investigations of real or potential scandals, often of a personal nature, or to chasten an agency created by the opposition party. Instead of engaging in the humdrum business of monitoring the activities and outcomes of agencies, Congress too often uses oversight either to embarrass or to applaud its witnesses for its own political benefit. As former Representative Lee Hamilton once observed:

[I]n recent years, congressional "oversight'" has come increasingly to mean a focus on personal investigations, possible scandals, and issues that are designed

to generate media attention . . . Congress has lost sight of the importance of traditional oversight. . . . It is often tedious, unglamorous work. But when done
well, it can display the activities of government to ordinary citizens, protect the
country from bureaucratic arrogance, expose and prevent misconduct, and give
voters influence over the activities of an administration.[87]

In the absence of hearings, agencies are monitored only by an occasional
investigative journalist, special-interest groups with limited resources, or the
Government Accounting Office (GAO), which is mainly concerned with financial matters. Because the intention of a candidate for office to engage in routine
oversight is not exactly the most gripping issue in a campaign (unless there has
been a recent scandal of huge proportions, such as with Enron), officeholders are
not held to a role of rigorous oversight as a campaign promise. And even if they
were, the flaws in our democratic electoral process would still give them a great
deal of leeway in how the role is performed. Indeed, it would be surprising if the
time spent on legislation for special-interest lobbies did not usurp time that
could more usefully be spent on oversight activities to benefit the public in general. In any case, few would argue that simply passing a law guarantees its effective implementation.

Here, then, is a mammoth, almost invisible domain that challenges the notion of a democratic panacea for what ails government—the elusive domain of
specialized, professional bureaucrats. In fact, government agencies can commit
errors of judgment and of action that fail egregiously to meet the originating
demands of the citizenry.

This is not the place to engage in a sociological analysis of the shortcomings of bureaucracy as a type of social organization (without which, by the way,
the modern world would be impossible), and particularly the tendency for self-
perpetuation to take priority over the achievement of goals. The following examples, however, show what can happen when Congress fails to perform its
oversight responsibilities, as is commonly the case in America.

It has been asserted persuasively that NASA's preoccupation with its image,
and the ascendancy of boastful, wishful thinkers, together with its cold-
shouldering of the older engineers who were most attuned to safety and budget
cuts, precipitated the Columbia disaster.[88] (This has been confirmed by a six-
month commission study.) A GAO report on security against terrorism before
the 9/11 attacks identified a range of problems: the ease of stealing weapons of
the military that are temporarily stored in private trucks when being moved; the
inability to identify where weapons and explosives are located during shipment;
the misplacement of Stinger missiles in a civilian storage area without anyone's
knowledge; the ease of gaining access to military storage facilities with phony
credentials; the absence of alarms to detect intruders in storage facilities; the
ease of access at five sites to a full military arsenal with cruise missiles, rockets,

bombs, rounds for howitzers, and more.[89] Months after 9/11, only 2 percent of
the shipments into U.S. ports were being inspected,[90] and an investigation found
that one out of four weapons could get through security checkpoints at airports.[91]
A law since 1952 requiring foreign visitors to register with INS [Immigration
and Naturalization Service] after 30 days was ignored,[92] and 15 of the 19 September 11 hijackers were given visas to enter the country in spite of their applications being incomplete and incorrect. In fact, Mohammad Atta (the hijacker
who failed to participate) was given a visa six months *after* 9/11 when the subsequent crackdown on security was in full force.[93] Bombs that were supposed to
be accurate were found to be hitting civilian houses in Afghanistan and Iraq, and
so on (as discussed in an earlier chapter).[94] Finally, back in this country, federal
prosecutors were found to be ignoring 98 percent of gun crimes, which resulted
in gun traffickers being rarely prosecuted.[95]

Of special interest is the case of the Occupational Safety and Health Administration (OSHA), a situation that highlights the solicitude of the American
government for corporate felicity. According to an eight-month investigation by
the *New York Times* in 2003,[96] of the 1,242 cases of workplace deaths since 1982
that were found by OSHA to have been caused by "willful" safety violations, 93
percent were not referred for prosecution. Furthermore, at least 70 employers
who had escaped prosecution continued to violate safety laws. In the past two
decades, in 17 states, the District of Columbia, and three territories there has not
been a single prosecution for willful violations that killed 423 workers. "The
honest to God truth," said one of the inspectors, "is that it's just going to slow
you down. They want numbers, lots of inspections, and it will hurt you to do one
of these [wrongful] death cases." The priority of the appearance of efficiency
over effectiveness could hardly be better demonstrated.

A program in the early '90s to train OSHA inspectors to work on criminal
investigations was terminated after fewer than 100 had been trained. And an
Enforcement Litigation Strategy Committee, set up in 1994, was discontinued
after a few meetings. The single federal prosecutor in the Environmental Protection Agency, who had worked almost exclusively on workplace safety crimes,
had never even met the director of OSHA's enforcement programs. The median
fine for willful violations that resulted in death and were prosecuted since 1991
has been only $30,240. The maximum sentence has been only six months. Sanc-
tions for breaking environmental or financial laws are greater than for willful
safety violations that cause the death of workers. It also suggests that violations
that have not yet resulted in death or injury have been rampant.

Apparently, the mere creation of an agency to protect the American people,
which is said to be the first responsibility of our government, is sometimes regarded as sufficient to allay anxieties and ensure reelection. One can only conclude from the case of OSHA that meaningful congressional oversight is a weak
element in the democratic equation in America, especially when the happiness

and good will of corporations are at stake. (The foregoing report by the *New York Times,* incidentally, demonstrates what can be achieved by the mainstream news media when they make a serious effort to earn the free-speech protections of the Constitution.)

An agency that has been subjected to even greater criticism than OSHA is the Environmental Protection Agency (EPA), and here we are reminded of the role of lawmakers in contributing to bureaucratic deficiencies. As a recent independent report on the status of environmental matters has observed: "The vagueness of many environmental statutes, the ad hoc permit and regulatory negotiations between agencies and private parties, and the abuse of administrative discretion combine to make the EPA one of the most arbitrary agencies in government."[97]

In the field of international affairs, American intelligence agencies in particular appear to have exhibited a special talent for incompetence. Their flaws were exhibited, for example, in the failure to anticipate and prevent the 9/11 attacks, as indicated by testimony and several investigative reports. Most obviously, information about the hijackers or their preparations was not shared by the FBI with the CIA, and vice versa. Representative Cynthia McKinney pointed out before the final official reports were released, for example, that "people were calling in to the FBI and the CIA and they were giving information that was critical . . . There was adequate warning. There were people who failed to act on the warning."[98] Tracking the mastermind of the attacks was given a low priority in spite of his having tried to blow up airliners over the Pacific. Hijackers were not put on a watch list, although their terrorist connections had been known, and so they easily entered the country.[99] And so on, as documented by recent government investigations.

Then, of course, there was the confident belief, fostered by intelligence sources, that Saddam Hussein harbored a huge arsenal of weapons of mass destruction, which ostensibly became the core reason for the administration's deciding to mount a preemptive attack on Iraq. And it was this threat that was given as the paramount reason for the American people to support the war. Yet, both a UN inspection team and the American military have been unable to find evidence of this arsenal before or after the war.[100] What seems far more plausible is that our intelligence sources were quite imperfect. As Hans Blix, the chief of the WMD inspection team under the UN, remarked: "I had been told that [the U.S.] would give the best intelligence they had [to the inspection team]. So I thought, My God, if this is the best intelligence they had and we find nothing, what about the rest?"[101] In short, the credibility of American intelligence was severely damaged by its performance with regard to Iraq.

We should not overlook the fact, however, that this state of affairs has prevailed for a number of years, and has involved far graver historical events than the snafu about Saddam's weapons of mass destruction. In the words of a recent book on American intelligence:

> The CIA's history . . . is rich with failures to predict major events, among them the first Soviet atomic bomb, the North Korean and Chinese invasions in Korea, the Hungarian revolt, Fidel Castro's victory and Khrushchev's subsequent placement of missiles in Cuba, the invasion of Czechoslovakia, and the invasion of Afghanistan. Above all, the CIA failed to predict—failed even to imagine—the collapse of Soviet Communism and the end of the cold war.[102]

In fact, during the years of the Cold War the Soviet threat was highly exaggerated by the CIA, not only with regard to weaponry and the size of its army, but with regard to the strength of the Soviet economy, which was said for years to be growing 50 percent faster than the American economy, when in fact it was far behind America and its allies.[103] These distortions about the Soviet Union, incidentally, are similar to the CIA's distortions about Iraq in 2002.

In at least one fateful instance, even the National Security Council (NSC) seems to have been derelict in dealing with a significant intelligence issue. In the early months of the current Bush administration before the 9/11 attacks, terrorism was a topic in only 2 out of 90 to 100 meetings of the NSC's *leadership,* according to an Associated Press story in 2002. This estimate of how often the topic was discussed in those formal meetings of the "principals" was confirmed by three White House officials, according to the story. And during those months, a remarkable spike occurred in signs of an imminent attack somewhere in the world. Nevertheless, the topic was relegated to midlevel committees for prolonged study and drafting of a new policy. In contrast, during the former administration the leadership of the NSC had met formally to discuss the threat of terrorism every 2 or 3 weeks following the 1998 attack on the vessel Cole.[104] In view of our political leaders' frequent reiteration of the policy that the nation's security is the government's number one responsibility, one is hard pressed to understand the persistent recurrence of such failures over the past few years

In addition to these spectacular shortcomings of government agencies and their overseers in Congress, government inspectors and auditors have identified a host of more run-of-the-mill failures involving the waste of billions of taxpayers' dollars and the occurrence of other organizational problems. In 1997, for example, there were estimated overpayments in Medicare's Fee-for-Service Program of $20 billion. And in 1999 there were concerns that the new $550 million computer system of the National Weather Service would not operate correctly. In addition, "ten of the 24 largest government agencies have confused or even contradictory missions, stove-piped or obsolete organizational structures or a lack of the proper mix of skills among their workforces . . . Fourteen of the agencies have problems managing grants and contracts; 19 of the 24 have serious financial management weaknesses; and 22 of the 24 have major information technology problems."[105] Further, $1.8 billion was wasted in the Federal Employees Health Benefits plan; and in the IRS, "two-thirds of all earned income tax credit claims were paid in error," amounting to $448 million. Agencies designated "at risk" for waste, fraud, and abuse included 10 that had been on the list since 1990.[106]

More recently, in 2003 the Department of Energy was reported to be $200 million over budget and 26 months behind schedule in cleaning up radioactive tritium that had leaked into groundwater. One and a half million dollars was found to have been wasted by the FAA in modernizing the air-traffic-control system. Et cetera. One million dollars was being wasted every day in HUD's disposal of its single-member housing inventory. Et cetera.[107]

These failings of federal agencies are consistent with the evaluations of top agency leaders by their staff members. A survey by the GAO in 2000 found that only 52 percent of the nonsenior executive members of federal agencies perceived their top leadership as "demonstrating a strong commitment to achieving results." And much the same percentage of nonsenior executive managers (56 percent) believed that "they have needed decision-making authority and are held accountable for results."[108] It would seem, therefore, that there is plenty of oversight work for Congress, and also plenty of reason to believe that it has been grievously neglected.

Conveniently, the low salience or importance to the public of Congress's oversight role precludes the members from being blamed for 9/11, the shuttle Columbia disaster, willful violations of workplace safety leading to death, or the killing of civilians in recent wars, just as it appears to exonerate them for rampant government waste by agencies under their oversight responsibility. Are these defaults of oversight due only to lack of time? If so, how did Congress find time to delve into the commodity transactions of Mrs. Clinton and the sex life of Mr. Clinton for several months when they could have been scrutinizing federal agencies to preclude or quickly remedy the kinds of gaffs and horrors mentioned above?

*   *   *

If the state of affairs disclosed in this chapter is a reasonably accurate reflection of our democracy, then the American version of this form of political system is not only messy, but a fairly abject failure. Quite possibly the main function of our democratic apparatus, that is, its contribution to the maintenance of American society, is simply the prevention of widespread revolt. If Americans were flatly denied voting rights by a cabal of authoritarian leaders, upheaval and mayhem would ensue, even though fewer than half of the eligible voters presently bother to vote and even fewer make a serious effort to understand the issues. At least we have the right to do so, and evidently that is good enough for the great majority of us. Meanwhile, the American Myth diligently reassures us that our democracy is not only healthily vibrant but the best in the world—whether or not we the people participate in it.

In the end, the slow eclipse of democracy, permitted and abetted by the public itself, means that the vacuum of power will be filled by something besides the will of the people. And that something is embarrassingly obvious: wealth. And so, while the legal structure of a democracy is retained, its control shifts from a broadly based, pluralistic electorate (at least in theory) to a narrow plutocracy whose members share an intensity of purpose focused on material enrichment at any cost, including the risk of imprisonment, and who collectively dominate the government.

Analogies to the Roman Empire have become platitudinous; but in one respect they are on target: Rome, too, became a plutocracy, although wealth was based on land instead of industry or commerce. Also, the power of the wealthy was rooted in the ancient electoral advantage of being able to afford costly weapons, including horses; and, of course, the wealthy ruled the Republic as senators and executive officers. This blend of wealth, rule, and military power (absorbed and legitimated by aristocratic traditions) eventually produced the deadly rivalries that were finally resolved by a single man called the emperor. Although the Roman situation was vastly different from America's today, the fact remains that the combination of interlocking relationships between government and wealth (reinforced by private clients and armies), on the one hand, and a weak system for representation of plebeians and the proletariat (e.g., there was no provision for voting anywhere in the Republic outside the Assembly in Rome), on the other, produced the classical Roman model of rule by the rich in spite of calling itself a republic. Although the reasons for the fall of Rome are complex and much disputed, "what we can say with confidence is that Rome fell gradually and that Romans for many decades scarcely noticed what was happening."[109]

12

Conclusions and a New Beginning

It is important to understand what this survey of contemporary America did *not* set out to accomplish so that its original intention is kept in focus. It did not set out to present a systematic analysis of American society or of current affairs, or a history of American institutions with the exception of a few side trips. These exclusions leave us with a social profile of selected areas of American life intended to serve as the empirical basis for an *evaluation* of the nation's performance.

I have characterized America's glowing image of itself and its place in the world today as a Myth because the nation fails to measure up to the highest standards of contemporary civilized society, either domestically or abroad. This disclosure is important because the nation will not endeavor to correct its deficiencies unless it is first able to acknowledge them, and to acknowledge that they are legion and deep-rooted. And yet, casting aside the crutches of a Myth that prevent us from standing on our own feet and advancing with the strength of unflinching self-knowledge is a task that is by no means easy for a proud nation to undertake.

Many obstacles of monumental proportions have been overcome in the past, however, and it is possible that we can do it again. It was done when we defeated the British Empire on one occasion and fought them to a standstill on another, spanned a continent, reunited North and South, attacked the Great Depression, and overcame our doubts and fears when attacked by Germany and Japan and threatened with annihilation by the Soviet Union. We even made it possible for Europe to reclaim its civilization and for Japan to sit in the hall of peaceful nations. That is the past that we must now try to emulate and not just nostalgically wallow in or evoke endlessly as grounds for supremacy in a world that has profoundly changed. In fact, the times that we now face are as daunting as any other in our history; and the enemy might be even more awesome than any we have faced before, namely, our own complacency.

To speak bluntly, our present conditions are an affront to the American Dream, a cause for dismay and contempt in foreign lands, and a prelude to real

311

disaster. Even if the reader does not accede to every fact or interpretation in this book as accurate or valid, he or she cannot easily dismiss the impression of a nation suffering from stagnation at best and deterioration at worst, a nation that is bringing up the rear among advanced industrial societies in a number of ways, with the main exceptions being an extreme concentration of wealth among the few and superior military firepower based on exorbitantly expensive technology.

It would be the height of egotistic folly for me to declare that I know the solutions to all the nation's problems identified in this book. Even if I were avidly running for the highest office in the land, I would not make such an absurd claim. It is possible, however, that a body of scholars and other authorities in many fields, authorized by all three branches of government and composed of individuals as devoid as possible of any personal or political stake in the outcomes, would be suitable for that solemn undertaking.

This group, which might be called a *National Commission for the Recovery of America*, should begin by examining and summarizing up-to-date data bearing on America's international standing and achievement of its own widely shared, basic goals, such as those proposed by Bok[1] in his careful study of America's achievement in the mid-1990s. With proper resources and a wide range of expertise, the commission could go far beyond my efforts here. It should then identify a set of problem areas under each basic goal and the intermediate goals pertaining to each of these problem areas. And finally, it should propose steps that might serve to achieve these intermediate goals. To facilitate this effort, many experts and esteemed public figures should be called upon to prepare research and position papers and to give public testimony. Even if several years were devoted to this effort, it would be well worth the time, money, and hard work. If it only succeeded in educating the public and dissolving the American Myth during the course of its inquiry, it would be a boon to the nation. In time, if the commission's work is heeded, its significance could be comparable to that of the Constitutional Convention in Philadelphia more than two hundred years earlier.

The work of any such commission should not focus exclusively on America, however. A host of problems in the management of our society are shared with other advanced nations. But according to my own research as well as that of Bok, it seems that these other nations have done a better job of coming to grips with these problems on the whole than we have. Some serious attention, therefore, must be given to our international peers, including an attempt to understand to what extent different *historical backgrounds* and *specific policies* have contributed to their greater progress in many areas.

In my earlier chapters, I referred briefly at a number of points to decisive differences in historical background and policies between America and Europe, such as the tradition of socialism and workers' organizations in Europe that ensured a much higher voter turnout than in America. Another example is the policy of proportional representation, which seems to have enhanced social performance as well as political involvement and democratic representation in other nations. Moreover, in some cases Europe has been able to profit from America's mistakes, which was apparently the case with the founding of vigorous media sources that remained independent of financial support from nonmedia businesses, such as the BBC, in contrast with our own mediocre, over-concentrated, profit-oriented mass communications industry discussed in chapter 10. And there is evidence that most other advanced nations have been much more successful in reducing child poverty than America, and also in providing affordable health care without compromising quality. In short, there might be much to learn from other countries, a task that will be undertaken only if we are able to lay aside the threadbare cloak of superiority that the American Myth has draped over our shoulders. This, then, is one of the important services that our commission could perform, and I have no doubt that any number of historians and other scholars would welcome the opportunity to investigate the subject (if they have not already done so).

As for the *kind* of recommendations for renewal that the commission might set forth, they should be addressed to American institutions and folkways as if they had never been looked at before, that is, almost anthropologically or perhaps from the perspective of a 22nd-century historian. In other words, our most basic assumptions and traditional modes of operating need to be unmercifully revealed and examined, and then perhaps fundamentally reformed. For example, a much greater investment in overcoming the crippling background of students who come from lower-income families—in their homes, neighborhoods, leisure activities, exposure to the mass media, peer relations, and so forth—might be a much more effective approach to the improvement of educational achievement than focusing almost exclusively on what goes on within the schools. As I point out in chapter 4, and as research suggests, there is little the schools themselves can do to overcome the most serious socioeconomic handicaps of their students. And yet, we are persistently occupied with, and spend great sums of money on, ways of improving curriculum and teaching while ignoring the more basic problem of breaking the cycle of poverty and poor educational achievement by attacking its roots in the local neighborhood or family. (See chapter 4 for a specific proposal along these lines.)

Note that my educational example requires a radical departure from current policies and practices. Turning funds over to America's thousands of PTAs or Rotary Clubs and offering them technical assistance, for instance, is not what the U.S. Department of Education normally regards as "educational innovation," and yet funds might be far better spent in that fashion than on new curricula or smaller classes or teacher education, although the latter are also important, of course. Thus, my educational example underscores my contention that what is needed is a new set of eyes, or even a new set of mind, to evaluate affairs from an impartial distance without subservience to traditional assumptions or practices.

Another such example pertains to economic vitality. If asked about our national well-being, most of us would think about productivity, the GDP, the Dow Jones Average, or consumer spending, and commissions of inquiry would also focus on these measures and the forces they presumably reflect. But are these traditional, taken-for-granted indicators of growth and vitality what we really need to be scrutinizing? Productivity hides a good deal of resulting job stress and technological unemployment, the GDP measures many transactions that reflect social or personal breakdown, the Dow Jones Average is mainly a measure of how well the more affluent are doing, and consumer spending glosses over the burden of debt and the failure of consumption to increase happiness. Even our gross measures of employment obscure the burden of holding multiple jobs, the many part-time workers who want full-time jobs, inadequate pay (especially at the bottom), job stress, racial and ethnic discrimination in hiring, assigning, and promoting, and so on— a collection of problems that I have referred to as posing an occupational crisis in America.

Insofar as the economy is of interest to us precisely because economic vitality is supposed to reflect the nation's degree of well-being, why not combine noneconomic indicators that *directly* measure how well off we are in an alternative set of "leading indicators"? A few examples of such indicators are: use of renewable resources, crime, infant mortality, job satisfaction, drug use, affordable medical care, level of R&D commitment, and child poverty, all of which have been measured and combined into indices in independent research studies. Shouldn't these indices be reported to the public by the government and the media *on a regular basis,* and studied in conjunction with the traditional measures of economic activity? I have little doubt that a commission that resolutely broke away from the conventional way of looking at the economy as the fountainhead and preserver of well-being, a view that leads to reliance on strictly economic measures for gauging how well off we are as a people, would advocate an alternative or at least supplementary approach to national self-evaluation. People are not just economic actors. They are complex creatures with a wide variety of needs and wants that have little to do with economic productivity.

Another example of broadening our perspective to accommodate a wholly new way of thinking about problems is to pay more attention to preventive health care and less to therapeutic care, at least with regard to so-called "lifestyle" therapies. The latter include drugs like Vioxx and Celebrex that cost millions just to advertise, but do nothing to help *prevent* the conditions they treat. As noted in chapter 3, it has been estimated that treatment of preventable illness accounts for 70 percent of the nation's medical costs, although a far greater share of medical R&D and practice is spent on therapeutic treatment than on prevention, as is well known but generally ignored in practical terms. That this perverse order of priority might be peculiar to the United States is shown by our much higher rate of premature mortality because of our failure to embrace preventive measures, as also mentioned in chapter 3. Only a highly prestigious commission that is not afraid to go against the grain could make Americans realize what harm they are doing to themselves by their inattention to preventive health care, and especially in a time when the cost of therapeutic care is soaring and thereby limiting our consumption of other goods and services. Shifting more resources to preventive care, then, provides another example of thinking "outside the box."

Still another example of this sort of liberated thinking about reform concerns the influence of demographic features on the crime rate, discussed in chapter 5. Instead of officials, politicians, and American apologists rushing to take credit for reducing crime in the '90s, when in all probability crime fell because of shrinkage in the crime-prone age bracket, should we not be asking why it is that generation after generation of younger males are tempted to commit crimes more often than older males? The answer can only be that younger American males are especially vulnerable to certain social pathologies, such as economic slowdowns (especially unemployment), disempowerment, intense pressure to achieve in a highly competitive society, stress on masculinity, cultural emphasis on materialism and consumerism, racial or ethnic discrimination, lack of rewarding leisure activities, recent separation from family of orientation, inadequate education, and so on. Therefore, when there are proportionately more young people in the population, we suffer a surge of crime. It is as simple as that. And what are we doing about this special vulnerability to social pathologies among younger males? Are we enlisting them by the millions in community organizations for youth where they can gain skills and guidance from mentors, self-esteem and civic involvement from community service, gratification from participation in creative activities in the neighborhood, healthy peer relationships through sports, and so on? Are we offering generous assistance for higher education? Do we have hoards of youth workers in the ghettos who virtually live with young people on the streets, and who were found many years ago to be highly successful? The answer to these questions is no; and we are paying for our neglect with crime and drug abuse, especially when the number of younger males mushrooms during certain periods.

As for our conduct of international affairs and how we might change course in that important domain, allow me to underscore the fact that our behavior abroad has appalled much of the world. (The full measure of animosity has been kept from us by the mainstream media.) Neither in humanitarian assistance nor in geopolitical affairs have we earned unequivocal respect. Our wholesale killing of innocent civilians in war, which we euphemize as "collateral damage," our support for dictatorships, our lack of understanding of foreign languages and cultures, our aggressive market orientation that has caused so much hardship in certain countries, our reluctance to contribute more than a tiny percentage of our GNP to foreign assistance in comparison with the greater generosity of other nations, our unilateral arrogance, and our materialism, crime, and so on—all of these features have marred our reputation abroad. The 9/11 attacks gave us a precious opportunity to start afresh in international relations because they aroused an outpouring of sympathy abroad, in spite of our bad reputation. But what did we do with that opportunity? We killed thousands of innocent civilians in two wars, threatened war against other Middle Eastern countries, failed to control the postwar havoc in Iraq, and continued to give military and diplomatic support to Israel throughout its ghastly handling of relations with the Palestinians. In light of these facts, perhaps the wisest thing we could do presently is to declare a moratorium on international interventionism and devote our time instead to mending our fences with the world's people by humanitarian aid and goodwill diplomacy. We could also cut back defense spending on such endeavors as "Star Wars" and divert money to social needs at home and in underdeveloped countries. But again, only a high-level commission composed of national leaders would have sufficient credibility to be able to confidently propose such a radical change of course without being met with aspersions and summary dismissal.

Perhaps the most controversial remedies for our nation, however, would flow from our taking a hard look at America's Constitution as a document that ostensibly advances and preserves democracy. For there seems to be little in that document that does either. (See chapter 11 for a critique of our system of democratic representation.) Consequently, we have been left behind by other advanced nations that have wisely spurned our 18th-century solution to organizing the body politic under a system of laws. Lack of proportional representation, which is found in Europe and elsewhere in contrast to our majoritarian system, is a good example of our failure to keep up. This observation, by the way, reminds us that America is an *older* nation than many other advanced countries. True, we were pioneers in the fostering of modern democracy, but our Constitutional Convention took place many, many yesterdays ago. Is it surprising, then, that we lag behind other democratic systems that have been founded more recently? We are not a dictatorship, aristocracy, or monarchy, but we are not a commendable democracy either. In short, recommendations for revising the Constitution in fundamental ways should definitely be on the agenda of a National Commission for the Recovery of America.

While we are on the subject of democracy, it is worth mentioning the need to promote and support America's alternative press. During the past decades of mainstream-media deterioration and increasing concentration, the alternative press has arisen to help answer America's need for reliable information and commentary about contemporary affairs that better fill the need of a democracy for an informed citizenry. And its Web sites have been especially helpful in promoting the rapid sharing of information on topics ignored by the mainstream media, and in stimulating new grassroots organizations and the electorate in general to vent collective desires and reactions to government policies. This trend is one of the most hopeful that I have identified in this book, for it points to the possibility that our democracy might be saved from decrepitude after all. But alternative presses need to be nurtured through foundation and government support, including special tax subsidies, and their readership needs to be enlarged through public awareness campaigns, also with help from the government and foundations. If public television and public radio receive some support from these sources, why shouldn't the alternative press? Our democracy deserves no less. No doubt there are some exceptions that receive such funding, but by and large the alternative presses are struggling for survival, and some media observers have predicted that the more successful will succumb to mainstream-media takeovers. In short, here again we witness the need to gaze beyond our traditional institutions and to support those "adaptive mechanisms" that have sprung up to serve the basic needs of our society when other, more familiar enterprises have failed do so.

These examples should suffice to show the kind of unconstrained "divergent" thinking that is needed in our country if we are to approach our fundamental problems in a serious fashion. But now I come to an even more offbeat mode of thinking, a perspective that calls for looking at not only the *good* things that could ensue from undertaking radical reform, but the *bad* things that could ensue as well. As suggested at several points in foregoing chapters, every innovation occurs within a system of socioeconomic and cultural variables that have become integrated over many years into relatively stable social systems, and sometimes these variables have been integrated for centuries. A major change in any one variable can have repercussions on the system that would make the most avid reformer rue the day that he or she ever ventured into policymaking. In fact, it sometimes seems as if policymakers spend half of their time designing and implementing change and the other half cleaning up the mess they have caused.

Because unintended consequences are inevitable, one needs to assess the effects of any reform in terms of *net* benefits, as well as in terms of the goals that one seeks to achieve. This means that *before* launching our most brilliant or compassionate ideas into the world, we need to note in a highly *systematic fashion* the kinds of undesirable consequences that are likely to ensue. Then, we need either to build in safeguards to thwart their occurrence or abandon the enterprise altogether.

Unfortunately, this odd way of looking at needed reform is not very popular in social planning, not even at the highest levels of policy formation. Partisan wrangling about the harm of proposed policies or commonsense efforts to avoid allegedly detrimental outcomes is not a substitute for impartial, systematic analysis of the probabilities of a host of carefully delineated unwanted effects.

Policymakers are familiar with so-called "goal attainment" models (that is, what steps should be taken to achieve goals), but not with "failure avoidance" models (that is, what steps should be taken to avoid undesirable side effects). In fact, the latter models hardly exist. Failure avoidance has not been regarded as something that requires modeling, check lists, or guidelines as with goal attainment, because failure is seen simply as the *absence of success*, and the assumption is that success will follow if only we take the right steps toward the goal. Thus, failure simply means that we did not take those steps. This is far from the truth, for "the right steps" can have unintended consequences that *cause* failure or at least havoc.

We are mentally geared to the rationalistic assumption that expertise in the choice of means to achieve ends is all that we need to know about—when, in fact, there are specific *mechanisms,* or automatic reactive patterns, in the context of all actions that *repeatedly* produce effects that can nullify our most slavish devotion to step-by-step implementation on behalf of goals. We need to know about these mechanisms if we wish to perform as astute social planners and implementers, yet we proceed in blissful ignorance of them. Simply put, we have embraced the rational, reformist tradition of the early Enlightenment, which scorned pessimism about the human condition. (Voltaire's satiric figure of Dr. Pangloss who lived in "the best of all possible worlds" epitomizes this outlook.) In other words, the possibility of failure is upstaged by our implicit reliance on goal-directed expertise, which is simply a form of institutionalized optimism. Its motto may be regarded as "we can do anything that we set our hearts and minds to," a familiar bit of political rhetoric. This motto might serve to inspire exertion, but it also invites a recklessness that can have shocking consequences.

What does this brief disquisition on unanticipated consequences have to do with our subject? First, any enterprise that is addressed to radical change in the nation's modus operandi will itself threaten to produce large, negative repercussions. At the very least, many citizens will attack some of its proposals on the grounds of their harmful side effects. The effects of massive renovation and the attacks on it that will occur—all of which might be perfectly realistic—must be *anticipated* and *planned for*. Second, existing government policies and practices need to be reevaluated in terms of their *net* benefits, which means taking into account all unanticipated detrimental side effects, including trade-offs and opportunity costs. To accomplish either of these tasks requires a systematic identification of side effects, some of which might be quite obscure. My own work in this area could serve as a starting point,[2] but a great deal of additional disciplined thinking about the subject still needs to be done.

For an example of how a familiarity with mechanisms that stimulate counterproductive effects can sensitize one to the potentially undesirable consequences of *any* intervention, the reader should refer to the first pages of "The Afghanistan War" in chapter 7, where I enumerate the hypothetical self-defeating effects of our technological superiority in warfare. The inventory of hypothetical effects presented there was not generated off the top of my head, but systematically derived from my own codification of unanticipated consequences based on my study of numerous regressive interventions (which work is cited above). The fact that I did not need to be an expert in military affairs or in weapon systems to identify the possible unintended effects of our high-tech superiority demonstrates the usefulness of guidelines for the pinpointing of such possible effects. Another, less elaborate example can be found in my introductory pages to chapter 3 on health care, where I suggest certain possibly undesirable consequences of improvements in the field of medicine. Note in particular the "lulling effect," a first cousin to the "Maginot Line mentality," which looms as a pitfall for every safeguard or effort at improvement in human affairs, but perhaps especially in the field of health.

Since we live in a world where policy formation by the government affects all of our lives, and where the failure or even detrimental effects of such policies are not exactly unknown (the pages of this book bulge with examples), the commission could perform a great service by highlighting the importance of *forestalling* undesirable consequences and supporting the formulation of guidelines to that end. Preventing unintended harm in human affairs is just as important as trying to do good. But this is a difficult message to get across in our era of audacious, self-confident optimism, a sentiment that is part and parcel of the American Myth.

The main point of my discussion about new beginnings, however, is that America desperately needs to be scrutinized afresh from the highest angles of vision without partisanship or special pleading, and with systematic attention to the possibly untoward consequences of fundamental policies—policies that might be proposed as well as those that are already being acted upon. This means, above all, that the country must disavow the American Myth and evaluate with dispassion the workings of its major institutions, including their defects and their *net* accomplishments. For it should not by any means be taken for granted that our society and its government, no matter how much we cherish them, will survive the shocks of world change that are now brewing *in combination with* the legacies of our own past and current miscalculations—and to survive in a way that history will applaud and that all American citizens will profit from, enjoy, and be proud of. Just muddling through, as we have been doing for years, may no longer be an option.

As for the panaceas of free enterprise and piecemeal legislative approaches to serving the public interest, it must be borne in mind that America is a mammoth, highly complex, and spectacularly unruly social system. To leave it up to the profit motive and purely political interests to set our affairs in order might appeal to our venturesome spirit of individualism, but it is Quixotic in the extreme. It is also suicidal.

The United States is not the center of the world any more than the world is the center of the universe. And yet, how natural it is for a once great nation to indulge in reassuring fantasies of nationalistic centrism in times of profound self-doubt and sense of peril. And how painful it will be to purge itself of those illusions and to forge a more praiseworthy identity.

Notes

Introduction

1. Robert J. McMahon, "The Republic as Empire," in *Perspectives on Modern America: Making Sense of the Twentieth Century,* ed. Harvard Sitkoff (New York: Oxford University Press, 2001), 217.

2. Ibid., 96.

3. George Eisen, "The United States and the World: The Changing Role of International Education," *U.S. Society and Values* 1, no. 15 (October 1996).

4. Immanuel Wallerstein, "Soft Multilateralism," *Nation*, February 2, 2004; and *The Decline of American Power: The U.S. in a Chaotic World* (New York: New Press, 2003).

5. Clifford Cobb, Ted Halstead, and Jonathan Rowe, "If the GDP is Up, Why is America Down?" *Atlantic Online,* October 1995.

6. Derek Bok, *The State of the Nation: Government and the Quest for a Better Society* (Cambridge, MA: Harvard University Press, 1996), 21.

7. Kevin Phillips, *Arrogant Capital* (Boston, MA: Back Bay Books, 1995), chap. 7.

8. Andrew Shapiro, *We're Number One* (New York: Vintage Press, 1992), 42–43.

9. Project for the New American Century (PNAC), "Rebuilding America's Defenses: Strategy, Forces and Resources for the New Century," Washington, D.C., September 2000.

10. Gerald Bordman, *American Musical Theatre—A Chronicle* (New York: Oxford University Press, 1986), 680–713.

11. Bok, *State of the Nation,* 375–76.

1. Overview of an Inferior Nation

1. "Americans Are World's Most Patriotic People, National Opinion Research Center at the University of Chicago Finds,"
http://www.news.uchicago.edu/releases/98/980630.patriotism.shtml.

2. Peter Ford, "Is America the 'Good Guy'? Many Now Say, 'No,'" *Christian Science Monitor,* September 11, 2002.

3. "College Students Speak Out," AVOT [Americans for Victory Over Terrorism], http://avot.org/stories/storyReader$72.

4. Michael Graham, "Those Crazy Kids," The Usual Suspects, http://www.free-times.com/Usual%20Suspects/suspects062602.html.

5. "Americans for Victory Over Terrorism Releases Poll of College and University Students," June 20, 2002, http://avot.org/stories/storyReader$73.

6. David Brooks, "Refuting the Cynics," *New York Times,* November 25, 2003.

7. Emily Gersema, "Poll: Europeans Blame U.S. Policies," Associated Press, September 4, 2002.

8. Brian Knowlton, "A Global Image on the Way Down," *International Herald Tribune,* December 5, 2002.

9. Robert A. Dahl, *How Democratic Is the American Constitution?* (New Haven: Yale University Press, 2001); Andrew Shapiro, *We're Number One* (New York: Vintage Books, 1992); Derek Bok, *The State of the Nation* (Cambridge, MA: Harvard University Press, 1996).

10. National Science Foundation, National Patterns of R&D Resources: 2002, Table 10.

11. Jonathan Rauch, "Taking Stock—The Real State of the Union," *Atlantic Monthly,* January/February 2003, 119–21.

12. Bill Wolman, interview with the chairman of Intel, *BusinessWeekOnline,* June 9, 2003.

13. Michael J. Mandel, "Commentary: Meeting the Asia Challenge," *Business-WeekOnline,* December 8, 2003. See also National Science Foundation, Science and Engineering Indicators, 2002.

14. Union of Concerned Scientists, "Restoring Scientific Integrity in Policy Making," February 19, 2004.

15. ASCE [American Society of Civil Engineers] Report Card for America's Infrastructure, 2003 Progress Report, http://www.asce.org/reportcard/.

16. Mercer Human Resource Consulting, Worldwide 2002 Quality of Life City Rankings; Mercer Inc. 2002, Geneva, Switzerland. All Rights Reserved. http://www.mercerHR.com.

17. EH.R: Social Health Index, Economic History Services, note posted by Fred Carstensen, April 29, 1999; Adam Kirschner, "How Are We Really Doing?" Ford Foundation Report, Winter 1999.

18. Gregg Easterbrook, *The Progress Paradox: How Life Gets Better While People Feel Worse* (New York: Random House, 2003).

19. Bok, *State of the Nation,* 387–89.

20. Ibid., 401.

21. Kevin Phillips, *Wealth and Democracy: A Political History of the American Rich* (New York: Broadway Books, Random House, 2002), 274.

22. Robert Pear, "Study Shows Poverty in U.S. Less Concentrated," *New York Times,* May 18, 2003.

23. The World Almanac Education Group, Inc., *The World Almanac and Book of Facts 2001* (Mahwah, NJ: World Almanac Book, 2000), 168. (Data are for 1998.)

24. Marc Miringoff and Marque-Luisa Miringoff, *The Social Health of the Nation: How America Is Really Doing* (New York: Oxford University Press, 1999), 27–31.

25. Ibid., 40.

26. Nancy Folbre and the Center for Popular Economics, *The New Field Guide to the U.S. Economy: A Complete and Irreverent Guide to Economic Life in America* (New York: New Press, 1995), 8.1.

27. Miringoff and Miringoff, *Social Health*, 27.

28. Redefining Progress, Community Indicators Project, July 19, 2003, http://www.redefiningprogress.org/projects/indicators.

2. The Economy, Work, Recent Federal Budgets, and Business and Government

The Paradox of Poverty in the Midst of Wealth

1. Tony Judt, "Its Own Worst Enemy," review of *The Paradox of American Power: Why the World's Only Superpower Can't Go It Alone,* by Joseph S. Nye, Jr., *New York Review of Books,* August 15, 2002; Howard Zinn, *A People's History of the United States: 1492–Present* (New York: HarperCollins, 1999), 640.

2. Mike Dowling, "Interactive Table of World Nations," updated July 12, 2002, http://www.mrdowling.com/800nations.html.

3. Ibid.

4. Isaac Shapiro, Center on Budget and Policy Priorities (Washington, D.C.), July 18, 2001.

5. Bread for the World Institute, "Hunger Basics: International Facts on Hunger and Poverty," United Nations Development Programme, Human Development Report 2002, 2004.

6. Vic Cox, "U.S. Consumption Deserves Reappraisal," http://www.instadv.ucsb.edu/93106/2001/nov19/consumption/consumption.html.

7. Lynette Clemetson, "Census Shows Ranks of Poor Rose by 1.3 Million," *New York Times,* September 3, 2003.

8. U.S. Census Bureau, "Poverty 2001 Highlights."

9. "Child Poverty Rate Improves Significantly in Many States Since 1993. But Recent Progress Leaves Most States with Higher Child Poverty Rates Than Two Decades Ago," *Columbia University News,* August 10, 2000.

10. Rodman B. Webb and Robert L. Sherman, *Schooling and Society,* 2nd ed. (New York: Macmillan, 1989), http://www.phenomenologycenter.org/course/class.htm.

11. Cassandra Cantave and Roderick Harrison, "Children Living in Poverty," Joint Center for Political and Economic Studies, September 1999. (Based on U.S. Census data.)

12. Economic Policy Institute, *The State of Working America 2004/2005*, Washington, D.C., September 2004.

13. Jacqueline Jones, "The History and Politics of Poverty in Twentieth-Century America," in *Perspectives on Modern America: Making Sense of The Twentieth Century,* ed. Harvard Sitkoff (New York: Oxford University Press, 2001), 128.

14. Jared Bernstein, "Who's Poor? Don't Ask the Census Bureau," *New York Times,* September 26, 2003.

15. National Coalition for the Homeless, "How Many People Experience Homelessness?" NCH Fact Sheet #2, September 2002.

16. Ibid., February 1999.

17. U.S. Conference of Mayors, A Status Report on Hunger and Homelessness in America's Cities (Washington, D.C.: 2001).

18. HUD News, "Cuomo releases historic report that paints most comprehensive picture ever of homelessness in America," news release, HUD No. 99-258, December 8, 1999.

19. National Coalition for the Homeless, "Why Are People Homeless?" NCH Fact Sheet #1, September 2002.

20. National Low Income Housing Coalition, "Bush Tax Plan Ignores the Housing Needs of Low Income Americans," February 11, 2003.

21. Sheila Crowley, President of the National Low Income Housing Coalition, NLIHC Briefing on the Bush Housing Budget, February 21, 2003, http://www.cspan.org.

22. Mark Engler, "Who Pays for Poverty?" September 8, 2003, http://www.tompaine.com/feature2.cfm/ID/8812.

23. Associated Press, "More U.S. Families Hungry or Too Poor to Eat, Study Says," *New York Times,* November 2, 2003.

24. Brian Knowlton, "A Global Image on the Way Down," *International Herald Tribune,* December 5, 2002.

25. Trudy Lieberman, "Hungry in America," *Nation,* August 18, 2003.

26. National Center of Health Statistics, July 30, 1998.

27. Centers for Disease Control and Prevention, National Center for Health Statistics, National Health Interview Survey, 1997.

28. Bok, *State of the Nation*, 205.

29. CNN, August 1, 2002.

30. "Sanders Scoop," newsletter of Congressman Bernie Sanders, April 2002.

31. Denny Braun, *The Rich Get Richer: The Rise of Income Inequality in the United States and the World,* 2nd ed. (Chicago: Nelson-Hall, 1997), 17.

32. American Association of Retired Persons Bulletin, September 2002.

33. Emory University, *Emory Magazine,* Spring 2003.

34. U.S. Census Bureau, International Statistics, http://Infoplease.com; United Nations Statistics Division, 2002.

35. Clifford J. Levy, "Mentally Ill, and Locked Away in Nursing Homes," *New York Times,* October 6, 2002.

36. Centers for Disease Control and Prevention, National Center for Health Statistics, *Health, United States, 2002,* 26th Annual Statistical Report.

37. Barbara Ehrenreich on the Plight of the Working Poor, interviewed by Jamie Passaro, *Sun,* January 2003.

38. Kevin Boyle, "Work Places. The Economy and the Changing Landscape of Labor, 1900-2000," in *Perspectives on Modern America,* 123.

39. Jacqueline Jones, "History and Politics of Poverty," 128–29.

Income Inequality and Social Mobility

40. Judt, "Its Own Worst Enemy."

41. Lester Thurow, quoted in Ben H. Bagdikian, *The Media Monopoly* (Boston: Beacon Press, 1997), 5.

42. *Lehrer News Hour*, PBS-TV, July 17, 2002.

43. Chuck Collins, Chris Hartman, and Holly Sklar, "Divided Decade: Economic Disparity at the Century's Turn," United for a Fair Economy, December 15, 1999.

44. Molly Ivins, "Enron: Think Bigger," *Texas Observer,* March 1, 2002.

45. Jacob M. Schlesinger, "Wealth Gap Grows; Why Does It Matter?" *Wall Street Journal,* September 13, 1999.

46. Sarah Anderson, John Cavanagh, and Ralph Estes of the Institute for Policy Studies, and Chuck Collins and Chris Hartman of United for a Fair Economy, "A Decade of Executive Excess: The 1990s," 6th Annual Executive Compensation Survey, September 1999.

47. Kirstin Downey, "The Pension Chasm: Disparity Between CEOs, Workers Under Scrutiny," *Washington Post,* April 13, 2003.

48. Hendrik Hertzberg, "Mine Shaft," *New Yorker,* August 19 & 26, 2002, 57.

49. Ibid.

50. *FOX TV News*, August 12 & 30, 2002.

51. Ben A. Franklin, ed., *Washington Spectator,* July 15, 2002.

52. MoveOn Bulletin, July 11, 2002.

53. Thomas B. Edsall, "Bush Has a Cabinet Full of Wealth," *Washington Post,* September 18, 2002.

54. Isaac Shapiro, Robert Greenstein, and Wendell Primus, "Pathbreaking CBO Study Shows Dramatic Increases in Income Disparities in 1980s and 1990s: An Analysis of the CBO Data," Center on Budget and Policy Priorities, May 31, 2001, http://www.cbpp.org/5-31-01tax.htm.

55. Edward N. Wolff and Richard C. Leone, *Top Heavy: The Increasing Inequality of Wealth in America and What Can Be Done About It,* 2nd ed. (New York: New Press, 2002).

56. David Cay Johnston, "Very Richest's Share of Income Grew Even Bigger, Data Show," *New York Times,* June 26, 2003.

57. *Economist of London,* January 20, 1990, 8.

58. Ibid.

59. Senator Joseph Lieberman, campaign newsletter, August 2002.

60. Julian Borger, "Why America's Plutocrats Gobble Up $1,500 Hot Dogs," *Guardian,* November 5, 2003.

61. Mehrun Etebari, "Trickle-Down Economics: Four Reasons Why It Just Doesn't Work," United for a Fair Economy, July 17, 2003.

62. "Read His Lips," Opinion, *New York Times,* August 16, 2003.

63. "Earned-Income Tax Harassment," *Progressive,* April 2002.

64. Stephen J. Rose, interview by Jeffrey Madrick, "The Truth about Social Mobility," *Challenge* 39, no. 3 (1996):4–8.

65. Paul Krugman, "The Death of Horatio Alger," *Nation,* January 5, 2004.

66. "Business Failures on the Upswing as Small Business Owners Repeat Tragic but Avoidable Mistakes," November 4, 2003,
http://www.click2newsites.com/pressrelease05112003-08.htm.

67. P. Gottschalk and T. M. Smeeding, "Empirical Evidence on Income Inequality in Industrialized Countries," Luxembourg Income Study Working Paper 154, February 1999.

68. Judt, "Its Own Worst Enemy."

69. "Economic Inequality Seen as Rising, Boom Bypasses Poor," Pew Research Center, Washington, D.C., June 21, 2001.

70. "Modest Increase in Nation's Alienation Index, According to Harris Poll." December 2003, Harris Alienation Index, harrisinteractive.com.

71. Tony Judt, "Anti-Americans Abroad," *New York Review of Books,* May 1, 2003.

The Rollover from Record Budget Surplus to Record Budget Deficit in Two Years

72. Various news sources.

The National Debt

73. Bureau of the Public Debt Online, The Debt to the Penny, January 29, 2004.

74. The National Debt Clock, August 2002.

75. David E. Rosenbaum and Edmund L. Andrews, "White House Projects Federal Deficit of More than $200 Billion," *New York Times,* January 15, 2003.

76. James Toedtman, "Deficit Disorder," July 16, 2003, *http://www.Newsday.com.*

77. National Debt Awareness Center, August 2002.

78. Scott Burns, "Lessons in How to Make $43 Trillion Disappear," *Houston Chronicle,* June 2, 2003.

79. Michael Hodges, Grandfather Economic Report, 2003,
http://mwhodges.home.att.net/.

80. Ibid.

The U.S. Trade Deficit

81. Elizabeth Becker, "U.S. Trade Deficit Reaches a Record $489.4 Billion," *New York Times,* February 14, 2004.

82. World Bank Group, World Development Indicators, Data by Country database, April 2003.

83. Judt, "Its Own Worst Enemy."

84. Dean Baker (co-director of the Center for Economic and Policy Research), "Why the Economy Will Go from Bad to Worse," *In These Times,* May 1, 2003.

85. Jeff Faux, "Fast Track to Trade Deficits," IPI Issue Brief No. 170, November 27, 2001.

86. Ibid.

87. Ibid.

State Deficits

88. Al Gore, C-Span, July 28, 2002.

89. *Lehrer News Hour,* PBS-TV, July 16, 2002.

90. Dale Russakoff, "A Grim Fiscal Forecast for States," *Washington Post,* December 24, 2002.

91. Robert Pear, "Rising Costs Prompt States to Reduce Medicaid Further," *New York Times,* September 23, 2003.

92. Jodi Wilgoren, "With Deadline Near, States Are in Budget Discord," *New York Times,* June 27, 2003.

93. Iris J. Lav and Nicholas Johnson, "State Budget Deficits for Fiscal Year 2004 Are Huge and Growing," The Center on Budget and Policy Priorities, mid-2003.

Bankruptcies

94. *Statistical Abstract of the U.S., 2001,* Table 1341.

95. Michael Calabrese and Maya MacGuineas, "Spendthrift Nation," *Atlantic Monthly,* January/February 2003, 102–6.

96. Al Gore, C-Span, July 28, 2002.

97. SiliconValley.com, February 19, 2002.

98. Bob Herbert, "Caught in the Credit Card Vise," *New York Times,* September 22, 2003.

99. Ibid.

Productivity, Job Stress, and Child Care for Working Parents

100. Judt, "Its Own Worst Enemy."

101. CNN/Money, June 5, 2001.

102. Bureau of Labor Statistics, Data, August 2003.

103. Glenn Somerville, "WRAP-UP-3-U.S. Productivity Up Sharply, Jobless Claims Wane," Reuters, August 7, 2003.

104. Judt, "Its Own Worst Enemy."

105. Molly Ivins, "S.O.S.tate of the Union," WorkingforChange (Public Campaign website), January 28, 2003.

106. Sanders for Congress newsletter, April 2002.

107. David Brooks, "Refuting the Cynics," *New York Times*, November 25, 2003.

108. American Institute of Stress, "Job Stress," http://www.stress.org/job.htm.

109. Gallup poll, "Attitudes in the American Workplace VII," sponsored by the Marlin Company (summarized by the American Institute of Stress, ibid.).

110. American Institute of Stress, "Job Stress," Integra Survey.

111. Dolores King, "Job Stress Linked to Heart Disease, Other Health Problems, Studies Say," *Boston Globe*, August 30, 1999.

112. John Burke, "American Businesses Taste the Bitter Fruit of Productivity," Bankrate.com.

113. Boyle, "Work Places," 120.

114. Karen Kornbluh, "The Parent Trap," *Atlantic Monthly*, January/February 2003.

Unemployment

115. United Nations Statistical Division, 2000.

116. Kevin Phillips, *Wealth and Democracy: A Political History of the American Rich* (New York: Broadway Books, Random House, 2002), 164–65.

117. Council of Economic Advisers, *Economic Report of the President*, February 2003.

118. David Leonhardt, "108,000 Jobs Lost in March, U.S. Says," *New York Times*, April 5, 2003.

119. Bureau of Labor Statistics, Employment Situation Summary, December 5, 2003.

120. Joseph E. Stiglitz, "Bush's Tax Plan—The Dangers," *New York Review of Books*, March 13, 2003.

121. Paul Krugman, "Too Low a Bar," *New York Times*, October 24, 2003.

Other Comparisons with Europe

122. *Statistical Abstract of the U.S., 2001*, Table 1345.

123. Ibid., Table 1349.

124. William Greider, "Deflation," *Nation*, June 30, 2002.

125. InflationData.com, Annual Inflation, June 27, 2003.

126. *Statistical Abstract of the U.S., 2001*, Table 1349.

127. World Bank Group, World Development Indicators, World Tables by Country database, April 2003.

128. Council of Economic Advisers, *Economic Report of the President,* International Statistics, February 2003.

129. Clifford Cobb, Ted Halstead, and Jonathan Rowe, "If the GDP is Up, Why is America Down?" *Atlantic Online,* October 1995.

130. Louis Uchitelle, "U.S. Economy Grows 4.2%; War Spending Provides Push," *New York Times,* April 30, 2004.

131. Marc Miringoff and Marque-Luisa Miringoff, *The Social Health of the Nation: How America Is Really Doing* (New York: Oxford University Press, 1999), 40.

132. Phillips, *Wealth and Democracy,* 343–46.

133. Redefining Progress, Genuine Progress Indicator, December 2001, http://www.redefiningprogress.org/projects/gpi/.

134. Miringoff and Miringoff, *Social Health,* 172.

135. Paul Krugman, "Our So-called Boom," *New York Times,* December 30, 2003.

Consumer Confidence and Spending

136. Reuters, September 17, 2002.

137. Louis Uchitelle, "As Stimulus, Tax Cuts May Soon Go Awry," *New York Times,* November 30, 2003.

138. Reuters, June 27, 2003.

139. Conference Board, "Consumer Confidence," July 2003.

140. WHIOTV.com and the Associated Press, "Survey: Holiday Spending to Be Constrained," November 25, 2003.

141. Dawn Anfuso, "Online Holiday Spending Up 37 Percent," imediaconnection.com, January 5, 2004; Melody Vargas, "2003 Consumer Holiday Retail Spending," Retail Industry, What You Need to Know, January 10, 2004.

142. Jenny Strasburg, "Retailers' Happy Holidays, S.F.'s Gap One of Few that Does Not Report Strong Sales," *San Francisco Chronicle,* January 9, 2004.

143. Associated Press, "U.S. Outlays Rose by a Scant 0.2 Percent in February," March 26, 2004, http://www.msnbc.msn.com/id/4607555/; Reuters, "U.S. Consumer Spending to Slow by Fall, Survey Shows," April 12, 2004, http://forbes.com/markets/economy/newswire/2004/04/12/rtr1329360.html.

Recent Federal Budgets

144. Jim Hightower, *Hightower Lowdown,* July 2002.

145. *Lehrer News Hour,* March 2002.

146. Democratic Policy Committee, "Senate Accomplishments under Democratic Leadership," *New York Times,* Politics, August 25, 2002.

147. *CNN News.*

148. Hightower, *Hightower Lowdown,* July 2002.

149. The White House, Office of Management and Budget, "Discretionary Outlays by Function," June 10, 2002.

150. Ibid.

151. The White House, "Discretionary Outlays," 2003.

152. Amy Goldstein and Mike Allen, "Budget Sharply Boosts Defense; Record Deficits Loom as Domestic Programs Slow," *Washington Post,* February 4, 2003.

153. Jeff Gates, "Sinking Fast," *Utne Magazine,* July-August 2003, 54.

154. Editorial, "Stealth Tax Reform," *Washington Post,* February 4, 2003.

155. Goldstein and Allen, "Budget Sharply Boosts Defense."

156. Larry Jones, quoting Senator Tom Daschle, "Congress Passes Fiscal Year 2002 Budget Resolution," *Front Page,* May 14, 2001.

157. *Nation,* March 25, 2002.

158. Coalition for Health Funding, Press Release on President's FY 2003 Budget, February 4, 2003.

159. Greg Palmer, "President's 2003 Budget Boosts Health Research, Redirects Training Funds," American Dental Association, February 11, 2002.

160. Coalition for Health Funding, press release.

161. The White House, "Discretionary Outlays," 2003.

162. National Council for Science and the Environment, "U.S. Geological Survey Faces Budget Cuts in FY 2003," 2002.

163. Natural Resources Defense Council, "The Bush Record," *Nature's Voice,* September/October 2002.

164. U.S. Conference of Mayors, "Mayors, Police Chiefs Fear Federal Budget Cuts Could Jeopardize Further Progress in Fighting Crime," Washington, D.C., March 14, 2002.

165. Ibid.

166. Frida Berrigan, "Sky High: The Military Busts the 2003 Federal Budget," *In These Times*, February 19, 2002.

167. Families USA, "900,000 Children in Jeopardy of Losing Health Coverage," September 12, 2002, http://www.familiesusa.org.

168. Alexander Cockburn, "Concerning Pee-Wee, Townshend and Ritter," *Nation,* February 17, 2003.

169. Robert A. Dahl, *How Democratic Is the American Constitution?* (New Haven: Yale University Press, 2001), 169.

170. Jeff Madrick, "Health for Sale," *New York Review of Books,* December 18, 2003.

171. "Spending Spree at the Pentagon," *New York Times,* February 10, 2003.

172. Goldstein and Allen, "Budget Sharply Boosts Defense."

173. Amy Goldstein and Jonathan Weisman, "Bush Seeks to Recast Federal Ties to the Poor," *Washington Post,* February 9, 2003.

174. Peter Edelman, "Is Anyone Watching as Welfare Becomes Unfair?" *Washington Spectator,* August 1, 2003.

175. Associated Press, "Church Head Responds to Ex-President Bush," January 30, 2003.

176. Edmund L. Andrews, "Greenspan Throws Cold Water on Bush Arguments for Tax Cut," *New York Times,* February 12, 2003.

177. Financial Times Information Limited, "Nobel Winners Pan Bush Tax Cuts," *Daily Telegraph,* February 8, 2003.

178. Paul Kennedy, *The Rise and Fall of the Great Powers* (New York: Random House, 1987), 445.

179. Citizens Against Government Waste, "The Pig Book," 2002.

180. Robert Pear, "Bush's Budget for 2005 Seeks to Rein in Domestic Costs," *New York Times,* January 4, 2004.

181. Immanuel Wallerstein, "The Limits of Economic Conservatism," *Commentary* no. 63, May 1, 2001; William Greider, "The Right's Grand Ambition: Rolling Back the Twentieth Century," *Nation,* May 12, 2003.

Consumption and Happiness

182. Alan During, "The Dubious Rewards of Consumption," *New Renaissance* (magazine) 3, no. 3, 1992. See also During's book *How Much Is Enough? The Consumer Society and the Future of the Earth* (New York: W.W. Norton Co., July 1992).

Enron and Beyond: Corporate Fraud, Regulatory Laxity, and Tax Evasion

183. Frank Portnoy, University of San Diego Law School, testimony at the hearings of the U.S. Senate Committee on Governmental Affairs, January 24, 2002.

184. Ibid.

185. Articles from *New York Times, Economist, Forbes,* and the Center for Responsive Politics, January 25, 2002.

186. Portnoy, testimony, January 24, 2002.

187. Felix G. Rohatyn, "The Betrayal of Capitalism," *New York Review of Books,* February 28, 2002.

188. Jim Hightower. "Don't Focus on Enron, Focus on the System," *Hightower Lowdown,* March 2002.

189. Robert Bryce, "The Rat Pack: How Enron Seduced Wall Street," *Texas Observer,* September 27, 2002.

190. Public Interest, newsletter, July 2002.

191. Ibid.

192. Hightower, *Hightower Lowdown,* July 2002.

193. Adam Lashinsky, "The Enron Story Is Nothing New," CNN/Money, February 4, 2002.

194. Bernie Sanders, "We Must Stop the Culture of Greed," *Bernie Buzz* (newsletter), July 2002.

195. Portnoy, testimony, January 24, 2002.

196. Richard A. Oppel, Jr., with Lowell Bergman, "Judge Concludes Energy Company Drove Up Prices," *New York Times,* September 23, 2002.

197. MSNBC-TV, July 24, 2002.

198. Hightower, "Don't Focus," March 2002.

199. Floyd Norris, "Help Wanted at the SEC; Help Needed for Reform," *New York Times,* November 13, 2002.

200. Stephen Labaton, "SEC Facing Deeper Trouble," *New York Times,* November 30, 2002.

201. Brookings Institute report, *Lehrer News Hour,* 2002.

202. *BBC-TV News,* July 11, 2002.

203. Stephen Labaton, "Bush Seeks to Cut Back on Raise for SEC's Corporate Cleanup," *New York Times,* October 18, 2002.

204. News interview, TV-News, August 2002.

205. Karlyn Bowman and Todd Weiner, "Attitudes toward Business," AEI Special Analysis, August 23, 2002.

206. Public Citizen, Congress Watch, "Public Citizen's Position on Corporate Welfare," June 21, 2001, http://www.citizen.org.

207. Robert S. McIntyre, "One for Oil," *American Prospect,* March 11, 2002.

208. LucyAfter Dirty Air, Dirty Money," *Nation,* June 18, 2001.

209. Phillips, *Wealth and Democracy,* 149.

210. James Fallows, "The Forgotten Home Front," *Atlantic Monthly,* January/February 2003, 81.

211. Will Hutton, "Bye Bye American Pie," *Observer,* June 30, 2002.

212. Lee Drutman, "Avoidance Issues," October 28, 2003, http://www.tompaine.com/feature2.cfm/ID/9252.

213. Dahl, "How Democratic Is the Constitution?"

214. Hightower, "Don't Focus."

215. Ibid.

216. Don Oldenburg, "Creator of 'Dilbert' Weasels Out," *Washington Post,* November 2, 2002. (Quotation of Scott Adams.)

217. William Greider, *Who Will Tell the People?* (New York: Touchstone Books, Simon and Shuster, 1992), 352.

218. C. Wright Mills, *The Power Elite* (New York: Oxford University Press, 1956), 347.

219. Rohatyn, "Betrayal of Capitalism."

Corporations as Persons and Their Political Ascendancy

220. Thom Hartmann, "Now Corporations Claim the 'Right to Lie,'" January 1, 2003, http://www.commondreams.org/views03/0101-07.htm.

221. Ibid.

222. Ibid.

223. Ibid.

224. Jan Edwards, "Thinking About Corporate Personhood," Big Medicine, Countercoup, 2002, http://www.nancho.net/corperson/cptalk.html.

225. Thom Hartmann, "Right to Lie."

226. George Draffan, "Comments on Corporations & Labor" (speech, 1996 Annual Meeting of Jobs with Justice, Seattle, WA., June 29, 1996).

227. "Timeline of Corporate Personhood," Big Medicine, Countercoup, 2002, http://www.nancho.net/corperson/corptime.html.

228. Edwards, "Corporate Personhood."

229. William Greider, "The Right and US Trade Law: Invalidating the 20th Century," N*ation,* October 15, 2001.

230. Draffan, "Corporations & Labor."

231. Ralph Nader and Carl J. Mayer, "Corporations Are Not Persons," *New York Times,* April 9, 1988, http://www.nancho.net/corperson/cpnader.html.

232. Ibid.

233. Ibid.

234. Ibid.

235. Thom Hartmann, "Now Your Vote Is the Property of a Private Corporation," March 6, 2003, http://www.commondreams.org/views03/0306-04.htm. See also http://www.thomhartmann.com and http://www.thomhartmann.com/unequalprotection.shtml.

236. William Meyers, "What Would Change if Corporations Lost Personhood?" Supplement to William Meyers, *Santa Clara Blues: Corporation Personhood versus Democracy* (Gualala, CA: III Publishing, 2000), http://www.iiipublishing.com/afd/changes.htm.

237. Ibid.

238. Hartmann, "Now Your Vote."

239. Phillips, *Wealth and Democracy,* 236.

240. Ibid., 237.

241. Ibid., 237–38.

242. Ibid., 238.

243. Ibid., 239.

244. Ibid., 241–42.

245. Ibid., 241.

246. Ibid., 242.

247. Ibid., 243.

248. Ibid., 248.

249. Kristal Brent Zook, "Hog-tied: Battling It Out (Again) at Smithfield Foods," *Amnesty Now,* Winter 2003, http://www.amnestyusa.org/amnestynow/smithfield.html.

250. Frances Fox Piven with Richard A. Cloward, *Why Americans Still Don't Vote: And Why Politicians Want It That Way* (Boston: Beacon Press, 2000), chap. 5.

251. Ibid., 10.

252. Gretchen Morgenson, "Waiting for the President to Pass the Tax-Cut Gravy," *New York Times,* January 11, 2003.

253. "Earned-Income Tax Harassment," *Progressive,* April 2002.

254. The Office of Dick Armey, "Washington's Lobbying Industry: A Case for Tax Reform," June 19, 1996, http://flattax.house.gov/armey/study/st-lobby.asp.

255. Jim Hightower, "Can You Hear Me Now?" *Texas Observer,* March 28, 2003.

256. Mills, *Power Elite,* 274–75.

257. Elizabeth Becker and Edmund L. Andrews, "I.M.F. Report Says U.S. Deficits Threaten World Economy," *New York Times,* January 7, 2004.

3. Health, Health Care, and Costs

Leading Causes of Death, Major Illnesses, and Disabilities

1. U.S. Department of Health and Human Services.

2. Ibid.

3. Centers for Disease Control and Prevention, National Center for Health Statistics.

4. CNN, September 15, 2002.

5. U.S. Department of Health and Human Services.

6. U.S. National Center for Health Statistics, *National Vital Statistics Report,* vol. 52, no. 3, September 18, 2003.

7. Agency for Healthcare Research and Quality, "Women and Heart Disease," *AHRQ* Publication No. 01-P016, September 2001, http://www.ahrq.gov/research/womheart.htm.

8. Ibid.

9. "Sparing No Expense," *Lehrer News Hour,* PBS-TV, August 22, 2002, http://www.pbs.org/newshour/bb/business/july-dec02/solman_8-22.html.

10. Kenneth Chang, *New York Times,* August 25, 2002.

11. Centers for Disease Control, "Self-Reported Asthma Prevalence among Adults — U.S. 2000," *MMWR Weekly,* August 17, 2001, http://www.cdc.gov/mmwr/preview/mmwrhtml/mm5032a3.htm.

12. Peter J. Gergen, M.D., "Understanding the Economic Burden of Asthma," *Journal of Allergy and Clinical Immunology* 107 (May 2001): S445–S448.

13. C-Span, Hearing before the Senate Subcommittee on Public Health, September 11, 2002.

14. "Managing Care," *Lehrer News Hour*, PBS-TV, July 22, 2002, http://www.pbs.org/newshour/bb/health/july-dec02/care_7-22.html.

15. TCM, TCM Hospital for Chronic and Difficult Diseases, *The Merck Manual of Medical Information*, Sec. 11, Chap. 124, April 1, 2002.

16. "Interstitial nephritis," *General Health Encyclopedia*, adam.com (1998).

17. University of Maryland Medicine, Septicemia, http://www.umm.edu/ency/article/001355.htm.

18. Dr. Darrell Rigel, dermatologist, CNN, July 7, 2002.

19. *Lehrer News Hour*, PBS-TV, July 8, 2003.

20. Centers for Disease Control and Prevention (CDC), National Center for Health Statistics, *Health, United States, 2002*, 26th Annual Statistical Report.

21. John Whitesides, "Democrat Lieberman to Propose Disease Cure Center," iVillage, Health, Reuters Health Information, May 21, 2003.

22. "Is Obesity a Disease?" CNN, July 24, 2002.

23. Ibid.

24. Centers for Disease Control, "New CDC Study Finds Obesity among Youth Exacts an Enormous Healthcare Burden, Jeopardizes Individual Health," *Prevention Report* 16, no. 4 (July 4, 2002), http://odphp.osophs.dhhs.gov/pubs/prevrpt/02Volume16/Issue4pr.htm.

25. U.S. Department of Health and Human Services, "HHS Report Shows 7 in 10 Adults Are Not Active Regularly," press release, *HHS News*, April 7, 2002.

26. Donald B. Brown, "About Obesity," International Task Force on Obesity, n.d.

27. Edward Kennedy, National Press Club address, C-Span, June 18, 2002, http://kennedy.senate.gov/spotlightnpc061802.html.

28. National Center for Health Statistics, *US Newswire*, June 30, 1998.

29. CDC, *Health, U.S., 2002*.

30. CNews, CANOE.CA, Law and Order, December 18, 2001.

31. Morgan O. Reynolds, National Center for Policy Analysis, "Europe Surpasses America—in Crime," *Wall Street Journal*, October 16, 1998.

32. David A. Vise and Lorraine Adams, "Despite Rhetoric, Violent Crime Climbs," *Washington Post*, December 5, 1999. (Based on a study issued by the National Commission on the Causes and Prevention of Violence.)

33. FBI, Uniform Crime Statistics, National Press, June 24, 2002.

34. Infoplease.com, August 8, 2002.

35. Tim Lambert, Department of Computer Science, University of Manitoba, September 26, 1993, lambert@silver.cs.umanitoba.ca.

36. William Cromie, *Harvard University Gazette*, Harvard Injury Research and Control Center, September 28, 2002.

37. John Bacon, "Gun Death," Nationline, *USA Today*, September 28, 2002.

38. Infoplease.com, FBI Statistics, August 30, 2002.

39. U.S. Census Bureau, International Statistics, Infoplease.com, 2002.

40. Illinois Department of Public Health, "State's Infant Mortality Rate Drops 22 Percent in the '90s," January 12, 2001.

41. *National Vital Statistics Report* 49, no. 8 (September 21, 2001).

42. Congressman Bernie Sanders, *Sanders Scoop,* April 2002.

Mental Illness

43. National Institute of Mental Health, "The Numbers Count: Mental Disorders in America," Publication No. 01-4584, updated January 1, 2001.

44. Robert Pear, "Mental Care Poor for Some Children in State Custody," *New York Times,* September 2, 2003.

45. Substance Abuse and Mental Health Services Administration (SAMHSA), *2001 National Household Survey on Drug Abuse,* http://www.DrugAbuseStatistics.samhsa.gov.

46. National Institute of Mental Health, "Depression in Children and Adolescents: a Fact Sheet for Physicians," 2000.

47. Paul von Zielbauer, "Report on State Prisons Cites Inmates' Mental Illness," *New York Times,* October 22, 2003.

48. Open Society Institute, "Mental Illness in U.S. Jails," Occasional Papers Series, No. 1, November, 1996.

49. U.S. Bureau of the Census, National Center for Health Statistics, "Suicide in the U.S." (1999 data)

50. Marc Miringoff and Marque-Lisa Miringoff, *The Social Health of the Nation: How America Is Really Doing* (New York: Oxford University Press, 1999), 90.

51. Ibid., 86.

52. Jedediah Purdy, "Suspicious Minds," *Atlantic Monthly,* January/February 2003, 83.

53. CNN, July 22, 2002.

54. National Institute of Mental Health, "Suicide Facts," 2002.

Domestic Violence

55. "National Domestic Violence Statistics," http://www.dopcampaign.org/stats.htm.

56. Ibid.

Child Abuse

57. Prevent Child Abuse America, Chicago, Ill., April 2, 2001, http://www.preventchildabuse.org.

58. National Clearinghouse on Child Abuse and Neglect Information, April 2004.

59. Prevent Child Abuse America.

60. Ibid.

Alcohol and the Use of Illicit Substances

61. "Alcohol Use and Abuse, a Special Report from Harvard Medical School," *Harvard Men's Health Watch*, 2002.

62. Media Awareness Project, *New York Times,* February 2, 2001, http://www.nytimes.com.

63. SAMHSA, *2001 Survey on Drug Abuse*.

64. Ibid.

Prevention of Illness, Deferment of Death

65. "Preventing and Treating Heart Disease," *Harvard Men's Health Watch, Special Supplement,* 2002.

66. *National Institutes of Health News,* January 14, 2002.

67. Center for Science in the Public Interest, *Nutrition Action Healthletter,* Washington, D.C., 2001.

68. American Academy of Periodontology, "Respiratory Diseases," February 11, 2002.

69. National Institute on Aging, "Pneumonia Prevention: It's Worth a Shot," *Multiplan, 2002.*

70. Centers for Disease Control, "High Blood Pressure Fact Sheet," August 21, 2002.

71. "More Evidence that Tomatoes Cut Risk of Prostate Cancer," *Nutrition Commentator,* Tufts University, March 2002.

72. "Studies Point to the Benefits of Whole Grain Food," *Nutrition Commentator,* Tufts University, September 27, 2000.

73. "Study Looks at Diet and Breast Cancer, *Nutrition Commentator,* Tufts University, February 20, 2001.

74. Ibid.

75. Centers for Disease Control, "Physical Activity and Fitness," *Prevention Report* 16, no. 4 (July 4, 2002), http://odphp.osophs.dhhs.gov/pubs/prevrpt/02Volume16/Issue4pr.htm.

76. Ibid.

77. Jonathan Rowe and Judith Silverstein, "The GDP Myth: Why 'Growth' Isn't Always a Good Thing," *Washington Monthly,* March 1999.

78. *New York Times,* May 30, 1978.

79. Columbia University College of Physicians and Surgeons, September 20, 2002.

80. Uwe E. Reinhardt, Peter S. Hussey, and Gerard F. Anderson, "Cross-National Comparisons of Health Systems Using OECD Data, 1999," *Project HOPE, the People-to-People Health Federation, Inc.,* May/June 2002, http://content.healthaffairs.org/cgi/reprint/21/3/169.pdf.

81. *Journal of the American College of Cardiology* 41, no. 1 (January 1, 2003): 56–61, cited in *Harvard Heart Letter* 13, no. 8 (April 3, 2003). See also Elizabeth A. McGlynn et al., "The Quality of Health Care Delivered to Adults in the United States," *New England Journal of Medicine* 348, no. 26 (June 26, 2003): 2635–45.

82. U.S. Food and Drug Administration, Office of Public Affairs, "FDA's Budget Proposal for FY 2003," Paper, T02-08, February 4, 2002.

83. Institute of Medicine report and National Academy of Sciences report cited in *Nation,* May 6, 2002.

The Cost of Health Care

Overall Costs

84. "Five Nation Survey Exposes Flaws in U.S. Health Care System," *Health Affairs,* press release, Commonwealth Fund, May-June 2002 issue.

85. Texas for Public Justice, Austin, Texas, April 5, 2002.

86. Bradley C. Strunk, Paul B. Ginsburg, and Jon R. Gabel, "Tracking Health Care Costs: Hospital Spending Spurs Double-Digit Increase in 2001," Data Bulletin no. 23, Center for Studying Health System Change, September 2002.

87. *Lehrer News Hour*, PBS-TV, August 22, 2002.

88. Reinhardt, Hussey, and Anderson, "Cross-National Comparisons."

89. CDC, *Health, U.S., 2002.*

Distribution of Health Costs

90. Ibid.

91. Public Citizen's Congress Watch, *America's Other Drug Problem: A Briefing Book on the Rx Drug Debate,* 2002.

92. Ibid.

93. Ibid.

94. Ibid.

95. Ibid.

96. "AHRQ Data Showing Rising Hospital Charges, Falling Hospital Stays," September 18, 2002, HCUPnet or FEnglert@ahrq.gov.

97. Reinhardt, Hussey, and Anderson, "Cross-National Comparisons."

98. Katherine Eban, "Waiting for Bioterror," *Nation,* December 9, 2002.

99. *Statistical Abstract of the U.S., 2001*, Table 1332.

100. Ibid.

101. *Emory Magazine,* Emory University, Spring 2003, 296.

102. Eban, "Waiting for Bioterror."

103. Sherwin B. Nuland, "Whoops!" *New York Review of Books,* July 18, 2002.

104. CNN, July 22, 2002.

105. Centers for Disease Control, Division of Media Relations, "Hospital Infections Cost U.S. Billions of Dollars Annually," March 6, 2000.

106. CNN, October 9, 2003; CNN.com/HEALTH, "Study: Hospital Errors Cause 195,000 Deaths," July 28, 2004.

107. CNN.com/HEALTH, September 9, 2002 (based on *Archives of Internal Medicine,* Institute of Medicine report, 1999).

108. *60 Minutes,* CBS-TV, June 9, 2002.

109. Cynthia Engel, "Health Services Industry: Still a Job Machine?" *Monthly Labor Review Online* 122, no. 3 (March 1999).

110. Agency for Healthcare Research and Quality, "Women and Heart Disease."

111. *Lehrer News Hour,* PBS-TV, November 18, 2002.

112. Ibid., November 19, 2002.

113. Reinhardt, Hussey, and Anderson, "Cross-National Comparisons."

114. Center for Studying Health System Change, "Spending on Hospital Care."

115. BizState.com, 2002.

116. Health Care Liability Alliance, "America Speaks Out on the Health Care Liability Crisis," April 2002.

117. Dr. Palmisano, CNN, June 22, 2002.

118. Texas for Public Justice, Austin, Texas, April 5, 2002.

119. BizState.com, 2002.

120. American College of Emergency Physicians, "Medical Liability Insurance Crisis," June 2003, http://www.acep.org/1,32158,0.html.

121. Ibid.

122. Ibid.

123. Texas for Public Justice.

124. American College of Emergency Physicians, "Crisis."

125. "At Deadline, November 2002," *AARP Bulletin,* November 2002, 2.

126. Ibid.

127. Patricia Barry, "Drug Profits vs. Research," *AARP Bulletin,* June 2002.

128. Public Citizen, *Briefing Book.*

129. Ibid.

130. Ibid.

131. Ibid.

132. Ibid.

133. Robert Pear, "Drug Companies Increase Spending to Lobby Congress and Governments," *New York Times,* June 1, 2003.

134. *Sanders Scoop,* Newsletter of Congressman Sanders, April 2002.

135. *Washington Spectator,* June 15, 2002.

136. Public Citizen, *Briefing Book.*

137. Pear, "Drug Companies Increase Spending."

138. Public Citizen, *Briefing Book.*

139. Ibid.

140. Ibid.

141. Ibid.

142. Ibid.

143. Barry, "Drug Profits vs. Research."

144. Public Citizen, *Briefing Book.*

145. Ibid.

146. *AARP Bulletin,* February 2002.

147. Public Citizen, *Briefing Book.*

148. *Washington Spectator,* June 15, 2002.

149. Public Citizen, *Briefing Book.*

150. "Prescription Drug Safety," *On Health, Consumer Reports* 15, no. 3, March 2003.

151. Public Citizen, *Briefing Book.*

152. Ibid.

153. Ibid.

154. *Washington Spectator,* June 15, 2002.

155. Melody Petersen, "Madison Avenue Plays Growing Role in Drug Research," *New York Times Online,* November 22, 2002.

156. Public Citizen, *Briefing Book.*

157. *Sanders Scoop,* April 2002.

158. Robert Pear, "Big Increase Seen in People Lacking Health Insurance," *New York Times,* September 30, 2003.

159. Robert Pear, "New Study Finds 60 Million Uninsured During a Year," *New York Times,* May 13, 2003.

160. National Center for Health Statistics, "Early Release of Selected Estimates Based on Data from the 2001 NHIS [National Health Interview Survey]," released July 15, 2002.

161. Pear, "Big Increase Seen in People Lacking Health Insurance."

162. Public Citizen, *Briefing Book.*

163. Agency for Healthcare Research and Quality, "State Differences in Job-Related Health Insurance, 1998," Medical Expenditure Panel Survey, MEPS-Ic-002, AHRQ Publication No. 01-DP04, December 2002.

164. Ibid.

165. *Lehrer News Hour,* PBS-TV, September 5, 2002.

166. Senate Ways and Means Committee Staff, *Medical Costs and the 2002 Budget,* January 28, 2002.

167. CNN, September 2002.

168. "Future Retirees Face Higher Health Care Costs" (based on a survey of 56 large employers with at least 5,000 employees), CNN.com/HEALTH, September 16, 2002.

169. Public Citizen, *Briefing Book.*

170. Public Citizen, "Medicare Privatization: The Case Against Relying on HMOs and Private Insurers to Offer Prescription Drug Coverage," September 2002.

171. Ibid.

172. Ibid.

173. *Lehrer News Hour*, PBS-TV, June 7, 2002.

174. Families USA, "900,000 Children in Jeopardy of Losing Health Coverage," September 12, 2002, http://www.familiesusa.org.

175. National Center of Health Statistics, Press Office, 1998.

176. *AARP Bulletin*, September 2002.

177. Dr. David W. Baker et al., "Lack of Health Insurance and Decline in Overall Health in Late Middle Age," *New England Journal of Medicine* 345 (October 11, 2001): 1106–12.

178. Speaker at the National Press Club, C-Span, June 10, 2002.

179. Governor Howard Dean, Vermont, *Meet the Press*, July 21, 2002.

The Quality of Health Care

180. Elizabeth A. McGlynn, Steven M. Asch, John Adams, et al., "Quality of Health Care Delivered to Adults in U.S." *New England Journal of Medicine* 348 (June 26, 2003): 2635–45.

181. Ibid.

182. Hillary Rodham Clinton, "Now Can We Talk About Health Care?" *New York Times Magazine*, April 18, 2004

183 Reuters, "U.S. States Do Poorly in Women's Health," Yahoo! News, May 6, 2004.

184. Dr. Thomas Insel, National Institute of Mental Health, C-Span, August 14, 2003.

185. President's Freedom Commission on Mental Health, September 2003.

186. Barbara McNeil, "Hidden Barriers to Improvement in the Quality of Care," *New England Journal of Medicine* 345 (November 29, 2001): 1612–20

The Health of Americans Compared with That of Citizens of Other Advanced Nations

187. CDC, *Health, U.S., 2002*.

188. Ibid.

189. United Nations Statistical Division, 2002.

190. Ibid.

191. CDC, *Health, U.S., 2002*.

192. United Nations Statistical Division, 2002.

193. "Report on the Global HIV/AIDS Epidemic," UNAIDS, June 2000.

194. "Sexually Transmitted Diseases in Canada: 1996 Surveillance Report" (with preliminary 1997 data), *Canada Communicable Disease Report Supplement* 25S1 (May 1999).

195. World Health Organization (WHO), Statistical Information System, "Cause of Death Statistics," *World Health Statistics Annual, 1997–1999.*

196. UNICEF, "A League Table of Child Deaths by Injury in Rich Nations," *Innocenti Report Card No. 2,* UNICEF Innocenti Research Centre, Florence, February 2001, http://www.unicef-icdc.org.

197. Ibid.

198. World Health Organization (WHO), Statistical Information System, "Cause of Death Statistics," *World Health Statistics Annual, 1994–1998.*

199. Ibid.

200. World Health Organization (WHO), "Health Behavior in School-Aged Children: A WHO Cross-National Study (HBSC) International Report," *Health Policy for Children and Adolescents Series No. 1,* 2000.

201. Ibid.

202. Ibid.

203. Ibid.

204. Ibid.

205. Ibid.

206. Ibid.

207. *Lehrer News Hour*, PBS-TV, 2002.

208. Bob Herbert, "A Second Opinion," Op-Ed, *New York Times*, June 28, 2004.

209. Elliott S. Fisher, "More Medicine Is Not Better Medicine," Op-Ed, *New York Times,* December 1, 2003.

210. Commonwealth Fund 1998 International Health Survey.

211. Centers for Disease Control, March 7, 2002; CNN, September 7, 2002.

212. Ibid.

213. Denise Grady and Lawrence K. Altman, "With Flu Cases Spreading, Demand for Vaccine Grows," *New York Times,* December 6, 2003.

214. Commonwealth Fund 1998 Survey.

An Afterword on the Medicare Prescription Drug and Modernization Act of 2003

214. Mark Sherman, "HMOs to Reap Benefits from Medicare Law," Associated Press, December 10, 2003.

215. Julie Rovner, "Analysts: Medicare Law to Do More Harm than Good," Reuters, Common Dreams News Center, December 5, 2003.

216. John Leland, "73 Options for Medicare Plan Fuel Chaos, Not Prescriptions," *New York Times,* May 12, 2004.

217. Knight Ridder News, "List of Medicare Law Losers Is Significant," Billings-gazette.com, December 7, 2003.

218. Andrea Louise Campbell and Theda Skocpol, "Politics and the Elderly: Down Goes Their Clout; The New Medicare Law Could Leave the AARP Toothless and the Elderly Upstaged by Business Lobbies," Newsday.com, November 30, 2003.

219. Andrew Shapiro, *We're Number One* (New York: Vintage Books, 1992), 3.

220. Campbell and Skocpol, "Politics and the Elderly."

4. Education

Educational Achievement Compared with Other Nations

1. National Center for Education Statistics (NCES), Trends in [Third] International Mathematics and Science Study (TIMSS), 1999. (1995 data)

2. OECD Programme for International Student Assessment (PISA), "Knowledge and Skills for Life: First Results from PISA 2000," http://www.pisa.oecd.org/knowledge/summary/intro.htm.

3. NCES, Trends in International Math and Science Study.

4. James S. Braswell, Mary C. Daane, and Wendy S. Grigg, *The Nation's Report Card: Mathematics*, National Center for Education Statistics, November 2003.

5. NCES, Trends in International Math and Science Study (TIMSS).

6. OECD Programme, "Knowledge and Skills."

7. Ibid.

8. National Assessment of Educational Achievement, cited in *New York Times,* August 31, 2002.

9. *New York Times,* June 1, 2003.

10. William H. Schmidt, Project Director, TIMSS, National Center for Education Statistics, 1999.

11. J. Patrick, "The National Assessment of Educational Progress in U.S. History," *ERIC Digest,* ED 412173, 1997-05-00, ERIC Clearinghouse for Social Studies/Social Science Education, Bloomington, Indiana, 1997.

12. Anthony D. Lutkus et al., "Civics Report Card for the Nation," National Assessment of Education Progress, NCES Electronic Catalog, 1998.

13. Associated Press, "Young Americans Are Flunking Geography, Survey Suggests," *Kansas City Star,* November 21, 2002.

14. "Survey Results: U.S. Young Adults Are Lagging," Global Geographic Literacy Survey, National Geographic-Roper, 2002.

15. Cheryl Russel, "What's Wrong with Schools?" *American Demographics,* September 1996.

16. NCES, Trends in International Math and Science Study.

Spending on Education as a Measure of National Commitment

17. National Center for Educational Statistics, International Comparisons of Expenditures for Education, Table 36-1, Annual expenditures on public and private institutions per student and as a percentage of GDP for OECD: 2000.

18. OECD Programme, "Knowledge and Skills."

19. OECD, 1998.

20. National PTA, "Funding for Education and Child-Related Programs," December 2003, http://www.pta.org/ptawashington/issues/funding.asp.

21. The White House, Home, August 29, 2002.

22. Ibid.

23. Jake Bernstein, "Test Case: Hard Lessons from the TAAS," *Texas Observer,* August 30, 2002.

24. Sam Dillon, "States Cut Test Standards to Avoid Sanctions," *New York Times,* May 22, 2002.

Factors Related to School Achievement

25. OECD Programme, "A Profile of Student Proficiency in Reading Literacy," 2000.

26. Ibid.

27. G. Bridge, J. Blackman, and M. Lopez-Morillas, "How Parents Choose Schools in Multiple Option Systems," paper delivered at the meeting of the American Educational Research Association, San Francisco, April 22, 1976.

28. 1994-1998 Digest of Educational Statistics, International Statistics, International Comparisons of Education, 1998.

29. National Center for Education Statistics, *Education in States and Nations: 1991* (1992 data), http://nces.ed.gov/pubs/esn/n18a.asp.

Innovation and the Organization of Education

30. F. Howard Nelson, "How and How Much the U.S. Spends on K-12 Education: An International Comparison," American Federation of Teachers, Washington, D.C., March 1996, http://www.aft.org/research/reports/interntl/sba.htm.

31. Ibid.

32. Margaret K. Nelson, "The Adoption of Innovations in Urban Schools," Bureau of Applied Social Research, Final Report Grant No. OEG-72-1611, U.S. Department of Health, Education and Welfare, March 1975, 82.

33. Ibid., 288.

34. Ibid., 290.

35. Sloan Wayland, "Interrelationship between School Districts," in Sam Sieber and David Wilder, eds., *The School in Society: Studies in the Sociology of Education* (New York: Collier-Macmillan, 1973), 230–34.

36. Ibid.

Dropping Out of Secondary Education and the Negative Role of the Federal Government

37. American Association of School Administrators, "With World Progress, U.S. No Longer Tops in Graduation Rate," *Leadership News,* May 18, 2000.

38. Phillip Kaufman, Martha Naomi Alt, and Christopher Chapman, "Dropout Rates in the United States: 2000," National Center for Education Statistics, November 2001, http://nces.ed.gov/pubsearch/pubsinfo.asp?pubid=2002114.

39. Ibid.

40. Ibid.

41. Bureau of Labor Statistics, "College Enrollment and Work Activity of 2001 High School Graduates," news release, May 14, 2002, USDL 02-288, ftp://ftp.bls.gov/pub/news.release/History/hsgec.05142002.news.

42. U.S. Census Bureau, Income Survey Branch, Historical Income Tables—People.

43. Cassandra Cantave and Roderick Harrison, "Children Living in Poverty," Joint Center for Political and Economic Studies, September 1999. (Based on U.S. Census data.)

44. Kaufman et al., "Dropout Rates in the United States: 2000."

45. Jayne Freeman, "What's Right with Schools." ERIC Clearinghouse on Educational Management, ERIC Digest No. 3, February 1995.

46. Candace Currie, Klaus Hurrelmann, Wolfgang Settertobulte, Rebecca Smith, and Joanna Todd, eds., *Health and Health Behavior Among Young People: Health Behavior in School-Aged Children,* a WHO Cross-National Study (HBSC) International Report, Health Policy for Children and Adolescents (HEPCA), Series No. 1, WHO, 2000.

47. Sam Dillon, "Thousands of Schools May Run Afoul of New Law," *New York Times,* February 16, 2003.

48. Diana Jean Schemo, "Rule on Failing Schools Draws Criticism," *New York Times,* December 1, 2002.

49. Bernstein, "Test Case."

50. Diana Jean Schemo, "Education Secretary Defends School System He Once Led," *New York Times,* July 26, 2003.

51. Bernstein, "Test Case."

52. Greg Winter, "More Schools Rely on Tests, but Study Raises Doubts," *New York Times,* December 28, 2002.

53. Ibid.

54. Diana Jean Schemo, "Schools Face New Policy on Transfers," *New York Times,* December 10, 2002.

55. Bernstein, "Test Case."

56. Bureau of Labor Statistics, "College Enrollment."

57. Ibid.

Access to Higher Education

58. Family Education Network, Infoplease.com, October 10, 2002.

59. Diana Jean Schemo, "Public College Tuitions Rise 10% Amid Financing Cuts," *New York Times,* October 21, 2002.

60. Ibid.

61. *Nation,* August 19/26, 2002.

62. Will Hutton, "The American Prosperity Myth," *Nation,* September 1/8, 2003.

63. *ABC TV-News,* August 27, 2002.

64. Jim Hightower, *Hightower Lowdown,* May 2002

65. Sarah Snelling, "The Rising Cost of Higher Education," Viewpoints, GenerationVote.com contributor, May 14, 2002.

66. Hightower, *Hightower Lowdown,* May 2002.

67. Ibid.

68. Greg Winter, "Change in Aid Formula Shifts More Costs to Students," *New York Times,* June 13, 2003.

69. NEA and AFT, *Higher Education,* October 10, 2002.

70. Richard Gephardt, "Bush Budget Fails to Make Education a Top Priority: Huge Tax Cut Is Crowding Out Investment in Our Schools," Democratic Policy Committee, April 4, 2001.

71. ASCE Report Card for America's Infrastructure, 1998; Eco.IQ.com., 1999; Concrete Products, ASCE, June 1, 1999.

72. Steven Kirscj, "Texas Miracle or Myth? Was Bush Telling the Truth?" *Silicon Valley Philanthropic,* n.d.

5. Crime and Punishment

Crime, Its Fluctuation, and Its Costs

1. John van Kesteren, Pat Mayhew, and Paul Nieuwbeerta, "Criminal Victimization in Seventeen Industrialized Countries: Key Findings from the 2000 International Crime Victims Survey," *Wetenschappelijk Onderzoek-en Documentatiecentrum.*

2. Institute Against Violence, "About Us," New York University, November 2001.

3. "International Homicide Comparisons," GunCite-Gun Control (1999 data), February 22, 2003.

4. U.S. Department of Justice, FBI National Press, June 24, 2002.

5. Gordon Barclay and Cynthia Tavores, "International Comparisons of Criminal Justice Systems," Home Office, London, Issue 5/02.

6. Disaster Center, "United States Uniform Crime Report: Crime Statistics Total and by State, 1960-2000," http://www.disastercenter.com/crime/.

7. David A. Anderson, "The Aggregate Burden of Crime," *Journal of Law and Economics,* October 1999.

8. National Law Enforcement Memorial Fund, Inc., Newsletter, August 2, 2002.

9. U.S. Department of Justice, Bureau of Justice Statistics, "Criminal Victimization 2000: Changes 1999–2000 with Trends 1993–2000."

10. *FBI Uniform Crime Reports, 1999.*

11. Families to Amend California's 3-Strikes, July 30, 1997, facts@attbi.com.

12. *OC-LA Times,* November 1995.

13. Morris Janowitz, *The Last Half-Century: Societal Change and Politics in America* (Chicago: University of Chicago Press, 1978).

14. "The Criminal Justice Sorting Machine," Right Sizing Justice, 1999.

Imprisonment, Rehabilitation, and Parole

15. Tara-Jen Ambrosio and Vincent Schiraldi, "Executive Summary: From Classrooms to Cell Blocks: A National Perspective," Justice Policy Institute, Washington, D.C., February 1997.

16. Meghan Cotter, "Technology Eases Corrections Crowding," *Government Technology,* G2 Research, Republic, Inc., June 1997.

17. "Prison Brief for United States of America," International Center for Prison Studies, n.d.; Reuters, "Number Imprisoned Exceeds 2 Million, Justice Dept.," April 7, 2003.

18. Barclay and Tavores, "International Comparisons."

19. Reuters, "Number Imprisoned Exceeds 2 Million."

20. Anne M. Piehl, Bert Useem, and John J. Dilulio, Jr., "Right-Sizing Justice: A Cost-Benefit Analysis of Imprisonment in Three States," Center for Civic Innovation at the Manhattan Institute, September 8, 1999.

21. Ambrosio and Schiraldi, "From Classrooms to Cell Blocks."

22. Ibid.

23. Fox Butterfield, "Mistreatment of Prisoners Is Called Routine in U.S.," nytimes.com, May 8, 2004.

24. CURE, "Correctional Education," http://www.curenational.org/Position/curepo5.html

25. Carla Rivera, "Study Finds Aid Outdoes '3 Strikes' in Crime Fight" (paraphrased).

26. U.S. Department of Justice, 2001.

27. State of Florida, "Key Juvenile Crime Trends and Conditions, 2000."

28. Florida Department of Corrections, "Factors Affecting Recidivism Rates," *Recidivism Report,* May 2001.

29. Memorial Fund, Inc. Newsletter, Washington, D.C., August 2002.

30. Ambrosio and Schiraldi, "From Classrooms to Cell Blocks."

31. Jacqueline Cohen, Daniel Nagin, Garrick Wallstrom, and Larry Wasserman, "Hierarchical Bayesian Analysis of Arrest Rates," *Journal of American Statistical Association* 93, no. 444 (December 1998).

32. "Prison Overcrowding—Decriminalizing Drugs Could Double Space," *Syracuse Newspaper,* Letter to the Editor.

33. *Washington Spectator,* March 1, 2002.

34. Cohen et al., "Hierarchical Bayesian Analysis."

35. *The World Revolution,* August 8, 2002, http://www.aworldrevolution.org.

36. Piehl et al., "Right-Sizing Justice."

37. Cohen et al., "Hierarchical Bayesian Analysis."

38. American Society of Addiction Medicine (ASAM), "Treatment for Prisoners with Addiction to Alcohol or Other Drugs," Public Policy Statement, October 19, 2001.

39. Alexandra Marks, "For Prisoners, It's a Nearly No-Parole World," *Christian Science Monitor,* July 10, 2001.

40. "From 'Scarlet Letter' to 1995, Americans Want Criminals to Suffer Shame with Punishment," University of Chicago News Office, October 16, 1995.

Privatization of Prisons

41. U.S. Justice Department, Bureau of Justice Statistics, *Bulletin,* "Prison and Jail Inmates at Midyear 2002," NCJ 198877, April 2003.

42. Brigette Sarabi and Edwin Bender, "The Prison Payoff: The Role of Politics and Private Prisons in the Incarceration Boom," Western Prison Project, Western States Center, November 2000.

43. Ibid., 6.

44. Ibid., 8.

45. Ibid., 10.

46. Ibid., 14–15.

47. House of Representatives, Committee on the Judiciary, *Report to the Committee on the Judiciary,* August 1996, "Private and Public Prisons: Studies Comparing Operational Costs and/or Quality of Service," GAO/GGD Private and Public Prisons (182827).

48. U.S. Justice Department, "Prison and Jail Inmates at Midyear 2002."

49. Center for Policy Alternatives, State Issues, "Privatizing Prisons," stateaction.org, 2003.

Drug Control: Enforcement or Prevention, Crime or Disease?

50. Bob Curley, "2003 Administration Drug-Budget: Analysis," *Join Together Online, Substance Abuse,* February 8, 2002.

51. Ibid.

52. "Changing Attitudes toward the Criminal Justice System," Summary of Findings, Peter D. Hart Associates, Inc., for The Open Society Institute, February 2002.

53. The White House, Office of Management and Budget, "The Drug Control Strategy, 2003 Budget."

54. Ibid.

55. Pew Research Center for the People and the Press, news release, March 3, 2001.

56. Women's International League for Peace and Freedom, "US Drug Policy Issue Committee Statement on Drugs," March 22, 2002.

57. Alexander Cockburn, "An Entire Class of Thieves," *Nation,* October 7, 2002.

Capital Punishment

58. Amnesty International USA newsletter, June 28, 2002.

59. Rosalynn Carter, American Bar Association Address, C-Span, August 19, 2002.

60. U.S. Department of Justice, Office of Justice Programs, "Number of Persons Under Sentence of Death, 1953-2002," Capital Punishment 2002; NCJ 201848, November 2003.

61. Death Penalty Information Center, "The Execution of Juveniles in Other Countries Since 1990," DPIC, Homepage, October 2002.

62. Death Penalty Information Center, "Juveniles and the Death Penalty," DPIC, Homepage, 2002.

63. Ibid.

64. Elliott Naishtat, "In Support of a Moratorium," *Texas Observer,* June 21, 2002.

65. Michael Radelet and Ronald L. Akers, "Deterrence and the Death Penalty: The Views of the Experts," *Journal of Criminal Law and Criminology* 87, no. 1 (1996): 1–16.

66. Ibid.

67. Ibid.

68. David C. Baldus, George G. Woodworth, and Charles A. Pulaski, *Equal Justice and the Death Penalty: A Legal and Empirical Analysis* (Boston: Northeastern University Press, 1990).

69. Phil Porter, phporter@mindspring.com.

70. Editorial, *New York Times,* February 23, 2002.

71. Carter, American Bar Association address.

72. Carl Limbacher and NewsMax.com Staff, "Liberals' Attack on Death Penalty Backfires," Newsmax.com, October 25, 2002.

73. Death Penalty Information Center, "A Watershed Year of Change—The Death Penalty in 2000: Year End Report," December 2000.

74. James Vicini, "Supreme Court Won't Review Juvenile Death Penalty," Reuters, October 21, 2002.

75. Death Penalty Information Center, "Watershed Year of Change" (2000).

76. Vicini, "Supreme Court Won't Review Juvenile Death Penalty."

77. Death Penalty Information Center, "Watershed Year of Change" (2000).

78. Humphrey Taylor, "Support for Death Penalty Still Very Strong in Spite of Widespread Belief That Some Innocent People Are Convicted of Murder," Harris Poll #41, Harris Interactive, Inc., August 17, 2001.

79. Limbacher and NewsMax.com, "Liberals' Attack."

80. Jeff Flock, "'Blanket Commutation' Empties Illinois Death Row," CNN.com./ LAW CENTER, January 13, 2003.

81. Benjamin Weiser and William Glaberson, "Ashcroft Pushes Executions in More Cases in New York," *New York Times,* February 6, 2003.

82. Julian Borger, "Ashcroft Pushes for More Death Sentences," *Guardian, UK,* February 7, 2003.

6. The Environment, Energy, and Natural Resources

Energy Consumption, Pollution, and Global Warming

1. *Statistical Abstract of the U.S., 2001,* Table 1369.

2. Ibid., Table 1335.

3. Andrew C. Revkin, "Climate Talks Will Shift Focus from Emissions," *New York Times,* October 23, 2002.

4. *New York Review of Books,* December 20, 2001, 97.

5. *Where We Stand,* "Environmental Comparisons of the U.S. to Other Rich Nations," *International Encyclopedia, The Long FAQ on Liberalism,* part of the Liberalism Resurgent Web Site. (Steve_Kangas@hotmail.com) Data is from the '90s.

6. Ibid.

7. Environmental Defense Pollution Locator, *Scorecard, A National Overview,* 2002.

8. "Half of Americans Breathing Bad Air," Health and Environmental Effects of Automobile Pollution, *I Don't Care about the Air,* May 1, 2002.

9. "Metro Washington Air Smog Levels Soar; Bush Administration Finalizes Plans to Weaken Clean Air Rules," *Progressive News Wire,* August 14, 2002.

10. Michael Moore, "Why Don't We Just Cut the Crap Right Now," May 1, 2001, http://www.geocities.com/no2capitalism/moore.htm.

11. Natural Resources Defense Council, "In Profile," 2002.

12. *CBS-TV News,* April 23, 2002.

13. *Now,* PBS-TV, July 19, 2002.

14. Elinor Mills Abreu, "Landfills," *Yahoo News,* October 26, 2002.

15. *Texas Observer,* May 9, 2003.

16. Eric Pianin, "Study Finds Net Gain from Pollution Rules," *Washington Post,* September 27, 2003.

17. U.S. Environmental Protection Agency (EPA), Region 7 Air Program, "Health Effects of Pollution," July 29, 2002.

18. Ibid.

19. Ibid.

20. Ibid.

21. Ibid.

22. Ibid.

23. Senate Subcommittee on Public Health, Hearings, September 11, 2002.

24. U.S. EPA, "Health Effects of Pollution."

25. "After Kyoto: A Realistic Approach to Climate Management," naturalSCIENCE: Editorial, April 17, 2001, http://naturalscience.com/ns/articles/edit/ns_ed08.html.

26. Robert E. Billings, "Hydrogen Fuel Cell Vehicles," International Academy of Science Hydrogen Technology Papers, 1997. (Based on testimony by Dr. James Hansen, head of NASA's Goddard Institute for Space Studies, at a congressional hearing.)

27. "Alaskan Senator Stevens: Disastrous Global Warming Consequence Already Happening in Alaska as Whole Towns Face Moving Due to Rising Sea Levels," May 1, 2001, http://arcticcircle.uconn.edu/NatResources/Globalchange/stevens.htm; Brethren Witness, Peace and Justice, "Global Warming Heating Up Alaska," 2002, http://www.brethren.org/genbd/witness/Alaska/GlobalWarming.htm.

28. "U.S. Holds Back Agreement on Global Warming," *Environment News Service,* October 30, 2002.

29. Natural Resources Defense Council Newsletter, February 2, 2002.

30. "Gas Guzzler Campaign Educates Against Car Pollution," *FACT ON LINE,* http://www.afn.org/~fact/energy3.htm.

31. "Half of Americans Breathing Bad Air."

32. Piero Scaruffi, "The Worst Problems of the United States," *Politics,* Piero Scaruffi, Editor, 2002 http://www.scaruffi.com/politics/problems.html.

33. *Where We Stand,* n.d.

34. Jonathan Rauch, "Taking Stock," *Atlantic Monthly,* January/February, 2003, 119.

35. "Study Proves Using Public Transportation Is the Best—and Possibly Only—Non-regulatory Strategy for Major Environmental and Energy Gains," *American Public Transportation News,* July 17, 2002.

36. Gretchen Randall, "National Academy of Sciences Issues Final Report on Corporate Average Fuel Economy (CAFE) Standards," *Ten Second Response: Fast Facts on the Environment,* National Center for Public Policy Research.

37. "Sales of SUVs, Minivans and Pickups Surpass Cars for First Time," Union of Concerned Scientists, news release, December 27, 2001.

38. Ibid.

39. *Washington Spectator,* review of *High and Mighty: SUVs – the World's Most Dangerous Vehicles and How They Got That Way* by Keith Bradsher, quoted in Tim Dunlop, "The Road to Surfdom," August 2, 2002, http://www.roadtosurfdom.com/surfdomarchives/000342.php.

40. Robert L. Redding, Jr., "CAFE Standards Unlikely to Change," ASA Washington, D.C., Representative, 2002.

41. Ralph Nader, "The Quest for the Fuel Efficient Car," *The Nader Page, In the Public Interest,* August 8, 2002.

42. Transportation Department, International Council for Local Environmental Initiatives, "Introduction—Cities for Climate Protection," 2002.

43. Natural Resources Defense Council, Newsletter, February 2002.

44. Ibid.

45. Alliance for Energy and Economy Growth.

46. Escapees RV Club, Coalition for Vehicle Choice, "Senate Defeats Stricter Gas Mileage Standards," March 19, 2002.

47. Sierra Club, "Selling-Out: An Interview with Mark Green," October 23, 2002.

48. Office of Transportation Technologies, "CAFE Standards Reduce Petroleum Use," Fact of the Week, Fact #208, March 18, 2002.

49. Competitive Enterprise Institute, 2002.

50. Transportation Research Board and National Academy of Sciences, "Effectiveness and Impact of Corporate Average Fuel Economy (CAFE) Standards (2002)."

51. Republic Conference, Energy Information Center, "Improving Fuel Economy," February 22, 2002.

52. *Washington Spectator,* review of *High and Mighty.*

53. Marc Ross and Tom Wenzel, "Losing Weight to Save Lives: A Review of Automobile Weight and Size in Traffic Fatalities," American Council for an Energy Efficient Economy, July 2001.

54. Fred de Sam Lazaro, "Clean Cars," *Online News Hour,* March 3, 2000.

55. Keith Bradsher, *High and Mighty—SUVs* (see note 39).

56. David Suzuki, "We've Heard This Story Before," September 27, 2002.

57. Working Assets, February 2, 2003.

58. David Suzuki, "Meeting Regulations Costs Less than Expected," Oct. 25, 2002.

59. Carl Pope, "Killing the CAFE Standards," TomPaine.com, March 21, 2002, http://www.alternet.org/story.html?StoryID=12665.

60. Center for Responsive Politics, "2002 Election Overview," OpenSecretsSociety.org.

61. Ibid.

62. Ibid.

63. Ibid.

64. Ibid.

65. Ibid.

66. Natural Resources Defense Council, "Bush Administration Fails to Boost Automobile Efficiency," April 1, 2002.

67. Office of Transportation Technologies, Fact of the Week, Fact #195, December 17, 2001.

68. PlanetSave.com, Energy Federation, Inc., "Hot-Selling Honda Civic May Stir Interest in Hybrids," May 15, 2002.

69. *Funny Times,* November 11, 2001.

70. "Sales of SUVs" (see note 37).

71. David Suzuki, "Industry Fights Progress—Again," *Environmental News Network,* October 1, 2002.

72. *The American Prospect,* March 11, 2002, 17.

73. Projectcensored.org, "#1 FCC Moves to Privatize Airwaves," *Censored 2003: Top 25 Censored Stories of 2000–2002.*

74. Bette Hileman, "California Law Cuts Emissions," "Today's Headlines," *Chemical & Engineering News* 80, no. 30 (July 29, 2002), 10.

75. *BBC-TV News,* July 22, 2002.

76. Natural Resources Defense Council, Newsletter, "The Bush Record," October 9, 2002.

77. Danny Hakin, "States Plan Suit to Prod U.S. on Global Warming," *New York Times,* October 4, 2003.

78. Back to Life Science, "Environment: Bush Rejects Kyoto Climate Treaty," March 29, 2001.

79. Rachel Coen, "Rare, Not Well Done: U.S. Coverage of Climate Change Talks," *FAIR—Fairness and Accuracy in Reporting,* March/April 2001.

80. Howard Geller and Toru Kubo, "National and State Energy Use and Carbon Emissions Trends," September 2000, ACE3 (American Council for an Energy Efficient Economy, Report E001).

81. Revkin, "Climate Talks" (see note 3).

82. UN Environment Programme, "2002: Natural Disasters Set to Cost Over $70 Billion," news release, 2002/78.

83. Geoffrey Lean, "Bush Ready to Wreck Ozone Layer Treaty," *Independent* (UK), July 20, 2003.

Actions of the Current Administration That Endanger the Nation's Environment

84. Natural Resources Defense Council (NRDC), "The Bush Record, 2001 and 2002," http://www.nrdc.org/bushrecord/.

85. Associated Press, "States Sue EPA Over New Rules," *New York Times,* December 31, 2002.

86. NRDC, "The Bush Record," October 31, 2001.

87. Ibid., July 21, 2002.

88. U.S. PIRG online, Public Interest Research Groups, February 11, 2002.

89. NRDC, "The Bush Record," August 17, 2001.

90. Ibid., October 4, 2002.

91. Ibid., October 3, 2002.

92. Ibid., September 15, 2002; June 12, 2002.

93. Ibid., October 25, 2001.

94. Natural Resources Defense Council, "In Profile," 2002.

95. Robert Pear, "Agency Proposes Relaxing Rules on Logging in National Forest," *New York Times,* November 27, 2002.

96. Wilderness Newsletter, Washington, D.C., September 2002.

97. Natural Resources Defense Council, Newsletter, July 2002.

98. NRDC, "The Bush Record," September 30, 2002.

99. Ibid., September 17, 2002.

100. Public Interest Research Groups, "Big Buck Awards," October 2002, http://www.pennenvironment.org/reports/BigBuckAwards10_02.pdf.

101. NRDC, "The Bush Record," June 9, 2003.

102. Ibid., April 11, 2002.

103. Ibid., December 14, 2001.

104. Ibid., November 6, 2001.

105. Ibid., February 5, 2002.

106. Ibid., November 28, 2001.

Other Crises of the Global Environment and America's Response

107. *BBC-TV News*, July 7, 2002.

108. Natural Resources Defense Council, "As Polar Ice Cap Melts, Senate Casts First Vote on Global Warming," *Nature's Voice,* January/February 2004.

109. PBS-TV, *International News*, April 3, 2002.

110. U.N. Development Programme, *Human Development Report* (New York: Oxford University Press, 1998).

111. *ABC-TV News*, April 3, 2002.

112. *BBC-TV News*, October 8, 2002.

113. World Bank, *World Development Report 2002,* cited by Steve Schifferes, *BBC-News*, Business, August 21, 2002, http://news.bbc.co.uk/2/low/business/2207027.stm.

114. Ibid.

115. Jim Hightower, *Hightower Lowdown,* June 2002.

116. Ibid.

117. Ibid.

118. Ibid.

119. Ibid.

120. Simon Retallack, "US Hijacks Johannesburg Summit," *Ecologist*, August 2, 2002.

121. http://www.climatenetwork.org/wssd/Call%20to%20Action.pdf.

122. Retallack, "US Hijacks Summit."

123. Jonathan Lash, "The Johannesburg Summit," World Resources Institute, September 2002.

124. Retallack, "US Hijacks Summit."

125. US Agency for International Development (USAID), Global Development Alliance Secretariat, 2002.

126. U.S. Department of State, International Information Programs, August 21, 2002.

127. USAID, FY 2003 Budget, May 2002.

128. U.S. Department of State, International Information Programs, "U.S. Officials Seek Real Development Results at Johannesburg Summit," August 21, 2002.

129. House Budget Committee, Democrats, 2002.

130. Conservation Action Network, 2002.

131. House Budget Committee, Democrats, 2002.

7. Foreign Affairs—Selected Issues

Foreign Assistance to Poor and Developing Countries

1. Bread for the World Institute, "Hunger Basics, International Facts on Hunger and Poverty," United Nations Development Programme, Human Development Report 2002, 2004.

2. Isaac Shapiro, Center on Budget and Policy Priorities (Washington, D.C.), July 18, 2001.

3. Steve Schifferes, "Attacking World Poverty," *BBC News Online: Business,* September 14, 2000.

4. Greg Palast, "Venezuela and Argentina: A Tale of Two Coups," *New Internationalist Magazine,* July 7, 2002.

5. *BBC News,* PBS-TV, June 26, 2002.

6. Schifferes, "World Poverty."

7. Azza Munif, "Poverty Snatches Childhood from Millions," Gulf News Research Centre, Dubai, November 20, 2002.

8. Ibid.

9. Ibid.

10. U.N. Development Programme, *Human Development Report* (New York: Oxford University Press, 1998).

11. Munif, "Poverty Snatches Childhood."

12. Bread for the World Institute, "Hunger Basics."

13. Bill Moyers, *NOW,* PBS-TV, July 8, 2002.

14. *Lehrer News Hour,* PBS-TV, July 8, 2002.

15. NewScientist.com news service, "Global AIDS epidemic 'in early phase,'" July 2, 2002.

16. CNN-TV, September 29, 2002.

17. *BBC-TV News, June 4, 2002.*

18. *Lehrer News Hour*, PBS-TV, May 9, 2002.

19. *BBC-TV News*, June 4,2002.

20. Ibid.

21. *Lehrer News Hour*, PBS-TV, October 1, 2002.

22. *Lehrer News Hour*, PBS-TV, July 8, 2002.

23. Doctors Without Borders, "Battling the World's Silent Emergencies," September 2002.

24. Ibid.

25. Jimmy Carter (fund-raising letter), 2002.

26. UN Development Programme, *Human Development Report.*

27. Howard Zinn, "Operation Enduring War," *Progressive,* March 2003.

28. *BBC-TV News*, September 16, 2002.

29. Lane Vanderslice, "Millions Threatened with Starvation in Ethiopia and Eritrea: Needs of Millions Worldwide Threaten to Overwhelm International Emergency Food Supplies," *Hunger Notes,* World Hunger Education Service, November 14, 2002.

30. TV newscast.

31. CNN, July 24, 2002.

32. UN Development Programme, *Human Development Report.*

33. Academy for Educational Development (AED), "Facts about Basic Education in Developing Countries," http://www.aed.org/education/edu_facts.html.

34. Kathleen Manzo, "UN Report: No School for 156 Million Children," *Education Week Online,* November 7, 2001.

35. AED, "Basic Education in Developing Countries."

36. Sean Cavanaugh, "Congress Mulls Aid for Education Overseas," *Education Week on the Web,* September 18, 2002.

37. AED, "Basic Education in Developing Countries."

38. World Bank, "Attacking Education," World Bank Development Background Paper for the World Development Report, 2000/2001.

39. Deborah Zabarenko, "Population to Double in 74 Poor Countries," Reuters, December 30, 1997.

40. Jared Diamond, "Why We Must Feed the Hands That Could Bite Us," *Washington Post,* January 13, 2002.

The U.S. Response to the Need for Assistance

41. Charles Sheketoff, "Take the War-on-Iraq IQ Test," Oregon Center for Public Policy, PO Box 7, Silverton, OR 97381.

42. Jimmy Carter (paraphrased), "Ex-US President Jimmy Carter Slams 'Arrogant' U.S. Foreign Policy," Agence France Presse, November 16, 2002.

43. George McGovern, "Questions for Mr. Bush," *Nation,* April 22, 2002.

44. Peter Singer, "The Singer Solution to World Poverty," *New York Times Magazine,* September 5, 1999, 63.

45. *ABC-TV News,* August 27, 2002.

46. "Foreign aid holds steady as US, EU make up fall in Japanese assistance," *Daily Star,* Business Page, May 14, 2002.

47. Office of Management and Budget, Congressional Budget Office, 2002.

48. Basic Education Coalition, "A Primer on Basic Education," *Education Week on the Web,* 2002.

49. Piero Scaruffi, "Corruption in America," *Politics,* A Review of Politics, U.S.A., 2002, scaruffi.com.

50. Population Action International, "Bush FY 2003 Budget Guts International Planning Funds," February 4, 2002, AED, http://www.planetwire.org/details/2265.

51. Paul Krugman, "Matter of Emphasis," *New York Times,* April 29, 2003.

52. Jim Hightower, *Hightower Lowdown,* July 2002.

53. Paul Blustein, "U.S. Resists Giving Poor Countries More Anti-Poverty Money," *Washington Post,* March 7, 2002.

54. Constant Brand, "UN: Rich Nations Not Helping Enough," quoting Mark Malloch Brown, head of the UN Development Program, *Detroit Free Press,* May 16, 2001.

55. Karen DeYoung, "Amid Prosperity, Country Is World's Least Generous in Helping Poor," *Herald Tribune,* November 26, 1999.

56. Ibid.

57. Isaac Shapiro and David Weiner, "The Administration's Proposed Millenium Fund—While Significant—Would Lift Foreign Aid to Just 0.13 Percent of GDP," Center for Global Development, March 21, 2002.

58. Berta Gomez, "Treasury Secretary O'Neill Calls for Effective Foreign Aid," Washington File, February 4, 2002.

59. U.S. Agency for International Development (USAID), "A Record of Accomplishment," June 18, 2003, http://www.usaid.gov/about_usaid/accompli.html.

60. World Bank Group, Aid Effectiveness Research, "Assessing Aid—Overview: Rethinking the Money and Ideas," http://www.worldbank.org/research/aid/overview.htm.

61. Ibid.

62. Bread for the World, " Development Aid to Africa Cut in 2003: Bush Administration Strong on Promises, Weak on Current Funding," press release, June 20, 2002.

63. Paul S. Zeitz, "Waging a Global Battle More Efficiently," *New York Times,* March 1, 2003.

64. Reuters, "Harvard Economist Challenges O'Neill on Poverty," June 19, 2002.

65. Per Pinstrup-Andersen, Mattias Lundberg, and James L. Garrett, "Foreign Assistance to Agriculture: A Win-Win Proposition," International Food Policy Research Institute, July 1995.

66. Craig Burnside and David Dollar, "Aid, Policies, and Growth," Policy Research Working Paper 1777 (Washington, D.C.: World Bank, 1997).

67. Michael Dobbs, "Aid Abroad Is Business Back Home—Washington Firms Profit from Overseas Projects," *Washington Post,* January 26, 2001.

68. World Bank Group, "Assessing Aid." .

69. Dobbs, "Aid Abroad."

70. Ibid.

71. Ibid.

72. Michael Dobbs, "Foreign Aid Shrinks, But Not for All," *Washington Post,* January 24, 2001.

73. Paul Blustein, "Bush to Call for New Foreign Aid Agency," *Washington Post,* November 26, 2002.

74. Glenn Somerville, "U.S. Treasury Chief Pushes More Foreign Aid Grants," Reuters, February 20, 2002.

75. Paul O'Neill, "Caring Greatly and Succeeding Greatly: Producing Results in Africa," *Foreign Policy,* June 5, 2002.

76. Judy Sarasohn, "Why Not Eritrea?" *Washington Post,* November 21, 2002.

77. James Dao, "With Rise in Foreign Aid, Plans for a New Way to Give It," *New York Times,* February 3, 2003.

78. *Lehrer News Hour,* PBS TV, July 10, 2002.

79. Eric J. Labs, "Development and the Role of Foreign Aid," Congressional Budget Office, May 1997, http://www.cbo.gov/showdoc.cfm?index=8&sequence=0.

80. Amy Waldman, "Poor in India Starve as Surplus Wheat Rots," *New York Times,* December 2, 2002.

81. Elizabeth Becker, "U.S. Official to Discuss Trade as Africa Hopes to Talk AIDS," *New York Times,* January 11, 2003.

82. Bill Clinton, *BBC News,* July 11, 2002.

Public Attitudes toward Foreign Assistance

83. James F. Miskel, "The Debate about Foreign Aid," *Journal of Humanitarian Assistance,* January 17, 1997.

84. Meg Bostrom, "Public Attitudes toward Foreign Affairs: An Overview of the Current State of Public Opinion," Frameworks Institute, October 1999.

85. Ibid.

86. Program on International Policy Attitudes (PIPA), "Americans on Foreign Aid and World Hunger: A Study of U.S. Attitudes," February 2, 2002.

87. Bostrom, "Public Attitudes toward Foreign Affairs."

88. PIPA, "Study of U.S. Attitudes."

89. Pew Research Center, "American and Europeans Differ Widely on Foreign Policy Issues," Introduction and Summary, April 17, 2002.

90. George W. Bush, All News Channel TV, August 31, 2002.

The Afghanistan War: A Case Study of Military Mismanagement with Tragic Consequences

91. Robert Dreyfuss, "The Home Front: The Military Mind and Civil Defense," *American Prospect,* November 5, 2001.

92. United Nations Department of Public Information, May 5, 1997.

93. Dru Oja Jay, "Civilian Casualties in Afghanistan," Monkeyfist.com, December 13, 2001.

94. Marc Herold, "3,500 Civilians Killed in Afghanistan by U.S. Bombs," *Global Policy Forum,* December 10, 2001. For the full-text version, see http://www.cursor.org/stories/civilian_deaths.htm. For details about the ongoing conflict, the reader is urged to see: http://pubpages.unh.edu/~mwherold/.

95. Pankaj Mishra, "The Afghan Tragedy," *New York Review of Books,* January 17, 2002.

96. Amnesty International, January 11, 1999.

97. John E. Rielly, "Americans and the World: A Survey at Century's End," *Foreign Policy,* Spring 1999, 97–114.

98. Naomi Klein, "A Time to Think about Collateral Damage," AlterNews.org, September 18, 2001.

99. Michael Ratner and Jules Lobel, "An Alternative to the U.S. Employment of Military Force," Center for Constitutional Rights, February 28, 2003; Francis A. Boyle, "The illegalities of the Bush, Jr., War Against Afghanistan," USA Patriot Act Briefing, National Lawyers Guild, Chicago, Illinois, July 17, 2002.

100. Herold, "3,500 Civilians Killed."

101. Carl Conetta, "Operation Enduring Freedom: Why a Higher Rate of Civilian Bombing Casualties," Project on Defense Alternatives Briefing Report No. 11, January 18, 2002 (revised January 24, 2002).

102. Jonathan Steele, "Forgotten Victims," *Guardian,* May 20, 2002.

103. Conetta, "Operation Enduring Freedom."

104. Ibid., executive summary.

105. Herold, "3,500 Civilians Killed."

106. Conetta, "Operation Enduring Freedom."

107. Richard Falk, "Appraising the War Against Afghanistan," http://www.ssrc.org/sept11/essays/falk.htm.

108. "Action Alert: CNN Says Focus on Civilian Casualties Would Be 'Perverse,'" FAIR, November 1, 2001.

109. Jim Rutenberg, "Fox Portrays a War of Good and Evil, and Many Applaud," *New York Times,* December 3, 2001.

110. Herold, "3,500 Civilians Killed."

111. "Action Alert: How Many Dead? Major Networks Aren't Counting," FAIR, December 12, 2001.

112. Herold, "3,500 Civilians Killed."

113. Carl Conetta, "Strange Victory: A Critical Appraisal of Operation Enduring Freedom and the Afghanistan War," Project on Defense Alternatives Research Monograph No. 6, January 30, 2002.

114. Herold, "3,500 Civilians Killed."

115. Ibid.

116. "The Afghan Killing Fields," *Al-Ahram Weekly Online,* January 24–30, 2002.

117. John Donnelly and Anthony Shadid, "Civilian Toll in US Raids Put at 1,000; Bombing Flaws, Manhunt Cited," *Boston Globe,* February 17, 2002.

118. Marc Herold, "A Dossier on Civilian Victims of United States' Aerial Bombing of Afghanistan: A Comprehensive Accounting" (revised), http://www.cursor.org/stories/civilian_deaths.htm. For details about the ongoing conflict, the reader is urged to see: http://pubpages.unh.edu/~mwherold/.

119. Ibid.

120. Ibid.

121. Conetta, "Strange Victory."

122. Robert Fisk, "Lost in the Rhetorical Fog of War," *Independent, UK,* October 9, 2001.

123. Kate Randall, "Civilian Casualties Mount in Afghanistan," World Socialist Web Site, October 13, 2001.

124. Ibid.

125. U.S. Department of State, "Fact Sheet: U.S. Military Efforts to Avoid Civilian Casualties," October 25, 2001.

126. Donnelly and Shadid, "Civilian Toll in US Raids."

127. Conetta, "Operation Enduring Freedom."

128. U.S. Committee for Refugees, "Worldwide Refugee Information: Afghanistan," 2002.

129. Ibid.

130. CNN, October 19, 2002.

131. Conetta, "Operation Enduring Freedom."

132. Vernon Loeb, "Bursts of Brilliance," *Washington Post,* December 15, 2002.

133. Conetta, "Operation Enduring Freedom."

134. Conetta, "Strange Victory."

135. Ibid.

136. Conetta, "Operation Enduring Freedom."

137. Herold, "3,500 Civilians Killed."

138. Conetta, "Strange Victory."

139. Associated Press, "Book [*Bush at War* by Bob Woodward]: U.S. Paid Off Afghan Warlords," November 16, 2002.

140. Nicholas J. Wheeler, "Protecting Afghan Civilians from the Hell of War," Social Science Research Council, n.d., http://www.ssrc.org/sept11/essays/wheeler.htm.

141. Michael Kamber, "Afghanistan's Environmental Crisis," MotherJones.com, March 6, 2002.

142. Calvin Woodward, "War May Be Costing $1 Billion a Month," Associated Press, November 11, 2001.

143. David Francis, "Postwar Afghanistan Will Come with a Hefty Bill," *Christian Science Monitor,* December 17, 2001.

144. Kathleen T. Rhem, American Forces Press Service, "Humanitarian Work Progressing in Afghanistan," December 19, 2002.

145. U.S. Department of State, International Information Programs, "USAID Helping to Create a Stable Afghanistan, Natsios Says," March 14, 2002, http://usinfo.state.gov/topical/pol/terror/02031408.htm.

146. Carlotta Gall, "Half a Million Afghan Refugees Left Homeless and Cold in Cities," *New York Times,* January 1, 2003.

147. Natasha Hunter, "Short on Change: Is America Building Nations or Tearing Them Down?" February 14, 2003, http://www.tompaine.com/feature2.cfm/ID/7280.

148. Conetta, "Strange Victory."

149. Ibid.

150. Joseph S. Nye, Jr., "Lessons from Afghanistan," *Boston Globe,* March 16, 2002.

151. Jack Kelley, "Al-Qaeda Fragmented, Smaller, but Still Deadly," *USA Today,* September 9, 2002.

152. Conetta, "Operation Enduring Freedom."

153. Rahimullah Yusufzai, "UN al-Qaeda Report Confounds Experts," *BBCnews World Edition,* December 19, 2002.

154. Eric Alterman, "USA Oui! Bush Non!" *Nation,* February 10, 2003.

155. Associated Press, "Afghanistan Is World's Largest Opium Producer, UN," October 25, 2002.

156. Associated Press, "Afghans Sign Pact with Six Neighbors," December 22, 2002.

157. Robert Fisk, "What Will the Northern Alliance Do in Our Name Now? I Dread to Think . . .," *Independent (London),* November 14, 2001.

158. Human Rights Watch, "Afghanistan: Return of the Warlords," Human Rights Briefing Paper, June 2002.

159. Ibid.

160. Ibid.

161. Mike Collett-White, "Warlords Are Afghanistan's New Worry Number One," Reuters, December 12, 2002.

162. Anne E. Brodsky, "Hollow Victory: Afghanistan Struggles Out of the Rubble," *In These Times,* August 30, 2002.

163. Anna Badkhen, "Widespread Abuse, Restrictions on Freedom Continue Almost Year After Fall of Taliban," *San Francisco Chronicle,* October 14, 2002.

164. Sayed Salahuddin, "Afghans Fear Being Eclipsed," March 20, 2003, http://www.dawn.com/2003/03/20/int17.htm.

165. Rhem, "Humanitarian work."

166. Wheeler, "Protecting Afghan Civilians."

167. Norman Solomon, "Spinning the Gulf War to Ignore the Cost in Lives," *Extra! Update* (the bimonthly newsletter of FAIR), February 2003.

168. Iraq Body Count, April 27, 2004.

The Iraq War of 2003 and More Military Mismanagement

169. Eric Schmitt and Joel Brinkley, "State Department Study Foresaw Troubles Now Plaguing Postwar Iraq," *New York Times,* October 19, 2003.

170. "Unclassified After Action Report from Iraq," April 24, 2003, Dirty Little Secrets, September 12, 2003.

171. Melinda Liu, John Barry, and Michael Hirsh, "The Human Cost," *Newsweek,* April 26, 2004.

172. "Iraqi Civilian Casualties Mount," *BBC News World Edition,* April 1, 2003.

173. Dennis J. Kucinich, "Kucinich Requests DOD Release Number of Iraqi Casualties," press release, April 21, 2003.

174. "Unclassified After Action Report."

175. Sandra Laville, David Blair, and John Steele, "Military Restrictions and Lawlessness Shut Aid Agencies Out of Iraq," *Daily Telegraph,* April 28, 2003.

176. "Chronology," War on Iraq Information Portal, RUSI, http://www.iraqcrisis.co.uk/.

177. Mark Perry, "Rummy Invades Iraq Aid," *Nation,* May 12, 2003.

178. Ibid.

179. Ibid.

180. Ibid.

181. Michael Massing, "The Unseen War," *New York Review of Books,* May 29, 2003.

182. Russell Smith, "The New Newsspeak," *New York Review of Books,* May 29, 2003.

183. Ibid.

184. Massing, "Unseen War."

185. John W. Dean, "Missing Weapons of Mass Destruction: Is Lying about the Reason for War an Impeachable Offense?" Findlaw.com, June 6, 2003.

186. Ibid.

187. William Douglas, "Poll: U.S. Image Abroad Worse Since Iraq War," *Newsday,* June 4, 2003.

188. Ibid.

189. Curt Goering, "Iraq Dispatch: Notes from the Field," *Amnesty International Newsletter,* October 2003.

190. Amnesty International, "Iraq: The US Must Ensure Humane Treatment and Access to Justice for Iraqi Detainees," news release, June 30, 2003.

191. Carlotta Gall, "An Afghan Gives His Own Account of U.S. Abuse," *New York Times,* May 12, 2004; Douglas Jehl, Steven Lee Myers, and Eric Schmitt, "Abuse of Captives More Widespread, Says Army Survey," *New York Times,* May 26, 2004.

192. Fox Butterfield, "Mistreatment of Prisoners Is Called Routine in U.S.," *New York Times,* May 8, 2004.

193. Douglas Jehl and Eric Schmitt, "In Abuse, a Portrayal of Ill-Prepared, Overwhelmed G.I.'s," *New York Times,* May 9, 2004.

194. Lee Wha Rang, review of *The Bridge at No Gun Ri: A Hidden Nightmare from the Korean War* by Charles J. Hanley, Sang-Hun Choe, and Martha Mendoza, http://www.kimsoft.com/2001/nogun-review.htm.

195. International Action Center, "The Korea International War Crimes Tribunal, The Final Judgment," http://www.kimsoft.com/2001/ica.htm.

196. Hanley et al., *Bridge at No Gun Ri.*

197. Philip Shenon, "Officer Suggests Iraq Jail Abuse Was Encouraged," *New York Times,* May 2, 2004; The Daily Mislead, "Administration Officials Knew of Abu Ghraib Report," misleader.org, May 5, 2004; Peter Schurman, "Fire Rumsfeld," MoveOn.org, May 6, 2004; "Petition: Rumsfeld Must Resign," Kerry for President, May 7, 2004; "The Abu Ghraib Spin," nytimes.com, May 12, 2004; Eric Schmitt, "2 Generals Outline Lag in Notification on Abuse Reports," *New York Times,* May 20, 2004; Andrea Elliott, "Unit Says It Gave Earlier Warning of Abuse in Iraq," *New York Times,* June 14, 2004.,

198. Ahmad Sabri, "U.S. to Establish Permanent Military Bases in Iraq," *Al-Arab Al-Yawm's,* November 19, 2003.

199. Christine Spolar, "14 'Enduring Bases' Set in Iraq," *Chicago Tribune,* March 23, 2004.

Corporate Influence on Military Preparedness

200. Michelle Ciarrocca, "Post-9/11 Economic Windfalls for Arms Manufacturers," *Foreign Policy in Focus* 7, no. 10 (September 2002).

201. Ibid.

202. Leslie Wayne, "So Much for the Plan to Scrap Old Weapons," *New York Times,* December 22, 2002.

203. William D. Hartung with Jonathan Reingold, "About Face: The Role of the Arms Lobby in the Bush Administration's Radical Reversal of Two Decades of U.S. Nuclear Policy," Arms Trade Resource Center, World Policy Institute, May 2002.

204. Ciarrocca, "Post-9/11 Economic Windfalls."

205. Niccolo Sarno, "The Military's Silent Role in Globalization," IPS World News, May 14, 1999, http://www.globalpolicy.org/globaliz/special/milglob.htm.

206. Hartung and Reingold, "About Face."

207. William D. Hartung, "Star Wars Unbound," *Nation,* April 8, 2002.

208. Bill Moyers, "Inside the Pentagon," *NOW,* PBS-TV, August 1, 2003.

The Sanctions Alternative

209. Dennis Halliday, former UN Assistant Secretary General and Humanitarian Aid Coordinator in Iraq, *Independent, UK,* October 15, 1998.

210. Ibid.

211. Ibid.

212. Ernest H. Preeg, *Feeling Good or Doing Good with Sanctions: Unilateral Economic Sanctions and the U.S. National Interest*, CSIS Significant Issues Series (Washington, D.C.: CSIS Press, 1999).

Unilateralism

213. John Van Oudenaren, "What Is 'Multilateral'?" *Policy Review Online*, February 2003, http://www.policyreview.org/feb03/oudenaren.html.

214. "Germany Warns U.S. against Unilateralism," *BBC News*, February 2, 2002.

215. Canadian Centre for Foreign Policy Development, "The Halifax Roundtable on US Foreign Policy: Summary of Key Points from Roundtable Sessions and Final Report," June 15, 2001,
http://www.ecommons.net/ccfpd/main.phtml?city=ha&show=report.

216. The White House, "The National Security Strategy of the U.S.," September 23, 2002, http://www.whitehouse.gov/nsc/nssall.html.

217. Daniel Bodansky, "What's So Bad about Unilateral Action to Protect the Environment? *European Journal of International Law* 11, no. 2 (2000): 339–47.

218. White House, "National Security Strategy."

219. Canadian Centre, "Halifax Roundtable."

220. Council for a Livable World, "U.S. Foreign Policy Turns Unilateralist: 'No' to Treaties," 2002.

221. John R. Hale, *The Civilization of Europe in the Renaissance* (New York: Macmillan, 1994), 137–42.

222. Van Oudenaren, "What Is 'Multilateral'?"

223. John Tirman, "Hegemon Down," AlterNet.org, January 17, 2003.

224. Brian Knowlton, "A Global Image on the Way Down," *International Herald Tribune,* December 5, 2002.

225. Jimmy Carter, "An Alternative to War," Carter Center of Public Information, January 31, 2003.

226. Alterman, "USA Oui! Bush Non!"

227. Richard Norton-Taylor, "Both the Military and the Spooks Are Opposed to War on Iraq," *Guardian,* February 24, 2003.

228. Glenn Kessler and Mike Allen, "Bush Faces Increasingly Poor Image Overseas," *Washington Post,* February 24, 2003.

229. Reuters, "U.S. Offers Turkey Big Aid Package for Help in Iraq," February 15, 2003.

230. Ibid.

231. Ibid.

232. Ibid.

233. David R. Francis, "Economist Tallies Swelling Cost of Israel to U.S.," *Christian Science Monitor,* December 9, 2002.

234. Antonia Juhasz, "The Hand-Over That Wasn't," *Los Angeles Times,* August 5, 2004.

8. Racial, Ethnic, and Gender Inequality

Black Inequality

1. Mary Pattillo-McCoy, "Middle Class, Yet Black: A Review Essay," Institute for Policy Research, Northwestern University, 1999,
http://www.rcgd.isr.umich.edu/prba/perspectives/fall1999/mpattillo.pdf.

2. *Statistical Abstract of the U.S., 1999,* Table 661.

3. U.S. Census Bureau, "People and Families in Poverty by Selected Characteristics: 2000 and 2001," Table 1.

4. Marc Morial, National Urban League, C-Span, August 7, 2003.

5. *Statistical Abstract of the U.S., 2000,* Table 24.

6. Ibid.

7. Tim Wise, "Why Whites Think Blacks Have No Problems," AlterNet, July 17, 2001.

8. *Statistical Abstract of the U.S., 2000,* Table 604.

9. Wise, "Why Whites Think."

10. Ibid.

11. *Statistical Abstract of the U.S., 1999,* Table 661.

12. Cedric Muhammad, "Last Hired, First Fired," BlackElectorate.com, October 8, 2001.

13. John M. Berry, "Jobless Rate Rose to 6% in November," *Washington Post,* December 7, 2002.

14. Alan B. Krueger, "Economic Scene; Sticks and Stones Can Break Bones, But the Wrong Name Can Make a Job Hard to Find," *New York Times,* December 12, 2002.

15. Marketplace: News Archives, December 19, 2002,
http://marketplace.publicradio.org/shows/2002/12/19_mpp.html.

16. "Black America Makes Economic Gains; Problems Persist," CNN.com, November 16, 1999.

17. Wise, "Why Whites Think."

18. Interview with William Julius Wilson, *Frontline,* PBS.org, "The Two Nations of Black America."

19. Morgan O. Reynolds, National Center for Policy Analysis, "Europe Surpasses America—in Crime," *Wall Street Journal,* October 19, 1998.

20. Ricco Villanueva Siasoco, "Defining Hate Crimes," Infoplease.com, August 18, 1999.

21. *FBI Uniform Crime Reports, 2000.*

22. Hanyu Ni and Robin Cohen, "Trends in Health Insurance Coverage by Race/Ethnicity Among Persons Under 65 Years of Age: United States, 1997–2001," National Center for Health Statistics.

23. Centers for Disease Control and Prevention (CDC), National Center for Health Statistics, "Visits to the Emergency Department Increase Nationwide," news release, April 22, 2002.

24. Richard Pérez-Peña, "Study Finds Asthma in 25% of Children in Central Harlem," *New York Times*, April 19, 2003.

25. CDC, National Center for Health Statistics, "Infant Mortality Statistics [from the 1998 Period] Show Variation by Race, Ethnicity, and State," July 20, 2000.

26. CDC, National Center for Health Statistics, *Health, United States, 2002,* 26th Annual Statistical Report.

27. Agency for Healthcare Research and Quality, "Women and Heart Disease," *AHRQ,* Publication No. 01-P016, September 2001.

28. National Center for Health Statistics, "New CDC Report on U.S. Mortality Patterns," September 25, 2001, http://www.cdc.gov/nchs/releases/01facts/99mortality.htm.

29. Esther Campi, "Trying to Bridge 'Health Gap' among Blacks in America," *Ithaca Journal,* November 9, 2002.

30. *Lehrer News Hour*, PBS-TV, interview with Dr. Blancourt, Harvard Medical School, April 2000.

31. Congressional Black Caucus, press release, April 22, 2001.

32. Howard Dean, Governor of Vermont, *Meet the Press*-TV, July 21, 2002.

33. Erica Goode, "For Good Health, It Helps to Be Rich and Important," *New York Times,* June 1, 1999.

34. Alexander Cockburn, "An Entire Class of Thieves," *Nation,* October 7, 2002.

35. Ibid.

36. David C. Baldus, George G. Woodworth, and Charles A. Pulaski, *Equal Justice and the Death Penalty: A Legal and Empirical Analysis* (Boston: Northeastern University Press, 1990).

37. Fox Butterfield, "Prison Rates among Blacks Reach a Peak, Report Finds," *New York Times,* April 7, 2003.

38. Harvard Graduate School of Education, "School Segregation on the Rise Despite Growing Diversity among School-Aged Children," *HGSE News,* 2001.

39. Caroline Hodges Persell and Giselle F. Hendrie, "Race, Education, and Inequality," in *Blackwell Companion to Social Inequalities,* ed. Mary Romero and Eric Margolis (New York: Blackwell (forthcoming)).

40. Congressional Black Caucus—Health Issues, 2003.

41. Congressional Black Caucus Foundation, Inc., Comcast, January 2003.

42. "Highlights of the U.S. Report to the UN on Racism" (9/22/00) prepared by the Clinton Administration for the Geneva-based UN Committee on the Elimination of Racial Discrimination, http://www.bluecorncomics.com/racerpt.htm.

43. National Urban League, "The State of Black America," 2001.

44. Tim Wise, "See No Evil: Perception and Reality in Black and White," Znet Daily Commentary, August 2, 2001, http://www.zmag.org/ZSustainers/ZDaily/2001-08/02wise.htm.

45. Pew Research Center, "Conservative Opinions Not Underestimated, But Racial Hostility Missed," March 2, 1998.

46. Wise, "See No Evil."

47. C-Span TV, August 19, 2002.

48. Wise, "See No Evil."

49. Robert M. Entman and Andrew Rojecki, *The Black Image in the White Mind: Media and Race in America* (Chicago: University of Chicago Press, 2000, 2001).

50. Diane McWhorter, "Dixiecrats and the GOP," *Nation,* January 27, 2003.

51. Ted Gioia, *The History of Jazz* (New York: Oxford University Press, 1997).

Other Victims of Prejudice and Discrimination

52. *FBI Uniform Crime Reports, 2000.*

53. "Anti-Semitism on the Rise in America: ADL Survey on Anti-Semitic Attitudes Reveals 17 Percent of Americans Hold 'Hard-Core' Beliefs," Highlights of a Survey Conducted by the Marttila Communications Group and SWR Worldwide for the Anti-Defamation League, ADL press release, June 11, 2002.

54. Ibid.

55. Ibid.

56. National Congress of American Indians, "Economic Development," http://www.ncai.org/main/pages/issues/community_development/economic_dev.asp.

57. North Dakota Indian Affairs Commission, http://www.health.state.nd.us/ndiac/statistics.htm.

58. U.S. Census Bureau, "2000 Income and Poverty Statistics," September 25, 2001.

59. North Dakota Indian Affairs Commission, http://www.health.stte.nd.us/ndiac/statistics.htm.

60. U.S. Public Health Service, "Minorities Lack Proper Mental Health Care," August 27, 2001, http://www.cnn.com/2001/HEALTH/08/26/mental.health/.

61. North Dakota Indian Affairs Commission.

62. Ibid.

63. Helen Rumbelow and Neely Tucker, "Interior's Norton Cited for Contempt in Trust Suit," *Washington Post,* September 18, 2002.

64. Associated Press, "Indians See Little from $8 Billion in Gambling Revenue," August 31, 2000.

Gender Inequality

65. Arend Lijphart, *Patterns of Democracy: Government Forms and Performance in Thirty-Six Countries* (New Haven: Yale University Press, 1999), 280.

66. Rein Taagepera, "Beating the Law of Minority Attrition," in *Electoral Systems in Comparative Perspective: Their Impact on Women and Minorities*, ed. Wilma Rule and Joseph F. Zimmerman (Westport, Conn.: Greenwood Press, 1994), 236.

67. Inter-Parliamentary Union, "Women in National Parliaments," April 30, 2004.

68. Steve Bates, "Peopleclick in the News: Women's Share of Executive Positions Decreases," SHRMOnline, February 24, 2004.

69. U.S. Department of Labor, Bureau of Labor Statistics, "Women in the Labor Force: A Databook," Report 973, February 2004 (2002 data); U.S. Department of Labor, Bureau of Labor Statistics, Mary Bowler, "Women's Earnings: An Overview," *Monthly Labor Review* (online) 122, no. 12 (December 1999).

70. "Women in the Labor Force," Table 22.

71. U.S. Department of Labor, Bureau of Labor Statistics, "Highlights of Women's Earnings in 1999," Report 943, May 2000.

72. "Women in the Labor Force," Table 31.

73. Leslie Kaufman, "Are Those Leaving Welfare Better Off Now? Yes or No," *New York Times,* October 20, 2003.

74. Barbara Ehrenreich, *Nickel and Dimed,* quoted on *Now with Bill Moyers,* PBS online, May 28, 2004.

75. Barbara Ehrenreich, *Nickel and Dimed: On (Not) Getting By in America* (New York: Metropolitan/Owl Book, Henry Holt, 2002).

76. Marlene Kim, "Women Paid Low Wages: Who They Are and Where They Work," *Monthly Labor Review* (online) 123, no. 9 (September 2000).

77. Joyce P. Jacobsen and Laurence M. Levin, "Effect of Intermittent Labor Force Attachment on Women's Earnings," *Monthly Labor Review* (online) 118, no. 9 (September 1995).

78. "Job Absence Rate Higher for Women Than for Men," *Monthly Labor Review* (online), March 25, 1999.

79. Kirstin Downey Grimsley and R. H. Melton, "Homemakers Get Plenty of Support," *Washington Post,* March 22, 1998.

80. Nikki V. Katz, "Domestic Violence Statistics," *Women's Issues* (online), May 2004.

81. U.S. Department of Justice, Bureau of Justice Statistics Special Report, "Intimate Partner Violence and Age of Victim, 1993–99," October 2001.

82. National Women's Health Information Center, "Sexual Assault," 4woman.gov, April 2001.

83. Christine Soares, "Gender Inequality: Women Under Stress," Stress Management (online), Copyright © 2004 Discovery Communications Inc., May 26, 2004.

84. National Women's Law Center, "Administration Rolling Back Progress for Women and Girls with Policies That Are Out of Sight & Out of Touch," press release, April 14, 2004; "National Women's Law Center Releases Report on Administration's Record," civilrights.org, May 5, 2004.

9. Civil Liberties

The Bill of Rights vs. the Patriot Act and Other Government Policies and Regulations

1. Amnesty International, *Amnesty Now*, Summer 2002, 14–15.

2. Nancy Chang, "The USA Patriot Act: What's So Patriotic about Trampling on the Bill of Rights?" Center for Constitutional Rights, November 2001.

3. David Williams Russell, "Patching the Dragnet: An Overview of the USA Patriot Act," January 16, 2002, http://www.dla.org/downloads/Patching_the_Dragnet.doc.

4. Center for Constitutional Rights, "The State of Civil Liberties: One Year Later; Erosion of Civil Liberties in the Post 9/11 Era," January 24, 2003.

5. Chang, "Trampling on the Bill of Rights?"

6. Ann Harrison, "Detained for Terror," AlterNet.org, November 7, 2001.

7. Eli Pariser, ed., "Can Democracy Survive an Endless 'War'?" *MoveOn Bulletin*, July 17, 2002, *http://www.moveon.org/moveonbulletin/bulletin2.html.*

8. Ann Harrison, "Behind the USA Patriot Act," AlterNet.org, November 5, 2001.

9. Ibid.

10. American Civil Liberties Union (ACLU), "Urge Congress to Stop the FBI's Use of Privacy-Invading Software," Action Alert, September 27, 2002, http://archive.aclu.org/action/carnivore107.html.

11. ACLU, "Stop the Government Plan to Mine Our Privacy [through the Total Information Awareness Program]," Action Alert, January 22, 2003, http://www.aclu.org/Privacy/Privacy.cfm?ID=11323&c=130.

12. Bernie Sanders, "The USA Patriot Act: What Are You Reading?" *Baltimore Sun*, January 19, 2003.

13. Harrison, "Behind the USA Patriot Act."

14. ACLU, " Stop Use of Privacy-Invading Software."

15. Brian Doherty, "Watching the AG: John Ashcroft vs. Civil Liberties," reasononline, June 2002.

16. Center for Constitutional Rights, "State of Civil Liberties."

17. Zadvydas v. Davis, 121 S. Ct. 2491, 2500 (2001).

18. David Cole, "The Ashcroft Raids," *Amnesty Now,* Spring 2002.

19. Ibid.

20. Harrison, "Detained for Terror."

21. Ibid.

22. Cole, "Ashcroft Raids."

23. Harrison, "Behind the USA Patriot Act."

24. Center for Constitutional Rights, "State of Civil Liberties."

25. Ibid.

26. Ibid.

27. Jesse J. Holland, "Key House Republican Not Sure He's Ready to Reauthorize Patriot Act," Associated Press, April 16, 2003, http://www.govtech.net/news/news.php?id=47455.

28. "EFF [Electronic Frontier Foundation] Analysis of the Provisions of the USA Patriot Act That Relate to Online Activities," October 27, 2003, http://www.eff.org/Privacy/Surveillance/Terrorism/20011031_eff_usa_patriot_analysis.php.

29. "Homeland Security: Justice Denied," *Washington Spectator,* March 1, 2003.

30. Charles Lewis and Adam Mayle, "Justice Dept. Drafts Sweeping Expansion of Anti-Terrorism Act," Center for Public Integrity, February 7, 2003.

31. Elisa Massimino, "What's Wrong with Military Trials of Terrorist Suspects?" *Human Rights,* American Bar Association, Winter 2002, http://www.abanet.org/irr/hr/winter02/massimino.html.

32. Ibid.

33. Ibid.

34. Ibid.

35. Ibid.

36. George P. Fletcher, Cass Sunstein, and Laurence Tribe, "The Military Tribunal Debate: An Exchange among George P. Fletcher, Cass R. Sunstein, Laurence Tribe," *American Prospect Online,* March 5, 2002.

Anecdotal Evidence of Abuse

37. Jason Halperin, "Patriot Raid," AlterNet.org, April 29, 2003.

38. Hank Hoffman, "Free Speech, R.I.P.," AlterNet.org, November 20, 2001.

39. Ibid.

40. Ibid.

41. Ibid.

42. Chip Berlet and Abby Scher, "Political Profiling: Police Spy on Peaceful Activists," *Amnesty Now,* Spring 2003.

43. Phil Hirschkorn, "Former 9/11 Detainee Files $20 Million Civil Rights Suit," CNN.com, December 17, 2002.

44. Turkmen v. Ashcroft, Synopsis, Center for Constitutional Rights, Legal Team (n.d.).

45. Eric Lichtblau, "Ashcroft Defends Detentions as Immigrants Recount Toll," *New York Times,* June 4, 2003.

46. Erwin Chemerinsky, " By Flouting War Laws, US Invites Tragedy," *Los Angeles Times*, March 25, 2003.

47. "Al Qaeda Hates the Constitution—So Does Ashcroft," NYC Independent Media Center, September 13, 2002.

48. Jim Defede, "He Respected the Badge, but 'Not in Miami,'" *Miami Herald,* November 23, 2003; Reuters Newsdesk, "Amnesty Says Miami Police May Have Broken UN Laws," amnesty.org, December 19, 2003; John Sweeney, "Letter Sent by AFL-CIO President John Sweeney to Attorney General John Ashcroft Urging an Independent Investigation into Miami Police Force Tactics During FTAA Demonstrations," aflcio.org/mediacenter, December 3, 2003; Leif Utne, "Union Calls for Miami Police Chief's Job, Congressional Investigation," *Utne Tradewatch,* November 25, 2003; "Groups Plan to Sue Miami over FTAA Actions by Police," *Miami Herald,* December 8, 2003; Jim Hightower, "Cops Were Told to Savage Their Fellow Americans: Ashcroft and the Bushites Unleash Madness in Miami," *Hightower Lowdown,* December 2003.

Public Reaction to Curtailment of Civil Liberties

49. J. D. Tuccille, "Americans Again Question Government Power," *Spotlight*, freemarket.net, November 6, 2002.

50. Dean Schabner, "Patriot Revolution? Cities from Cambridge to Berkeley Reject Anti-Terror Measure," July 1, 2002,
http://abcnews.go.com/sections/us/DailyNews/usapatriot020701.html.

51. Bill of Rights Defense Committee, Local Efforts, copyright 2002–2004, http://www.bordc.org/OtherLocalEfforts.htm.

52. Evelyn Nieves, "Local Officials Rise Up to Defy the Patriot Act," *Washington Post,* April 21, 2002.

53. Tuccille, "Americans Question Government Power."

54. Ibid.

55. Renana Brooks, "A Nation of Victims," *Nation,* June 30, 2003.

10. The Media and Their Relationships with Corporations, the Government, and the Public

Media Mediocrity and Concentration

1. James Fallows, "The Forgotten Home Front," *Atlantic Monthly,* January/February 2003, 78–81.

2. Edward S. Herman and Noam Chomsky, *Manufacturing Consent: The Political Economy of the Mass Media* (New York: Pantheon Books, Random House, 1988), 298.

3. Robert W. McChesney, *Rich Media, Poor Democracy: Communications Politics in Dubious Times* (Urbana and Chicago: University of Illinois Press, 1999), 76–77.

4. Rachel Coen, "The FTAA Is None of Your Business: Media Look Away as Democracy Is Traded Away," *Extra! FAIR,* January/February 2003.

5. Zeynep Toufe, "Let Them Eat Cake: TV Blames Africans for Famine," *Extra! FAIR,* November/December 2002.

6. Rachel Coen, "Another Day, Another Mass Arrest: Media Unfazed by Erosion of Right to Assemble," *Extra! FAIR,* November/December 2002.

7. Andrew Jacobs of *The New York Times* quoted in "#17 Corporate Media Ignores Key Issues of the Anti-Globalization Protests" of "The 25 Top Censored Stories of 2001–2002," Projectcensored.org, 2003.

8. A silver elf, "Corporate Media and the Anti-Globalization Movement in the U$," Infoshop.org.

9. Jacobs, "Corporate Media Ignores."

10. CNN, July 15, 2002.

11. Alan Cooperman, "New Antiwar Ad Launched," *Washington Post,* January 31, 2003.

12. Norman Solomon, "When Journalists Report for Duty," *Free Press,* September 20, 2001.

13. Rachel Coen and Jim Naureckas, "Connic Chung: Skeptical of Skepticism," *Extra! Update, FAIR,* December 2002.

14. CNN, January 5, 2003.

15. Paul Krugman, "Behind the Great Divide," *New York Times,* February 18, 2003.

16. Jim Hightower, "Chickenhawks," *Texas Observer,* October 25, 2002.

17. Margaret Bald, "Top Ten Stories of 2003," *World Press Review*, March 2004.

18. Michael Parenti, "Monopoly Media Manipulation," *Political Archive*, May 2001.

19. Russell Baker, "What Else Is News?" review of *Media Unlimited: How the Torrent of Images and Sounds Overwhelms Our Lives,* by Todd Gitlin, *New York Review of Books*, July 18, 2002.

20. "Elections Shot Down," *Extra! Update, FAIR, December 2002.*

21. McChesney, *Rich Media*, 54.

22. Herbert Gans, *Democracy and the News* (New York: Oxford University Press, 2003), 28.

23. Ibid., 23.

24. Brian Eno, "The U.S. Needs to Open Up to the World," *Time,* January 12, 2003.

25. *Lehrer News Hour*, PBS-TV, interview of Tom Phillips, August 27, 2002.

26. PEW Research Center, August 4, 2002.

27. Gans, *Democracy and the News*, 34.

28. Ibid., 31.

The Media and Corporate Enterprise

29. Herman and Chomsky, *Manufacturing Consent.*

30. Ibid., 18.

31. Ibid., 21.

32. McChesney, *Rich Media*, 22.

33. Ibid., 23.

34. Ben H. Bagdikian, *The Media Monopoly* (Boston: Beacon Press, 1997), Summary, 8.

35. Herman and Chomsky, *Manufacturing Consent*, 17.

36. Barbara Ehrenreich, interview by Jamie Passaro, *Sun,* January 2003.

37. McChesney, *Rich Media*, 56–57.

38. Ibid., 58.

39. Ibid., 40.

40. Bagdikian, *Media Monopoly*, 8.

41. Ibid., 5.

42. *Sanders Scoop,* Congressman Bernie Sanders Newsletter, April 2002.

43. Arthur Kent, "Breaking Down the Barriers," *Nation,* June 8, 1998, and *Risk and Redemption: Surviving the Network News Wars* (Tortola, British Virgin Islands: Interstellar, 1997), quoted in McChesney, *Rich Media.*

44. "Action Alert: NBC Slams Universal Healthcare," *FAIR Online,* Nov. 12, 2002.

45. McChesney, *Rich Media*, 52.

46. Ibid., 54.

47. Ibid., 19.

48. *Extra! Update, FAIR,* December 2002.

49. Baker, "What Else Is News?"

50. Bob Long, news director of WRC, quoted in Leonard Downie, Jr. and Robert G. Kaiser, *The News about the News: American Journalism in Peril* (New York: Knopf, 2002).

51. Bagdikian, *Media Monopoly*, 5.

52. Kent, in McChesney, *Rich Media*, 52.

53. "Stay Tuned—You Won't Have Much Choice from Now ON," *Washington Spectator,* July 1, 2003.

54. Paul Wellstone, "Media & Democracy," *Extra! FAIR,* December 2002.

55. Jeff Chester and Gary O. Larson, "Whose First Amendment?" *American Prospect,* December 17, 2001.

56. Peter Hart and Rachel Coen, "The FCC: Asking the Wrong Questions," *Extra! Update, FAIR,* February 2003.

57. Brent Staples, "The Trouble with Corporate Radio: The Day the Protest Music Died," *New York Times,* February 20, 2003.

58. "Stay Tuned."

59. Ibid.

60. Ibid.

61. Scott Gordon and Laura Huntington, "#1 FCC Moves to Privatize Airwaves," of "The 25 Top Censored Stories of 2001–2002," Projectcensored.org, 2003.

62. Molly Ivins, "Media Concentration Is a Totalitarian Tool," *Boulder Daily Camera,* January 31, 2003, http://www.commondreams.org/views03/0131-09.htm.

63. McChesney, *Rich Media*, 78–118.

64. Ibid., 78–80.

65. Ibid., 98.

66. Ibid., 62.

67. Ibid.

68. Steve Rendall, "Fox's Slanted Sources: Conservatives, Republicans Far Outnumber Others," *Extra! FAIR* newsletter, August 2001.

69. Ivins, "Media Concentration."

70. Steve Rendall, "CNN's Reliably Narrow Sources," *Extra! FAIR,* March/April 2003.

71. Steve Rendall and Tara Broughel, "Amplifying Officials, Squelching Dissent, *Extra! FAIR,* May/June 2003.

A Brief History of Corporate Control of the Media

72. McChesney, *Rich Media*, 191–92.

73. Ibid., 192.

74. Ibid., 193.

75. Ibid., 192.

76. Ibid., 193.

77. Ibid., 194.

78. Ibid., 200.

79. Ibid., 202.

80. Ibid.

81. Ibid., 253.

82. Ibid., 212.

83. Ibid., 218.

84. Ibid., 222.

85. Bagdikian, *Media Monopoly*, 3.

86. Ibid.

87. McChesney, *Rich Media*, 76.

88. Ibid., 77.

89. Nicholas Lemann, "The Chairman," *New Yorker,* October 7, 2002, 48–55.

90. Robert W. McChesney and John Nichols, "Media Democracy's Moment," *Nation,* February 24, 2003.

91. McChesney, *Rich Media,* 68.

92. McChesney and Nichols, "Media Democracy's Moment," 17.

93. Ibid., 16.

94. John B. Judis, "Michael Powell v. The Economy," *New Republic,* Sept. 2, 2002.

95. Miranda Spencer, "Making the Invisible Visible: Poverty Activists Working to Make Their Own Media," *Extra! FAIR,* January/February, 2003.

96. John Naughton, "The Genius of Blogging," *Guardian Unlimited,* February 23, 2003.

The Media and Government

97. Mark A. Smith, *American Business and Political Power: Public Opinion, Elections, and Democracy* (Chicago: University of Chicago Press, 2000), 212–13.

98. Lemann, "The Chairman."

99. William Greider, "*Washington Post* Warriors," *Nation,* March 24, 2003.

100. Gans, *Democracy and the News,* 46–49.

101. *Extra! FAIR* newsletter, 2002.

102. Herman and Chomsky, *Manufacturing Consent.*

103. Seth Ackerman, "Withholding the News: The *Washington Post* and the UNSCOM Spying Scandal," *Extra! FAIR,* March/April 1999.

104. McChesney, *Rich Media,* 59–60.

105. Timothy E. Cook, *Governing with the News: The News Media as a Political Institution* (Chicago: The University of Chicago Press, 1998), 111. © 1998 by the University of Chicago. All rights reserved.

106. Ibid., 113.

107. Ibid., 112–13.

108. Ibid., 94.

109. Jim Naureckas with the staff of *FAIR,* "Gulf War Coverage: The Worst Censorship Was at Home," *Extra! FAIR,* Special Gulf War Issue 1991.

110. Cook, *Governing with the News.*

111. Gans, *Democracy and the News,* 63.

112. Norman Solomon, "Spinning the Gulf War to Ignore the Cost of Lives," *Extra! Update, FAIR,* February 2003.

113. Ibid.

114. David Goodman, "Reporters Wary of Pentagon Promises," Associated Press, January 28, 2003.

115. Laura Flanders, "Pushing the Media Right," AlterNet.org, November 12, 2001.

116. Maureen Dowd, "Powell without Picasso," *New York Times,* February 5, 2003.

117. Kelly-Cullivan Smith, "Reporters Without Borders Ranks U.S. 17th in World Press Freedom Survey," jsons.collegepublisher.com, November 2, 2002.

11. Democracy

The American Model

1. Robert A. Dahl, *How Democratic Is the American Constitution?* (New Haven: Yale University Press, 2002), 3. Copyright © 2002 by Yale University. All rights reserved.

2. Ibid., 43

3. Ibid., 165.

4. Ibid.

5. Ibid.

6. Ibid.

7. Ibid., 56.

8. Ibid., 100–1.

9. Steven Hill and Rob Richie, "In Texas, Gerrymandering Gets a New Name – Perrymandering," *Washington Spectator,* November 1, 2003.

10. Dahl, *How Democratic Is the Constitution?* 104.

11. Ibid., 62.

12. Ibid., 81–82.

13. Ibid., 80–81.

14. Ibid., 49.

15. Ibid., 115.

16. Alexander Keyssar, *The Right to Vote: The Contested History of Democracy in the United States* (New York: Basic Books, 2000), 328–29.

To Vote or Not to Vote

17. Greg Palast, *The Best Democracy Money Can Buy* (New York: Plume, Penguin Books, 2003).

18. Keyssar, *Right to Vote.*

19. Frances Fox Piven and Richard A. Cloward, *Why Americans Still Don't Vote and Why Politicians Want It That Way* (Boston: Beacon Press, 2000), 8.

20. Keyssar, *Right to Vote,* 313.

21. Ibid., 313.

22. Ibid., 315.

23. Ibid.

24. Ibid., 320.

25. Center for Voting and Democracy, "International Voter Turnout, 1991–2000," http://www.fairvote.org/turnout/.

26. Rashad Robinson, "After 227 Years, Isn't It Time We Claim Our Democracy?" Center for Voting and Democracy, October 14, 2003.

27. Frances Fox Piven, interview by David Barsamian, "Why Americans Still Don't Vote," July–August, 2001, http://www.zmag.org/ZMag/articles/jul01barpiven.htm.

28. Rob Richie and Steven Hill, "The Dinosaur in the Living Room," Center for Voting and Democracy, November 11, 1997.

29. "2000 Votes," *Gender Gap,* October 5, 2002.

30. Keyssar, *Right to Vote,* 320.

31. Piven and Cloward, *Why Americans Still Don't Vote,* 9.

32. Public Citizen, "Public Citizen's Analysis of the Help America Vote Act of 2002," http://www.citizen.org/congress/govt_reform/election/articles.cfm?ID=8510.

33. Leadership Conference on Civil Rights, Letter to the Honorable John D. Ashcroft, October 25, 2002.

34. Alexander Keyssar, "The Project of Democracy," http://ni4d.us/library/keyssarpaper.pdf.

Filling the Electoral Power Vacuum with Special Interest Wealth and Influence

35. Lawrence R. Jacobs and Robert Y. Shapiro, *Politicians Don't Pander: Political Manipulation and the Loss of Democratic Responsiveness* (Chicago: University of Chicago Press, 2000), Preface. © 2000 by the University of Chicago. All rights reserved.

36. Mark A. Smith, *American Business and Political Power. Public Opinion, Elections, and Democracy* (Chicago: University of Chicago Press, 2000).

37. Mark A. Smith, "Do Corporations Own Political Process?" interview with *University Week* (faculty and staff publication of the University of Washington), October 5, 2000, http://depts.washington.edu/~uweek/archives/2000.10.OCT_05/_article5.html.

38. Common Cause, "Soft Money: What Is It and Why Is It a Problem?" http://www.commoncause.org/laundromat/stat/softmoney.cfm.

39. Common Cause, "The Enormous Growth of Soft Money," http://www.commoncause.org/laundromat/stat/growing.cfm.

40. Common Cause, "Soft Money," and "Pocketbook Politics: How Special-Interest Money Hurts the American Consumer, Executive Summary," February 24, 1998, http://www.commoncause.org/publications/pocketbook1.htm/

41. Public Citizen, "Public Citizen's Analysis of How the FEC Is Undermining the Bipartisan Campaign Reform Act (BCRA) of 2002," October 23, 2002.

42. Ibid.

43. Ibid.

44. Ibid.

45. Ibid.

46. Ibid.

47. Glen Justice and Jim Rutenberg, "Special Interests Unfazed by New Campaign Limits," *New York Times,* December 20, 2003.

48. Molly Ivins, "S.O.S.tate of the Union," Working for Change, January 28, 2003.

49. The Center for Responsive Politics, "2000 Presidential Race: Total Raised and Spent" (n.d.).

50. David Stout, "Tab for Washington Lobbying: $1.42 Billion," *New York Times*, July 29, 1999 (based on an analysis by the Center for Responsive Politics).

51. Robert Tanner, "State-Level Lobbying Costs $570 M," Associated Press, May 1, 2002.

52. Kevin Phillips, *Arrogant Capitalism* (Boston, MA: Back Bay Books, 1995), 52.

53. Chuck Neubauer and Richard T. Cooper, "Senator's Way to Wealth Was Paved with Favors," *Los Angeles Times*, December 18, 2003.

What Difference Does It Make If Democracy Is Weak?

54. Patrick E. Tyler and Janet Elder, "Poll Shows Most Want War Delay," *New York Times*, February 14, 2003.

55. Ibid.

56. Ibid.

57. Ibid.

58. Pew Research Center, "Tax Plan Fails to Connect, Bush's Economic Ratings Sag," February 25, 2002.

59. CBS News Poll, *New York Times*, July 18, 2002.

60. Pew Research Center, "Tax Plan Fails to Connect."

61. Ibid.

62. *Lehrer News Hour*, PBS-TV, June 30, 2003,
http://www.pbs.org/newshour/bb/terrorism/jan-june03/unprepared_6-30.html.

63. Eric Alterman, "Bush Goes AWOL," *Nation*, May 5, 2003.

64. Paul Krugman, "Dereliction of Duty," *New York Times*, June 17, 2003.

65. Hendrik Hertzberg, "Framed Up: What the Constitution Gets Wrong," *New Yorker*, July 29, 2002.

66. Howard Zinn, *A People's History of the United States: 1492–Present* (New York: HarperCollins, 1999), 611–12.

67. Dana Milbank, "From Bush, Some Flexibility on Election Promises; Observers See Administration Changing Course on International Trade, Campaign Finance, Foreign Policy," *Washington Post*, March 25, 2002.

68. Ibid.

69. Ibid.

70. Ibid.

71. Ibid.

72. Ibid.

73. Ibid.

74. Jim Hightower, *Hightower Lowdown*, July 2003.

75. Dana Milbank, "President's Compassionate Agenda Lags," *Washington Post*, December 26, 2002.

76. Ibid.

77. Robert Pear, "The President's Budget Proposal: The Poor; Aid to Poor Faces Tighter Scrutiny," Abstract, *New York Times,* February 5, 2003.

78. Jacobs and Shapiro, *Politicians Don't Pander,* Preface.

79. Henry Kaiser Foundation, "Government by the People: A Data Essay," *Public Perspective,* July/August 2001, 16–17.

80. PEW Research Center, "Performance and Purpose; Constituents Rate Government Agencies," April 12, 2000,
http://people-press.org/reports/display.php3?ReportID=41.

81. John Samples, "Americans Don't Trust Big Government on Home Front, Says ABC Poll," Cato Institute, April 5, 2003.

82. Jedediah Purdy, "Suspicious Minds," in "The Real State of the Union" issue, *Atlantic Monthly,* January/February, 2003.

83. Herbert Gans, *Democracy and the News* (New York: Oxford University Press, 2003), 15.

84. Ibid.

85. Samples, "Americans Don't Trust Big Government."

86. Associated Press-Ipsos Poll conducted by Ipsos Public Affairs, May 3-5, 2004, Right Track/Wrong Track, PollingReport.com..

Where the Rubber Hits the Road: The Elusive Realm of Bureaucratic Performance

87. Lee Hamilton, "True Congressional Oversight," Center on Congress, Indiana University, n.d., http://congress.indiana.edu/outreach/opeds/oped11.htm.

88. Alcestis Oberg, "NASA Forsakes Integrity to Enhance Public Image," *Detroit News,* February 5, 2003,
http://www.detnews.com/2003/editorial/0302/05/a13-77015.htm.

89. Joseph Farah, "Trust the Government?" Between the Lines, WorldNet-Daily.com, October 30, 2001,
http://www.worldnetdaily.com/news/article.asp?ARTICLE_ID=25122.

90. *Lehrer News Hour,* PBS-TV, May 21, 2002.

91. CNN, "Tests Reveal Security Shortfalls at Airports," July 1, 2002.

92. CNN, June 6, 2002.

93. Molly Ivins, "9-11 Report Offers Findings that Were Obvious from the Get-Go," Creators Syndicate, August 4, 2003.

94. Jim Naureckas, "Gulf War Coverage: The Worst Censorship Was at Home," *Extra! FAIR,* Special Gulf War Issue 1991.

95. Eric Lichtblau, "Justice Dept. Plans to Step Up Gun-Crime Prosecutions," *New York Times,* May 14, 2003.

96. David Barstow, "When Workers Die: US Rarely Seeks Charges for Deaths in Workplace," *New York Times,* December 22, 2003.

97. Steven F. Hayward with Ryan Stowers, *2003 Index of Leading Environmental Indicators,* 8th ed. (San Francisco: Pacific Research Institute, 2003).

98. Cynthia McKinney, interview by Dennis Bernstein, Pacifica Radio, March 25, 2002.

99. Lorraine Adams, "Getting Smarter," Book World section, *Washington Post National Weekly Edition,* April 21–27, 2003.

100. Jay Bookman, "Trust in Leaders Is Lost If WMD Are Not Found," *Atlanta Journal–Constitution,* May 22, 2003.

101. Associated Press, "Blix Questions Coalition's Intelligence," June 6, 2003.

102. Thomas Powers, *Intelligence Wars: American Secret History from Hitler to Al-Qaeda* (New York: New York Review of Books, 2002). Reprinted with permission from *The New York Review of Books.* Copyright © 2002 NYREV, Inc.

103. William Greider, *Who Will Tell the People?* (New York: Touchstone Books, Simon and Schuster, 1992), 363.

104. Ted Bridis, "Before 9-11, Terror Was Low Priority," Associated Press, June 28, 2002.

105. Brian Friel, "IGs Detail Management Problems for Lawmakers," GovExec.com, January 22, 1999, http://www.govexec.com/dailyfed/0199/012299b1.htm.

106. John R. Kasich, Chairman, House Committee on the Budget, press release, "Wasted $19 Billion Just the Tip of the Iceberg," January 13, 2000, http://www.house.gov/budget/press/011300release.pdf.

107. "Government Waste and Fraud: Government Waste at an All Time High!" Justice Junction, February 12, 2003, http://www.justicejunction.com/government_waste_all_time_high.htm.

108. GAO Strategic Supplement, "Support Congressional Oversight of the Federal Government's Progress toward Being More Results-Oriented, Accountable, and Relevant to Society's Needs," 2002–2007, http://www.gao.gov/sp/strobj33.pdf.

109. Thomas Cahill, *How the Irish Saved Civilization* (New York: Doubleday, 1995), 14.

12. Conclusions and a New Beginning

1. Derek Bok, *The State of the Nation: Government and the Quest for a Better Society* (Cambridge, MA: Harvard University Press, 1996), 9–11.

2. Sam D. Sieber, *Fatal Remedies: The Ironies of Social Intervention* (New York: Plenum Press, 1981).

Index

A

AARP (American Association of Retired Persons), 104, 106
Abu Ghraib prison. *See* prisoner abuse
accidental deaths, 77
Afghanistan war
  aftermath, 187, 192–96, 218
  civilian casualties, 182–86, 189, 196–97
  conditions
    before war, 180
    postwar, 192
  cost, 191
  environmental damage, 191
  media coverage, 182–84, 190
  Northern Alliance, 190, 194, 196, 220
  precision bombs and missiles, 187–88
  public attitudes toward, 181
  refugees, 186
  success and failures, 193–96
  unintended consequences, 180
AIDS, 6, 9, 47, 78, 100, 101, 102, 164, 165, 170, 171, 175, 177, 227, 258
al Qaeda, 188, 192, 193, 197, 205, 206, 249, 257, 299
alcoholic consumption, 83–84
alienation of public, 9
Alzheimer's disease, 77, 81
America compared with other nations, 6–8, 10, 23–24, 27
American Dream, xix, xxi, 311
American Myth, xix, xxi, 2, 3, 10–14, 18, 19, 24, 25, 32, 33, 46, 48, 63, 73, 120, 177, 181, 205, 209, 219, 221, 230, 231, 240, 253, 263, 266, 275, 281, 287, 293, 310, 311–15, 319
anti-Semitism, 233
antiwar demonstrations, 258
arthritis, rheumatoid, 77
asthma, 47, 77, 78, 145, 155, 227
atrocities

in Iraq, 207–10
in Korea, 209
in Vietnam, 209

B

bankruptcies, 38, 45, 59, 62, 72, 299
Bin Laden, Osama, xvii, 181
black Americans, 223–32
    contributions to American culture, 232
    inequality, 223–32
        anti-discrimination enforcement, 230
        corporations' role in maintaining, 231
        criminal justice, 137, 226, 227, 230
        death penalty, 228
        discrimination reported by blacks, 230
        drug arrests, 137
        education, 224–25, 228–29
        employment, 223, 224, 225, 226
        health, 227
        health insurance, 226, 227
        housing, 226, 230
        imprisonment, 227, 228
        income and poverty, 223, 225, 229, 230
        victimization, 226, 232
        voting rights, 228
    racist hate groups, 226
blogging, 274
bonanza mentality, 57, 62, 63, 71, 270
budget, federal
    deficits, 33–35, 36. *See also* trade deficit; state deficits
    recent budgets, 50–56
    rollover from surplus to debt, 33–35. *See also* social expenditures
Bush, President George (father of George W. Bush), 204
Bush, President George W., xvi, xvii, 70, 253
    campaign promises broken, 302–3

C

campaign financing, 9, 68, 71, 293, 297, 293–98
cancer, 77, 78, 79, 82, 85, 100, 101, 144, 145, 146, 155
    skin, 78
capital punishment, 7, 137, 138, 139, 140, 141, 219

blacks vs. whites, 139

Cheney, Vice President Richard, 30, 218

child abuse, 5, 9, 15, 16, 47, 81, 83

child care programs and subsidies, 41

cigarette smoking, 79, 80, 85

cities, quality of life in, 8

civil liberties, xiii, xxi, 7, 241, 249, 250, 251, 252, 274, 301
  constitutional rights
    Fifth Amendment, 66, 244
    First Amendment, 66, 242, 261, 268
    Fourteenth Amendment, 65, 66, 244
    Fourth Amendment, 66, 243, 244
    Right of Privacy, 243
    Sixth Amendment, 242, 244
  International Covenant on Civil and Political Rights, 246, 247, 249
  journalists, arrests of, 257, 280
  President's military order of November 13, 2001, 246–47
  preventive detention, 245
  violations, 247–51. *See also* Patriot Act

class, social, 33, 113, 229, 291

Cold War, xiv, xv, xvi, xvii, 197, 211, 215, 216, 308

congressional oversight, 301, 306

Constitution of the U.S.
  need for revision, 316. *See also* chap. 11 on democracy

consumer confidence and spending, 49, 50, 262, 299, 314

consumer debt, 9, 39, 46, 50

consumption and happiness, 56–57

corporations
  and military, 211–13
  background of Bush administration, 59, 150–51, 157
  campaign financing, 68, 133–34, 150–51, 294–98
  illegalities, 63. *See also* Enron
  lobbying, 68, 294–96, 297–98
  media relations with, 261–74
  political ascendancy of, 67–71
  public attitudes toward, 61
  regulatory oversight, 58–60, 63
  taxes, 9, 61, 70

crime, 9, 125–37
  age distribution effect, 126, 315
  cost, 125
  drug control, 135, 136, 193

drug offenses, 130, 132, 137
rate compared with other nations, 125. *See also* imprisonment; parole and
    probation
criminal justice system as charade, 141

D

death, major causes of, 76–80
debt
    consumer and business, 38–39, 50
    national, 6, 33, 35, 36, 37, 54, 55, 71
defense. *See* Afghanistan war; Gulf War of 1990–1991; Iraq war; military;
    terrorism; unilateralism; WMD
deflation, 36, 45, 126
democracy, 283–310
    American model, 283–89
    campaign contributions and lobbying, 295–98
    disenfranchisement of felons, 292
    electoral college, 62, 286, 288, 292, 297, 303
    its performance in America, 298–304
    majoritarian system, 284, 316
    media's role, 266, 267–69
    presidency, 285–87, 288–89
    proportional representation, 284–85, 313
    public attitudes toward, 303–4
    senators per state, 287
    special interest wealth, 295–98
    two-party system, 283, 284, 285
    voting barriers, 289–90, 292–93
    voting turnout, 290–92
    women's parliamentary representation, 235–34
deunionization, xix, 72
diabetes, 27, 77, 78, 85, 97, 98
dictators, America's support of, 137, 220
disempowerment, sense of, 9, 293
domestic violence, 47, 81, 82, 238
drug control, 135, 136, 193
    imprisonment for drug offenses, 129–30
drug offenses, 130, 132, 137
drugs
    illicit, 83, 84
    prescription. *See* health care, prescription drugs

E

education, 107–23, 313–14. *See also* higher education
  achievement, 10, 107–9, 112–13, 228–29
  blacks and, 116, 228–29
  Bush administration's harm to, 122–23
  curriculum, 108, 115, 116, 118, 194, 313
  dropping out, 43, 107, 119, 122
  employment and, 117–18
  enjoyment of school, 7, 118
  factors related to achievement, 112–14
  income and, 117, 121–22
  innovation, 115–16
  No-Child-Left-Behind program, 54, 72, 111, 118, 120, 122
  organization of, 115–16
  segregation, 9, 228
  spending on, 7, 107, 113
  textbook industry, 116
energy consumption, 143, 148, 154
Enron, xx, 13, 57, 58, 59, 60, 62, 63, 64, 72, 159, 305
environment, 143–61
  Afghanistan, 191
  energy consumption, 146–49, 151–52
  EPA (Environmental Protection Agency), 66, 78, 144, 153, 154, 155, 156, 306, 307
  foreign aid for, 158–61
  fuel efficiency of motor vehicles, 146–52, 272, 296
  global degradation of, 157
  global warming, 73, 145, 146, 147, 153, 154, 156, 159, 160, 166. *See also* Kyoto Treaty
  harm to, by Bush administration, 155–57
  media coverage, 153–54
  pollution compared with other nations, 143
  water shortage and privatization of, 158
Europe, 3, 5–8, 10, 16, 29, 32, 37, 38, 39, 40, 41, 42, 44, 45, 46, 62, 69, 72, 79, 84, 100, 101, 103, 113, 118, 130, 143, 146, 154, 165, 176, 215, 219, 228, 232, 256, 271, 280, 291, 311, 312, 316. *See also* international comparisons

F

firearms, 79, 80
foreign affairs, xiv–xviii, xx, 3–4, 198, 163–221, 264, 299, 315–16
foreign assistance, 159, 169, 172, 163–75, 231, 316

conditions in poor countries, 163–67
level of funding for, 167–68
policies of USAID and Millennium Challenge Corporation, 169, 171–73
public attitudes toward, 175–78
U.S. response to need, 167–75
foreign debt, 8
foreign relations. *See* foreign affairs; foreign assistance
Fourteenth Amendment, 65, 66, 244
and corporations as persons, 65–67
Fourth Amendment, 66, 243, 244
FTAA (Free Trade Area of America), 250
fuel efficiency of motor vehicles. *See* environment, fuel efficiency of motor vehicles
fundamentalism in America, xviii, 233

G

GDP (Gross Domestic Product), 23, 46–49, 72, 73
gender inequality, 234–39
Genuine Progress Indicator, 15. *See also* social report
global warming, 73, 145, 146, 147, 153, 156, 159, 160, 166. *See also* Kyoto Treaty
Gulf War of 1990–1991, xv, xvi, xvii, 190, 197, 204, 220, 259, 265
media coverage, 278–79

H

health, 26
health care, 80, 84–99, 102–4
cost of, 6, 9, 80, 86–95, 103, 104
distribution of, 87–88
health insurance, 96
hospitals, 88–91
liability insurance, 91–92
nurses, 88
physicians, 87–88, 91
prescription drugs, 87–88, 95, 92–95, 104–5
HMOs, 88, 96, 103
liability insurance, 91–92, 98
medical errors, 86, 90, 104
nurses, shortage of, 88, 89, 90, 98
prescription drugs, 6, 10, 91, 92, 93, 95, 103, 104
preventive, 84–86, 314–15

public attitudes toward, 87, 104
quality of, 98–99
health in America, 76–102
compared with other countries, 80, 83–84, 100–104
death, causes of, 76–81
illnesses and disabilities, causes of, 76–80. *See also* specific illnesses
improvements, 100–101
heart disease, attack, 41, 77, 79, 81, 85, 88, 90, 100, 102, 227
higher education
and employment, 117
and income, 117
cost of, 9, 72, 121–22, 275
Hispanics, 27, 102, 117, 118, 137, 223, 227, 232
HMOs (Health Maintenance Organizations), 88, 96
homelessness, xiii, 5, 16, 26, 28, 104, 196, 255, 280
homicide, 79–80
hospitals. *See* health care
housing, 9, 26

I

imprisonment, xiii, 7, 9, 46, 65, 127–34, 140, 280, 310. *See* black Americans,
inequality; capital punishment
alternatives to, 131
compared with other nations, 127
cost of, 127–29, 132
for drug offenses, 129–30, 135–37
increase in prison population and construction, 127, 129, 132–34, 134
privitization of, 132–34
rehabilitation, 9, 126, 129, 135, 136, 137
income, 24. *See also* education; income inequality; poverty; wealth
income inequality, xiii, 6, 9, 12, 29–33, 48, 50, 72, 122, 299
Indians, Native American, 225, 233, 234
infant mortality, 4, 6, 10, 16, 27, 80, 100, 102, 227, 314
inflation, 6, 30, 37, 44, 45, 49, 52, 55, 87, 88, 91, 93, 96, 122
infrastructure, 1, 8, 9, 52, 170, 179, 192, 203
insurance
health, 6, 27, 87, 95–98, 104, 226, 227, 272, 293, 294, 300
medical liability, 91–92
intelligence (security)
failures, xix, 304, 305–8
international affairs. *See* foreign affairs

international comparisons, xviii, 4–8, 23–24, 26, 27, 100–104, 137–38, 166. *See also* Europe
International Criminal Court
  rejected by U.S., 215, 216
Iraq war, xvi, 193, 197–211, 219, 269, 274, 279, 299
  aftermath, 198, 203–4, 219
  aid after invasion, 202–3
  al Qaeda connection, 205–6, 257
  civilian casualties, 197, 201–2, 203, 206
  intelligence, 205–6
  invasion, conduct of, 199–200
  media coverage of, 184, 200, 201, 205, 269, 279
  menace of Iraq, 220
  military bases, xvi, 211
  preemptive war, 216–17
  regime change, xvi, 189, 197
  Saddam Hussein, xvi, xvii, 197, 204, 205, 206, 207, 210, 220, 257, 307, 308
  sanctions, effect of, 214
Islam, Islamic culture, 2, 3, 181
  attitudes toward America, 206
isolation, geographical, 16
Israel, xvi, 12, 109, 181, 198, 233, 241, 316
  American payments to, 221

J

Jews. *See* anti-Semitism, Israel
job stress, 40–42, 48–49, 72

K

Kuwait, xvi, 220
Kyoto Treaty, 73, 147, 153–54, 215

L

lobbying, 9, 68, 70, 71, 92, 93, 133, 150, 158, 212, 293–98, 303
lower respiratory tract disease, 77

M

media, 175, 183–84, 189, 191, 197, 231, 255–81
  alternative press, 273–74
  bias, 255–59, 274–77

blogging, 274
concentration of, 9, 266–68, 303
corporate enterprise and, 261–74
coverage of civilian war casualties, 201
coverage of protests, 257
coverage of trivia and crime, 259–60
democracy and, 260, 264, 266, 267, 271, 272, 281, 293, 317
FCC (Federal Communications Commission), 259, 271, 272, 273, 274, 300
FRC (Federal Radio Commission), 269–70
government relations with, 274–81
history of corporate control, 269–74
mediocrity of, 175, 255–61
public attitudes toward, 261
Telecommunications Act of 1996, 272
think tank relations with, 262
transformative relations with government, mutuality, 261
Web, 274
mental illness, 16, 47, 81, 82, 99, 275
Miami demonstration against FTAA (Free Trade Area of America), 250–51
Middle East, xvii, 10, 220
oil, xvi, 198, 233
military. *See also* Afghanistan war; Gulf War of 1990–1991; Iraq war
bases in Iraq, xvi, 211
corporate influence on, 211–13
high-tech weapons and unanticipated consequences, 7–8
preemptive war, 206, 216
public attitudes toward, 9
spending for, 50–52, 191, 212
mobility, social, 31–32
motor vehicles, 6, 77, 101, 146, 147
fuel efficiency. *See* environment, fuel efficiency of motor vehicles
pollution by, 146–47

N

NAFTA (North American Free Trade Agreement), 144, 259, 294
NASA (National Aeronautics and Space Administration), 145, 157, 212, 274, 305
natural resources. *See* environment
Nazism, xviii
neoconservatism, 70
nephritis, 77, 78

nine eleven (9/11), xvi, xvii, xix, 3, 10, 13, 179, 180, 183, 197, 198, 205, 244, 245, 252, 257, 264, 303, 304, 306, 307, 308, 309, 316
NSC (National Security Council), 308

O

obesity and overweight, 79
occupational crisis, 9, 10, 39–44, 72–73, 314
oil, xvi, xx, 23, 61, 146, 147, 148, 151, 156, 158, 198, 233
Osama bin Laden. *See* Bin Laden
OSHA (Occupational Safety and Health Administration) failures, 67, 306
overweight. *See* obesity and overweight

P

Palestinian-Israeli conflict, 10, 233
parole and probation, 131
Patriot Act, 241, 245, 241–46, 247, 248, 249, 250, 251, 301. *See also* civil liberties
    evidence of its abuse, 247–50
Patriot Act II, 246, 301
physical activity, 79, 80, 85
physicians. *See* health care
pneumonia/influenza, 77, 78, 85, 103, 144
pollution. *See* environment
poor countries. *See* underdeveloped and poor countries, conditions in
poverty, 9, 15, 24–28
    and health, 26–27
    and health care, 26–27
    and shelter, 26
    and violence, 27
    media coverage of, 275
power sectors and relations between, 17–19, 59, 73, 106, 152, 154, 157, 261–65, 276, 277
preemptive war, 206, 216–17
President's military order of November 13, 2001, 246
prisoner abuse
    in Afghanistan, 208
    in Guantanamo, 208
    in Iraq, 207–10
    in U.S., 208
prisons. *See* imprisonment

productivity, 15, 39, 40, 44, 73, 85, 127, 314
public attitudes toward
  America
    held by Americans, 1–2
    held by foreigners, 3, 206, 219–20, 315–16
  business, 62
  civil liberty curtailments, 251–52
  major institutions, 9
  terrorism before 9/11, 181
  war, xvi, 181
public opinion. *See* public attitudes

Q

quality of life, 8, 16, 46, 72, 73, 152

R

R&D, 7, 8, 71, 94, 115, 116, 232, 314
regulatory oversight, 58, 60, 63, 159
religion, xviii, 9, 12, 13, 266
Rice, Condoleezza, National Security Adviser, 218–19

S

Saddam Hussein, xvi, xvii, 197, 204, 205, 206, 207, 210, 220, 257, 307, 308
sanctions, 111, 204, 214, 215
  in Iraq, 214–15, 276
savings, 38–39, 71
SEC (Securities and Exchange Commission), 59, 60, 308
septicemia, 77, 78
social class, 32–33
social expenditures by government, 7, 11, 50–55
social health index, 15
social mobility, 31, 33
social report, 14, 16, 43, 46, 47, 73, 137, 265, 276, 314
Social Security, employer's contribution to, 46
Soviet Union, demise of, xiv–xvi
stagflation, xix, xx
state deficits, 37
stock market, 29, 37, 44, 45, 60, 61, 134, 265
stroke. *See* heart attack
suicide, 6, 9, 16, 77, 80, 81, 82, 86, 101, 234, 249

Sustainable Economic Welfare Index, 15. *See also* social report

T

tax cuts of Bush administration, 30–31, 49, 72
tax havens, 56, 61, 63
tax structure, 30, 72
terrorism, xvii, xviii, xix, 2, 10, 11, 50, 51, 53, 82, 163, 176, 178, 181, 193, 197, 198, 204, 205, 206, 212, 217, 241, 242, 247, 248, 249, 250, 252, 253, 259, 279, 301, 303, 304, 305, 308
trade deficit, 4, 6, 10, 37, 71
transformative effects of symbiosis between power sectors, 261–62, 274, 277, 279
treaties rejected by U.S., 215
trends, social, 9–10, 11
trust
   in institutions, 9
   in others, 9, 82

U

UN (United Nations), xvii, 198, 210, 216–17, 219, 229, 276
unanticipated consequences. *See* unintended consequences
underdeveloped and poor countries, conditions in
   education, 166
   exploitation of children, 164
   health, 164–65
   natural resources, environment, 166
   population growth, 167
unemployment, 4, 6, 9, 10, 31, 39, 40, 42, 43, 44, 48, 50, 72, 117, 126, 129, 224, 225, 226, 234, 275, 279, 299, 300, 314, 315
   coverage by media, 275
   insurance, 6, 44
unilateralism, xvi, xvii, 215, 217, 218
unintended consequences
   need to foresee, 178–80, 204, 218, 266, 317–19
   of Afghanistan war, 178–80
   of drug enforcement, 136–37
   of high-tech weapons, 178–79
   of Iraq war, 198–99
   of media's control, 266
   of therapeutic medicine, 75–76
   public attitudes toward U.S. of others, 206

unions
   decline of. *See* deunionization
United Nations, 203

V

Vietnam War, xiv, xviii, 48, 221, 274

W

war. *See* Afghanistan war; antiwar demonstrations; Gulf War of 1990–1991;
   Iraq war; military; WMD
Washington, D.C., demonstration against the World Bank, 257
wealth, 23–24
weapons of mass destruction. *See* WMD
WMD (weapons of mass destruction), 178, 198, 205, 206, 210, 211, 216, 217,
   220, 253, 275, 307, 308
Wolfowitz, Paul, Deputy Secretary of Defense, 249
work. *See* occupational crisis

Y

youth, vulnerability to social pathologies of, 315